Using Poetry Across the Curriculum

Library of Congress Cataloging-in-Publication Data

Chatton, Barbara.
Using poetry across the curriculum : learning to love language / Barbara Chatton. — 2nd ed.
p. cm.
Includes bibliographical references and index.
ISBN 978–1–59158–697–5 (hard copy : alk. paper)
1. Poetry—Study and teaching (Elementary) 2. Language experience approach in education. 3. Interdisciplinary approach in education. I. Title.
LB1575.C53 2010
372.64—dc22 2009036711

14 13 12 11 10 1 2 3 4 5

This book is also available on the World Wide Web as an eBook.
Visit www.abc-clio.com for details.

ABC-CLIO, LLC
130 Cremona Drive, P.O. Box 1911
Santa Barbara, California 93116-1911

This book is printed on acid-free paper ∞

Manufactured in the United States of America

For My Teachers

Milton John Chatton 1916–1992

Mildred Vick Chatton 1916–1994

Charlotte S. Huck 1923–2005

and Leah Griffin 1942–2009

Contents

Preface

Using Poetry Across the Curriculum: Learning to Love Language offers elementary and middle school librarians and teachers ideas for integrating poetry into all areas of study. Just as aspects of language usage (reading, writing, listening, and speaking) overlap, each of the major disciplines overlaps and interconnects with others. It is difficult, for example, to teach science without thinking about its links to mathematics, reading, writing, and social studies. Any one of the curricular areas can be a starting point for studies that interconnect several or all of the other curriculum areas.

POETRY ACROSS THE CURRICULUM

Generally, poetry study is an aspect of the language arts, but for purposes of this book, it will be considered broadly. *Using Poetry Across the Curriculum: Learning to Love Language* focuses on reading and sharing poetry to communicate and interrelate all areas of study. Poetry is regarded as part of everyday classroom life, rather than a topic or unit to be covered on a special week or month. Ideas for sharing poems and for reading and writing poems are included throughout the book when relevant to the subject matter. Poetry writing ideas are offered as optional activities but never required. Students should be invited to see the many forms of poems as different ways of expressing what they now. This book is not designed to help teach specific methods of reading, discussing, or writing poetry. The References section in Chapter One lists materials about how to teach poetry to young people.

Units are included in the book when poems seem to cluster around one subject or theme. These units are deliberately kept very open, with lists of materials and suggestions for activities, but without clear blueprints for what should occur in the study. The material in the poetry and prose will evoke responses from teachers and students. Depending upon one's curriculum, studies of these subjects can go in a number of different directions. The unit on Jazz, for instance, is included in the Fine Arts chapter under Music. Certainly, listening and responding to this music is critical to any jazz study. But the poetic and prose materials include other possible connections. These include biography of jazz musicians and singers, study of the poetic elements of rhythm (meter) and onomatopoeia, poetic writing, performance poetry, the history of jazz, and the role of African American musical roots in its creation. Other topics may arise as students and teachers reflect on the poetic works they read.

Rather than teach poetry out of context as part of a poetry unit, these units encourage teachers and librarians to put together poetic materials in an open way so that a variety of responses across a number of curriculum areas can result.

DIVERSITY AND MULTICULTURALISM

As educators have become more aware of diversity and seek to honor the backgrounds and beliefs of all students, more and better poetry has become available for enriching school collections. Poems in other languages and dialects are included in Chapter Two: Language Arts. Poetry about various cultures around the world and in the United States is included in Chapter Five: Social Studies. Poems about the music, art, and dance traditions of various cultural groups are included in Chapter Six: Fine Arts. A successful approach to treating diversity in the classroom or library is to regard it as part of everyday life, rather than as a subject addressed only during special weeks. Poetry by and about members of many cultural groups is included in all of the standards to encourage this approach.

CHAPTER ORGANIZATION BY SUBJECT

Chapter One provides a broad overview of the standards, poetry and language. Each succeeding chapter focuses on the standards in one or two subject areas. The standards appear in bold type with discussion and lists of poems following them. Some standards don't have direct links to poetry, but for purposes of continuity, they are included in the text, immediately followed by the next standards. If material is useful in two standards but has been placed in one area, a **See** reference will lead readers to that location. Cross-references used in catalogs are used throughout the book. **See also** references will take the reader to the standards under which useful material can be located. For example, because some aspect of problem solving or critical thinking is included in each set of standards, see also references will take the reader to the mathematics standard where poems relating to this subject are located. These references will also help librarians and teachers to locate poems listed in other curriculum areas that might be helpful. When units of study are included in a chapter, they will be preceded by **Links with** references to show which standards are being covered.

SOURCES FOR AND CITATION OF POETRY

The suggested poems in each chapter are discussed and then listed following the discussion. If the poem is available in the poet's own works, that edition of the work is cited. If not, another source is cited. If another common source for the poem is available it appears by title in parentheses after the first citation. Most of these poems can be found in other sources as well. An effort has been made to cite books that are still in print and readily available. The poems selected here comprise only a sampling of possible choices in each curriculum area. As librarians and teachers develop classroom, library, and personal poetry collections, they and their students will find other poems appropriate for their studies.

Acknowledgments

No one writes a book alone. Sharon Coatney and the staff of Libraries Unlimited made it possible for me to create this second edition. The faculty of the College of Education at the University of Wyoming granted me a sabbatical so that I could write it. Dean Kay Persichitte, department chair Alan Buss and Office Associate Dorie Gallegos protected, encouraged, and supported me throughout the process. Colleague Kate Muir Welsh (Dr. Science) shared materials with me and answered standards questions. Deb Parkinson cheerfully took over my advising. Judy Ellsworth stepped in for committee work. Librarians Anita Trout and Mary Henning taught my courses in Children's Literature. Without their willingness to help me out, I could not have accomplished this project.

The helpful staffs of the Albany County Public Library and the University of Wyoming, particularly Cathy Dodgson and the student workers at the University libraries, kept the process of interlibrary loans and check-outs cordial and orderly.

On the home front, my husband Andy provided gourmet meals and roaring fires to sit by. Cats Guy Noir and Dolly popped in and out, around, and over the computer station, letting me know I was never alone with this work.

Two teachers deserve my special thanks. Leah Griffin and her daughter Shari provided tea and brownies, stories, laughter, and wonderful ideas in our visits. Shari's students in Highlands Ranch, Colorado, took to poetry with enthusiasm, and I thank them for their efforts. They became poets because their own "Miss Stretchberry" created a classroom in which words, critical thought, and supporting one another were daily graces.

Introduction

Much has changed since *Using Poetry Across the Curriculum: A Whole Language Approach* was published in 1994. Curriculum has changed. Although the range of subject areas to be covered in elementary and middle schools is still broad, the focus has changed to creating curriculum to meet standards. The previous edition featured chapters on major discipline areas. In this edition, those areas remain in place, but within each chapter the poems are organized under the major headings of the national standards. As I did in the first edition, I emphasize that including all areas of study in the curriculum is vital to educating the young.

Poetry for children and young adults has changed. About one-third of the materials featured in the earlier edition of this book have gone out of print. Some of these are losses to the field, including volumes by award-winning poets Eve Merriam, Myra Cohn Livingston, and X. J. Kennedy. There have been remarkable gains in other areas of poetry. More collections of poems are designed for use across the curriculum, particularly collections selected by Lee Bennett Hopkins. Avis Harley, Paul Janeczko, and J. Patrick Lewis, among others, have provided readers with lively collections featuring an impressive array of poetic forms. New young poets speak directly to the concerns of upper elementary and middle school students. Beautifully illustrated poetry books enhance the meanings of the poems and invite readers. The image of poetry for young people has in the past been one of sweetness and innocence, but this is no longer true. The range of subjects and variety of forms of poems for the young has never been greater. Poetry is a strong and lively presence that deserves to be highlighted in schools and libraries.

When I wrote the first edition of the book, I struggled to find poetry that represented the experiences of diverse groups within the United States and around the world. Since that time, poetry about people of differing cultural backgrounds and poems about the contributions of girls and women has proliferated. Many more collections of poems are bilingual in English and Spanish. Anthologies of poems from around the world are appearing more frequently. While there are still gaps, with some languages and ethnicities represented by only one or two poets, the increase in numbers of poetry books that represent the diversity of human experience is heartening.

Definitions and genres of poetry have increasingly blurred. In 1994, novels in verse were almost exclusively a small subcategory of adult fiction, but are now a flourishing literary form for young people. Poets are creating biographies and histories in verse. Concrete poetry, combining visual and sound qualities, is widely available. Poets are writing free verse texts for picture books and nonfiction. Poetry collections in response to art and photography have increased in number. All of these have enriched poetry for young people.

Since the first edition of this book, oral presentation of poetry has become very popular. Rap music, poetry jams, poetry slams, and open mike nights for poetry reading at clubs have encouraged young people to write and share their poems with others. Programs such as Poetry Out Loud are attracting young poets. The National Poets Laureate have become more visible in their efforts to popularize poetry. The National Poetry Society has created a position of Poet Laureate for Children, and these Poets Laureate have also worked to make poetry more visible including public performances of poems.

While books of poetry can quickly go out of print, changes in technology have made it easier to access them in a variety of ways. Some on-line booksellers carry used editions for sale. Some books will be reprinted on demand. New publishers who specialize in reprints are offering many collections. Some poets have reclaimed copyrights for out of print books and self-publishing them with self-publishing services. Hard-to-find poems can sometimes be found on websites.

I continue to believe in the power of poetry to change the world one person at a time. Students who are allowed to explore the intricacies of language, to play with words and their sounds, and to think and make sense of the world through poems of all kinds will see that world differently. Words can give them power. Poets for the young have led the way in suggesting that students can handle the big, tough ideas. Poetry about war and peace, about how we treat our environment, and about how we treat one another invites us to ponder these hard issues with our students. Poetry that allows them to think like scientists, like historians, and like artists will enrich their lives. Their thoughts, words and poems can create a better future.

CHAPTER 1

Poetry and The National Standards for Education

THE STANDARDS

During the 1990s, under considerable pressure from the U.S. Department of Education, professional organizations began developing national standards for education in their disciplines. The standards were intended to encourage education of all students to high levels of content knowledge, conceptual understanding, and skills in the disciplines taught in school. The process of creating these standards was neither simple nor clear, enmeshed in politics both from outside the disciplines and from splits within them. The number of disciplines for which standards were created began to grow. National Standards were created for Civics, Foreign Language, Geography, History, Language Arts, Mathematics, Music, Physical Education, Science, Social Studies, Technology, and the Visual and Performing Arts (Including Drama, Art, and Dance). Additional standards emerged for specialized areas such as American Indian Education, Business Education, ESL, and Gifted Programs, among others. Not surprisingly, the national standards were quite broad and inclusive. States and then school districts took these sets of standards and translated them to fit local needs, adding more layers of meaning.

Every discipline naturally views knowledge through its own lens. Each set of standards uses the language of the discipline, in some cases, as a teacher friend told me, so oblique as to require a translator. A web search of the standards with the accompanying books, state and commercial websites, and other published materials needed to translate these standards into classroom use is revealing. So much is asked in each content area that no one teacher, classroom, or child could reasonably expect to accomplish these goals. Instead they tend to represent the philosophies of the organizations charged with producing them. Standards repeat themselves, overlap, and seem to omit some areas of fundamental knowledge. When faced with the lists of standards for all of the disciplines, elementary and middle school teachers and librarians, who strive to educate students in all of these areas, can feel overwhelmed. What began with the expectation that all students should have access to similar content and process knowledge has become a nightmare of regulations, interpretations, and accountability.

An odd outcome of the Standards movement is schools where Standards and Objectives must be posted in classrooms so that administrators and visitors can enter at any time and be assured that teachers (and students) can point to a standard on which they are working. I can't help wondering what kind of language students develop when they are surrounded by the jargon of many disciplines rather than rich natural language with which they live. Another outcome, far more disturbing, is that in most cases the standards contain nothing that speaks to finding joy in new ideas or in linking together the areas of the curriculum into a larger conceptual framework that is essential to being a lively and interesting and educated human being.

A Path through the Standards

There is nothing wrong with having standards. The difficulty for teachers and librarians comes because the education standards are hardly standardized. It is difficult to wade through all the materials because of the sheer number of standards, differences in discipline language, and their overlapping nature. The purpose of this book is to provide a poetic path through the disciplines that are taught by elementary and middle school teachers and librarians.

Some processes cross the curriculum areas covered by this book, although they are called by different names. One crossover is the ability to use content knowledge for critical thinking and problem solving. Another is to be able to communicate what one knows and understands about a subject. Language is a critical link across the standards. Poetry gives students and teachers a means of communicating what they understand and enjoy about each discipline and a means of linking the disciplines together.

This commonality is acknowledged by the standards themselves. Each set of standards includes one or more that encourage students to make links across the curriculum but does not necessarily discuss how this is to be accomplished. Poets generally "live" in the Language Arts, but in fact they come from and write about every subject area. Some are trained scientists or historians. Some love mathematics or art. Because of the range of topics of poetry, poems move freely across the discipline areas.

In an attempt to make teaching to the standards easier, writers and educators have created lessons and units that incorporate one or more standards. Typically, these describe an activity and cite the standard or standards that activity would address. This volume begins with the standards to show the ways that poetry moves around and across the curriculum. The standards appear in bold type, followed by poems and collections that can be used to support that standard. Some standards are quite technical and focus on material that seems designed for students majoring in a subject area. When there does not seem to be a poetry connection for a standard, standards are clumped together. For sheer lack of space and time, some standards will not be considered in this volume. The broader *Curriculum Standards for Social Studies* encompasses the major ideas of history, geography, and economics, so the specific content standards for these disciplines are not included. The standards for technology, and specific areas of instruction for specific populations are not included.

Using Poetry Across the Curriculum: Learning to Love Language is designed to use poetry and poetic language as a means of translating the numerous standards into creative, engaging, and stimulating activities. Poetry can act as a bridge across and a path between the many areas of required study in elementary and middle schools.

DEFINING POETRY

When I ask students what a poem is, most tell me that it is something that rhymes. Given that children's introduction to poetry is through nursery rhymes, rhyming songs, and playground chants, this answer is not surprising. Some students have told me that it is not rhyme that makes a poem; it is the way the words are arranged on the page. Poems sit in the middle of a page and don't go all of the way to the edges. Some students think that poetry is only about certain subjects, about nature and love and other subjects they don't care for. Ralph Fletcher answers the concern that poems are only about "sweet" things with his "Squished Squirrel Poem" in which the writer quarrels with his teacher that it is a good subject for a poem. Others see poetry as a certain way of using words or as using certain devices such as metaphor and meter when one writes. Poetry does not define easily. Melissa, who has been thinking a lot about poetry, gave these definitions:

> Poetry is like a small page, a small word, a big difference.
> Poetry is like a page full of memories hidden in words of black.
> Poetry is like opening a hundred year old box of feelings.
>
> Melissa
> Grade 5

Melissa shows in her definitions that one has to define poetry by talking about what it does, rather than what it is. Poets have written many poems about poetry. They try to capture what a poem is through imagery or comparison. They might write about how it makes them feel when they read it, speak it, or hear it spoken. Eleanor Farjeon's classic poem "Poetry" suggests that poetry is not the actual rose, but the image or sense of the rose. In *A Poet's Bird Garden*, Laura Nyman Montenegro uses the metaphor of "capturing" the bird to show the complexities of explaining poetry. Poet William Stafford has written, "A poem is anything said in such a way as to invite from the hearer or reader a certain kind of attention." (Stafford, 1978)

Stafford's idea of paying attention is significant. Poems ask us to notice the small things, natural acts, and kindnesses we tend to pass by. Poems ask us to pay attention to love, to grief, and to events around us. Ralph Fletcher speaks for the power of poetry to tell important truths in his poem "Poetry Stands." In her "Forward" to Arnold Adoff's collection, *I Am the Darker Brother*, Nikki Giovanni speaks of African Americans turning to poetry to give them a voice, to give them hope, to raise their spirits, and to tell the truth, "And poetry did not let them down."

The following list of books and poems includes works about many aspects of poetry. Each of the poems speaks to the power of poetic language. Bobbye S. Goldstein has selected some of her favorite poems on poetry for *Inner Chimes: Poems on Poetry*. Ralph Fletcher's *A Writing Kind of Day* includes a number of poems on poetry, as does Eloise Greenfield's *In the Land of Words*.

Afif, Kaissar. "The Bridge." In Nye, Naomi Shihab. *The Space Between Our Footsteps*.S & S, 1998. (Also in *The Flag of Childhood*)

Appelt, Kathi. "Homeroom." *Poems from Homeroom*. Holt, 2002.

Bogart, Sandra. "Poems Can Give You." In Booth, David. *'Til All the Stars Have Fallen*. Illus. by Kady MacDonald Denton. Viking, 1990.

Clarke, John Henrik. "The Poet Speaks." In Slier, Deborah. *Make a Joyful Sound*. Illus. by Cornelius Van Wright & Ying-Hwa Hu. Checkerboard, 1991.

Colby, Joan. "Processes." In Nye, Naomi Shihab. *What Have You Lost?* Greenwillow, 1999.

Collins, Billy. "Introduction to Poetry." In Hopkins Lee Bennett. *Days to Celebrate*. Illus. by Stephen Alcorn. HarperCollins, 2005.

Dakos, Kalli. "I Gotcha." *Don't Read This Book, Whatever You Do*. Illus. by G. Brian Karas. S & S, 1993.

Esbensen, Barbara Juster. "Homework" & "Pencils." *Who Shrank My Grandmother's House?* Illus. by Eric Beddows. HarperCollins, 1992.

Farjeon, Eleanor. "Poetry." In Goldstein, Bobbye S. *Inner Chimes*. Illus. by Jane Breskin Zalben. Boyds Mills, 1992.

Fletcher, Ralph. "Squished Squirrel Poem" & "Poetry Stands." *A Writing Kind of Day.* Illus. by April Ward. Boyds Mills, 2005.

Forester, Victoria. "A Poem So Spun." In Hopkins, Lee Bennett. *Small Talk.* Illus. by Susan Gaber. Harcourt, 1995.

Ghigna. Charles. "A Poem Is a Little Path." In Prelutsky, Jack. *The 20th Century Children's Poetry Treasury.* Illus. by Meilo So. Knopf, 1999.

———. "Writer's Block," "Porcupine Poems," & "What's a Poem?" *A Fury of Motion.* Boyds Mills, 2003.

Giovanni, Nikki. "Forward: The Poem Speaks." In Adoff, Arnold. *I Am the Darker Brother.* S & S, 1996.

Goldstein, Bobbye S. *Inner Chimes: Poems on Poetry.* Illus. by Jane Breskin Zalben. Boyds Mills, 1992.

Grandits, John. "The Little House." *Technically, It's Not My Fault.* Clarion, 2004.

Greenfield, Eloise. *In the Land of Words.* Illus. by Jan Spivey Gilchrist. HarperCollins, 2004.

———. "Things." In Giovanni, Nikki. *Hip-Hop Speaks to Children.* Sourcebooks, 2008. (Includes CD) (Also in *Make a Joyful Sound*)

Harris, William J. "An Historic Moment." In Hopkins, Lee Bennett. *Good Books, Good Times.* Illus. by Harvey Stevenson. HarperCollins, 1990. (Also in *Knock at a Star*)

Hopkins, Lee Bennett. "Why Poetry?" In Heard, Georgia. *Falling Down the Page.* Roaring Brook, 2009.

Johnson, Angela. "Preface." *The Other Side.* Orchard, 1998.

Jordan, Norman. "August 8." In Slier, Deborah. *Make a Joyful Sound.* Illus. by Cornelius Van Wright & Ying-Hwa Hu. Checkerboard, 1991.

Koriyama, Naoshi. "Unfolding Bud." In Dunning, Stephen, et al. *Reflections on a Gift of Watermelon Pickle.* HarperCollins, 1967.

Kuskin, Karla. "Dig Deep in You," "Take a Word Like Cat," "Thoughts That Were Put Into Words," "Where Do You Get an Idea for a Poem?" & "Write About a Radish." *Moon, Have You Met My Mother?* Illus. by Sergio Ruzzier. HarperCollins, 2003.

Lewis, J. Patrick. "Acknowledgements." *Please Bury Me in the Library.* Illus. by Kyle M. Stone. Harcourt, 2005.

———. *The Brothers' War.* National Geographic, 2007.

Little, Jean. "About Notebooks," "About Poems, Sort of," "After English Class," & "Writers." *Hey World, Here I Am!* Illus. by Sue Truesdell. HarperCollins, 1989.

Lyon, George Ella. "Invocation." In Janeczko, Paul B. *Hey You!* Illus. by Robert Rayevsky. HarperCollins, 2007.

Medina, Tony. "Poetry Means the World to Me." *Love to Langston.* Illus. by R. Gregory Christie. Lee & Low, 2002.

Merriam, Eve. "How to Eat a Poem." In Dunning, Stephen, et al. *Reflections on a Gift of Watermelon Pickle.* HarperCollins, 1967.

———. "Verse Play," "Prose and Poetry," "Reply to the Question: How Can You Become a Poet?" "Ways of Composing," "The Poem as a Door," & "Where Is a Poem?" *The Singing Green.* Illus. by Kathleen Collins Howell. Morrow, 1992.

Micklos, John, Jr. "A Poem for Me." *Daddy Poems.* Illus. by Robert Casilla. Boyds Mills, 2000.

Mitton, Tony. "Instructions for Growing Poetry." *Plum.* Illus. by Mary Grand Pré. Scholastic, 2003.

Montenegro, Laura Nyman. *A Poet's Bird Garden.* Farrar, 2007.

Moore, Marianne. "Poetry." In Clinton, Catherine, *A Poem of Her Own.* Illus. by Stephen Alcorn. Abrams, 2003.

Mora, Pat. "One Blue Door." *This Big Sky.* Illus. by Steve Jenkins. Scholastic, 1998.

———. "Recitation." *My Own True Name.* Arté Público, 2000.

Myers, Walter Dean. "Ernest S." *Here in Harlem.* Holiday, 2004.

Natal, Jim. "Dedication." In Nye, Naomi Shihab. *What Have You Lost?* Greenwillow, 1999.

Nye, Naomi Shihab. "Because of Poems." *A Maze Me.* Greenwillow, 2005.

———. Section: "Words and Silences." *This Same Sky.* Macmillan, 1992.

———. "Valentine for Ernest Mann." In Janeczko, Paul B. *The Place My Words Are Looking For.* Macmillan, 1990.

Prelutsky, Jack. "I Have to Write a Poem for Class." *What a Day It Was at School!* Illus. by Doug Cushman. HarperCollins, 2007.

———. "There Was a Little Poet." *In Aunt Giraffe's Green Garden.* HarperCollins, 2007.

Prince Redcloud. "And Then." In Bauer, Caroline Feller. *Snowy Day.* Illus. by Margot Tomes. HarperCollins, 1986.

Sanchez, Sonia. "To P. J. (2 yrs old who sed write a poem for me in Portland, Oregon.)" In Adoff, Arnold. *My Black Me.* Dutton, 1974. (Also in *Oxford Illustrated Book of American Children's Poetry; A Family of Poems*)

Sandburg, Carl. "Paper I," "Paper II," "Sketch of a Poet," & "From . . . Pencils." In Hopkins, Lee Bennett. *Rainbows Are Made.* Illus. by Fritz Eichenberg. Harcourt, 1982.

Schertle, Alice. "Question." In Hopkins, Lee Bennett. *Hamsters, Shells, and Spelling Bees.* Illus. by Sachiko Yoshikawa. HarperCollins, 2008.

———. "Right Here," "Poem About Rabbit," & "Writing Past Midnight." *A Lucky Thing.* Illus. by Wendell Minor. Harcourt, 1999.

Shields, Carol Diggory. "Poetry Dances." *English, Fresh Squeezed!* Illus. by Tony Ross. Handprint, 2004.

Sidman, Joyce. "To Anthony: Some Reasons Why." *This Is Just to Say.* Illus. by Pamela Zagarenski. Houghton, 2007.

Viorst, Judith. "Sometimes Poems." *If I Were in Charge of the World.* Illus. by Lynne Cherry. Atheneum, 1981.

Walker, Alice. "How Poems Are Made: A Discredited View." In Rochelle, Belinda. *Words with Wings.* Harper Collins, 2001.

Wallace, Ronald. "Hippopotamus." In Janeczko, Paul B. *Dirty Laundry Pile.* Illus. by Melissa Sweet. Harper Collins, 2001.

Young, Al. "For Poets." In Adoff, Arnold. *I Am the Darker Brother.* S & S, 1996.

Zimmer, Tracie Vaughan. "The Poems I Like Best." In Janeczko, Paul B. *A Foot in the Mouth.* Illus. by Chris Raschka. Candlewick, 2009.

Poetic Language

The sheer number of poems and essays about what poetry is and what makes it good indicates its complexity and power. Some would like a narrow definition of poetry that adheres precisely to form. Others would like students to be steeped in the classics rather than in contemporary poems. Some think that verse is frivolous and only serious poems should be addressed. Others feel most comfortable with light and humorous works, fearing they don't understand deeper poetry.

Students in Shari Griffin's fourth and fifth grade classroom struggled to understand what made a poem. When she shared Kristine O'Connell George's *Hummingbird Nest: A Journal of Poems* with them, they were surprised that this could be both a journal and poetry. They also thought it read like a story. They wondered if when someone really pays attention, the words come out as poems. One commented on "the shell poem" and feeling all "curled up" when it was read. One child said, "I've never heard of raisin black . . . That's a cool way to describe a bird color." Another observed that if you read out just the titles they would make their own poem. When Shari asked the students if they thought there was a poem in everything we do, some students were fairly sure there was. What Shari's students were beginning to notice was that George uses imagery and careful descriptions that are both scientific and poetic. As the year went on, students tried writing their own poems as they responded to the science they were learning.

In this book poetry will be defined very broadly: Poetry is the act of paying thoughtful attention to language and using that language to carefully express thoughts, feelings, and observations. For purposes of this book examples will be included because they use poetic language rather than because they adhere to strict definitions of poetry. Two of America's greatest orators were masters of poetic language. Abraham Lincoln's *Gettysburg Address* captures the pain of war and the resoluteness needed to continue to act. Martin Luther King Jr.'s *I Have a Dream* speech is a litany filled with imagery and emotion. Each of these poetic writings has been published in picture book form, with the words carefully arranged so that the power of each line is expressed. "The Preamble to the

Constitution of the United States" is written poetically, with careful phrasing and rich language that indicate the serious intent of the document. David Catrow has used these powerful words as the text for his picture book *We the Kids*.

Poetic Language in Picture Books

Increasingly, the text of picture books is arranged in the form of free verse, with lines of text floating beside or inside illustrations, rather than in prose style, with the text at the top or bottom of the page. The brief lines of Ntozake Shange's *Coretta Scott* are arranged in short bursts to give this poetic biography its power. The longer text of Robert Burleigh's *One Giant Leap* is arranged in poetic lines. Even when lines are not arranged as poems, some authors write terse, carefully worded images that could be poems. The quiet rendering of the hard life of prairie settlers is arranged as free verse in Ann Turner's *Dakota Dugout*. The strong images and repetition of Cynthia Rylant's *Night in the Country* and *Snow* are poetry.

Many picture books use rhymed text, from the works of Dr. Seuss to contemporary works such as Kristine O'Connell George's *One Mitten* and Nancy Shaw's *Raccoon Tune*. Rhyme in picture books allows beginning readers to predict what will happen next. Rhymed picture books are included throughout this volume in the appropriate subject areas. Many others can be located under the Library of Congress heading "Stories in Rhyme" in catalogs.

Burleigh, Robert. *One Giant Leap*. Illus. by Mike Wimmer. Philomel, 2009.
Catrow, David. *We the Kids: The Preamble to the Constitution of the United States*. Dial, 2005
George, Kristine O'Connell. *One Mitten*. Illus. by Maggie Smith. Clarion, 2004.
King, Martin Luther, Jr. *I Have a Dream*. Illus. by 15 Coretta Scott King Award & Honor Book Artists. Scholastic, 1997.
Lincoln, Abraham. *The Gettysburg Address*. Illus. by Michael McCurdy. Houghton, 1995.
Rylant, Cynthia. *Night in the Country*. Illus. by Mary Szilagyi. Bradbury, 1986.
———. *Snow*. Illus. by Lauren Stringer. Harcourt, 2008.
Shange, Ntozake. *Coretta Scott*. Illus. by Kadir Nelson. HarperCollins, 2009.
Shaw, Nancy. *Raccoon Tune*. Illus. by Howard Fine. Holt, 2003.
Turner, Ann. *Dakota Dugout*. Illus. by Ronald Himler. Macmillan, 1985.

Novels in Verse

Authors and poets are blurring the genre lines and using poetic language in novels as well as picture books. The best novels in verse use carefully selected, evocative language to share powerful emotions with young readers. Karen Hesse's *Out of the Dust*, for example, richly describes the bleakness of the Oklahoma Dust Bowl during the Depression, as well as a personal tragedy so great a father and daughter cannot articulate their pain to one another. The free verse allows readers to feel the horror of life that has turned to dust both literally and metaphorically, as the characters slowly make their way toward a new beginning.

Some of these novels are autobiographical, some historical, and some are contemporary. A number of novel-length collections of poems have a common thread and common characters. For purposes of space, not all of these are mentioned here, but they are included in appropriate subject areas of this book. When the subject of a novel listed here fits study in another curriculum area, the novel will also be included in that chapter. Sometimes poems in these novels are distinctive enough to stand alone, and these are included in the appropriate subject area. Other examples of novels in verse appear under the Library of Congress subject heading "Novels in Verse" in catalogs.

Appelt, Kathi. *My Father's Summers: A Daughter's Memoir*. Holt, 2004.
Applegate, Katherine. *Home of the Brave*. Feiwel & Friends, 2007.

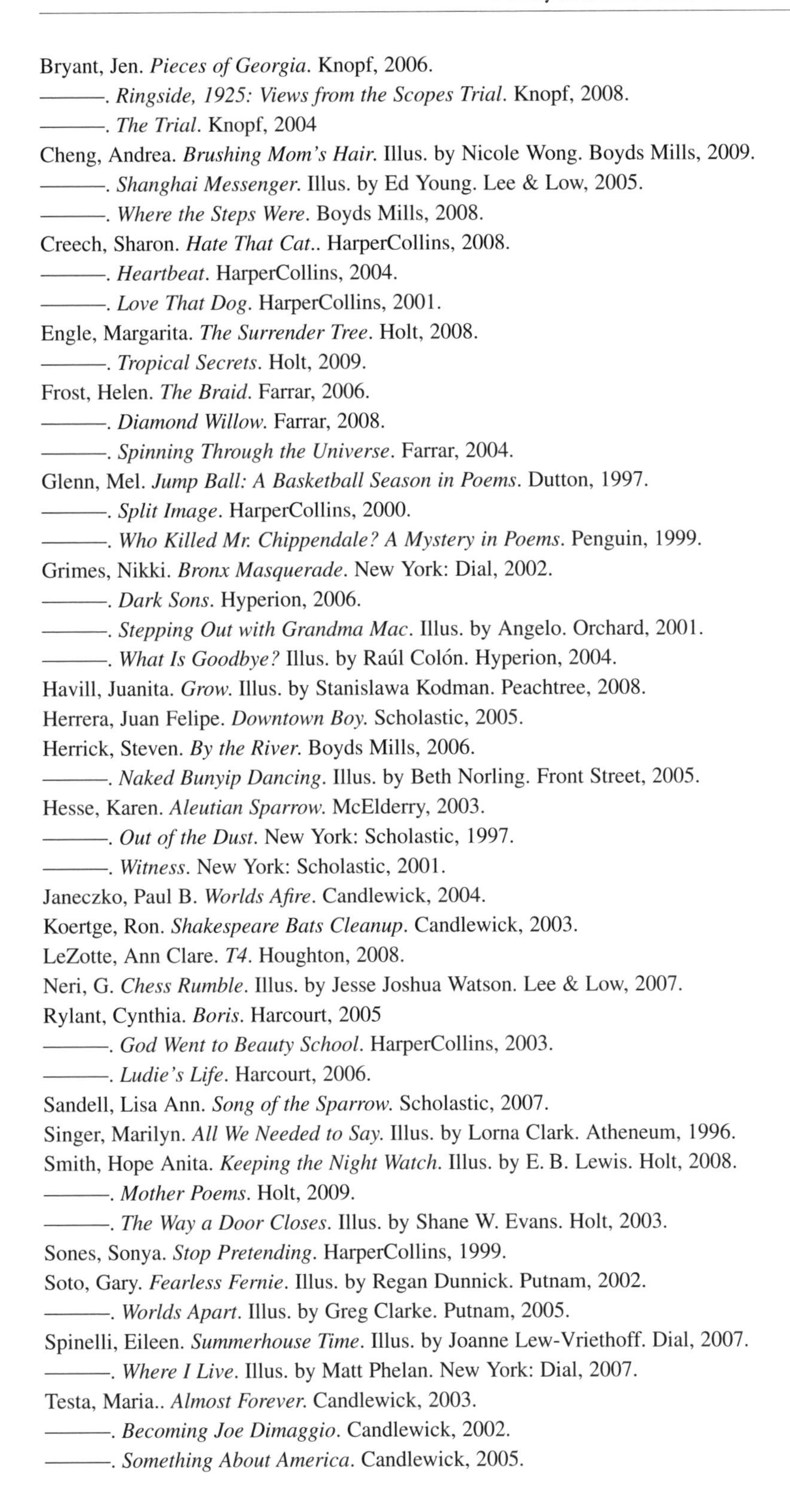

Bryant, Jen. *Pieces of Georgia*. Knopf, 2006.
———. *Ringside, 1925: Views from the Scopes Trial*. Knopf, 2008.
———. *The Trial*. Knopf, 2004
Cheng, Andrea. *Brushing Mom's Hair*. Illus. by Nicole Wong. Boyds Mills, 2009.
———. *Shanghai Messenger*. Illus. by Ed Young. Lee & Low, 2005.
———. *Where the Steps Were*. Boyds Mills, 2008.
Creech, Sharon. *Hate That Cat.*. HarperCollins, 2008.
———. *Heartbeat*. HarperCollins, 2004.
———. *Love That Dog*. HarperCollins, 2001.
Engle, Margarita. *The Surrender Tree*. Holt, 2008.
———. *Tropical Secrets*. Holt, 2009.
Frost, Helen. *The Braid*. Farrar, 2006.
———. *Diamond Willow*. Farrar, 2008.
———. *Spinning Through the Universe*. Farrar, 2004.
Glenn, Mel. *Jump Ball: A Basketball Season in Poems*. Dutton, 1997.
———. *Split Image*. HarperCollins, 2000.
———. *Who Killed Mr. Chippendale? A Mystery in Poems*. Penguin, 1999.
Grimes, Nikki. *Bronx Masquerade*. New York: Dial, 2002.
———. *Dark Sons*. Hyperion, 2006.
———. *Stepping Out with Grandma Mac*. Illus. by Angelo. Orchard, 2001.
———. *What Is Goodbye?* Illus. by Raúl Colón. Hyperion, 2004.
Havill, Juanita. *Grow*. Illus. by Stanislawa Kodman. Peachtree, 2008.
Herrera, Juan Felipe. *Downtown Boy*. Scholastic, 2005.
Herrick, Steven. *By the River*. Boyds Mills, 2006.
———. *Naked Bunyip Dancing*. Illus. by Beth Norling. Front Street, 2005.
Hesse, Karen. *Aleutian Sparrow*. McElderry, 2003.
———. *Out of the Dust*. New York: Scholastic, 1997.
———. *Witness*. New York: Scholastic, 2001.
Janeczko, Paul B. *Worlds Afire*. Candlewick, 2004.
Koertge, Ron. *Shakespeare Bats Cleanup*. Candlewick, 2003.
LeZotte, Ann Clare. *T4*. Houghton, 2008.
Neri, G. *Chess Rumble*. Illus. by Jesse Joshua Watson. Lee & Low, 2007.
Rylant, Cynthia. *Boris*. Harcourt, 2005
———. *God Went to Beauty School*. HarperCollins, 2003.
———. *Ludie's Life*. Harcourt, 2006.
Sandell, Lisa Ann. *Song of the Sparrow*. Scholastic, 2007.
Singer, Marilyn. *All We Needed to Say*. Illus. by Lorna Clark. Atheneum, 1996.
Smith, Hope Anita. *Keeping the Night Watch*. Illus. by E. B. Lewis. Holt, 2008.
———. *Mother Poems*. Holt, 2009.
———. *The Way a Door Closes*. Illus. by Shane W. Evans. Holt, 2003.
Sones, Sonya. *Stop Pretending*. HarperCollins, 1999.
Soto, Gary. *Fearless Fernie*. Illus. by Regan Dunnick. Putnam, 2002.
———. *Worlds Apart*. Illus. by Greg Clarke. Putnam, 2005.
Spinelli, Eileen. *Summerhouse Time*. Illus. by Joanne Lew-Vriethoff. Dial, 2007.
———. *Where I Live*. Illus. by Matt Phelan. New York: Dial, 2007.
Testa, Maria.. *Almost Forever*. Candlewick, 2003.
———. *Becoming Joe Dimaggio*. Candlewick, 2002.
———. *Something About America*. Candlewick, 2005.

Turner, Ann. *Hard Hit*. Scholastic, 2006,
Williams, Julie. *Escaping Tornado Season*. HarperCollins, 2004.
Williams, Vera B. *Amber Was Brave, Essie Was Smart*. Greenwillow, 2001.
Wong, Janet. *Minn and Jake*. Illus. by Geneviève Côté. Farrar, 2003.
———. *Minn and Jake's Almost Terrible Summer*. Illus. by Geneviève Côté. Farrar, 2008.
Woodson, Jacqueline. *Locomotion*. Putnam, 2003.
Zimmer, Tracie Vaughn. *42 Miles*. Illus. by Elaine Clayton. Clarion, 2008.
———. *Reaching For the Sun*. Bloomsbury, 2007.
———. *Sketches From a Spy Tree*. Illus. by Andrew Glass. Clarion, 2005.

LEARNING TO LOVE LANGUAGE

Early childhood educators and scholars have written a great deal on the importance of play in human growth and development (Paley, 2004, Roskos & Christie, 2007). In play we can practice what we will need in the broader, less controlled world. . The young child's forays into language seem playful, with the child trying out words she has heard in new contexts and situations. But play is hard work. Poets work hard to find the perfect word to say what they want to say. Eve Merriam has written that she sometimes has "spent weeks looking for the precisely right word." (Cullinan, 1996, p. 33) Carol Niven talks about how much poet Carl Sandburg loved words, commenting that he collected words in a notebook including both the Swedish his parents spoke at home and the English he learned at school. He plays with the meanings of words and talks about their power in many of his poems. Bilingual poets have talked about this love of words in two languages.

Anyone who works at something she loves is playing at the same time. No one ever fell in love with words by memorizing them for vocabulary tests. Farstrup and Samuels' review of research on vocabulary includes a number of strategies used by poets, a sign that playing with words is an effective method of learning (2008).

A love of words comes from the work of playing around with language. We learn words by hearing them, rolling them around on our tongues and in our minds like a small child does as she learns language. A person who loves language plays with it—hears words and links them with other sounds, other meanings, and other words. The patterns and sounds of language are fascinating to the lover of words. From these connections, many poets find poems. Poetry comes as Harry Behn writes (1968) from falling in love with language. We "learn to love words, to know how they look, what they mean, how they sound." Rebecca Kai Dotlich says in "A Kingdom of Words," that a word may seem to be just a word, but a poet can create "a kingdom around it."

Playing with Words

Poetry speaks to the power of words. The children's chant "Sticks and Stones May Break My Bones but Names Will Never Hurt Me" is used to ward off a powerful weapon, which, in reality, can hurt a great deal. Carl Sandburg's "Little Girl, Be Careful What You Say" and "Primer Lesson" speak to the power of words to hurt or heal. "Magic Words," an anonymous Inuit poem, is about the ancient power of words to create the world. In "Old Mountains Want to Turn to Sand," Tommy Olofsson suggests that the power of words is like water on rock; words can move mountains. In her Introduction to *By Definition*, Sara Holbrook tells young readers that in our fast-paced world, it is more important than ever to "nurture our words, respect them as individuals, and handle them with care."

Poets comment on the natural and pleasing sounds of words in their poems. In his poem "Take Sky," David McCord asks why the word sky "sounds so well out loud" and then mentions other words that sound like what they represent. In his poem "The Look and Sound of Words," he suggests that the sound of a word matters. Mary O'Neill explores the sounds of words in her poem "Feelings About Words"; words actually sound like the size, shape, or movement of the object or action they represent. Karla Kuskin has written "Cow Sounds Heavy" and "Worm" about how the names for creatures are appropriate for their size, shape, and abilities. Patricia Hubbell comments on "the gagging a" in "Rat." Barbara Juster Esbensen's collection of animal poems, *Words With Wrinkled Knees*, focuses on the sounds of animal names.

Sometimes poets will play with words. Homophones, antonyms, differing meanings, word roots and origin are all fodder for poems. Any interesting aspect of language is material for a poet's work. Lee Bennett Hopkins has collected a number of poems that discuss the importance of words in *Wonderful Words: Poems About Reading, Writing, Speaking and Listening*. Eloise Greenfield's *In the Land of Words* is a collection of her poems about words and poetry. Teachers and librarians can post these poems and share them with students to encourage them to think about and savor words.

Alarcón, Francisco X. "Words Are Birds." *Laughing Tomatoes = Jitomates Risueños*. Illus. by Maya Christina Gonzalez. Children's, 1997.

Angelou, Maya, "I Love the Look of Words." In Feelings, Tom. *Soul Looks Back in Wonder.* Dial, 1993.

Baer, Edith. *Words Are Like Faces*. Illus. by Kyra Teis. Star Bright, 2007.

Barretta, Gene. *Dear Deer: A Book of Homophones*. Holt, 2007.

Bonazzi, Robert. "Ah Words." In Nye, Naomi Shihab. *Is this Forever, or What?* HarperCollins, 2004.

Brown, Margaret Wise. "Cadence." *Nibble Nibble*. Illus. by Leonard Weisgard. HarperCollins, 1959, 1985.

Curtis, Jamie Lee. *Big Words for Little People*. Illus. by Laura Cornell. HarperCollins, 2008.

Dickinson, Emily. "A Word Is Dead" & "The Wind Begun to Knead the Grass." In Rosen, Michael. *Classic Poetry*. Illus. by Paul Howard. Candlewick, 2009.

Dotlich, Rebecca Kai. "Treasure Words." In Hopkins, Lee Bennett. *Days to Celebrate*. Illus. by Stephen Alcorn. *HarperCollins*, 2005.

Esbensen, Barbara Juster. *Words with Wrinkled Knees*. Illus. by John Stadler. HarperCollins, 1987.

George, Kristine O'Connell. "Quiddling with Words." *The Great Frog Race*. Illus. by Kate Kiesler. Clarion, 1997.

Gildner, Gary. "A Word." In Greenberg, Jan. *Heart to Heart*. Abrams, 2001.

Greenfield, Eloise. "In the Land of Words," "Oh, Words," & "I Go to the Land." *In The Land of Words*. Illus. by Jan Spivey Gilchrist. HarperCollins, 2004.

Hoberman, Mary Ann. "Opposites." *The Llama Who Had No Pajama*. Illus. by Betty Fraser. Harcourt, 1998.

Holbrook, Sara. "Introduction." *By Definition*. Illus. by Scott Mattern. Boyds Mills, 2003.

Hopkins, Lee Bennett, sel. *Wonderful Words: Poems About Reading, Writing, Speaking and Listening*. Illus. by Karen Barbour. S & S, 2004.

Hubbell, Patricia. "Rat." *Earthmates*. Illus. by Jean Cassels. Cavendish, 2000.

Hymes, Lucia & James L. Hymes Jr. "My Favorite Word." In De Regniers, Beatrice Schenk. *Sing a Song of Popcorn*. Scholastic, 1988.

Kuskin, Karla. "Cow Sounds Heavy," "What Separates Each One of Us . . . " & "Worm." *The Sky Is Always the Sky*. Illus. by Isabelle Dervaux. HarperCollins, 1998.

Lewis, J. Patrick. *Big Is Big (And Little, Little)*. Illus. by Bob Barner. Holiday, 2007.

———. "The Big-Word Girl." *Please Bury Me in the Library*. Illus. by Kyle M. Stone. Harcourt, 2005.

———. "Tickle Tackle Botticelli." *Black Cat Bone*. Illus. by Gary Kelley. Creative, 2006.

McCord, David. "The Look and Sound of Words," "Goose, Moose, & Spruce," & "Take Sky." *One At a Time*. Illus. by Henry B. Kane. Little, 1986.

"Magic Words." (Anonymous Inuit Poet). Trans. by Edward Field. In Paschen, Elise. *Poetry Speaks to Children*. Sourcebooks, 2005. (With CD)

Merriam, Eve. "Latch, Catch." *Blackberry Ink*. Illus. by Hans Wilhelm. Morrow, 1985.

———. "A Nanny for a Goat." *You Be Good and I'll Be Night*. Illus. by Karen Lee Schmidt. Morrow, 1988. (Compound Words)

Mora, Pat. "Words as Free as Confetti." *Confetti*. Illus. by Enrique O. Sanchez. Lee & Low, 1996.

Nye, Naomi Shihab. "Words in My Pillow." In Heard, Georgia. *Falling Down the Page*. Roaring Brook, 2009.

Olofsson, Tommy. "Old Mountains Want to Turn to Sand." In Nye, Naomi Shihab. *This Same Sky*. Macmillan, 1992.

O'Neill, Mary. "Feelings Abut Words." In Goldstein, Bobbye S. *Inner Chimes*. Illus. by Jane Breskin Zalben. (Also in *The Random House Book of Poetry for Children*)

Park, Linda Sue. "Word Watch." *Tap Dancing on the Roof*. Illus. by Istvan Banyai. Clarion, 2007.

Pomerantz, Charlotte. "Where Do These Words Come From?" In De Regniers, Beatrice Schenk, *Sing a Song of Popcorn*. Scholastic, 1988.

Salinger, Michael. *Well-Defined: Vocabulary in Rhyme*. Boyds Mills, 2009.

Sandburg, Carl. "Little Girl, Be Careful What You Say" & "Primer Lesson." In Hopkins, Lee Bennett. *Rainbows Are Made*. Illus. by Fritz Eichenberg. Harcourt, 1982.

Shields, Carol Diggory. "Speaking Greek," "36 Ways to Say Cool," "The Word," & "What's Another Word for Thesaurus?" *English, Fresh Squeezed*. Illus. by Tony Ross. Handprint, 2004.

Sidman, Joyce. "Fashion Sense." *This Is Just to Say*. Illus. by Pamela Zagarenski. Houghton, 2007.

Silverstein, Shel. "Bituminous." *Falling Up*. HarperCollins, 1996.

Wagner, Ann. "Vocabulary Lesson." In Hopkins, Lee Bennett. *America at War*. Illus. by Stephen Alcorn. McElderry, 2008.

Wilbur, Richard. *Opposites, More Opposites, and a Few Differences*. Harcourt, 2000.

———. *The Pig in the Spigot*. Illus. by J. Otto Seibold. Harcourt, 2000.

Zephaniah, Benjamin. "For Word." In Giovanni, Nikki. *Hip Hop Speaks to Children*. Sourcebooks, 2008. (With CD)

SHARING POETRY

Too often poetry is limited to one or two week units. This results in rushed instruction, memorization of terminology, and hastily written poems. Poetry that is naturally shared all year long becomes part of the fabric of classrooms, and students initiate the sharing and writing on their own terms. Sharing poetry—reading it during Sustained Silent Reading, reading it aloud, and writing it—should be a natural part of the classroom day. Poetry can become just one of the ways that students respond to science, social studies, and mathematics, as well as language arts.

Fourth-Fifth grade teacher Shari Griffin decided to feature poetry in her classroom during the 2008–2009 school year. Here are some of her thoughts from an email sent to me in February, 2009:

> I wanted to start with poetry but not end it there—it's not just a unit or a genre; it's a way of thinking, a way of communicating, a way of learning. Typically, it seems like poetry is "saved" for the end of the year .... it's like geometry ... seems simple yet really is so complex the teacher needs to know way more than she does to really serve kids well and develop a greater conceptual understanding. And because of that it gets relegated to the status of extra rather than essential.
>
> Well Shazam! Since we started with it, writing has been MUCH different, MUCH better. Our conversations are richer, kids seem to have a better grasp of the idea that having a reader doesn't just mean that a teacher will assess something or a peer will read it and give a few comments, but that there are dynamic people who might be able to interact with what they write. The kids seem much more willing to share genuine responses through poetry than through 5 paragraph essays or even a sentence or paragraph—they're more free with their thoughts, precise with their words, and exact in their thinking.

Writing Poetry

Students should be given many opportunities to play with language, try out forms (rather than be required to write poems in specific forms at specific times), and to write poems as one of a number of ways of expressing their knowledge. Several novels have served as inspiration for students to try poetry as the characters learn to use poetry to express their thoughts and feelings. Sharon Creech's *Love That Dog* and *Hate That Cat* feature poems that young Jack writes even as he insists he doesn't care for poetry. Walter Dean Myers is featured as the poet whose work opens the door for Jack, and other classic poems are included in the work. In Jacqueline Woodson's *Locomotion*, poetry is essential to Lonny's struggle to heal from the tragic deaths of his parents and his painful separation from his younger sister. In *Shakespeare Bats Cleanup*, Kevin Boland has mononucleosis and, having been given a blank notebook by his poet father, begins to write poems in a number of forms during his recovery simply as a way to pass the time. Gary Crew's *Troy Thompson's Excellent Peotry Book* (a deliberate misspelling) is a mock journal in which Troy writes all of his notes and attempts at various forms of poetry for school.

Some novelists have used poems by their young protagonists intermittently throughout a story to help readers to understand their thoughts and feelings. Norma Fox Mazer's *What I Believe* includes prose and many types of poems. Nikki Grimes' *Jazmin's Notebook* features one young writer, and her *Bronx Masquerade*, many writers of both prose and poetry that help classmates discover much about each other that they had not known or appreciated. High school student Kate Bloomfield's ironic and funny poems are scattered throughout Jean Little's *Hey World, Here I Am!* Each of these volumes can serve as a model for capturing one's thoughts in the form of poems. In the February email mentioned above, Shari Griffin wrote about what happened when she began her school year with a novel that featured poetry:

> We began with Sharon Creech's *Love That Dog*. We chose it because we wanted a whole class experience that would lead to deeper thinking and richer conversations. I love what the book did for the kids. It came up in all sorts of contexts, as a reference for behavior, thinking, events, and weaving a story together. So, I bought several copies of *Hate That Cat*. This book took our conversation to a whole new level. From these two books together we learned about the character, talked about the connections, reveled in the "aha" of discoveries, and how the pieces of the story added up.
>
> In my quest to be more "Miss Stretchberry" I gave the students binders, and new poems daily. I started with the poems in the back of Creech's books, then branched out to a variety of others I found, then to those recommended by students who at some point begun their own quests for poetry that mattered to them. (Griffin, email correspondence, 2009)

Creech, Sharon. *Hate That Cat*. HarperCollins, 2008.

———. *Love That Dog*. HarperCollins, 2001.

Crew, Gary. *Troy Thompson's Excellent Peotry Book*. Illus. by Craig Smith. Kane Miller, 2004.

Grimes, Nikki. *Bronx Masquerade*. Dial, 2002.

———. *Jazmin's Notebook*. Dial, 1998.

Koertge, Ron. *Shakespeare Bats Cleanup*. Candlewick, 2003.

Little, Jean. *Hey World, Here I Am!* Illus. by Sue Truesdell. HarperCollins, 1989.

Mazer, Norma Fox. *What I Believe*. Harcourt. 2005.

Woodson, Jacqueline. *Locomotion*. Putnam, 2003.

Advice on Writing Poetry

Some poets include writing advice in their poetry collections, so that as students read poems, they are also learning about how the poem came to be and what the poet was trying to express. Karla Kuskin's *Dogs and Dragons, Trees and Dreams* includes comments on how she chose the subjects of her poems and how she went about writing them. Her "Write About a Radish" is an amusing poem about how to choose a subject. Patricia Hubbell's "When Writing a Poem About a Carrot," seems to echo Kuskin's poem. J. Patrick Lewis includes notes on why and how he wrote each of his poetic responses to Civil War photographs in *The Brothers' War*. Naomi Shihab Nye's poignant introduction to her volume of poems of the Middle East, *19 Varieties of Gazelle*, talks about turning to writing poetry after September 11, 2001.

Paul B. Janeczko's *The Place My Words Are Looking For* and *Seeing the Blue Between* combine poets' thoughts on their writing processes with writing advice and examples of their poems. Bernice E. Cullinan's *A Jar of Tiny Stars: Poems by NCTE Award-Winning Poets* includes the poets' comments on their writing processes. X. J. and Dorothy M. Kennedy, Ralph Fletcher, and Jack Prelutsky have written reader-friendly guides for students. Some poets have written collections of poems that focus on how poetry is written. Sometimes a poet will write a single poem about the writing process. A list of useful references for adults on how to teach poetry is included at the end of this chapter.

Alarcón, Francisco X. "To Write Poetry" & "A Blank White Page." *Iguanas in the Snow = Iguanas en la Nieve* Illus. by Maya Christina Gonzales. Children's 2001.

Appelt, Kathi. *Poems from Homeroom: A Writer's Place to Start.* Holt, 2002.

Fletcher, Ralph. *Poetry Matters: Writing a Poem from the Inside Out.* HarperCollins, 2002.

Holbrook, Sara. *Wham! It's a Poetry Jam: Discovering Performance Poetry.* Honesdale, PA: Boyds Mills, 2002.

Hubbell, Patricia. "When Writing a Poem about a Carrot." *Black Earth, Gold Sun.* Illus. by Mary Newell DePalma. Cavendish, 2001.

Janeczko, Paul B. *How to Write Poetry.* Scholastic, 1999.

———, Comp. *The Place My Words Are Looking For.* S & S, 1990.

———. *Poetry from A to Z: A Guide for Young Writers.* Illus. by Cathy Bobak. S & S, 1994.

———. *Seeing the Blue Between: Advice and Inspiration for Young Poets.* Candlewick, 2002.

Kennedy, X. J. & Dorothy M. Kennedy. *Knock at a Star: A Child's Introduction to Poetry.* Little, 1999.

Kuskin, Karla. *Dogs and Dragons, Trees and Dreams.* HarperCollins, 1980.

Lewis, J. Patrick. *The Brothers' War: Civil War Voices in Verse.* National Geographic, 2007.

Nye, Naomi Shihab. "Introduction." *19 Varieties of Gazelle: Poems of the Middle East.* HarperCollins, 2002.

Prelutsky, Jack. *Pizza, Pigs, and Poetry: How to Write a Poem.* Greenwillow 2008.

———. *Read a Rhyme, Write a Rhyme.* Illus. by Meilo So. Knopf, 2005.

Soto, Gary. "Chatting with Gary Soto." *A Fire in My Hands.* Harcourt, 2006.

Poems on Writing Poetry

Bagert, Brod. "My Writer's Notebook." In Hopkins, Lee Bennett. *School Supplies.* Illus. by Renée Flower. S & S, 1996.

Berry, James. "Big Page Writer." *A Nest Full of Stars.* Illus. by Ashley Bryan. Greenwillow, 2004.

Esbensen, Barbara Juster. "Homework" & "Pencils." *Who Shrank My Grandmother's House?* Illus. by Eric Beddows. HarperCollins, 1992.

Ghigna, Charles. "Writer's Block." *A Fury of Motion.* Boyds Mills, 2003.

Greenfield, Eloise. "Things." In Giovanni, Nikki. *Hip-Hop Speaks to Children.* Sourcebooks, 2008. (Includes CD) (Also in *Make a Joyful Sound*)

Levertov, Denise. "Writing in the Dark." In Willard, Nancy. *Step Lightly.* Harcourt, 1998.

Little, Jean. "About Notebooks" & "Writers." *Hey World, Here I Am!* Illus. by Sue Truesdell. HarperCollins, 1989.

Magliaro, Elaine. "Things to Do if You Are a Pencil." In Heard, Georgia. *Falling Down the Page.* Roaring Brook, 2009.

Merriam, Eve. "Ways of Composing" & "Rainbow Writing." *The Singing Green.* Illus. by Kathleen Collins Howell. Morrow, 1992.

Sandburg, Carl. "Paper I," "Paper II," & "From . . . Pencils." In Hopkins, Lee Bennett. *Rainbows Are Made.* Illus. by Fritz Eichenberg. Harcourt, 1982. (Also in *School Supplies*)

Schertle, Alice. *A Lucky Thing*. Illus. by Wendell Minor. Harcourt, 1999.
Thurman, Judith. "New Notebook." In Hopkins, Lee Bennett. *School Supplies*. Illus. by Renée Flower. S & S, 1996.
Wong, Janet. *You Have to Write*. Illus. by Teresa Flavin. McElderry, 2002.
Worth, Valerie. "Pencil." *Peacock*. Illus. by Natalie Babbitt. Farrar, 2002.
Zimmer, Tracie Vaughan. "Writer." *Steady Hands*. Illus. by Megan Halsey & Sean Addy. Clarion, 2009.

Poetry by Young Poets

Listening to or reading poems by students who are close to one's age can provide an incentive to write. The following works are collections of poems by young people of differing backgrounds who take on a variety of subjects. Librarians and teachers can include these poems in appropriate areas of the curriculum to encourage students to see that poems are one way of responding to issues being studied.

Adedjouma, Davida, ed. *The Palm of My Heart: Poetry by African-American Children*. Illus. by R. Gregory Christie. Lee & Low, 1996.
Brenner, Barbara, ed. *The Earth Is Painted Green: A Garden of Poems About Our Planet*. Illus. by S. D. Schindler. Scholastic, 1994.
Franco, Betsy, ed. *Falling Hard: One Hundred Love Poems by Teenagers*. Candlewick, 2008.
———. *Things I Have to Tell You: Poems and Writings by Teenage Girls*. Illus. by Nina Nickles. Candlewick, 2001.
———. *You Hear Me? Poems and Writings by Teenage Boys*. Illus. by Nina Nickels. Candlewick, 2001.
Franklin, Kristine L. & Nancy McGirr, eds. *Out of the Dump: Writings and Photographs by Children from Guatemala*. Lothrop, 1995.
Giovanni, Nikki, ed. *Paint Me Like I Am: Teen Poems from Writerscorps*. HarperCollins, 2003.
Hirschfelder, Arlene B. & Beverly R. Singer. *Rising Voices: Writings of Young Native Americans*. Scribners, 1992.
Lowe, Ayana, ed. *Come and Play: Children of Our World Having Fun*. Bloomsbury, 2008.
Michael, Pamela, ed. *River of Words: Images and Poetry of Water*. Heydey, 2003.
———. *River of Words: Young Poets and Artists on the Nature of Things*. Milkweed, 2008.
Nye, Naomi Shihab, sel. *Salting the Ocean: 100 Poems by Young Poets*. Illus. by Ashley Bryan. Greenwillow, 2000.
Ochoa, Annette Piña, Betsy Franco & Traci L. Gourdine, eds. *Night Is Gone, Day Is Still Coming: Stories and Poems by American Indian Teens And Young Adults*. Candlewick, 2003.
Tell the World (From Writerscorps). Illus. by Richard Newirth. HarperCollins, 2008.
Volavková, Hana, ed. *I Never Saw Another Butterfly: Children's Drawings and Poems from Terezín Concentration Camp, 1942–1944*. Knopf, 1994.
Watson, Esther Pearl & Mark Todd, eds. *The Pain Tree: And Other Teenage Angst-Ridden Poetry*. Houghton, 2000.

Posting and Sharing Poems

Posting poems has become a popular way to share poetry. Cities have created campaigns with poems on the advertising panels of buses and subways. Towns have put lines of poetry on park benches, on paving stones, and in parks. These public postings proclaim the power of poetry in the world. Because the vocabulary and language of poetry is rich, it makes sense to post poems in schools and libraries. Students can help teachers find (or they can write) poems to drinking fountains (or to water), pencil sharpeners (or to pencils), and the cafeteria (or to food), then post them near their subjects. Poems with perhaps two or three differing perspectives on the seasons, or a subject of study could be posted together. Librarians and teachers can post poems for students to ponder in places where they wait in lines. Posted poems provide access to vocabulary beyond the word lists; teachers and librarians can help children to relish the sounds of the words of these poems by sharing them aloud.

Poems can be shared as a transition from one subject to another. Librarians sometimes share Shel Silverstein's "Invitation" or another poem to begin story hours. A teacher friend shared Jean Little's "Today," a humorous poem about not living up to expectations to tell her students about her own mood. I generally stop and share Arnold Adoff's "Love Song" to chocolate with great feeling to get a laugh from my students when they seem to be flagging. Once this atmosphere of sharing is introduced, poems may come in response to any type of reading.

Here are some more comments from Shari Griffin:

I read *Wabi Sabi* (Reibstein, 2008) to my students. After reading it, the students had about five minutes before going to PE. I flippantly said something inspiring like, "You have a few minutes to read or write, or do something useful to you . . . who knows, maybe there's a haiku waiting to be written . . . " (Forgive me, this was after many hours of testing and we were all tired.) I walked the kids to PE and returned to find these haiku (we've not talked much about them, don't think we've written them, one student mentioned the 5-7-5 idea as we looked at the way *Wabi Sabi* was presented.) Avery wrote three haiku in those brief minutes. Here is one:

Days passing by slow
Learning meanings of haikus
Loving I'm alive

Adoff, Arnold. "Love Song." *Eats*. Illus. by Susan Russo. Lothrop, 1979. (Op)
Little, Jean. "Today." *Hey World, Here I Am!* Illus. by Sue Truesdell. HarperCollins, 1989.
Reibstein, Mark. *Wabi Sabi*. Illus. by Ed Young. Little, 2008.
Silverstein, Shel. "Invitation." *Where the Sidewalk Ends*. HarperCollins, 1974.

National Poetry Month

April is National Poetry Month, and the third week of April is National Young People's Poetry Week. While poetry can be shared all year long, it should be especially honored during this month of spring and renewal. Posters for National Poetry Month appear in a number of professional magazines for teachers and librarians. The Children's Book Council sponsors and provides posters and ideas for celebrating National Young People's Poetry Week.

"National Pocket Poetry Day" is another celebration in April. The idea of a pocket poem originated with Beatrice Schenk De Regniers' "Keep a Poem in Your Pocket." A number of poets have created "pocket poems" that can be shared on this day. John Grandits' pocket poem says keeping one there is "a little snack for your soul." This celebration doesn't have to be limited to one day. Pulling out and reading a poem that is appropriate to an occasion, that makes us laugh, that links the subject being studied to another idea, or that is shared specifically in honor of one of our students is a hit any time. You can also keep a favorite poem in your pocket just to enjoy anytime all by yourself. I like to keep Eloise Greenfield's "Things," about when you write a poem, you will always have it, as a poem for my pocket. Students might want to choose poems to keep in their own pockets.

De Regniers, Beatrice Schenk. "Keep a Poem in Your Pocket." In Goldstein, Bobbye S. *Inner Chimes*. Illus. by Jane Breskin Zalben. Boyds Mills, 1992. (Also in *Pocket Poems*)
Grandits, John. "Pocket Poem (A Note from the Author.)" *Blue Lipstick*. Clarion, 2007.
Greenfield, Eloise. "Things." In Giovanni, Nikki. *Hip-Hop Speaks to Children*. Sourcebooks, 2008. (Includes CD) (Also in *Make a Joyful Sound*)

Katz, Bobbi. *More Pocket Poems*. Illus. by Deborah Zemke. Dutton, 2009.

———. *Pocket Poems*. Illus. by Marylin Hafner. Dutton, 2004.

Kooser, Ted. "Pocket Poem." In Janeczko, Paul B. *Pocket Poems*. Macmillan, 1985. (op, but poem is readily available on the web)

Lewis, J. Patrick. "Keep a Pocket in your Poem." *Countdown to Summer: 180 Poems for Every Day of the School Year*. Little, 2009.

LEARNING ABOUT THE POETS

Sometimes, reading about a poet's life is an impetus to read and write poetry. The works listed here include biographical material, novels, and poems in praise of the poet, as well as collections that include biographies. Sterling publishes the *Poetry for Young People* series, which includes works about a number of classic poets. These volumes also contain examples of these poets' best-known poems. Several of these are listed below. Richard C. Owens has published the autobiographies of several contemporary poets in a series of author autobiographies.

Some poets have written autobiographies. Others write autobiographical poetry that reflects their childhood experiences. These poems are found throughout this book. Biographical collections for use by teachers and librarians and individual articles from professional magazines are included in the references at the end of this chapter. Many contemporary poets have extensive websites that include biographical information and suggestions or ideas for responding to their poetry.

Anthologies

Bryan, Ashley. *Ashley Bryan's ABC of African-American Poetry*. S & S, 1997.

Clinton, Catherine, ed. *I, Too, Sing America: Three Centuries of African American Poetry*. Illus. by Stephen Alcorn. Houghton, 1998.

———. *A Poem of Her Own: Voices of American Women Yesterday and Today*. Illus. by Stephen Alcorn. Abrams, 2003.

Giovanni, Nikki. *Shimmy Shimmy Shimmy Like My Sister Kate: Looking at the Harlem Renaissance Through Poems*. Holt, 1995.

Janeczko, Paul, comp. *The Place My Words Are Looking For*. S & S, 1990.

———. *Seeing the Blue Between: Advice and Inspiration for Young Poets*. Candlewick, 2002.

Individual Poets

Bedard, Michael. *Emily*. Illus. by Barbara Cooney. Doubleday, 1992. (Emily Dickinson) (Fiction)

———. *William Blake: The Gates of Paradise*. Tundra, 2006.

Bober, Natalie S. *A Restless Spirit: The Story of Robert Frost*. Holt, 1991.

Bolin, Frances Schoomaker, ed. *Carl Sandburg*. Illus. by Steve Arcella. Sterling, 1995.

Bruchac, Joseph. *Seeing the Circle*. Richard C. Owens, 1999. (Autobiography)

Bryant, Jen. *Call Me Marianne*. Illus. by David A. Johnson. Eerdmans, 2006. (Marianne Moore)

———. *A River of Words: The Story of William Carlos Williams*. Illus. by Melissa Sweet. Eerdmans, 2008.

Clinton, Catherine. *Phillis's Big Test*. Illus. by Sean Qualls. Houghton, 2008. (Phyllis Wheatley)

Dana, Barbara. *A Voice of Her Own: Becoming Emily Dickinson*. HarperCollins, 2009. (Fiction)

Dickinson, Emily. *My Letter To the World: And Other Poems*. Illus. by Isabelle Arsenalt. Kids Can, 2008.

Fletcher, Ralph. "Frost in the Woods." *A Writing Kind of Day*. Boyds Mills, 2005. (Robert Frost)

Florian, Douglas. *See for Your Self*. Richard C. Owen, 2005. (Autobiography)

Frampton, David. *Mr. Ferlinghetti's Poem*. Eerdmans, 2006.
Hemphill, Stephanie. *Your Own Sylvia: A Verse Portrait of Sylvia Plath*. Knopf, 2007.
Hopkins, Lee Bennett. *Been to Yesterdays: Poems of a Life*. Boyds Mills, 1995.
———. *The Writing Bug*. Richard C. Owen, 1992. (Autobiography)
Kerley, Barbara. *Walt Whitman: Words for America*. Illus. by Brian Selznick. Scholastic, 2004.
Kuskin, Karla. *Thoughts, Pictures, and Words*. Richard C. Owen, 1995. (Autobiography)
Lasky, Katherine. *A Voice of Her Own: The Story of Phillis Wheatley, Slave Poet*. Illus. by Paul Lee. Candlewick, 2003.
Levin, Jonathan, ed. *Walt Whitman*. Illus. by Jim Burke. Sterling, 1997.
Lewis, J. Patrick. "My Agile Loom." *Vherses: A Celebration of Outstanding Women*. Illus. by Mark Summers. Creative, 2005. (Emily Dickinson)
Mitchell, Barbara. *Good Morning Mr. President: A Story About Carl Sandburg*. Illus. by Dane Collins. Carolrhoda, 1988.
Mora, Pat. *A Library for Juana: The World of Sor Juana Inés*. Illus. by Beatriz Vidal. Knopf, 2002.
———. "The Young Sor Juana." *My Own True Name*. Arté Público, 2000.
Myers, Tim. *Basho and the Fox*. Illus. by Oki S. Han. Cavendish, 2000. (Prose & Poems of Basho)
———. *Basho and the River Stones*. Marshall Cavendish, 2004. (Prose & Poems of Basho)
Niven, Penelope. *Carl Sandburg*. Illus. by Marc Nadel. Harcourt, 2003.
Pomerantz, Charlotte. "Good Night, Margaret Wise Brown." *Thunderboom!* Illus. by Rob Shepperson. Front Street, 2005.
Ray, Deborah Kogan. *To Go Singing Through the World: The Childhood of Pablo Neruda*. Farrar, 2006.
Reef, Catherine. *e. e. Cummings: A Poet's Life*. Clarion, 2006.
Rinaldi, Ann. *Hang a Thousand Trees with Ribbons: The Story of Phillis Wheatley*. Harcourt, 1996. (Fiction)
Rylant, Cynthia. *Best Wishes*. Richard C. Owen, 1992.
Schmidt, Gary, ed. *Robert Frost*. Illus. by Henri Sorensen. Sterling, 2008.
Serrano, Francisco. *The Poet King of Tezcoco: A Great Leader of Ancient Mexico*. Illus. by Pablo Serrano. Groundwood, 2007.
Spivak, Dawnine. *Grass Sandals: The Travels of Basho*. Illus. by Demi. Atheneum. 1997.
Wheatley, Phillis. "A Hymn to Evening." In Clinton, Catherine. *A Poem of Her Own*. Illus. by Stephen Alcorn. Abrams, 2003. (With biography)
Winter, Jeanette. *Emily Dickinson's Letters to the World*. Farrar, 2002.
Wong, Janet. *Before It Wriggles Away*. Richard C. Owen, 2006. (Autobiography)
Yolen, Jane. *A Letter from Phoenix Farm*. Richard C. Owens, 1992. (Autobiography)
———. *My Uncle Emily*. Illus. by Nancy Carpenter. Philomel, 2009. (Emily Dickinson)

Langston Hughes

Langston Hughes is the subject of many poems for young people, an indication of his impact on American poetry. Hughes' "I, Too" is a response to Walt Whitman's earlier poem, "I Hear America Singing." In this poem Hughes hopes for the day when others see how beautiful the "darker brother" is and are ashamed of the way he has been treated. Several collections of poems have titles that feature phrases from this poem, including Adoff's *I Am the Darker Brother* and Catherine Clinton's *I, Too, Sing America*. The Serbian American narrator of Marie Testa's *Something About America* alludes to another Hughes poem, "A Dream Deferred," in "A Dream Divided." She is afraid, not that her dream will explode, but that it will implode.

Adoff, Arnold, ed. *I Am the Darker Brother*. S & S, 1996.
Burleigh, Robert. *Langston's Train Ride*. Illus. by Leonard Jenkins. Orchard, 2004.
Cheng, Andrea. "Kayla: Dreams." *Where the Steps Were*. Boyds Mills, 2008.
Clinton, Catherine, sel. *I, Too, Sing America*. Illus. by Stephen Alcorn. Houghton, 1998.

Cooper, Floyd. *Coming Home: From the Life of Langston Hughes*. Philomel, 1994.
Frost, Helen. "Perfect (by) Shawna." *Spinning Through the Universe*. Farrar, 2004.
Giovanni, Nikki. "A Poem (for Langston Hughes)" *Shimmy Shimmy Shimmy Like My Sister Kate*. Holt, 1995.
Grimes, Nikki. "Long Live Langston, by Wesley Boone." *Bronx Masquerade*. New York: Dial, 2002.
Hughes, Langston. "I, Too." In *The Dream Keeper*. Illus. by Brian Pinkney. Knopf, 1994.
Lewis, J. Patrick. "Because My Mouth Is Wide With Laughter." *Freedom Like Sunlight: Praisesongs for Black Americans*. Illus. by John Thompson. Creative, 2000.
Medina, Tony. *Love to Langston*. Illus. by R. Gregory Christie. Lee & Low, 2002.
Meltzer, Milton. *Langston Hughes*.HarperCollins, 1968.
Myers, Walter Dean. "Jesse C." *Here in Harlem*. Holiday, 2004.
Osofsky, Audrey. *Free to Dream: The Making of a Poet*. Lothrop, 1996.
Perdomo, Willie. *Visiting Langston*. Illus. by Bryan Collier. Holt, 2002.
Testa, Maria. "A Dream Divided." *Something About America*. Candlewick, 2005. (Novel in Verse)
Walker, Alice. *Langston Hughes*. Illus. by Catherine Deeter. HarperCollins, 2002.

CREATING A POETRY COLLECTION

Classroom and library collections of all types of poems, both humorous and serious, allow students to pick up poetry books and browse them in spare moments. Collections by Shel Silverstein, Jack Prelutsky, and Douglas Florian are good humorous selections for Sustained Silent Reading. Librarians and teachers should have access to collections of poems to share with individual students or the entire class as the mood or topic comes up.

The anthologies listed here are basic volumes for classrooms and school libraries, most of which are arranged by subject. For suggestions on books that contain poems in one content area only, go to the first sections of each set of standards. You will find that Lee Bennett Hopkins, J. Patrick Lewis, and Carol Diggory Shields have been publishing collections of poems for the content areas. These are useful for all school library and classroom collections.

Anthologies

See also Chapter Two: Classic Poetry

One or two good collections of nursery rhymes
One or two collections of classic poems

Cullinan, Bernice. *A Jar of Tiny Stars: Poems by NCTE Award-Winning Poets*. Illus. by Andi McLeod. Boyds Mills, 1996. (All Ages)
De Regniers, Beatrice Schenk, et al, eds. *Sing a Song of Popcorn*. Scholastic, 1988. (Primary)
Giovanni, Nikki. *Hip Hop Speaks to Children: A Celebration of Poetry with a Beat*. Sourcebooks, 2008. (With CD) (All ages)
Hopkins, Lee Bennett, sel. *Days to Celebrate*. Illus. by Stephen Alcorn. HarperCollins, 2005. (All Ages)
———, sel. *My America: A Poetry Atlas of the United States*. Illus. by Stephen Alcorn. S & S, 2000. (Middle Elementary to Middle School)
———, sel. *Climb into My Lap: First Poems to Read Together*. Illus. by Kathryn Brown. S & S, 1998. (Primary)
Kennedy, X. J. and Dorothy M. Kennedy. *Knock at a Star: A Child's Introduction to Poetry*. Illus. by Karen Lee Baker. Little, 1999. (Middle Elementary to Middle School)
Kennedy, X. J. & Dorothy Kennedy. *Talking Like the Rain: A Read-to-Me Book of Poems*. Illus. by Jane Dyer. Little, 1992. (Primary and Middle Elementary)
Martin, Bill, Jr. and Michael Sampson, eds. *The Bill Martin Jr. Big Book of Poetry*. S & S, 2008. (Primary and Middle Elementary)

Nye, Naomi Shihab. *This Same Sky: A Collection of Poems from Around the World.* Macmillan, 1992. (Upper Elementary and Middle School)

Panzer, Nora, ed. *Celebrate America: In Poetry and Art.* Smithsonian/Hyperion, 1994. (Upper Elementary and Middle School)

Paschen, Elise, ed. *Poetry Speaks to Children.* Sourcebooks, 2005. (With CD) (All Ages)

Prelutsky, Jack, sel. *The Beauty of the Beast: Poems from the Animal Kingdom.* Illus. by Meilo So. Knopf, 1997. (All Ages)

———, sel. *The Random House Book of Poetry for Children.* Illus. by Arnold Lobel. Random, 1983. (Middle and Upper Elementary)

———, sel. *Read-Aloud Rhymes for the Very Young.* Illus. by Marc Brown. Knopf, 1986. (Primary)

———, sel. *The 20th Century Children's Poetry Treasury.* Illus. by Meilo So. Knopf, 1999. (All ages)

Rochelle, Belinda, sel. *Words with Wings.* HarperCollins, 2001. (Upper Elementary and Middle School)

Yolen, Jane & Andrew Fusek Peters, comp. *Here's a Little Poem: A Very First Book of Poetry.* Illus. by Polly Dunbar. Candlewick, 2007. (Primary)

Award-Winning Poets

A good poetry collection should contain works by award-winning poets. The National Council of Teachers of English Award for Excellence in Poetry for Children is given for a body of a poet's work every three years. The Lee Bennett Hopkins Poetry Award was established in 1993 and is presented annually to an American poet or anthologist for the most outstanding new book of children's poetry the previous calendar year. It is fitting that in 2009 Lee Bennett Hopkins, who has done so much for children's poetry, will receive the NCTE Award. The Poetry Foundation named Jack Prelutsky as the first Children's Poet Laureate "to raise awareness that children have a natural receptivity to poetry and are its most appreciative audience, especially when the poems are written for them." He completed his two-year term in 2008, and Mary Ann Hoberman is the second poet to be so honored.

Poets have also been awarded the Coretta Scott King prize, an occasional Newbery or Caldecott award and the American Library Association's Notable Children's Book award. A number of states give prizes for poetry. The websites for some of these awards are included in the references at the end of the chapter. Works by award-winning poets are featured throughout this book.

Works by any of the following poets will add depth and richness to school and library poetry collections. The titles included here are ones that were helpful in creating this book. Librarians and teachers will need to keep in mind the subjects highlighted in their own curricula and the interests of their students as they create their own poetry collections. Note that several of these poets have also edited anthologies listed above.

Adoff, Arnold. *In for Winter, Out for Spring.* Illus. by Jerry Pinkney. Harcourt, 1991. (Primary and Middle Elementary)

Esbensen, Barbara Juster. *Who Shrank My Grandmother's House? Poems of Discovery.* Illus. by Eric Beddows. HarperCollins, 1992. (Middle and Upper Elementary)

Fisher, Aileen. *I Heard a Bluebird Sing: Children Select Their Favorite Poems by Aileen Fisher.* Illus. by Jennifer Emery. Boyds Mills, 2002. (Primary)

George, Kristine O'Connell. *Hummingbird Nest; A Journal of Poems.* Illus. by Barry Moser. Harcourt, 2004. (Middle and Upper Elementary)

Greenfield, Eloise. *In the Land of Words: New and Selected Poems.* Illus. by Jan Spivey Gilchrist. HarperCollins, 2004. (All Ages)

Grimes, Nikki. *Thanks a Million.* Illus. by Cozbi A. Cabrera. HarperCollins, 2006. (Primary and Middle Elementary)

Hoberman, Mary Ann. *The Llama Who Had No Pajama: 100 Favorite Poems.* Illus. by Betty Fraser. Harcourt, 1998. (Primary)

Hopkins, Lee Bennett. *Good Rhymes, Good Times.* Illus. by Frané Lessac. HarperCollins, 1995. (Primary and Middle Elementary)

Kuskin, Karla. *Moon, Have You Met My Mother?* Illus. by Sergio Ruzzier. HarperCollins, 2003. (All Ages)

Levy, Constance. *I'm Going to Pet a Worm Today: And Other Poems.* Illus. by Ronald Himler. McElderry, 1991. (Middle and Upper Elementary)

Lewis, J. Patrick. *The Brothers' War: Civil War Voices in Verse.* National Geographic, 2007. (Upper Elementary and Middle School)

McCord, David. *One at a Time: His Collected Poems for the Young.* Illus. by Henry B. Kane. Little, 1986. (All Ages)

Merriam, Eve. *The Singing Green: New and Selected Poems for All Seasons.* Illus. by Kathleen Collins Howell. Morrow, 1992. (Primary and Middle Elementary)

Myers, Walter Dean. *Here in Harlem: Poems in Many Voices.* Holiday, 2004. (Upper Elementary and Middle School)

Nelson, Marilyn. *The Freedom Business: Including A Narrative of the Life and Adventures of Venture, a Native of Africa.* Illus. by Deborah Dancy. Boyds Mills, 2008. (Upper Elementary and Middle School)

Nye, Naomi Shihab. *Come With Me: Poems for a Journey.* Illus. by Dan Yaccarino. Greenwillow, 2000. (Upper Elementary and Middle School)

Prelutsky, Jack . *My Dog May Be a Genius.* Illus. by James Stevenson. HarperCollins, 2008. (Primary and Middle Elementary)

Sidman, Joyce. *This Is Just to Say: Poems of Apology and Forgiveness.* Illus. by Pamela Zagarenski. Houghton, 2007. (Middle and Upper Elementary)

Weatherford, Carole Boston. *Remember the Bridge: Poems of a People.* Philomel, 2002. (Upper Elementary and Middle School)

Worth, Valerie. *All the Small Poems and Fourteen More.* Illus. by Natalie Babbitt. Farrar, 1994. (All Ages)

Additional Readings About the Poets

Barrera, R. B. (1998). "Profile: Pat Mora, Fiction/Nonfiction Writer and Poet." *Language Arts* 75 (March): 221–227.

Basurto, I. (2002). "The Poet Behind the Series: An Interview with Francisco X. Alarcón." *The New Advocate* 15 (Winter): 1–8.

Burns, M. M. (1997). "The Last Hello and the First Goodbye: David McCord, 1897–1997." *The Horn Book* LXXIII (November): 660–665.

Copeland, J. S. *Speaking of Poets: Interviews with Poets Who Write for Children and Young Adults.* National Council of Teachers of English, 1993.

Copeland, J. S. & V. L. Copeland. *Speaking of Poets 2: More Interviews with Poets Who Write for Children and Young Adults.* National Council of Teachers of English, 1994.

Cox, E. J. (2009). "Talking with Joyce Sidman." *Book Links* 18 (March): 24–27.

Gallo, D. R. *Speaking for Ourselves, Too: More Autobiographical Sketches by Notable Authors of Books for Young Adults.* National Council of Teachers of English, 1993. (Paul Fleischman, Ron Koertge, Cynthia Rylant, Gary Soto)

Grimes, N. (2004). "Where Do Poems Come From? A CLA Workshop Presentation." *Journal of Children's Literature* 30 (Spring): 7–12.

Kiefer, B. *Getting to Know You: Profiles of Children's Authors Featured in Language Arts, 1985–1990.* National Council of Teachers of English, 1991. (Arnold Adoff, Byrd Baylor, Lilian Moore)

McElmeel, S. L. *The Poet Tree.* Illus. by Deborah L. McElmeel. Libraries Unlimited, 1993.

Schertle, A. (1996). "Up the Bookcase to Poetry." *The Horn Book* LXXII (July-August): 430–435.

Vardell, S. M. *Poetry People: A Practical Guide to Children's Poets.* Libraries Unlimited, 2007.

Wong, J. (2001). "Crafting Images: A Writer's Perspective." *Journal of Children's Literature* 27 (Fall): 37–38.

Teaching Poetry

Ambrosini, M. & T. M. Moretta. *Poetry Workshop for Middle School: Activities that Inspire Meaningful Language Learning*. International Reading Association, 2003.

Behn, H. *Chrysalis: Concerning Children and Poetry*. Harcourt, Brace, Jovanovich, 1986

Booth, D. and B. Moore. *Poems Please: Sharing Poetry with Children*. Stenhouse, 2003.

Carey, M. A. *Poetry: Starting from Scratch: How to Teach and Write Poetry*. Foundation Books, 1989.

Corbett, P. *Jumpstart! Poetry: Games and Activities for Ages 7–12*. Routledge, 2008.

Cullinan, B., M. Scala, & V. Schroder. *Three Voices: An Invitation to Poetry Across the Curriculum*. Stenhouse, 1995.

Denman, G. *When You've Made It Your Own: Teaching Poetry to Young People*. Heinemann, 1988.

Dias, Patrick X. *Reading and Responding to Poetry: Patterns in the Process*. Heinemann, 1996.

Dotlich, R. K. (2005). "A Kingdom of Words." Journal of Children's Literature. 31 (Fall):8.

Dunning, S & W. Stafford. *Getting the Knack: 20 Poetry Writing Exercises*. National Council of Teachers of English, 1992.

Esbensen, B. J. *A Celebration of Bees: Helping Children Write Poetry*. Winston, 1975.

Florian, D. *Teaching with the Rib-Tickling Poetry of Douglas Florian*. Scholastic, 2003.

Foale, J. & L. Pagett. *Creative Approaches to Poetry for the Primary Framework for Literacy*. Routledge, 2009.

Franco, B. *Conversations with a Poet: Inviting Poetry into K-12 Classrooms*. Richard C. Owen, 2005.

Glazer, J. I. & L. L. Lamme. (1990). "Poem Picture Books and Their Uses in the Classroom." *Reading Teacher* 44 (October): 102–109.

Heard, G. *Awakening the Heart: Exploring Poetry in Elementary and Middle School*. Heinemann, 1999.

———. *For the Good of Earth and Sun: Teaching Poetry*. Heinemann, 1989.

Hermsen, T. *Poetry of Place: Helping Students Write Their Worlds*. National Council of Teachers of English, 2009.

Holbrook, S. *Practical Poetry: A Nonstandard Approach to Meeting Content-Area Standards*. Heinemann, 2005.

Hopkins, L. B. *Pass the Poetry, Please!* 3rd. ed. HarperCollins, 1998.

Kutiper, K. & P. J. Wilson. (1993)."Updating Poetry Preferences: A Look at the Poetry Children Really Like." *Reading Teacher* 47 (September): 28–34.

Lewis, R. *When Thought Is Young: Reflections on Teaching and the Poetry of the Child*. New Rivers Press, 1984.

Lies, B. B. *The Poet's Pen: Writing Poetry with Middle and High School Students*. Illus. by Brian Lies. Teacher Ideas, 1993.

Livingston, M. C. *The Child as Poet: Myth or Reality*. Horn Book, 1990.

———. *Climb into the Bell Tower: Essays on Poetry*. HarperCollins, 1984.

McClure, A. A., with P. Harrison & S. Reed. *Sunrises and Songs: Reading and Writing Poetry in the Elementary Classroom*. Heinemann, 1990.

O'Connor, J. S. *Wordplaygrounds: Reading, Writing, and Performing Poetry in the English Classroom*. National Council of Teachers of English, 2004.

Perry, A. Y. *Poetry Across the Curriculum: An Action Guide for Elementary Teachers*. Allyn & Bacon, 1997.

Sloan, G. *Give Them Poetry! A Guide for Sharing Poetry with Children K–8*. Teachers College, 2003.

Strickland, D. & M. (1997). "Language and Literacy: The Poetry Connection." *Language Arts* 74 (March): 201–205.

Terry, A. *Children's Poetry Preferences: A National Survey of Upper Elementary Grades*. National Council of Teachers of English, 1962.

Thomas, J. T., Jr. *Poetry's Playground: The Culture of Contemporary American Children's Poetry*. Wayne State University, 2007.

Tiedt, I. *Tiger Lilies, Toadstools, and Thunderbolts: Engaging K–8 Students with Poetry*. International Reading Association, 2002.

Vardell, S. M. *Poetry Aloud Here! Sharing Poetry with Children in the Library*. American Library Association, 2006.

———. Column: "Everyday Poetry." *Book Links* (Beginning 11/2007).

———. Poetry for Children Blog. http://poetryforchildren.blogspot.com/.

Poetry Award Web Sites

National Council of Teachers of English Award for Excellence in Children's Poetry. http://www.ncte.org/awards/poetry

Poetry Foundation, Children's Poet Laureate Award. http://www.poetryfoundation.org

Coretta Scott King and Notable Children's Book Awards. http://www.ala.org/ala/awardsgrants/booksprintmedia/childrenyngadults/index.cfm

Lee Bennett Hopkins Award/Pennsylvania Center for the Book. http://www.pabook.libraries.psu.edu/activities/hopkins

REFERENCES

Behn, H. *Chrysalis: Concerning Children and Poetry.* Harcourt, Brace, Jovanovich, 1968: 19

Children's Book Council Young People's Poetry Week. http://www.cbcbooks.org

Cullinan, B. E. "Eve Merriam: 'I've Sometimes . . .' " *A Jar of Tiny Stars.* Boyds Mills, 1996: 33.

Farstrup, A. E. & S. J. Samuels, eds. *What Research Has to Say About Vocabulary Instruction.* International Reading Association, 2008.

Paley, V. *A Child's Work: The Importance of Fantasy Play.* University of Chicago, 2004.

Roskos, K. A. & J. F. Christie, eds. *Play and Literacy in Early Childhood: Research from Multiple Perspectives.* Lawrence Erlbaum, 2007.

Stafford, W. *Writing the Australian Crawl: Views on the Writer's Vocation.* The University of Michigan Press, 1978: 61.

CHAPTER 2

Poetry and the Language Arts Standards

Standard One: Students read a wide range of print and non-print texts to build an understanding of texts, of themselves, and of the cultures of the United States and the world; to acquire new information; to respond to the needs and demands of society and the workplace; and for personal fulfillment. Among these texts are fiction and nonfiction, classic and contemporary works.

See also Chapter One: Poetry and the National Standards (Writing Poetry)

STANDARD ONE: THE LANGUAGE ARTS

This first standard is very broad, encompassing all of the purposes of the language arts. The poetry collections included here feature poems on all aspects of reading, writing, listening, and speaking. These are followed by poems about oral language through storytelling, and poems about books and reading.

Greenfield, Eloise. *In the Land of Words: New and Selected Poems*. Illus. by Jan Spivey Gilchrist. HarperCollins, 2004.

Hopkins, Lee Bennett, sel. *Good Books, Good Times*. Illus. by Harvey Stevenson. HarperCollins, 1990.

———. *Wonderful Words: Poems About Reading, Writing, Speaking and Listening*. Illus. by Karen Barbour. S & S, 2004.

Shields, Carol Diggory. *English: Fresh Squeezed*. Illus. by Tony Ross. Handprint, 2004.

Storytelling

See also Chapter Six: Theatre Standard One (Performing Poetry)

Since the earliest times, people have been telling stories to one another. As Anne Haas Dyson and Celia Genishi point out (Dyson, 1994) stories are the way people organize their experiences to give them meaning. Oral storytelling contains the roots of written story, and children hear stories before they can read or write them. Early stories were often in the form of epic poems or songs, so it is not surprising that poets write about storytelling. Storytelling exists on the personal level in family stories passed down from one generation to another. Storytelling also exists at the cultural level, in stories passed on to explain values, beliefs, and traditions. Both types of storytelling are captured in these poems.

Argueta, Jorge. "My Grandma's Stories = Los Cuentos de Mi Abuelita." *A Movie in My Pillow = Una Pelicula en Mi Almohada.* Illus. by Elizabeth Gómez. Children's, 2001.

Borden, Louise. *Across the Blue Pacific.* Illus. by Robert Andrew Parker. Houghton, 2006.

Brand, Dionne. "Old Men of Magic." In Brenner, Barbara. *The Earth Is Painted Green.* Illus. by S. D. Schindler. Scholastic, 1994.

Bryan, Ashley. "Storyteller." *Sing to the Sun.* HarperCollins, 1992.

Collett, Andrew. "Story Time." In Nicholls, Judith. *Someone I Like.* Illus. by Giovanni Manna. Barefoot, 2000.

Gunning, Monica. "Storyteller Nana." In Hittleman, Carol G. & Daniel R. Hittleman *A Grand Celebration.* Illus. by Kay Life. Boyds Mills, 2002.

Harjo, Joy. "Remember." In Panzer, Nora. *Celebrate America.* Hyperion, 1994.

Harper, Frances Ellen Watkins. "Learning to Read." *Hour of Freedom.* Boyds Mills, 2003.

Hoberman, Mary Ann. "Four Generations." *Fathers, Mothers, Sisters, Brothers.* Illus. by Marylin Hafner. Little, 1991.

Hughes, Langston. "Aunt Sue's Stories." *The Dream Keeper.* Illus. by Brian Pinkney. Knopf, 1993.

———. "Grandpa's Stories." In Martin, Bill, Jr. & Michael Sampson. *The Bill Martin Jr. Big Book of Poetry.* S & S, 2008.

Lee, Dennis. "I Know It's Time." *The Ice Cream Store.* Illus. by David McPhail. Scholastic, 1991.

Martin, Bill, Jr. & Michael Sampson. "Once Upon a Time." *The Bill Martin Jr. Big Book of Poetry.* S & S, 2008.

Medina, Tony. "Grandma's Stories." *Love to Langston.* Illus. by R. Gregory Christie. Lee & Low, 2002.

Micklos, John, Jr. "I Only Know the Stories." *Grandparent Poems.* Illus. by Layne Johnson. Boyds Mills, 2004.

Mora, Pat. "Tigua Elder." *My Own True Name.* Arté Público, 2000.

Nichols, Grace. "I Like to Stay Up Late." In Agard, John & Grace Nichols. *Under the Moon and Over the Sea.* Illus. by Cathie Felstead, et al. Candlewick, 2002.

Olaleye, Isaac. "Village Tales-Teller." *The Distant Talking Drum.* Illus. by Frané Lessac. Boyds Mills, 1995.

Silko, Leslie Marmon. "In Cold Storm Light." In Clinton, Catherine. *A Poem of Her Own.* Illus. by Stephen Alcorn. Abrams, 2003.

Sneve, Virginia Driving Hawk. *Dancing Teepees.* Illus. by Stephen Gammell. Holiday, 1989.

Spinelli, Eileen. "Summer Twilight." *Tea Party Today.* Illus. by Karen Dugan. Boyds Mills, 1999.

Unobagha, Uzo. "Grandpa! Grandpa!" *Off to the Sweet Shores of Africa.* Illus. by Julia Cairns. Chronicle, 2000.

Viorst, Judith. "Lady, Lady." *Sad Underwear.* Illus. by Richard Hull. Atheneum, 1995.

Weatherford, Carole Boston. "The Slave Storyteller." *Remember the Bridge.* Philomel, 2002.

Yeahpau, Thomas M. "Oral Tradition." In Ochoa, Annette Piña, et al. *Night Is Gone, Day Is Still Coming.* Candlewick, 2003.

Yolen, Jane. *Miz Berlin Walks.* Illus. by Floyd Cooper. Philomel, 1997.

———. "Once Upon a Time, She Said." In Janeczko, Paul B. *Seeing the Blue Between.* Candlewick, 2002.

Books and Reading

Armour, Richard. "Two Lives Are Yours." In Hopkins, Lee Bennett. *Days to Celebrate.* Illus. by Stephen Alcorn. HarperCollins, 2005.

Bertram, Debbie & Susan Bloom. *The Best Book to Read.* Illus. by Michael Garland. Random, 2008.

———. *The Best Place to Read.* Illus. by Michael Garland. Random, 2003.

———. *The Best Time to Read.* Illus. by Michael Garland. Random, 2005.

Brug, Sandra Gilbert. "Listening." In Hopkins, Lee Bennett. *Hamsters, Shells, and Spelling Bees.* Illus. by Sachiko Yoshikawa. HarperCollins, 2008.

Dahl. Roald. "Concerning Mike TeaVee." *Vile Verses.* Illus. by Quentin Blake et al. Viking, 2005.

Dakos, Kalli. "Don't Read This Book, Whatever You Do!" *Don't Read This Book, Whatever You Do!* Illus. by G. Brian Karas. S & S, 1993.

Dasgupta, Manjush. "Companion." In Nye, Naomi Shihab. *This Same Sky.* Macmillan, 1992.

Dove, Rita. "The First Book." In Paschen, Elise. *Poetry Speaks to Children.* Sourcebooks, 2005. (With CD)

English, Karen. "The Reading Boy {Malcolm}." *Speak to Me (And I Will Listen Between the Lines).* Illus. by Amy June Bates. Farrar, 2004.

Esbensen, Barbara Juster. "Bat" & "Giraffe." *Words with Wrinkled Knees.* Illus. by John Stadler. HarperCollins, 1991.

Fisher, Aileen. "After the End." *Always Wondering.* Illus. by Joan Sandin. HarperCollins, 1991.

Florian, Douglas. "Pages" & "Mr. Crook." *Bing Bang Boing.* Harcourt, 1994.

Giovanni, Nikki. "Ten Years Old." *Spin a Soft Black Song.* Illus. by George Martins. Farrar, 1985.

———. "Winter" & "The Reason I Like Chocolate." *The Sun Is So Quiet.* Illus. by Ashley Bryan. Holt, 1996.

Graves, Donald. "Lost in a Book." *Baseball, Snakes, and Summer Squash.* Boyds Mills, 1996.

Greenfield, Eloise. "Books," "Story," & "I Don't Care." *In the Land of Words.* Illus. by Jan Spivey Gilchrist. HarperCollins, 2004.

Grimes, Nikki. "Dear Author." *Thanks a Million.* Illus. by Cozbi A. Cabrera. HarperCollins, 2006.

Harley, Avis. "Booktime." In Heard, Georgia. *Falling Down the Page.* Roaring Brook, 2009.

Harrison, David L. "Bedtime." In Micklos, John, Jr. *Daddy Poems.* Illus. by Robert Casilla. Boyds Mills, 2000.

Hines, Anna Grossnickle. "Lights Out." *Winter Lights.* HarperCollins, 2005.

Hopkins, Lee Bennett, sel. *Good Books, Good Times!* Illus. by Harvey Stevenson. HarperCollins, 1990.

Jimenez, Gladiz. "Reading Lesson." In Franklin, Kristine L. & Nancy McGirr. *Out of the Dump.* Lothrop, 1995.

Katz, Bobbi. "When You Can Read." In Prelutsky, Jack. *The 20th Century Children's Poetry Treasury.* Illus. by Meilo So. Knopf, 1999.

Kennedy, X. J. "Summer Cooler." In Hopkins, Lee Bennett. *Small Talk.* Illus. by Susan Gaber. Harcourt, 1995.

Kuskin, Karla. Section: "I Need to Read." *Moon, Have You Met My Mother?* Illus. by Sergio Ruzzier. Harper Collins, 2003.

Lewis, Claudia. "Not in a Hundred Years." *Long Ago in Oregon.* Illus. by Joel Fontaine. HarperCollins, 1987.

Lewis, J. Patrick. "Read . . . Think . . . Dream" & "Two Good Books." *The Bookworm's Feast.* Illus. by John O'Brien. Dial, 1999.

Little, Jean. "Condensed Version." *Hey World, Here I Am!* Illus. by Sue Truesdell. HarperCollins, 1989.

Livingston, Myra Cohn. "A Book." In Hopkins, Lee Bennett. *School Supplies.* Illus. by Renée Flower. S & S, 1996.

———. "Reading: Summer." In Prelutsky, Jack. *The 20th Century Children's Poetry Treasury.* Illus. by Meilo So. Knopf, 1999.

McCord, David. "Books Fall Open" & "When I Would." *One at a Time.* Illus. by Henry B. Kane. Little, 1986.

Medina, Jane. "Invisible Blue Flowers = Las Flores Azules Invisibles." *The Dream on Blanca's Wall = El Sueño Pegado en la Pared de Blanca.* Illus. by Robert Casilla. Boyds Mills, 2004.

Micklos, John, Jr. "When Grandpa Reads to Me." *Grandparent Poems.* Illus. by Layne Johnson. Boyds Mills, 2004.

Mora, Pat. *Book Fiesta!* Illus. by Rafael López. HarperCollins, 2009.

Nye, Naomi Shihab. "The List." *A Maze Me.* Greenwillow, 2005.

Pinkney, Sandra L. *Read and Rise.* Illus. by Myles C. Pinkney. Scholastic, 2006.

Prelutsky, Jack. "Boys Are Big Experts" & "Look! Look!" *My Dog May Be a Genius.* Illus. by James Stevenson. HarperCollins, 2008.

Schoenherr, Ian. *Read It, Don't Eat It!* HarperCollins, 2009.

Shapiro, Karen Jo. "If." *I Must Go Down to the Beach Again.* Illus. by Judy Love. Charlesbridge, 2007.

Sierra, Judy. *Born to Read.* Illus. by Marc Brown. Knopf, 2008.

———. *Wild About Books.* Illus. by Marc Brown. Knopf, 2004.

Silverstein, Shel. "Invitation." *Where the Sidewalk Ends.* HarperCollins, 1974.
Soto, Gary. "Eating While Reading." *Canto Familiar.* Illus. by Annika Nelson. Harcourt, 1995.
Spinelli, Eileen. "Adventure" & "Seaside." *Tea Party Today.* Illus. by Karen Dugan. Boyds Mills, 1999.
Stevenson, Robert Louis. "The Land of Storybooks" & "Picture Books in Winter." *A Child's Garden of Verses.* Illus. by Diane Goode. Morrow, 1998.
Tobin, Jim. *Sue MacDonald Had a Book.* Illus. by Dave Coverly. Holt, 2009.
Turner, Ann. "Read." *Street Talk.* Illus. by Catherine Stock. Houghton, 1986.
Viorst, Judith. "My—Oh Wow!—Book." *If I Were in Charge of the World.* Illus. by Lynne Cherry. Atheneum, 1981.
Worth, Valerie. "Book." *All the Small Poems and Fourteen More.* Illus. by Natalie Babbitt. Farrar, 1994.
Zolotow, Charlotte. "The Present." *Snippets.* Illus. by Melissa Sweet. HarperCollins, 1992.

Standard Two: Students read a wide range of literature from many periods in many genres to build an understanding of the many dimensions of human experience.

STANDARD TWO: CLASSIC POETRY

Folk literature and nursery rhymes are the basis of the written literature of all cultures. They are the first "classics" for children. Other literature frequently alludes to these rhymes and stories. Students without a background with these stories may miss the meanings of more sophisticated works. Librarians and primary grade teachers can provide students with an important grounding by introducing children to nursery rhymes. Collections of nursery rhymes from some world cultures are now available so that children can both honor their own heritages and learn that these simple rhymes and their subjects cross cultures. Children can share rhymes they may have learned in their own family traditions as well.

Anthologies of Nursery Rhymes

Ada, Alma Flor & F. Isabel Campoy. *Mamá Goose.* Illus. by Maribel Suárez. Hyperion, 2004.
———. *Pío Peep!* Illus. by Viví Escrivá. HarperCollins, 2003.
Chorao, Kay. *Rhymes Around the World.* Dutton, 2009.
Crews, Nina. *The Neighborhood Mother Goose.* Greenwillow, 2004.
Delacre, Lulu, sel. *Arroz con Leche.* Scholastic, 1992.
DePaola, Tomie. *Tomie De Paola's Mother Goose.* Penguin, 2005.
Dillon, Leo, ed. *Mother Goose: Numbers on the Loose.* Illus. by Leo & Diane Dillon. Harcourt, 2007.
Engelbreit, Mary. *Mary Engelbreit's Mother Goose.* HarperCollins, 2005.
Hall, Nancy Abraham & Jill Syverson-Stork, coll. *Los Pollitos Dicen = The Baby Chicks Sing.* Illus. by Kay Chorao. Little, 1994.
Hoberman, Mary Ann. *You Read to Me, I'll Read to You: Very Short Mother Goose Tales to Read Together.* Illus. by Michael Emberley. Little, 2005.
Hopkins, Lee Bennett, sel. *Mother Goose Around the World.* Sadlier, 1999.
Jaramillo, Nelly Palacio, comp. *Las Nanas de Abuelita = Grandmother's Nursery Rhymes.* Illus. by Elivia Savadier. Holt, 1994.
Lobel, Arnold. *The Arnold Lobel Book of Mother Goose.* Random, 2003.
Marshall, James. *James Marshall's Mother Goose.* Farrar, 1986.
Opie, Iona, ed. *Here Comes Mother Goose.* Illus. by Rosemary Wells. Candlewick, 1999.
———. *Mother Goose's Little Treasures.* Illus. by Rosemary Wells. Candlewick, 2007.
———. *My Very First Mother Goose.* Illus. by Rosemary Wells. Candlewick, 1996.

Orozco, José Luis, sel. *Diez Deditos = Ten Little Fingers*. Illus. by Elisa Kleven. Dutton, 1997.
Rosen, Michael, sel. *Poems for the Very Young*. Illus. by Bob Graham. Houghton, 1993.
Ross, Tony. *Three Little Kittens: And Other Favorite Nursery Rhymes*. Holt, 2009.
Wyndam, Robert, sel. *Chinese Mother Goose Rhymes*. Illus. by Ed Young. Putnam, 1989.

Picture Book Nursery Rhymes

Individual nursery rhymes are sometimes used as the text for picture books. Not all of these are for young children. Maurice Sendak's illustrations for *We Are Down in the Dumps with Jack and Guy* turn the rhyme into a modern parable. Students might want to give an old rhyme a new twist by creating modern illustrations.

Aylesworth, Jim. *The Completed Hickory Dickory Dock*. Illus. by Eileen Christelow. Atheneum, 1990.
Baker, Keith. *Big Fat Hen*. Harcourt, 1994.
———. *Hickory Dickory Dock*. Harcourt, 2007.
DePaola, Tomie, ret. *The Comic Adventures of Old Mother Hubbard and Her Dog*. Harcourt, 1981.
Emberley, Barbara, adapt. *Drummer Hoff*. Illus. by Ed Emberley. Weston Woods, 1967. (With Cassette)
Hines, Anna Grossnickle. *1, 2, Buckle My Shoe*. Harcourt, 2008.
Jones, Carol. *Old MacDonald Had a Farm*. Houghton, 1989.
Loveless, Liz. *1, 2, Buckle My Shoe*. Hyperion, 1993.
Sendak, Maurice, ret. *Hector Protector and As I Went Over the Water*. HarperCollins, 1990.
———. *We Are All In the Dumps With Jack and Guy: Two Nursery Rhymes With Pictures*. HarperCollins, 1993.
Taback, Simms. *This Is the House That Jack Built*. Putnam, 2004.

Anthologies of Classic Poems

Ferris, Helen, ed. *Favorite Poems Old and New*. Illus. by Leonard Weisgard. Random, 1957, 2009.
Foster, John, comp. *A Very First Poetry Book*. Oxford, 1980.
Hall, Donald, ed. *The Oxford Illustrated Book of American Children's Poems*. Oxford, 1999.
Harrison, Michael & Christopher Stuart-Clark. *Oxford Book of Story Poems*. Oxford, 1990.
Philip, Neil, ed. *The New Oxford Book of Children's Verse*. Oxford, 1998.
Rosen, Michael, sel. *Classic Poetry*. Illus. by Paul Howard. Candlewick, 2009.

Classic Poems as Texts for Picture Books

Illustrated versions of classic poems can help students to better comprehend their meanings. When a poem provides the text for a picture book, however, the reader's choice of responses may narrow to the explanation provided by the illustrations. It is important to help students understand that the illustrator provides only one of a number of possible responses. Sometimes, it is helpful to share a poem with students before they see the illustrations so they can form their own images and responses. Using two illustrated versions of the same poem can help students do this as well, particularly when the sets of illustrations are very different.

Murray Kimber's modern interpretation of Alfred Noyes' *The Highwayman* as a motorcycle rider, Charles R. Smith''s photographic interpretation of Rudyard Kipling's *If*, and Christopher Myers' interpretation of *Jabberwocky* as a basketball game give older students food for thought as they reinterpret classic poems in new contexts.

Behn, Harry. *Trees.* Illus. by James Endicott. Holt, 1992.
Carroll, Lewis. *Jabberwocky.* Illus. by Christopher Myers. Hyperion, 2007.
———. *Jabberwocky.* Illus. by Stephane Jorisch. Kids Can. 2004.
———. *The Walrus and the Carpenter.* Illus. by Jane Zalben. Holt, 1986.
Carryl, Charles Edward. *The Camel's Lament.* Illus. by Charles Santore. Random, 2004.
Cummings, E. E. *Little Tree.* Illus. by Chris Raschka. Hyperion, 2001.
———. *Little Tree.* Illus. by Deborah Kogan Ray. Crown, 1987.
Field, Eugene. *Wynken, Blynken, and Nod.* Illus. by Giselle Potter. Random, 2008.
———. *Wynken, Blynken, and Nod.* Illus. by Johanna Westerman. North-South, 1995.
Field, Rachel. *General Store.* Illus. by Nancy Winslow Parker. Greenwillow, 1988.
———. *General Store.* Illus. by Giles Laroche. Little, 1988.
———. *Prayer for a Child.* Illus. by Elizabeth Orton Jones. S & S, 2005.
Frost, Robert. *Birches.* Illus. by Ed Young. Holt, 1988.
———. *Christmas Trees.* Illus. by Ted Rand. Holt, 1990.
———. *Stopping by Woods on a Snowy Evening.* Illus. by Susan Jeffers. Dutton, 2001.
Hughes, Langston. *My People.* Illus. by Charles R. Smith, Jr. Atheneum, 2009.
———. *The Negro Speaks of Rivers.* Illus. by E. B. Lewis. Disney, 2009.
Kipling, Rudyard. *If.* Illus. by Charles R. Smith Jr. S & S, 2007.
Lear, Edward. *A Was Once an Apple Pie.* Illus. by Suse MacDonald. Scholastic, 2005.
———. *A Was Once an Apple Pie.* Illus. by Julie Lacome. Candlewick, 1992.
———. *An Edward Lear Alphabet.* Illus. by Vladimir Radunsky. HarperCollins, 1999.
———. *The Owl and the Pussycat.* Illus. by Stephane Jorisch. Kids Can, 2007.
———. *The Owl and the Pussycat.* Illus. by Anne Mortimer. HarperCollins, 2006.
———. *The Owl and the Pussycat.* Illus. by James Marshall. HarperCollins, 1998.
———. *The Pelican Chorus.* Illus. by Fred Marcellino. HarperCollins, 2004.
———. *The Quangle Wangle's Hat.* Illus. by Louise Voce. Candlewick, 2005.
———. *The Quangle Wangle's Hat.* Illus. by Janet Stevens. Harcourt, 1988.
———. *The Scroobius Pip.* Illus. by Nancy E. Burkert. HarperCollins, 1987.
———. *There Was an Old Man.* Illus. by Michelle Lemieux. Kids Can, 1994.
Longfellow, Henry Wadsworth. *The Children's Hour.* Illus. by Glenna Lang. Godine, 1993.
———. *Hiawatha.* Illus. by Keith Mosely. Putnam, 1988.
———. *Hiawatha and Megissogwon.* Illus. by Jeffrey Thompson. National Geographic, 2001.
———. *Hiawatha's Childhood.* Illus. by Errol Le Cain. Farrar, 1984.
———. *The Midnight Ride of Paul Revere.* Illus. by Christopher Bing. Handprint, 2001.
———. *Paul Revere's Ride.* Illus. by Ted Rand. Dutton, 1990.
———. *Paul Revere's Ride: The Landlord's Tale.* Illus. by Charles Santore. HarperCollins, 2003.
Nash, Ogden. *The Adventures of Isabel.* Illus. by James Marshall. Little, 1991.
———. *Custard the Dragon and the Wicked Knight.* Illus. by Lynn Munsinger. Little, 1996.
———. *The Tale of Custard the Dragon.* Illus. by Lynn Munsinger. Little, 1995.
Noyes, Alfred. *The Highwayman.* Illus. by Murray Kimber. Kids Can, 2005.
———. *The Highwayman.* Illus. by Charles Keeping. Oxford, 1987.
Poe, Edgar Allan. *The Raven.* Illus. by Ryan Price. Kids Can, 2006.
Riley, James Whitcomb. *The Gobble-Uns'll Git You Ef You Don't Watch Out!* Illus. by Joel Schick. HarperCollins, 1975.
———. *When the Frost Is on the Punkin'.* Illus. by Glenna Lang. Godine, 1992.
Rossetti, Christina. *What Is Pink? A Poem about Colors.* Illus. by Judith Hoffman Corwin. HarperCollins, 2000. (Abridged version of the poem)
———. *Color.* Illus. by Mary Teichman. HarperCollins, 1992.

Service, Robert. *The Cremation of Sam McGee*. Illus. by Ted Harrison. Kids Can, 2006.

———. *The Shooting of Dan McGrew*. Illus. by Ted Harrison. Kids Can, 1992.

Shakespeare, William. *Winter Song*. Illus. by Melanie Hall. Boyds Mills, 2006.

Stevenson, Robert Louis. *Block City*. Illus. by Daniel Kirk. S & S, 2005.

———. *The Moon*. Illus. by Tracey Campbell Pearson. Farrar, 2006.

———. *My Shadow*. Illus. by Glenna Lang. Godine, 1989.

Tennyson, Alfred Lord. *The Lady of Shalott*. Illus. by Geneviève Côté. Kids Can, 2005.

Thayer, Ernest Lawrence. *Casey at the Bat*. Illus. by Joe Morse. Kids Can, 2006.

———. *Casey at the Bat: A Ballad of the Republic Sung in the Year 1888*. Illus. by Patricia Polacco. Putnam, 1988.

Whitman, Walt. *Nothing But Miracles*. Illus. by Susan Roth. National Geographic, 2003.

———. *When I Heard the Learn'd Astronomer*. Illus. by Loren Long. S & S, 2004.

STANDARD TWO: RETELLING THE CLASSICS

Poets retell classic stories and poems by adding verses or by borrowing their plots and characters to tell a different story. Sometimes poets borrow the rhyme scheme, rhythms, and often the first line of a classic piece and then rewrite it as a parody of the original. Sometimes, poets provide a modern comment on the traditional message. Judith Viorst, for example, provides a pleasing balance to the saccharine film version of *The Little Mermaid* by taking the story back to Andersen's original in which the mermaid does not win the prince, suggesting she might have been better off being true to herself. Viorst includes retellings in two of her poetry collections. Many of Shel Silverstein's poems retell or allude to classic literature. Students might want to see how many allusions to folk stories they can find in his poems. Sometimes poets use the plot structure of a traditional verse to create an entirely new story. Several of the most popular of these plot structures are included below.

Retelling Nursery Rhymes

Aylesworth, Jim. *The Completed Hickory Dickory Dock*. Illus. by Eileen Christelow. Atheneum, 1990. (Added verses)

Baker, Keith. *Hickory Dickory Dock*. Harcourt, 2007. (Added verses)

———. *Potato Joe*. Harcourt, 2008. ("One Potato, Two Potato")

Brown, Calef. "New Utensil." *Flamingos on the Roof*. Houghton, 2006. ("I Eat My Peas . . .")

Bunting, Eve. *Sing a Song of Piglets*. Illus. by Emily Arnold McCully. Clarion, 2002.

Carroll, Lewis. "Twinkle, Twinkle Little Bat," In Prelutsky, Jack. *Read-Aloud Rhymes for the Very Young*. Illus. by Marc Brown. Knopf, 1986

Dehn, Paul. "Hey Diddle Diddle" & "Little Miss Muffet." In Dunning, Stephen, et al. *Reflections on a Gift of Watermelon Pickle*. HarperCollins, 1967.

Florian, Douglas. "Twinkle, Twinkle" & "Pease-Porridge Not." *Bing Bang Boing*. Harcourt, 1994.

Henri, Adrian. "What Are Little Girls?" In Hollyer, Belinda. *She's All that!* Illus. by Susan Hellard. Kingfisher, 2006.

Hoberman, Mary Ann. *You Read to Me, I'll Read to You: Very Short Mother Goose Tales to Read Together*. Illus. by Michael Emberley. Little, 2005.

"Humpty Dumpty" & "Mary Had a Little Lamb." In Prelutsky, Jack. *For Laughing Out Loud*. Illus. by Marjorie Priceman. Knopf, 1991.

"Humpty Dumpty," "Mary Had Some Bubble Gum," "Mary Had a Little Lamb," "That's the Way to Do it," & "Twinkle, Twinkle." In Katz, Bobbi. *Pocket Poems*. Illus. by Marylin Hafner. Dutton, 2004.

Lawson, JonArno. "Humpty Dumpty." *Black Stars in a White Night Sky*. Illus. by Sherwin Tjia. Boyds Mills, 2006.

Lechner, Jack. *Mary Had a Little Lamp*. Illus. by Bob Staake. Bloomsbury, 2008.

Lenski, Lois. *Sing a Song of People*. Illus. by Giles Laroche. Little, 1987.

McCord, David. "Jack, Jill, Sprats, and Horner." *One at a Time*. Illus. by Henry B. Kane. Little, 1986.

McNaughton, Colin. "Monday's Child Is Red and Spotty." In Prelutsky, Jack. *For Laughing Out Loud*. Knopf, 1991.

Miranda, Anne. *To Market, To Market*. Illus. by Janet Stevens. Harcourt, 1997.

Phillips, Louis. "On Eating Porridge Made of Peas." In Martin, Bill, Jr. & Michael Sampson. *The Bill Martin Jr. Big Book of Poetry*. S & S, 2008. (Also in *Poem Stew*)

Pomerantz, Charlotte. "For Humpty My Dumpty." *Thunderboom!* Illus. by Rob Shepperson. Front, 2005.

Potter, Beatrix. "The Old Woman." In Prelutsky, Jack. *Read Aloud Rhymes for the Very Young*. Illus. by Marc Brown. Knopf, 1986.

Rosen, Michael. "Humpty Dumpty Went to the Moon." In Foster, John. *A Very First Poetry Book*. Oxford, 1981.

Schoenherr, Ian. *Cat and Mouse*. HarperCollins, 2008.

Shannon, George. "Zucchini." *Busy in the Garden*. Illus. by Sam Williams. HarperCollins, 2006. ("Eeny, Meeny, Miney, Mo")

Sierra, Judy. *Monster Goose*. Illus. by Jack E. Davis. Harcourt, 2001.

Silverstein, Shel. "One Two." *A Light in the Attic*. HarperCollins, 1981.

Trapani, Iza. *Rufus and Friends*. Charlesbridge, 2008.

Retelling Myths and Legends

Bernier-Grand, Carmen T. "Quetzalcoatl." In Greenberg, Jan. *Side by Side*. Abrams, 2008.

Bourinot, Arthur S. "Paul Bunyan." In Booth, David. *'Til All the Stars Have Fallen*. Illus. by Kady MacDonald Denton. Viking, 1990.

Brown, Calef. "Sally" & "Poseidon's Hair." *Flamingos on the Roof*. Houghton, 2006.

Fleischman, Paul. "The Phoenix." *I Am Phoenix*. Illus. by Ken Nutt. HarperCollins, 1985.

Hovey, Kate. *Ancient Voices*. Illus. by Murray Kimber. S & S, 2004.

———. *Arachne Speaks*. Illus. by Blair Drawson. McElderry, 2001.

Lewis, J. Patrick & Rebecca Kai Dotlich. "Bran Castle: Romania" & "The Castle in the Air: A Viking Legend." *Castles*. Illus. by Dan Burr. Boyds Mills, 2006.

Norris, Leslie. "Merlin and the Snake's Egg." In Harrison, Michael & Christopher Stuart-Clark. *Oxford Book of Story Poems*. Oxford, 1990.

Silverstein, Shel. "Medusa." *Falling Up*. HarperCollins, 1996.

———. "Paul Bunyan." *Where the Sidewalk Ends*. HarperCollins, 1974.

———. "Squishy Touch." *A Light in the Attic*. HarperCollins, 1981.

Smith, Charles R., Jr. *The Mighty 12: Superheroes of Greek Myth*. Illus. by P. Craig Russell. Little, 2008.

Soto, Gary. "Ode to La Llorona." *Neighborhood Odes*. Illus. by David Diaz. Harcourt, 1992.

Yolen, Jane. "Delphi." *Sacred Places*. Illus. by David Shannon. Harcourt, 1996.

Retelling Fables and Folk Tales

Ahlberg, Janet & Allan Ahlberg. *Each Peach Pear Plum*. Scholastic, 1978.

Allen, Lillian. "Anancy." In Agard, John & Grace Nichols. *Under the Moon and Over the Sea*. Illus. by Cathie Felstead, et al. Candlewick, 2002.

Bennett, Rowena. "The Gingerbread Man." In De Regniers, Beatrice Schenk, et al. *Sing a Song of Popcorn*. Scholastic, 1988.

Cedering, Siv. "The Changeling." In Janeczko, Paul B. *Seeing the Blue Between*. Candlewick, 2002. (Also in *What Have You Lost?*)

Ciardi, John. "The Wise Hen." *You Read to Me, I'll Read to You*. Illus. by Edward Gorey. HarperCollins, 1961.

Crawley, Dave. "City Cat, Country Cat." *Cat Poems*. Illus. by Tamara Petrosino. Boyds Mills, 2005.

Dahl. Roald. *Revolting Rhymes*. Illus. by Quentin Blake. Knopf, 1982.

Fisher, Aileen. "Fairy Tale." *I Heard a Bluebird Sing*. Illus. by Jennifer Emery. Boyds Mills, 2002.

Fletcher, Ralph. "Beanstalk Poem." *A Writing Kind of Day*. Illus. by April Ward. Boyds Mills, 2005.

Grandits, John. "The Tower." *Technically, It's Not My Fault*. Clarion, 2004.

Harrison, Michael. "Miss! Sue Is Kissing." In Hollyer, Belinda. *She's All That!* Illus. by Susan Hellard. Kingfisher, 2006. ("The Frog Prince.")

Havill, Juanita. "The Pumpkin's Revenge." *I Heard It from Alice Zucchini*. Illus. by Christine Davenier. Chronicle, 2006.

Hoberman, Mary Ann. *You Read to Me, I'll Read to You: Very Short Fairy Tales to Read Together*. Illus. by Michael Emberley. Little, 2004.

Horowitz, Dave. *The Ugly Pumpkin*. Putnam, 2005.

Lawson, JonArno. "Handsome Prince." *Black Stars in a White Night Sky*. Illus. by Sherwin Tjia. Boyds Mills, 2006.

Millay, Edna St. Vincent. "La, What a Climb." In Schoonmaker, Francis. *Edna St. Vincent Millay*. Illus. by Mike Bryce. Sterling, 1999. ("Jack and the Beanstalk")

Patten, Brian. "The Complacent Tortoise." In Harrison, Michael & Christopher Stuart-Clark. *Oxford Book of Story Poems*. Oxford, 1990.

Perry, Andrea. "Acme's Super Spider Spotter." *Here's What You Do When You Can't Find Your Shoe (Ingenious Inventions for Pesky Problems)*. Illus. by Alan Snow. Atheneum, 2003.

Prelutsky, Jack. "A Princess Laments." *It's Raining Pigs and Noodles*. Illus. by James Stevenson. Greenwillow, 2000. ('The Frog Prince.")

Silverstein, Shel. "In Search of Cinderella." *A Light in the Attic*. HarperCollins, 1981.

———. "Golden Goose." *Falling Up*. HarperCollins, 1996.

———. "The Silver Fish." *Where the Sidewalk Ends*. HarperCollins, 1974.

Singer, Marilyn. "Frog Prince." *How to Cross a Pond*. Illus. by Meilo So. Knopf, 2003.

Stafford, William. "A Story That Could Be True." In Kennedy, X. J. & Dorothy M. Kennedy. *Knock at a Star*. Little, 1999.

Viorst, Judith. Section: "Fairy Tales." *If I Were in Charge of the World*. Illus. by Lynn Cherry. Macmillan, 1984.

———. Section: "Fairy Tales." *Sad Underwear*. Illus. by Richard Hull. Atheneum, 1995.

Wax, Wendy. *City Witch, Country Witch*. Illus. by Scott Gibala-Broxholm. Cavendish, 2008.

Yeats, William Butler. "The Song of Wandering Aengus." In Willard, Nancy. *Step Lightly*. Harcourt, 1998.

Yolen, Jane. "Gingerbread Boy." In Janeczko, Paul B. *Seeing the Blue Between*. Candlewick, 2002.

———. "Ice Bridge." *Once Upon Ice*. Illus. by Jason Stemple. Boyds Mills, 1997.

Retelling Classic Poems

Beard, Henry. *Poetry for Cats: The Definitive Anthology of Distinguished Feline Verse*. Illus. by Gary Zamchick. Villard, 1994.

"The Boy Stood on the Burning Deck," & "Somebody Said It Couldn't Be Done." In Prelutsky, Jack. *For Laughing Out Loud*. Knopf, 1991.

Dahl. Roald. "Gray's Eulogy, or Energy in a Country Bypass." *Vile Verses*. Illus. by Quentin Blake et al. Viking, 2005.

Dickman, Conrad. "Winter Trees." In Morrison, Lillian. *Sprints and Distances*. HarperCollins, 1990. (Joyce Kilmer's "Trees")

Florian, Douglas. "Styropoem." *Bing Bang Boing*. Harcourt, 1994. (Joyce Kilmer's "Trees")

Hoberman, Mary Ann. *And to Think That We Thought That We'd Never Be Friends*. Illus. by Kevin Hawkes. Crown, 1999. (Structure of *And to Think That I Saw It on Mulberry Street*)

Janeczko, Paul B. "Teresa's Red Adidas (For T. G.)" In Katz, Bobbi. *More Pocket Poems*. Illus. by Deborah Zemke. Dutton, 2009. (Joyce Kilmer's "Trees")

Kennedy, X. J. & Dorothy M. Kennedy. Section: "Takeoffs." *Knock at a Star.* Illus. by Karen Lee Baker. Little, 1999.
Lewis, J. Patrick. "Acknowledgements." *Please Bury Me in the Library.* Illus. by Kyle M. Stone. Harcourt, 2005. ("Stopping by Woods on a Snowy Evening")
Little, Jean. "After English Class." *Hey World, Here I Am!* Illus. by Sue Truesdell. HarperCollins, 1986. ("Stopping by Woods on a Snowy Evening")
Rex, Adam. *Frankenstein Makes a Sandwich.* Harcourt, 2006.
———. *Frankenstein Takes the Cake.* Harcourt, 2008.
Rex, Michael. *Goodnight Goon.* Putnam, 2008.
———. *The Runaway Mummy.* Putnam, 2009.
Sandburg, Carl. "Fog." In Niven, Penelope. *Carl Sandburg: Adventures of a Poet.* Illus. by Marc Nadel. Harcourt, 2003. (Parody of his own poem)
Schwartz, Alvin, col. *And the Green Grass Grew All Around.* Illus. by Sue Truesdell. HarperCollins, 1992.
Scieszka, Jon. *Science Verse.* Illus. by Lane Smith. Viking, 2004.
Shapiro, Karen. *Because I Could Not Stop My Bike.* Illus. by Matt Faulkner. Charlesbridge, 2003.
———. *I Must Go Down to the Beach Again.* Illus. by Judy Love. Charlesbridge, 2007.
Silverstein, Shel. "Pinocchio." *Falling Up.* HarperCollins, 1996.
Soto, Gary. "My Meow." *A Fire in My Hands.* Harcourt, 2006. ("For I Will Consider My Cat, Jeoffry.")
Swanson, Susan Marie. *The House in the Night.* Illus. by Beth Krommes. Houghton, 2008. ("This Is the Key to the Kingdom")
Willard, Nancy. "The Tiger Asks Blake for a Bedtime Story." *A Visit to William Blake's Inn.* Illus. by Alice Provensen & Martin Provensen. Harcourt, 1981. ("The Tyger")

Variations on "This Is the House That Jack Built"

The plot pattern and repetition of this traditional poem are used to explain processes such how a potter creates in *The Pot That Juan Built* or the water cycle in *This Is the Rain.* Students might want to try to write up an explanation for a process they know using this form.

Aardema, Verna. *Bringing the Rain to Kapiti Plain.* Illus. by Beatriz Vidal. Dial, 1981.
Alborough, Jez. *Duck in the Truck.* HarperCollins, 2000.
Alexander, Jessica & Diane Z. Shore. *This Is the Dream.* Illus. by James Ransome. HarperCollins, 2006.
Andrews-Goebel, Nancy. *The Pot That Juan Built.* Illus. by David Diaz. Lee & Low, 2002.
Beil, Karen Magnuson. *Jack's House.* Illus. by Mike Wohnoutka. Holiday, 2008.
Dragonwagon, Crescent. *This Is the Bread I Baked for Ned.* Illus. by Isadore Seltzer. Atheneum, 1989.
Edwards, Pamela Duncan. *Jack and Jill's Treehouse.* Illus. by Henry Cole. HarperCollins, 2008.
Ernst, Lisa Campbell. *This Is the Van That Dad Cleaned.* S & S, 2005.
Fleming, Candice. *This Is the Baby.* Illus. by Maggie Smith. Farrar, 2004.
Godwin, Laura. *This Is the Firefighter.* Illus. by Julian Hector. Hyperion, 2009.
Greene, Rhonda Gowler. *This Is the Teacher.* Illus. by Mike Lester. Dutton, 2004.
———. *The Very First Thanksgiving Day.* Illus. by Susan Gaber. Atheneum, 2002.
Krebs, Laurie. *The Beeman.* Illus. by Melissa Iwai. National Geographic, 2002.
Rosenberg, Liz. *This Is the Wind.* Illus. by Renée Reichert. Roaring Brook, 2008.
Schaeffer, Lola M. *This Is the Rain.* Illus. by Jane Wattenberg. HarperCollins, 2001.
Shore, Diane Z. *This Is the Feast.* Illus. by Megan Lloyd. HarperCollins, 2008.
Sierra, Judy. *The House That Drac Built.* Illus. by Will Hillenbrand. Harcourt, 1995.
Sloat, Teri. *This Is the House That Was Tidy and Neat.* Illus. by R. W. Alley. Holt, 2005.

Variations on "The Night Before Christmas"

James Rice has issued fifteen variants of Clement Moore's classic story, the best-known being *The Cajun Night Before Christmas*. Natasha Wing has written thirteen variants about holidays and school events.

Murray, Margaret. *Halloween Night*. Illus. by Brandon Dorman. Greenwillow, 2008.
Rice, James. *Cajun Night before Christmas*. Pelican, 1992. (And many others)
Sierra, Judy. *'Twas the Fright Before Christmas*. Illus. by Will Hillenbrand. Harcourt, 2005.
Wing, Natasha. *The Night Before First Grade*. Illus. by Deborah Zemke. Grosset, 2005. (And many others)
Yolen, Jane. *Beneath the Ghost Moon: A Halloween Tale*. Illus. by Laurel Molk. Little, 1994.

Variations on "Over in the Meadow"

Bateman, Donna M. *Deep in the Swamp*. Illus. by Brian Lies. Charlesbridge, 2007.
Crum, Shutta. *The House in the Meadow*. Illus. by Paige Billin-Frye. Whitman, 2003.
Shulman, Lisa. *Over in the Meadow at the Big Ballet*. Illus. by Sarah Massini. Putnam, 2007.
Silverman, Erica. *The Halloween House*. Illus. by Jon Agee. Farrar, 1997.
Wilson, Anna. *Over in the Grassland*. Illus. by Alison Bartlett. Little, 1999.

Variations on "There Was an Old Lady Who Swallowed a Fly"

Arnold, Tedd. *There Was an Old Lady Who Swallowed Fly Guy*. Scholastic, 2007.
Colandro, Lucille. *There Was an Old Lady Who Swallowed a Bell*. Scholastic, 2006.
Jackson, Alison. *I Know an Old Lady Who Swallowed a Pie*. Illus. by Judith Byron Schachner. Dutton, 1997.
Sierra, Judy. *Thelonius Monster's Sky-High Fly Pie*. Illus. by Edward Koren. Knopf, 2006.
Silverman, Erica. *There Was a Wee Woman*. Illus. by Rosanne Litzinger. Farrar, 2008.

STANDARD TWO UNIT: HALLOWEEN

See also Chapter Three: Science Standard Four (Bats), Chapter Three: Science Standard Four (Crows), Chapter Three: Science Standard Four (Pumpkins)

There are more poetry books about Halloween and its various monsters than about any other holiday. Rather than look at the holiday as an occasion for sweets and costumes, teachers and librarians can treat the holiday as an occasion for the study of traditional literary character motifs. A character motif is one that recurs in many stories. Characters that come down through time in folklore reappear in fantasy novels for children and young adults, as well as adult fiction. Students can get to know the historic qualities of these characters, then compare them with characters in poems and in fiction. Jack Prelutsky's collections of poems for older readers, for example, are filled with poems about folk characters known to young readers of the Harry Potter books and other fantasy series. The poet describes behaviors of ogres, trolls, ghosts, and goblins using alliteration, onomatopoeia, and repetition to add to the eerie sense of each character. Older students will enjoy presenting these poems in spooky read-alouds. W. Nikola-Lisa's *Shake dem Halloween Bones*, a rhythmic chant filled with traditional folk tale characters, makes a great read aloud or oral presentation for a younger audience.

Several poets allude to other literature in their Halloween poems. Middle elementary children will enjoy Michael Rex's *Goodnight Goon*, a "Petrifying Parody" of Margaret Wise Brown's *Goodnight Moon*, and his *Runaway Mummy*, a modern *Runaway Bunny*. In *Dracula Makes a Sandwich* and *Dracula Takes the Cake*, Adam Rex's books of poems for older readers, he includes characters from literature and popular culture such as *The Phantom of the Opera* and *The Invisible Man*.

Halloween Poetry

Alarcón, Francisco X. "El Día de los Muertos = Day of the Dead." *Angels Ride Bikes = Los Ángeles Andan en Bicicleta*. Children's, 1999.

Bauer, Caroline, Feller, ed. *Halloween: Stories and Poems*. Illus. by Peter Sis. HarperCollins, 1989.

Brown, Marc. *Scared Silly!* Little, 1994.

Carlstrom, Nancy White. *Who Said Boo?* Illus. by R. W. Alley, Simon & Schuster, 1995.

Cooper, Harriet. "October Nights." In Booth, David. *'Til All the Stars Have Fallen*. Illus. by Kady MacDonald Denton. Viking, 1990.

Cummings, e. e. "From 'Chansons Innocetes, II' " ("Hist Whist") in Hopkins, Lee Bennett. *Days to Celebrate*. Illus. by Stephen Alcorn. HarperCollins, 2005.

Fleming, Denise. *Pumpkin Eye*. Holt, 2001.

Hopkins, Lee Bennett, ed. *Halloween Howls*. Illus. by Stacey Schuett. HarperCollins, 2005.

Hubbell, Patricia. *Boo!* Illus. by Jeff Spackman. Cavendish, 1998.

Huck, Charlotte S. *A Creepy Countdown*. Illus. by Jos. A Smith. Greenwillow, 1998.

Johnston, Tony. "The Day of the Dead = El Día de los Muertos." *My Mexico = México Mío*. Illus. by F. John Sierra. Putnam, 1996.

Keep, Richard. *Clatter Bash! A Day of the Dead Celebration*. Peachtree, 2004.

Larrick, Nancy, ed. Section: "I Saw a Spooky Witch Out Riding Her Broom." *Piping Down the Valleys Wild*. Illus. by Ellen Raskin. Topeka, 1968.

Leuck, Laura. *One Witch*. Illus. by S. D. Schindler. Walker, 2003.

Livingston, Myra Cohn. "El Día de Muertos = The Day of the Dead." *Festivals*. Illus. by Leonard Everett Fisher. Holiday, 1996.

———. "Halloween." *Celebrations*. Illus. by Leonard Everett Fisher. Holiday, 1985.

Merriam, Eve. *Halloween ABC*. Illus. by Lane Smith. Simon & Schuster,1987.

Murray, Marjorie Dennis. *Halloween Night*. Illus. by Brandon Dorman. HarperCollins, 2008.

Neitzel, Shirley. *Who Will I Be? A Halloween Rebus Story*. Illus. by Nancy Winslow Parker. HarperCollins, 2005.

Nikola-Lisa, W. *Shake dem Halloween Bones*. Illus. by Mike Reed. Houghton, Mifflin, 1997.

Riley, James Whitcomb. *The Gobble-Uns'll Git You Ef You Don't Watch Out!* Illus. by Joel Schick. HarperCollins, 1975.

Schertle, Alice, *The Skeleton in the Closet*. Illus. by Curtis Jobling. HarperCollins, 2003.

Schulman, Janet. *10 Trick-or-Treaters*. Illus. by Linda Davick. Knopf, 2005.

Shaw, Nancy. *Sheep Trick or Treat*. Illus. by Margot Apple. Houghton Mifflin, 1997.

Sierra, Judy. *The House That Drac Built*. Illus. by Will Hildenbrand. Harcourt, 1995.

———. *Monster Goose*. Illus. by Jack E. Davis. Harcourt, 2001.

Silverman, Erica. *The Halloween House*. Illus. by Jon Agee. Farrar, 1997.

Sklansky, Amy E. *Skeleton Bones and Goblin Groans*. Illus. by Karen Dismukes. Holt, 2004.

Soto, Gary. "Description of the Suspect." *Fearless Fernie*. Illus. by Regan Dunnick. Putnam, 2002. (Novel in Verse)

Turner, Ann. "Halloween." *Street Talk*. Illus. by Catherine Stock. Houghton, Mifflin, 1986.

Updike, John. "October." *A Child's Calendar*. Illus. by Trina Schart Hyman. Holiday, 1999.

Whitehead, Jenny. "Halloween Leftovers." *Holiday Stew*. Holt, 2007.

Winthrop, Elizabeth. *Halloween Hats*. Illus. by Sue Truesdell. Holt, 2002.

Woodson, Jacqueline. "Halloween Poem." *Locomotion*. Putnam, 2003. (Novel in Verse)

Worth, Valerie. "Skeletons." *All the Small Poems and Fourteen More*. Illus. by Natalie Babbitt. Farrar, 1994.

Yolen, Jane. *Beneath the Ghost Moon*. Illus. by Laurel Molk. Little, 1994.

More Scary Characters

Andrews, Sylvia. *Rattlebone Rock.* Illus. by Jennifer Plecas. HarperCollins, 1995.

Bunting, Eve. *The Bones of Fred McFee.* Illus. by Kurt Cyrus. Harcourt, 2002.

Fox, Mem. *Guess What?* Illus. by Vivienne Goodman. Harcourt, 1988.

Hoberman, Mary Ann. *You Read to Me, I'll Read to You: Very Short Scary Tales to Read Together.* Illus. by Michael Emberley. Little, 2007.

Pearson, Susan. *Grimericks.* Illus. by Gris Grimly. Cavendish, 2005.

Prelutsky, Jack. *The Dragons Are Singing Tonight.* Illus. by Peter Sis. Greenwillow, 1993.

———. *The Gargoyle on the Roof.* Illus. by Peter Sis. Greenwillow, 1999.

———. *The Headless Horseman Rides Tonight.* Illus. by Arnold Lobel. Greenwillow, 1980.

———. *Monday's Troll.* Illus. by Peter Sis. Greenwillow, 1996.

———. *Nightmares.* Illus. by Arnold Lobel. Greenwillow, 1976.

Rex, Adam. *Frankenstein Makes a Sandwich.* Harcourt, 2006.

———. *Frankenstein Takes the Cake.* Harcourt, 2008.

Rex, Michael. *Goodnight Goon: A Petrifying Parody.* Putnam, 2008.

———. *The Runaway Mummy: A Petrifying Parody.* Putnam, 2009.

Sierra, Judy. *Beastly Rhymes to Read After Dark.* Illus. by Brian Biggs. Knopf, 2008.

———. *Thelonius Monster's Sky-High Fly Pie.* Illus. by Edward Koren. Knopf, 2006.

Wax, Wendy. *City Witch, Country Witch.* Illus. by Scott Gibala-Broxholm. Cavendish, 2008.

Wong, Janet. *Knock on Wood: Poems About Superstitions.* Illus. by Julie Paschkis. McElderry, 2003.

Zalben, Jane Breskin & Steven Zalben. *Saturday Night at the Beastro.* HarperCollins, 2004.

Standard Three: Students apply a wide range of strategies to comprehend, interpret, evaluate, and appreciate texts. They draw on their prior experience, their interactions with other readers and writers, their knowledge of word meaning and of other texts, their word identification strategies, and their understanding of textual features (e.g., sound-letter correspondence, sentence structure, context, graphics).

Standard Four: Students adjust their use of spoken, written, and visual language (e.g., conventions, style, vocabulary) to communicate effectively with a variety of audiences and for different purposes.

STANDARD FOUR: LANGUAGE CONVENTIONS

Poets like to play with the elements of language, including the letters of the alphabet, grammar, spelling, parts of speech, and punctuation. In some poems, the poet has struggled just as students do. In others, the poet takes joy in playing around with the parts we put together to make our language flow.

Lewis, Alan F. G. "Propper English." In Kennedy, Dorothy M. *I Thought I'd Take My Rat to School.* Illus. by Abby Carter. Little, 1993.

Shields, Carol Diggory. Sections: "The Rules" & "The Tools." *English, Fresh Squeezed.* Illus. by Tony Ross. Handprint, 2004.

Letters of the Alphabet

Alarcón, Francisco X. "Keys to the Universe." *From the Bellybutton of the Moon = Del Ombligo de la Luna.* Illus. by Maya Christina Gonzalez. Children's, 1988.

Brown, Calef. "Alphabet Sherbet." *Flamingos on the Roof.* Houghton, 2006.

Chesworth, Michael. *Alphaboat.* Farrar, 2002.

Dakos, Kalli. "Elemenopee." *Mrs. Cole on an Onion Roll.* Illus. by JoAnn Adinolfi. S & S, 1995.

Hoberman, Mary Ann. "X" & "O Is Open." *The Llama Who Had No Pajama.* Illus. by Betty Fraser. Harcourt, 1998.

Hollander, John. "Vowel Owl." In Paschen, Elise. *Poetry Speaks to Children.* Sourcebooks, 2005. (With CD)

Lewis, J. Patrick. "Eating Alphabet Soup." *Please Bury Me in the Library.* Illus. by Kyle M. Stone. Harcourt, 2005.

McCord, David. "Alphabet (Eta Z)," "LMNTL," "The Likes and Looks of Letters," "V," "X and Y," & "Z." *One at a Time.* Illus. by Henry B. Kane. Little, 1986.

Merriam, Eve. "A Jamboree for J" & "Quibble." *The Singing Green.* Illus. by Kathleen Collins Howell. Morrow, 1992.

Reeves, James. "W." In Attenborough, Liz. *Poetry by Heart.* Scholastic, 2001.

Seuss, Dr. *On Beyond Zebra.* Random, 1955.

Shannon, Angela. "First Signature." In Giovanni, Nikki. *Hip Hop Speaks to Children.* Sourcebooks, 2008. (With CD)

Tobin, Jim. *Sue MacDonald Had a Book.* Illus. by Dave Coverly. Holt, 2009.

Spelling

Adams, Charles. "Orthographic Lament." In Janeczko, Paul B. *A Foot in the Mouth.* Illus. by Chris Raschka. Candlewick, 2009.

Baylor, Byrd. *The Best Town in the World.* Illus. by Ronald Himler. Macmillan, 1983.

Bingham, Shirlee Curlee. "From English Is a Pain (Pane?)" In Katz, Bobbi. *Pocket Poems.* Illus. by Marylin Hafner. Dutton, 2004.

Cole, Joanna & Stephanie Calmenson, sels. "Spelling Rhymes." *Miss Mary Mack.* Illus. by Alan Tiegreen. Morrow, 1990.

Dakos, Kalli. "The Star." *Don't Read This Book, Whatever You Do.* Illus. by G. Brian Karas. S & S, 1993.

———. "Worried About Being Worried." *Put Your Eyes Up Here.* Illus. by G. Brian Karas. S & S, 2003.

Holbrook, Sara. "Spellbound." *The Dog Ate My Homework.* Boyds Mills, 1996.

Lewis, J. Patrick. "Book Editor." *Once Upon a Tomb.* Illus. by Simon Bartram. Candlewick, 2006.

McCord, David. "Spelling Bee." *One at a Time.* Illus. by Henry B. Kane. Little, 1986. (Also in *I Thought I'd Take My Rat to School*)

McElroy, Butch. "One." In Nye, Naomi Shihab. *Salting the Ocean.* Illus. by Ashley Bryan. Greenwillow, 2000.

Prelutsky, Jack. "I Wish I'd Studied Harder." *What a Day It Was at School!* Illus. by Doug Cushman. Harper Collins, 2006.

———. "My Dog May Be a Genius." *My Dog May Be a Genius.* Illus. by James Stevenson. HarperCollins, 2008.

Roemer, Heidi Bee. "Spelling Bee." In Hopkins, Lee Bennett. *Hamsters, Shells, and Spelling Bees.* Illus. by Sachiko Yoshikawa. HarperCollins, 2008.

Rylant, Cynthia. "Spelling Bee." *Waiting to Waltz.* Illus. by Stephen Gammell. Macmillan, 1984.

Schertle, Alice. "Consider Cow." *How Now Brown Cow?* Illus. by Amanda Schaffer. Harcourt, 1994.

Sidman, Joyce. "Lucky Nose" & "Spelling Bomb." *This Is Just to Say.* Illus. by Pamela Zagarenski. Houghton, 2007.

Silverstein, Shel. "One Out of Sixteen." *Falling Up.* HarperCollins, 1996.

Smith, William Jay. "X Is for X." In Janeczko, Paul B. *Poetry from A to Z.* Illus. by Cathy Boback. S & S, 1994.

Soto, Gary. "Spelling Bee." *Fearless Fernie.* Putnam, 2002. (Novel in Verse)

Viorst, Judith. *The Alphabet from Z to A (With Much Confusion on the Way)*. Illus. by Richard Hull. Atheneum, 1994.

———. "We Interrupt This Program." *If I Were in Charge of the World*. Illus. by Lynne Cherry. Atheneum, 1981.

Punctuation

Alarcón, Francisco X. "Question." *From the Bellybutton of the Moon = Del Ombligo de la Luna*. Illus. by Maya Christina Gonzalez. Children's, 1988.

Armour, Richard. "The Period." In Hopkins, Lee Bennett. *Wonderful Words*. Illus. by Karen Barbour. S & S, 2004.

Bruno, Elsa Knight. *Punctuation Celebration*. Illus. by Jenny Whitehead. Holt, 2009.

Dakos, Kalli. "Call the Periods, Call the Commas." *If You're Not Here Please Raise Your Hand*. Illus. by G. Brian Karas. Macmillan, 1990.

Emin, Gevorg. "The Question Mark." In Nye, Naomi Shihab. *This Same Sky*. Macmillan, 1992.

Fisher, Aileen. "Comma in the Sky." *Always Wondering*. Illus. by Joan Sandin. HarperCollins, 1991. (Also in *Sing of the Earth and Sky*)

Florian, Douglas. "Commas." *Bing Bang Boing*. Harcourt, 1994. (Also in *Knock at a Star*)

Nye, Naomi Shihab. "Ellipse." *A Maze Me*. Greenwillow, 2005.

Prelutsky, Jack. "The Flotz." *The New Kid on the Block*. Illus. by James Stevenson. Greenwillow, 1984.

———. "Squirrels." *Something Big Has Been Here*. Illus. by James Stevenson. Greenwillow, 1990. (Question Mark)

Worth, Valerie. "The Water Lily." *All the Small Poems and Fourteen More*. Illus. by Natalie Babbitt. Farrar, 1994.

Parts of Speech

Heller, Ruth. *Behind the Mask: A Book About Prepositions*. Penguin, 1988.

———. *Fantastic! Wow! And Unreal! A Book About Interjections and Conjunctions*. Grosset, 1998.

———. *Kites Sail High: A Book About Verbs*. Penguin, 1998.

———. *Many Luscious Lollypops: A Book About Adjectives*. Penguin, 1998.

———. *Merry-Go-Round: A Book About Nouns*. Grosset, 1990.

———. *Mine, All Mine: A Book About Pronouns*. Penguin, 1999.

———. *Up, Up, and Away: A Book About Adverbs*. Grosset, 1991.

Koch, Kenneth. "Permanently." In Smith, William Jay. *Here Is My Heart*. Illus. by Jane Dyer. Little, 1999. (All)

Kraus, Ruth. *A Hole Is to Dig*. Illus. by Maurice Sendak. Harper, 1952.

Merriam, Eve. "Skywriting." *The Singing Green*. Illus. by Kathleen Collins Howell. Morrow, 1992.

Prelutsky, Jack. "An Unassuming Owl." *The New Kid on the Block*. Illus. by James Stevenson. Greenwillow, 1984. (Who and whom)

Collective Nouns

Heller, Ruth. *A Cache of Jewels: And Other Collective Nouns*. Penguin, 1998.

Lipton, James. *An Exaltation of Larks*. Penguin, 1977. (Adult prose)

Maddox, Marjorie. *A Crossing of Zebras: Animal Packs in Poetry*. Illus. by Philip Huber. Boyds Mills, 2008.

McMillan, Bruce. *The Baby Zoo*. Scholastic, 1992.

Pomerantz, Charlotte. "Here They Come." *Thunderboom!* Illus. by Rob Shepperson. Front, 2005.

Handwriting

Dakos, Kalli. "If My Hand . . ." & "My Writing Is an . . ." *Don't Read This Book, Whatever You Do!* Illus. by G. Brian Karas. S & S, 1993.

Graves, Donald. "Handwriting." *Baseball, Snakes, and Summer Squash*. Boyds Mills, 1996.

Heaney, Seamus. "Alphabets. Part 1." In Paschen, Elise. *Poetry Speaks to Children*. Sourcebooks, 2005. (With CD)

Salas, Laura Purdie. "Printer Problems." *Stampede!* Illus. by Steven Salerno. Clarion, 2009.

Shannon, Angela. "First Signature." In Giovanni, Nikki. *Hip Hop Speaks to Children*. Sourcebooks, 2008. (With CD)

Thurman, Judith. "New Notebook." In Hopkins, Lee Bennett. *School Supplies*. Illus. by Renée Flower. S & S, 1996.

Standard Five: Students employ a wide range of strategies as they write and use different writing process elements appropriately to communicate with different audiences for a variety of purposes.

See also Chapter One: Poetry and the National Standards (Writing Poetry)

See also Chapter Six: Music Standard One (Blues Poems)

STANDARD FIVE: POETIC FORMS

The works listed in this standard highlight the wide array of poetic forms available to young poets. The first set of books includes description and examples of many forms. These are followed by specific examples of some of the forms. Librarians and teachers can post examples of individual forms with invitations to try them out. A student might become interested in one or two of these types of poetry and be encouraged to write in the form.

Harley, Avis. *Fly with Poetry: An ABC of Poetry*. Boyds Mills, 2000.

———. *Leap into Poetry: More ABC's of Poetry*. Boyds Mills, 2001.

Janeczko, Paul B. sel. *A Kick in the Head: An Everyday Guide to Poetic Forms*. Illus. by Chris Raschka. Candlewick, 2005.

Kennedy, X. J. & Dorothy M. Kennedy. *Knock at a Star: A Child's Introduction to Poetry*. Illus. by Karen Lee Baker. Little, 1999.

Marsalis, Wynton. *Jazz A B Z*. Illus. by Paul Rogers. Candlewick, 2005.

McCord, David. "Write Me a Verse" & "Write Me Another Verse." *One at a Time*. Illus. by Henry B. Kane. Little, 1986.

Terse Verse (Hink Pinks or Hinky Pinkies)

Feldman, Eve B. *Billy and Milly, Short and Silly*. Illus. by Tuesday Mourning. Putnam, 2009.

Janeczko, Paul B. "August Ice Cream Cone Poem." In Rosen, Michael J. *Food Fight*. Harcourt, 1996. (Also in *Least Things*)

McCall, Francis & Patricia Keeler. *A Huge Hog Is a Big Pig*. HarperCollins, 2002.

Rex, Michael. *Dunk Skunk*. Putnam, 2005.

Couplets

Banks, Kate. *Max's Dragon*. Illus. by Boris Kulikov. Farrar, 2008. (Character speaks in couplets)

Ehlert, Lois. *Oodles of Animals*. Harcourt, 2008.

Fleming, Denise. *Pumpkin Eye*. Holt, 2001.

Gaiman, Neil. *The Dangerous Alphabet*. Illus. by Chris Grimly. HarperCollins, 2008.

Knowles, Sheena. *Edward the Emu*. Illus. by Rod Clement. HarperCollins, 1998.

———. *Edwina the Emu.* Illus. by Rod Clement. HarperCollins, 1996.
Thomas, Patricia. *Red Sled.* Illus. by Chris Demarest. Boyds Mills, 2008.
Zolotow, Charlotte. *Some Things Go Together.* Illus. by Ashley Wolff. HarperCollins, 1999.

Haiku

Chaikin, Miriam. *Don't Step on the Sky.* Illus. by Hiroe Nakata. Holt, 2002.
Demi, ed. *In the Eyes of the Cat.* Trans. by Tze-si Huang. Holt, 1992.
Gollub, Matthew. *Cool Melons Turn to Frogs!* Illus. by Kazuko G. Stone. Lee & Low, 1998.
Grimes, Nikki. *A Pocketful of Poems.* Illus. by Javaka Steptoe. Clarion, 2001.
Kobayashi, Issa. *Today and Today.* Illus. by G. Brian Karas. Scholastic, 2007.
Lin, Grace & Ranida T. McKneally. *Our Seasons.* Charlesbridge, 2006.
Mannis, Celeste Davidson. *One Leaf Rides the Wind.* Illus. by Susan Kathleen Hartung. Viking, 2002.
Mora, Pat. *¡Yum! Mm Mm! Qué Rico! America's Sproutings.* Illus. by Rafeal López. Lee & Low, 2007.
Prelutsky, Jack. *If Not for the Cat.* Illus. by Ted Rand. HarperCollins, 2004.
Reibstein, Mark. *Wabi Sabi.* Illus. by Ed Young. Little, 2008.
Rosen, Michael J. *The Cuckoo's Haiku.* Illus. by Stan Fellows. Candlewick, 2009.
Shannon, George, sel. *Spring: A Haiku Story.* Illus. by Malcah Zeldis. Greenwillow, 1996.
Spivak, Dawnine. *Grass Sandals.* Illus. by Demi. Atheneum, 1997.

Limericks

Ciardi, John. *The Hopeful Trout and Other Limericks.* Illus. by Susan Meddaugh, Houghton, 1989.
Hubbell, Patricia. *Boo!* Illus. by Jeff Spackman. Cavendish. 1998.
Kennedy, X. J. *Uncle Switch.* Illus. by John O'Brien. McElderry, 1997.
Lear, Edward. *There Was an Old Man.* Illus. by Michele Lemieux. Kids Can, 1994.
Lobel, Arnold. *The Book of Pigericks.* HarperCollins, 1983
Pearson, Susan. *Grimericks.* Illus. by Gris Grimly. Cavendish, 2005.

More Small Poems

De Regniers, Beatrice Schenk, sel. Section: "In a Few Words." *Sing a Song of Popcorn.* Scholastic, 1988.
James, Simon, ed. *Days Like This.* Candlewick, 1999.
Katz, Bobbi. *More Pocket Poems.* Illus. by Deborah Zemke. Dutton, 2009.
———. *Pocket Poems.* Illus. by Marylin Hafner. Dutton, 2004.
Worth, Valerie———. *All the Small Poems and Fourteen More.* Illus. by Natalie Babbitt. Farrar, 1987.

———. *Animal Poems.* Illus. by Steve Jenkins. Farrar, 2007.
———. *Peacock.* Illus. by Natalie Babbitt. Farrar, 2002.

Concrete Poems (Shape Poems)

Cyrus, Kurt. *Hotel Deep.* Harcourt, 2005.
Esbensen, Barbara Juster. *Words with Wrinkled Knees.* Illus. by John Stadler. Crowell, 1986
Graham, Joan Bransfield. *Flicker, Flash.* Illus. by Nancy Davis. Houghton, 1999.
———. *Splish, Splash.* Illus. by Steve Scott. Houghton, 1994.
Grandits, John. *Blue Lipstick.* Clarion, 2006.
———. *Technically, It's Not My Fault.* Clarion, 2004.
Janeczko, Paul B. sel. *A Poke in the I.* Illus. by Chris Raschka. Candlewick, 2001.

Lewis, J. Patrick. *Doodle Dandies*. Illus. by Lisa Desimini. S & S, 1998.

Roemer, Heidi B. *Come To My Party*. Illus. by Hideko Takahashi. Holt, 2004.

Sidman, Joyce. *Meow Ruff*. Illus. by Michelle Berg. Houghton, 2006.

Smith, Charles R. *Diamond Life: Baseball Sights, Sounds, and Swings*. Orchard, 2004.

Stevenson, James. *Popcorn*. Greenwillow, 1998. (Also *Candy Corn*, *Cornflakes*, *Just Around the Corner*, *Corn-Fed*, and *Corn Chowder*)

Odes

An ode is a celebration of an animal, a place, an object, or a person. Contemporary odes are often lighthearted. Pablo Neruda's adult collection, *Odes to Common Things*, provides a model for this approach to the ode. Gary Soto includes "Ode to Pablo's Tennis Shoes" in *Neighborhood Odes*; perhaps it is a nod to Neruda,

Alarcón, Francisco X. "Ode to Corn." *Laughing Tomatoes = Jitomates Risueños*. Illus. by Maya Christina Gonzalez. Children's, 1997.

———. "Ode to My Shoes." *From the Bellybutton of the Moon = Del Ombligo de la Luna*. Illus. by Maya Christina Gonzalez. Children's, 1998.

Dakos, Kalli. "An Ode To a Toe." *Don't Read This Book, Whatever You Do!* Illus. by G. Brian Karas. S & S, 1993.

Marsalis, Wynton "J: Jellyroll Morton." *Jazz A B Z*. Illus. by Paul Rogers. Candlewick, 2005.

Mora, Pat. "Ode to Pizza." *My Own True Name*. Arté Público, 2000.

Neruda, Pablo. "From 'Ode to a Pair of Sox.' " In Kennedy, Caroline. *A Family of Poems*. Illus. by Jon J. Muth. Hyperion, 2005.

———. *Odes to Common Things*. Illus. by Ferris Cook. Bulfinch, 1994.

O'Shaughnessy, Arthur. "Ode to Writers." In Krull, Kathleen. *A Pot O' Gold*. Illus. by David McPhail. Hyperion, 2004.

Sidman, Joyce. "Ode to a Slow Hand." *This Is Just to Say*. Illus. by Pamela Zagarenski. Houghton, 2007.

Soto, Gary. *Neighborhood Odes*. Illus. by David Diaz. Harcourt, 1992.

———. "Ode to Pablo's Tennis Shoes." *Neighborhood Odes*. Illus. by David Diaz. Harcourt, 1992. (Also in *A Kick in the Head*)

Valdes, Gina. "Ode to the Tortilla." In Carlson, Lori Marie, *Red Hot Salsa*. Holt. 2005.

Ballads

Ballads are stories told in poetry with rhythmic, singing qualities. They come from musical traditions, and many students learn them first as songs. This is only a small sample of poems that could be called ballads. Those who have heard *Casey at the Bat* will enjoy J. Patrick Lewis' parody, *Tulip at the Bat*.

"Ballad of John Henry." In Slier, Deborah. *Make a Joyful Sound*. Illus. by Cornelius Van Wright & Ying-Hwa Hu. Checkerboard, 1991.

"Cockles and Mussels." In Krull, Kathleen. *A Pot O' Gold*. Illus. by David McPhail, Hyperion, 2004.

Harley, Avis. "Bluebottle Fly."*Leap into Poetry*. Boyds Mills, 2001.

Jackson, Alison. *The Ballad of Valentine*. Illus. by Tricia Tusa. Dutton, 2002.

Lewis, J. Patrick. *Tulip at the Bat*. Little, 2006.

Marsalis, Wynton. "X: Bix Beiderbecke." *Jazz A B Z*. Illus. by Paul Rogers. Candlewick, 2005.

Parton, Dolly. *Coat of Many Colors*. Illus. by Judith Sutton. HarperCollins, 1994.

"El Señor Don Gato" = "The Ballad of Sir Cat." In Ada, Alma Flor & F. Isabel Campoy. *Mamá Goose*. Illus. by Maribel Suárez. Hyperion, 2004.

Service, Robert. *The Cremation of Sam McGee*. Illus. by Ted Harrison. Kids Can, 2007.

———. *The Shooting of Dan McGrew.* Illus. by Ted Harrison. Kids Can, 1992.
Thayer, Ernest Lawrence. *Casey at the Bat.* Illus. by Joe Morse. Kids Can, 2006.
———. *Casey at the Bat: A Ballad of the Republic Sung in the Year 1888.* Illus. by Patricia Polacco. Putnam, 1988.
Yolen, Jane. *The Ballad of the Pirate Queens.* Illus. by David Shannon. Harcourt, 1995.

Sonnets

Students who have struggled to write sonnets for school assignments might like Avis Harley's "A Bite-Sized Sonnet," which has fourteen lines, but only one word per line. They might enjoy reading Shakespeare's "Sonnet Number Twelve" paired with April Halprin Wayland's "My Version of Shakespeare's Sonnet Number Twelve" in *A Kick in the Head.* Marilyn Nelson has created a "heroic crown of sonnets" in *A Wreath for Emmett Till.* The book features fifteen interlinked sonnets; the last sonnet uses the first lines of all of the others.

Cotter, Joseph Seaman, Jr. "Sonnet to Negro Soldiers." In Panzer, Nora. *Celebrate America.* Smithsonian/Hyperion, 1994
Harley, Avis. "A Bite-Sized Sonnet." *Fly with Poetry.* Boyds Mills, 2000.
Hirsch, Robin. "Sonnet." *F.E.G. Ridiculous (Stupid) Poems for Intelligent Children.* Illus. by Ha. Little, 2002.
Lewis, J. Patrick. "Letter from Home . . ." & "Letter Home . . ." *The Brothers' War.* National Geographic, 2007.
Marsalis, Wynton. "V: Sarah Vaughan." *Jazz A B Z.* Illus. by Paul Rogers. Candlewick, 2005.
Nelson, Marilyn. *A Wreath for Emmett Till.* Houghton, 2005.
Shakespeare, William. "Sonnet Number Twelve." In Janeczko, Paul B. *A Kick in the Head.* Illus. by Chris Raschka. Candlewick, 2005.
Wayland, April Halprin. "My Version of Shakespeare's Sonnet Number Twelve." In Janeczko, Paul B. *A Kick in the Head.* Illus. by Chris Raschka. Candlewick, 2005.

List/Catalog Poems

At times a poet tries to describe an animal, person, or object with a list of traits in a list poem. Because many people write lists, this is a popular form of poetry. Georgia Heard's *Falling Down the Page* collects list poems by a number of contemporary poets so that students can see the artful arrangement of words that makes a list poem out of an ordinary list. Lisa Nola's *My Listography: My Amazing Life in Lists* is set up like a blank journal, but with lots of ideas for lists to keep. Students might want to use some of her ideas for lists as they try these poems.

Some poems are lists of questions or questions and answers. Nancy Van Laan's poem *When Winter Comes* and Barbara Seuling's *Winter Lullaby* both pose a series of questions about what happens to animals and plants when winter comes followed by simple answers. These can be paired with Lee Bennett Hopkins' "How?" which asks questions about where insects go in the winter.

Some poems are lists of rules. Some poems are litanies. Each line of the litany begins with the same word or phrase, often of praise, blessings, or thanks. Christopher Smart's "For I Will Consider My Cat Jeoffry" is a praise poem for his cat; each line describes a particular admirable characteristic. Margaret Wise Brown's *Goodnight Moon* is a litany as a child would write one, a blessing of all of the comforting things in the child's room.

Ciardi, John. "A Short Checklist of Things to Think about Before Being Born." *You Read to Me, I'll Read to You.* Illus. by Edward Gorey. HarperCollins, 1961.
Heard, Georgia, ed. *Falling Down the Page.* Roaring Brook, 2009.

Holder, Julie. "Sad Things," "Mad Things," "Scary Things," & "Glad Things." In Foster, John. *A Very First Poetry Book.* Oxford, 1987.
Kuskin, Karla. *Green As a Bean.* Illus. by Melissa Iwai. HarperCollins, 2007.
Little, Jean. "Today. "*Hey World! Here I Am.* Illus. by Sue Truesdell. HarperCollins, 1989. (Also in *She's All That*)
Mabry, Oisin. "Nine Ways to Step Into a Tree." In Nye, Naomi Shihab. *Is This Forever or What?* HarperCollins, 2004.
Marsalis, Wynton. "C: John Coltrane." *Jazz A B Z.* Illus. by Paul Rogers. Candlewick, 2005.
Nola, Lisa. *My Listography: My Amazing Life in Lists.* Illus. by Nathaniel Russell. Chronicle, 2008. (Prose)
Nye, Naomi Shihab. "How Long Peace Takes." *19 Varieties of Gazelle.* Greenwillow, 2002.
Pearson, Susan. "A Ferret's Morning." *Who Swallowed Harold?* Illus. by David Slonim. Cavendish, 2005.
Ryder, Joanne. "Toad's Summer To-Do List" & "Toad's Winter To-Do List." *Toad by the Road.* Illus. by Maggie Kneen. Holt, 2007.
Sandburg, Carl. "Arithmetic" & "Tentative (First Model) Definitions of Poetry." In Hopkins, Lee Bennett. *Rainbows Are Made.* Illus. by Fritz Eichenberg. Harcourt, 1982.
Singer, Marilyn. """Ears," "Fur," And "Tails." *It's Hard to Read a Map with a Beagle on Your Lap.* Illus. by Clement Oubrerie. Holt, 1993.
Smith, Charles R. "Excuses, Excuses." *Diamond Life.* Orchard, 2004.
Stevens, Wallace. "From 13 Ways of Looking at a Blackbird." In Rogasky, Barbara. *Winter Poems.* Illus. by Trina Schart Hyman. Scholastic, 1994.
Weisburd, Stefi. "Morning Chores For Feet." *Barefoot.* Illus. by Lori McElrath-Eslick. Boyds Mills, 2008.

Questions and Answers

Hopkins, Lee Bennett. "How?" *Spectacular Science.* Illus. by Virginia Halstead. S & S, 1999.
Kuskin, Karla. "Where Have You Been, Dear?" *Dogs and Dragons, Trees and Dreams.* HarperCollins, 1980.
Levy, Constance. "Questions to Ask a Butterfly." *I'm Going to Pet a Worm Today.* Illus. by Ronald Himler. Macmillan, 1991
Seuling, Barbara. *Winter Lullaby.* Illus. by Greg Newbold. Harcourt, 1998.
Van Laan, Nancy. *When Winter Comes.* Illus. by Susan Gaber. Atheneum, 2000.
Zolotow, Charlotte. *Do You Know What I'll Do?* Illus. by Javaka Steptoe. HarperCollins, 2000.

Rules

Baylor, Byrd. *Everybody Needs a Rock.* Illus. by Peter Parnall. Scribners, 1974.
Ciardi, John. "Rules." *Someone Could Win a Polar Bear.* Illus. by Edward Gorey. Boyds Mills, 2002.
Kuskin, Karla. "Rules." *Dogs and Dragons, Trees and Dreams.* HarperCollins, 1980.
Lewis, J. Patrick. "Rules for the Elephant Parade" & "A Tomcat Is." *A Hippopotamusn't.* Illus. by Victoria Chess. Dial, 1990.
Medina, Jane. "The Sign." *The Dream on Blanca's Wall = El Sueño Pegado en la Pared de Blanca.* Illus. by Robert Casilla. Boyds Mills, 2004.
Prelutsky, Jack. "My Mother Says I'm Sickening." *The New Kid on the Block.* Illus. by James Stevenson. Greenwillow, 1984.
Sidman, Joyce. "Dog Lore." *The World According to Dog.* Illus. by Doug Mindell. Houghton, 2003.
Soto, Gary. "Eating Mexican Food." *A Fire in My Hands.* Harcourt, 2006.

Litanies

Brown, Margaret Wise. *Another Important Book.* Illus. by Chris Raschka. HarperCollins, 1999.
———. *Goodnight Moon.* HarperCollins, 1947.
———. *The Important Book.* HarperCollins, 1947.

Edens, Cooper. *If You're Afraid of the Dark, Remember the Night Rainbow.* Chronicle, 2002.
———. *Add One More Star to the Night.* Chronicle, 2003.
Goble, Paul. *Song of Creation.* Eerdmans, 2004.
Jordan, June. "What Great Grief Has Made the Empress Mute?" In Nye, Naomi Shihab, *What Have You Lost?* HarperCollins, 1999.
Prelutsky, Jack. "I'm Thankful." *The New Kid on the Block.* Illus. by James Stevenson. Greenwillow, 1984
Rylant, Cynthia. *Bless Us All.* S & S, 1998.
Smart, Christopher. "For I Will Consider My Cat Jeoffry" In Willard, Nancy. *Step Lightly.* Harcourt, 1998.
Walker, Alice. *There Is a Flower at the Tip of My Nose Smelling Me.* Illus. by Stefano Vitale. HarperCollins, 2006.

Acrostics

Acrostics are poems in which the first letters of each line of a poem form a word when read downward. These have been heavily used in schools as a way for children to describe themselves. Examples of acrostic poems can show them more complexity in this form. In *Fly with Poetry*, Avis Harley shows how an acrostic can have two meanings; she uses a butterfly to create an acrostic on the letter "A Poem" in "Editing the Chrysalis." She also includes a triple acrostic, a much more difficult form to try. Another of her collections contains acrostic poems of many types, and features a clever subtitle: *African Acrostics: A Word in Edgeways.*

Appelt, Kathi. "Elegies for Those We Lost Too Soon." *Poems from Homeroom.* Holt, 2002. (Seven Acrostics)
Belle, Jennifer. *Animal Stackers.* Illus. by David McPhail. Hyperion, 2005.
Harley, Avis. *African Acrostics: A Word in Edgeways.* Illus. by Deborah Noyes. Candlewick, 2009.
———. "Worldly Wise," "Getting Ready," "Final Finery," & "Wintering Over." *The Monarch's Progress.* Boyds Mills, 2008.
———. "Editing the Chrysalis" & "A Rock Crossing." *Fly with Poetry.* Boyds Mills, 2000.
Lewis, J. Patrick. "Necessary Gardens." *Please Bury Me in the Library.* Illus. by Kyle M. Stone. Harcourt, 2005.
———. "Notes from a Day in the Bush." *Vherses.* Illus. by Mark Summers. Creative, 2005.
Marsalis, Wynton. "Q: Modern Jazz Quartet." *Jazz A B Z.* Illus. by Paul Rogers. Candlewick, 2005.
Paolilli, Paul & Dan Brewer. *Silver Seeds.* Illus. by Steve Johnson & Lou Fancher. Viking, 2001.
Schnur, Steven. *Autumn: An Alphabet Acrostic.* Illus. by Leslie Evans. Clarion, 1997.
———. *Spring: An Alphabet Acrostic.* Illus. by Leslie Evans. Clarion, 1998.
———. *Summer: An Alphabet Acrostic.* Illus. by Leslie Evans. Clarion, 2001.
———. *Winter: An Alphabet Acrostic.* Illus. by Leslie Evans, Clarion, 2002.

Letters, Notes, and Postcard Poems

Sometimes poems take the form of a letter or a note. In Andrea Cheng's novel in verse, *Where the Steps Were*, the third graders write thank you notes, letters of protest, get-well cards, and other forms of correspondence as they try to save their school and fight injustice. Nikki Grimes' *Danitra Brown Leaves Town* includes the letters that best friends Zuri and Danitra write to each other when they spend the summer apart.

William Carlos Williams' "This Is Just to Say" is a short apologetic note. The poem is the opening frame for a collection of apologetic poems by a fictional class of sixth graders in Joyce Sidman's *This Is Just to Say.* The recipients of the notes write back to the students in the second half of the book. Sharon Creech includes Williams' poem, with young Jack's attempts to make sense of it, followed by his attempt to write an apology poem to his mother, in *Hate That Cat.*

Anderson, David. A. "Promises." In Steptoe, Javaka. *In Daddy's Arms I Am Tall*. Lee & Low, 1997. (Also in *Bill Martin Jr.s' Big Book of Poetry*)

Berry, James. "Postcard Poem: Solo." *A Nest Full of Stars*. Illus. by Ashley Bryan. Greenwillow, 2004.

Cheng, Andrea. *Where the Steps Were*. Boyds Mills, 2008. (Novel in Verse)

Creech, Sharon. "March 6." *Hate That Cat*. HarperCollins, 2008. (Novel in Verse)

Dakos, Kalli. "A Good-bye Note to Mrs. Roys." *Put Your Eyes up Here*. Illus. by G. Brian Karas. S & S, 2003.

———. "Love Note." *Mrs. Cole on an Onion Roll*. Illus. by JoAnn Adinolfi. S & S, 1995.

———. "Dear Brothers and Sisters." *Don't Read This Book, Whatever You Do!* Illus. by G. Brian Karas. S & S, 1993.

Dickinson, Emily. "Bee, I'm Expecting You!" In Janeczko, Paul B. *Hey You!* Illus. by Robert Rayevsky. HarperCollins, 2007. (Also in *Poetry Speaks to Children*)

———. *My Letter to the World*. Illus. by Isabelle Arsenault. Kids Can, 2008.

Graham, Joan Bransfield. "A Soldier's Letter to a Newborn Daughter." In Hopkins, Lee Bennett. *America at War*. Illus. by Stephen Alcorn. McElderry, 2008.

Grandits, John. "The Thank-You Letter." *Technically, It's Not My Fault*. Clarion, 2004.

Grimes, Nikki. "Dear Author" & "Dear Teacher." *Thanks a Million*. Illus. by Cozbi A. Cabrera. HarperCollins, 2006.

———. *Danitra Brown Leaves Town*. Illus. by Floyd Cooper. HarperCollins, 2002.

Lewis, J. Patrick. "Letter from Home . . ." & "Letter Home, July, 1864." *The Brothers' War*. National Geographic, 2007.

———. "Postcard Poem." *The Bookworm's Feast*. Illus. by John O'Brien. Dial, 1999.

Maddox, Marjorie. "Letter Poem to a Mailbox." In Janeczko, Paul B. *Hey You!* Illus. by Robert Rayevsky. HarperCollins, 2007

Moore, Lilian. "Letter to a Friend." In Janeczko, Paul B. *Poetry from A to Z*. Illus. by Cathy Boback. S & S, 1994.

Noda, Takayo. *Dear World*. Dial, 2003.

Prelutsky, Jack. "A Letter from Camp." *My Dog May Be a Genius*. Illus. by James Stevenson. HarperCollins, 2008.

———. "Awful Ogre Pens a Letter." *Awful Ogre's Awful Day*. Illus. by Paul O. Zelinsky. Greenwillow, 2001.

Rex, Adam. "An Open Letter from Wolfman's Best Friend." *Frankenstein Makes a Sandwich*. Harcourt, 2006.

Schertle, Alice. "Secretary Bird." *Advice for a Frog*. Illus. by Norman Green. Lothrop, 1995.

Shehadeh, Mohammed. "From 'Letters to Childhood.' " In Nye, Naomi Shihab. *The Space Between Our Footsteps*. S & S, 1998. (Also in *The Flag of Childhood*)

Sidman, Joyce. *This Is Just to Say*. Illus. by Pamela Zagarenski. Houghton. 2007.

———. "Letter to the Sun" & "Letter to the Rain." *Butterfly Eyes*. Illus. by Beth Krommes. Houghton, 2006.

Viorst, Judith. "Thank-You Note." *If I Were in Charge of the World*. Illus. by Lynne Cherry. Macmillan, 1981.

Weatherford, Carole Boston. *Dear Mr. Rosenwald*. Illus. by R. Gregory Christie. Scholastic, 2006.

Williams, William Carlos. "This Is Just to Say." In Sidman, Joyce. *This Is Just to Say*. Illus. by Pamela Zagarenski. Houghton, 2007. (Also in *Hate That Cat* and *Reflections on a Gift of Watermelon Pickle*)

Yolen, Jane. "Letter to the Moon." In Hopkins, Lee Bennett. *Blast Off!* Illus. by Melissa Sweet. HarperCollins, 1995.

Valentines

Valentines Day, which began in friendship and love, is too often an occasion for hurt feelings. Robert Sabuda's *St. Valentine*, a retelling of the legend, highlights the friendship between Valentine and a young blind girl, and the letter he sends her from prison. In honor of Valentine, teachers and students could think about sending a note or letter of friendship to someone who might appreciate it. Cynthia Rylant's *If You'll Be My Valentine* shows Valentines being given to pets, family, friends, and others, encouraging good wishes rather than romantic love. The illustrations in Martine Kindermans'

You and Me show a tender relationship between a mother and child, but the poetic lines, when read without showing the illustrations are also about friendship.

Dakos, Kalli. "Love Note." *Mrs. Cole on an Onion Roll.* Illus. by JoAnn Adinolfi. S & S, 1995.
Hall, Donald. "Valentine." In Paschen, Elise. *Poetry Speaks to Children.* Sourcebooks, 2005. (With CD) (Also in *Here Is My Heart*)
Hopkins, Lee Bennett. "Valentine Feelings." *Good Rhymes, Good Times.* Illus. by Frané Lessac. HarperCollins, 1995.
———, sel. *Valentine Hearts.* Illus. by JoAnn Adinolfi. HarperCollins, 2005.
Jackson, Alison. *The Ballad of Valentine.* Illus. by Tricia Tusa. Dutton, 2002.
Kindermans, Martine. *You and Me.* Eng. trans. by Sasha Quinton. Philomel, 2006.
Noda, Takayo. "Dear Valentines." *Dear World.* Dial, 2003.
Prelutsky, Jack. *It's Valentine's Day.* Illus. by Yossi Abolafia. Mulberry, 1996.
Rylant, Cynthia. *If You'll Be My Valentine.* Illus. by Fumi Kosaka. HarperCollins, 2005.
Sabuda, Robert. *St. Valentine.* S & S, 1999. (Prose)
Smith, William Jay, comp. *Here Is My Heart.* Illus. by Jane Dyer. Little, 1999.
Zolotow, Charlotte. "Valentine's Day." *Snippets.* Illus. by Melissa Sweet. HarperCollins, 1992.

Persona Poems (Mask Poems)

Persona poems, in which the poet takes on the character of another person, an animal or object, are typically written in free verse. They are a good way to think about another point of view. A number of novels in verse consist of persona poems as characters speak directly to the reader in the first person. Rather than address the reader as a character, Joanne Ryder's poems ask the reader to imagine what her day would be like if she were a particular animal.

Barker, George. "Snake." In Prelutsky, Jack. *The Beauty of the Beast.* Illus. by Meilo So. Knopf, 1997.
Janeczko, Paul B. *Dirty Laundry Pile: Poems in Different Voices.* Illus. by Melissa Sweet. HarperCollins, 2001.
Kirk, Daniel. *Cat Power!* Hyperion, 2007. (With CD)
———. *Dogs Rule!* Hyperion, 2003. (With CD)
Kuskin, Karla. "The Night Is Black and So Am I," "My Home Is a White Dome Under Me," & "If You Stood with Your Feet in the Earth." *Moon, Have You Met My Mother?* Illus. by Sergio Ruzzier. HarperCollins, 2003. (And many others)
Levy, Constance. "The Collector." *I'm Going to Pet a Worm Today.* Illus. by Ronald Himler. McElderry, 1991.
Ryder, Joanne. *Earthdance.* Illus. by Norman Gorbaty. Holt, 1996.
———. *Jaguar in the Rain Forest.* Illus. by Michael Rothman. Morrow, 1996.
———. *Tyrannosaurus Time.* Illus. by Michael Rothman. Morrow, 1999.
———. *Where Butterflies Grow.* Illus. by Lynne Cherry. Lodestar, 1989.
———. *Winter Whale.* Illus. by Michael Rothman. Morrow, 1991.
Spires, Elizabeth. *I Heard God Talking to Me.* Farrar, 2009.

Notebook, Diary, and Journal Poems

Sometimes a poet will provide an entry from a notebook or journal in poem form to provide just a glimpse of someone's thinking. Sometimes, as in a number of novels in verse, an entire collection of poems appears as journal entries. Kristine O'Connell George's *Hummingbird Nest* is a series of poems written with the careful observations of a scientific journal.

Fleischman, Paul. "Chrysalis Diary." *Joyful Noise*. Illus. by Eric Beddows. HarperCollins, 1988.

Fletcher, Ralph. "Writer's Notebook." *A Writing Kind of Day*. Illus. by April Ward. Boyds Mills, 2005.

Florian, Douglas. "Dog Log." *Bow Wow Meow Meow*. Harcourt, 2003.

George, Kristine O'Connell. *Hummingbird Nest*. Illus. by Barry Moser. Harcourt, 2004.

Lewis, J. Patrick. "Notes from a Day in the Bush." *Vherses*. Illus. by Mark Summers. Creative Ed, 2005. (As Jane Goodall)

Sierra, Judy. "Diary of a Very Short Winter Day." *Antarctic Antics*. Illus. by José Aruego & Ariane Dewey. Harcourt, 1998.

Recipe Poems

Buck, Nola. "Seashore Recipe." In Shaw, Alison. *Until I Saw the Sea*. Holt, 1995.

Ciardi, John. "Some Cook!" In Larrick, Nancy. *Piping Down the Valleys Wild*. Dell, 1982.

Duggar, John Paul. "Licorice." In Booth, David. *'Til All the Stars Have Fallen*. Illus. by Kady MacDonald Denton. Viking, 1989.

Farmiloe, Dorothy. "Recipe for Thanksgiving Day Soup." In Booth, David. *'Til All the Stars Have Fallen*. Illus. by Kady MacDonald Denton. Viking, 1990.

Fletcher, Ralph. "Poetry Recipes." *A Writing Kind of Day*. Illus. by April Ward. Boyds Mills, 2005.

Frasier, Debra. *A Birthday Cake Is No Ordinary Cake*. Harcourt, 2006.

Katz, Bobbie. "Recipe." In Cole, William. *Poem Stew*. Illus. by Karen Ann Weinhaus. Lippincott, 1981.

Peters, Lisa Westberg. "Recipe for Granite." *Earthshake*. Illus. by Cathie Felstead. HarperCollins, 2003.

Weinstock, Robert. "Recipe." *Food Hates You, Too*. Hyperion, 2009.

Wong, Janet. "Grandmother's Almond Cookies." *A Suitcase of Seaweed*. Booksurge, 2008.

Worth, Valerie. "Pie." *All the Small Poems and Fourteen More*. Illus. by Natalie Babbitt. Farrar, 1994.

Yolen, Jane. "Recipe for Green." *Here's a Little Poem*. Illus. by Polly Dunbar. Candlewick, 2007.

Prayers

Alarcón, Francisco X. "Prayer of the Fallen Tree." *Laughing Tomatoes = Jitomates Risueños*. Illus. by Maya Christina Gonzalez. Children's, 1997.

Bernos de Gasztold, Carmen. "Prayer of the Cat." In Janeczko, Paul B. *Dirty Laundry Pile*. Illus. by Melissa Sweet. HarperCollins, 2001.

Field, Rachel. *Prayer for a Child*. Illus. by Elizabeth Orton Jones. Macmillan, 1984.

Gaiman, Neil. *Blueberry Girl*. Illus. by Charles Vess. HarperCollins, 2009.

Harjo, Joy. "Eagle Poem." In Paschen, Elise. *Poetry Speaks to Children*. Sourcebooks, 2005. (With CD)

Hubbell, Patricia. "Prayer for Reptiles." In Larrick, Nancy. *Piping Down the Valleys Wild*. Illus. by Ellen Raskin. Dell, 1968.

"Iroquois Prayer. "In Hopkins, Lee Bennett. *Days to Celebrate*. Illus. by Stephen Alcorn. HarperCollins, 2005.

Kennedy, X. J. "Little Elegy (For a Child Who Skipped Rope.)" In Janeczko, Paul B. *A Kick in the Head*. Illus. by Chris Raschka. Candlewick, 2005.

Lach, William. *I Imagine Angels*. Metropolitan Museum of Art/ Atheneum, 2000.

Lindbergh, Reeve. *The Circle of Days: From 'Canticle of the Sun' by St. Francis of Assisi*. Illus. by Cathie Felstead. Candlewick, 1998.

Livingston, Myra Cohn. "Prayer for Earth." In Prelutsky, Jack. *The 20th Century Poetry Treasury*. Illus. by Meilo So. Knopf, 1999.

Milne, A. A. "Vespers." *When We Were Very Young*. Illus. by E. H. Shepard. Dutton, 1924.

Myers, Walter Dean. "Prayer." *Brown Angels*. HarperCollins, 1993.

Nye, Naomi Shihab. "Prayer In My Boot." *19 Varieties of Gazelle*. Greenwillow, 2002.

Pederson, Cynthia. "Prayer of the Snowflake." In Janeczko, Paul B. *Dirty Laundry Pile*. Illus. by Melissa Sweet. HarperCollins, 2001.

"Prayer to the Corn in the Field." In Nye, Naomi Shihab. *The Tree Is Older Than You Are*. S & S, 1995.

Swamp, Chief Jake. *Giving Thanks*. Illus. by Erwin Printup Jr. Lee & Low, 1995.

Viorst, Judith. "Prayer of the Good Green Boy." *Sad Underwear*. Illus. by Richard Hull. Atheneum, 1995.

Other Forms of Poetry

Janeczko, Paul B. & J. Patrick Lewis. *Wing Nuts*. Illus. by Tricia Tusa. Little, 2006. (Senryu)

Lewis, J. Patrick. *Once Upon a Tomb: Gravely Humorous Verses*. Illus. by Simon Bartram. Candlewick, 2006. (Epitaphs)

Lewis, J. Patrick & Paul B. Janeczko. *Birds on a Wire*. Illus. by Gary Lippincott. Boyds Mills, 2008. (Renga)

Liu, Siyu & Orel Protopopescu. *A Thousand Peaks: Poems from China*. Pacific View, 2002. (Shi)

Mora, Pat. *Join Hands! The Ways We Celebrate Life*. Illus. by George Ancona. Charlesbridge, 2008. (Pantoum)

Neitzel, Shirley. *The Jacket I Wear in the Snow*. Illus. by Nancy Winslow Parker. Greenwillow, 1989. (Rebus) (And others by this author and illustrator)

Park, Linda Sue. *Tap Dancing on the Roof (Poems)*. Illus. by Istvan Banyai. Clarion, 2007. (Sijo)

Standard Six: Students apply knowledge of language structure, language conventions (e.g., spelling and punctuation, media techniques, figurative language, and genre) to create, critique, and discuss print and non-print texts.
See also Chapter One: Poetry and the National Standards (Writing Poetry)
See also Chapter Six: Dance Standard One (Rhythm)
See also Standard Four (Language Conventions)

STANDARD SIX: POETIC CONVENTIONS—IMAGERY AND FIGURATIVE LANGUAGE

Both poets and writers of prose use imagery, figurative language, and sound techniques when they write. Learning about these techniques simply by memorizing definitions and seeing examples is not nearly as powerful for young writers as sharing poetry in such a way that students can themselves begin to see how poets are using these tools to create the effect they want from a poem.

Imagery

Sensory exploration and description of the world, or imagery, is a tool the poet uses to help the reader or listener see, hear, taste, feel, or smell the world in a new way. A poet may use images to appeal to all of the senses as Heidi Mordhorst does in "Honeysuckle Hunting." Byrd Baylor's *Everybody Needs a Rock* asks readers to choose a rock based on satisfying all of their senses. Mary Ann Hoberman explores things that feel, smell, sound, taste, and look cozy in *The Cozy Book*. Joyce Sidman's *Red Sings from Treetops: A Year in Colors* uses imagery in many ways as does Christine San José and Bill Johnson's collection of 60 poems to appeal to the senses. Paul Janeczko opens his collection, *A Foot in the Mouth*, with Tracie Vaughan Zimmer's "The Poems I Like Best," a poem that uses all five senses to explain what poems do.

Poets may focus on one or two senses to capture the best image of a person, an object, or something from nature. The poems included here provide examples of strong appeal to one or two senses. These images are not always positive. Poems about biting into a worm in one's peach, the smell of dirty laundry, and the slimy texture of mold show that imagery is powerful whether the appeal is pleasant or not.

Baylor, Byrd. *Everybody Needs a Rock*. Illus. by Peter Parnall. Macmillan, 1974. (All)

———. *I'm In Charge of Celebrations*. Illus. by Peter Parnall. Scribners, 1986. (All)

———. *The Other Way to Listen*. Illus. by Peter Parnall. Macmillan, 1978. (Hearing)

Black, Marcy Barack. "Dirty Laundry Pile." In Janeczko, Paul B. *Dirty Laundry Pile*. Illus. by Melissa Sweet. HarperCollins, 2001. (Smell)

Cisneros, Sandra. "Good Hot Dogs." In Paschen, Elise. *Poetry Speaks to Children*. Sourcebooks, 2005. (With CD) (Also in *Knock at a Star*) (Taste)

Cole, William. "It's Such a Shock . . ." *Poem Stew*. Illus. by Karen Ann Weinhaus. Lippincott, 1981. (Taste and Texture)

Collins, Pat Lowery. *I Am An Artist*. Illus. by Robin Brickman. Millbrook, 1992. (All)

Edwards, Richard. "To a Maggot in an Apple." In Janeczko, Paul. *Hey You!* Illus. by Robert Rayevsky. Harper Collins, 2007. (Taste and Texture)

Fox, Paula. *Traces*. Illus. by Karla Kuskin. Boyds Mills, 2008. (All)

Harley, Avis. "Feet Treat." *The Monarch's Progress*. Boyds Mills, 2008. (Texture)

Hines, Anna Grossnickle. "The Nose Knows." *Pieces*. HarperCollins, 2001. (Smell)

Hoberman, Mary Ann. *The Cozy Book*. Illus. by Tony Chen. Viking, 1982. (All)

Merriam, Eve. "Silence." *The Singing Green*. Illus. by Kathleen Collins Howell. Morrow, 1992. (Hearing)

Moffett, James. "To Look at Anything." In Dunning, Steven, et al. *Reflections on a Gift of Watermelon Pickle*. HarperCollins, 1967. (In many collections) (Sight)

Moore, Lilian. "Snowy Morning." *Mural on Second Avenue*. Illus. by Roma Karas. Candlewick, 2005. (Hearing)

Mordhorst, Heidi. "Honeysuckle Hunting." *Squeeze*. Illus. by Jesse Torrey. Boyds Mills, 2005. (All)

O'Neill, Mary. *The Sound of Day, the Sound of Night*. Illus. by Cynthia Jabar. Farrar, 2003. (Hearing)

Prelutsky, Jack. "Mold, Mold." *Something Big Has Been Here*. Illus. by James Stevenson. Greenwillow, 1990. (Texture)

———. "Winter's Come." *It's Snowing! It's Snowing!* Illus. by Yossi Abolafia. HarperCollins, 2006. (Hearing)

Rauter, Rose. "Peach." In Kennedy, X. J. & Dorothy M. Kennedy. *Knock at a Star*. Illus. by Karen Lee Baker. Little, 1982. (Taste and Smell)

Ryan, Pam Muñoz. *Hello Ocean*. Illus. by Mark Astrella. Charlesbridge, 2001. (All)

Rylant, Cynthia. *Night in the Country*. Illus. by Mary Szilagyi. Macmillan, 1986. (Hearing)

San José, Christine & Bill Johnson, sels. *Every Second Something Happens: Poems for the Mind and Senses*. Illus. by Melanie Hall. Boyds Mills, 2009.

Sandburg, Carl. "From 'Blossom Thoughts.' " In Rogasky, Barbara. *Winter Poems*. Illus. by Trina Schart Hyman. Scholastic, 1994. (Smell)

Shapiro, Karen Jo. "The Smells." *I Must Go Down to the Beach Again*. Illus. by Judy Love. Charlesbridge, 2007. (Smell)

Sidman, Joyce. "Always Take a Dog." *The World According to Dog*. Illus. by Doug Mindell. Houghton, 2003. (Smell)

———. *Red Sings from Treetops: A Year in Colors*. Illus. by Pamela Zagarenski. Houghton, 2009. (All)

Stafford, William. *The Animal That Drank Up Sound*. Illus. by Debra Frasier. Harcourt, 1992 (Hearing)

Weisburd, Stefi. *Barefoot*. Illus. by Lori McElrath-Eslick. Boyds Mills, 2008. (Texture)

Wolff, Ashley. *Only the Cat Saw*. Putnam, 1985. (Sight)

Worth, Valerie. "Magnifying Glass" & "Barefoot." *All the Small Poems and Fourteen More*. Illus. by Natalie Babbitt. Farrar, 1994. (Sight)

Zimmer, Tracie Vaughan. "The Poems I Like Best." In Janeczko, Paul B. *A Foot in the Mouth*. Illus. by Chris Raschka. Candlewick, 2009. (All)

Zolotow, Charlotte, *If You Listen*. Illus. by Marc Simont. HarperCollins, 1980. (Hearing)

Figurative Language

Figurative language, the use of comparisons to describe one thing in terms of another, is not only essential to poetry but to all language in which we strive to communicate effectively. In our daily talk we may rely on heavily used figures of speech or clichés. Loreen Leedy and Pat Street have created *There's a Frog in My Throat! 440 Animal Sayings A Little Bird Told Me*, a book of common figures of speech involving animals. A picture book, *Monkey Business*, elaborately illustrates a few figures of speech. Tedd Arnold's silly *Parts* series plays with figures of speech about the human body. Poets play with figures of speech as well. Alice Schertle creates poems from several figures of speech about cows in *How Now Brown Cow?*

Arnold, Tedd. *Even More Parts*. Penguin, 2004.

———. *More Parts*. Penguin, 2001.

———. *Parts*. Penguin, 1997.

Edwards, Wallace. *Monkey Business*. Kids Can, 2004.

Fisher, Aileen. "Timid as a Mouse?" *The House of a Mouse*. Illus. by Joan Sandin. HarperCollins, 1988.

Florian, Douglas. "The Clam." *In the Swim*. Harcourt, 1997. ("Happy as a Clam")

———. "Swallowed Pride," "You Don't Say," & "Lost Head." *Bing Bang Boing*. Harcourt, 1994.

———."Winter Lives." *Winter Eyes*. Greenwillow, 1999. ("Dead of Winter")

Franco, Betsy. "Anatomy Class." *Messing Around on the Monkey Bars*. Illus. by Jessie Hartland. Candlewick, 2009.

Lawson, JonArno. "Clam." *Black Stars in a White Night Sky*. Illus. by Sherwin Tjia. Boyds Mills, 2006. ("Happy as a Clam")

Leedy, Loreen & Pat Street. *There's a Frog in My Throat*. Holiday, 2003.

McCord, David. "Figures of Speech." *One at a Time*. Illus. by Henry B. Kane. Little, 1986.

Moses, Will. *Raining Cats and Dogs: A Collection of Irresistible Idioms and Illustrations To Tickle the Funny Bones of Young People*. Philomel, 2008

Schertle, Alice. *How Now Brown Cow?* Illus. by Amanda Schaffer. Harcourt, 1994.

Terban, Marvin. *In a Pickle: And Other Funny Idioms*. Illus. by Giulio Maestro. Houghton, 2007.

———. *Mad as a Wet Hen! And Other Funny Idioms*. Illus. by Giulio Maestro. Houghton, 2007.

Similes

Similes make comparisons using "like" or "as," in both poetry and prose. In a book discussion group, some third graders noticed how often Eleanor Coerr used comparisons in *Sadako and the Thousand Paper Cranes*. They decided to make a list of those they found in one chapter. The teacher had them try to write one or two comparisons themselves, using things they knew about, and they shared the best ones with one another. After they had used this figurative language for a while and gotten comfortable with looking for it and trying it themselves, she told them this device had a name: Similes. Several weeks later, a child commented that she was finding lots of "similars" in the book she was currently reading. "Similars" describes quite well what these phrases do.

Audrey Wood's picture book *Quick as a Cricket* uses similes as a young narrator finds ways to describe himself by comparing himself to animals. Some of these are clichés, while others are original. The son of one of my students liked Wood's "cold as a toad" to describe how he felt on chilly Wyoming days.

Coerr, Eleanor. *Sadako and the Thousand Paper Cranes*. Putnam, 1977. (Prose)

Leedy, Loreen. *Crazy Like a Fox: A Simile Story*. Holiday, 2008.

Wood, Audrey. *Quick as a Cricket*. Illus. by Don Wood. Child's Play, 1982

Metaphors

See Also Chapter Four: Mathematics Standard Five (Riddles)

Metaphors are comparisons in which one thing is described as if it is another. Two picture books by Dianna Aston, *An Egg Is Quiet* and *A Seed Is Sleepy*, use metaphors to explain the science of these seemingly simple things. John Updike uses a list of metaphors to describe the ocean in "Winter Ocean." Metaphors can be like small riddles. Valerie Worth's "Safety Pin," for example, in which she describes a closed safety pin as if it were a fish, can be shared without its title, as a riddle.

Aston, Dianna. *An Egg Is Quiet*. Illus. by Sylvia Long. Chronicle, 2006.
———. *A Seed Is Sleepy*. Illus. by Sylvia Long. Chronicle, 2007.
Fletcher, Ralph. "Metaphor," *A Writing Kind of Day*. Illus. by April Ward. Boyds Mills, 2005.
Updike, John. "Winter Ocean." In Nichols, Judith. *The Sun in Me*. Illus. by Beth Krommes. Barefoot, 2003.
Worth, Valerie. "Safety Pin." *All the Small Poems and Fourteen More*. Illus. by Natalie Babbitt. Farrar, 1987.

STANDARD SIX: POETIC CONVENTIONS—SOUND

Poets consider the element of sound in many ways as they write their poems. The many types of rhyme are the best-known sound devices. Students also respond to alliteration and onomatopoeia.

Rhyme

When children first write poetry, they often create nonsense poems full of rhyme. As teachers and librarians share rhymed poems with children, it is important to help them see that there is sense as well as sound in a good poem. David McCord suggests a simple rhyming form that children can try on their own in "Jamboree." Each line of the poem begins with "A rhyme for . . .." with the name of a food and then supplies a rhyme (e.g., "A rhyme for ham? *Jam*.") Children could try this type of rhyme with any topic you might be studying, from frogs to names of friends. The only rule is that the rhyme must make sense.

Children who like to play with rhyme will enjoy Nancy Shaw's *Sheep in a Jeep* and its sequels, and her more recent *Raccoon Tune*. In these picture books, Shaw uses end rhyme, internal rhyme and onomatopoeia to create humorous stories. Beatrice Schenk de Regniers and Betsy Lewin have both written picture book poems about cats that feature internal rhyme. John Ciardi's "I Met a Man That Was Playing Games" and Karla Kuskin's "Alexander Soames: His Poems" are about people who like to rhyme.

De Regniers, Beatrice Schenk. *So Many Cats!* Illus. by Ellen Weiss. Clarion, 1988.
Kuskin, Karla. "Alexander Soames: His Poems." *Dogs and Dragons, Trees and Dreams*. HarperCollins, 1980.
Lewin, Betsy. *Cat Count*. Holt, 2003.
McCord, David. "Jamboree." *One at a Time*. Illus. by Henry B. Kane. Little, 1986.
Shaw, Nancy. *Raccoon Tune*. Illus. by Howard Fine. Holt, 2003.
———. *Sheep in a Jeep*. Illus. by Margot Apple. Houghton, 1986. (Also *Sheep in a Shop*, *Sheep Out to Eat*, *Sheep on a Ship*, *Sheep Take a Hike*, *Sheep Trick or Treat*, & *Sheep Blast Off*)

Alphabet Books and Alliteration

Alphabet books often use rhyme and alliteration, the repetition of initial letter sounds in a series of words. Typically, an alphabet book links a letter with a single word that begins with that letter, a simple form of alliteration. Some alphabet books include blends of letter sounds. In Susan Middleton Elya's *N Is For Navidad*, she includes four letter sounds that aren't found in English. A number of alphabet books are simple introductions to the vocabulary of a particular subject, such as Sherry Shahan's *A Jazzy Alphabet.*

Some alphabet books contain several alliterative words with each letter, as Graeme Base does in *Animalia* and Margriet Ruurs does in *A Mountain Alphabet.* In both of these books, additional items with that initial sound can be found in the illustrations. Some poets create collections of poems including a poem for every letter of the alphabet. Some poets create Alphabet or Abecedarian poems; single poems with each line beginning with a letter, in alphabetical order.

The jump-rope game *A My Name Is Alice* is a good way to try out alliteration. Students have to think of personal names, names of animals, occupations, and places that begin with the same initial letter in order to play the game. Lesa Cline-Ransom's *Quilt Alphabet* asks younger students to predict the noun that begins with each letter by looking at the illustration. Chris Van Allsburg's *The Z Was Zapped* shows verbs that readers must try to predict.

It's important to help students savor alliteration in poems and prose. Teachers and librarians can highlight poems that use two or three alliterative words in a series, sometimes with other word sounds among them, to create a unique sound. Karla Kuskin's "Thistles" uses the tongue-twisting quality of "th" words with other sounds to capture the prickly qualities of these plants. Judi Barrett's *A Snake Is Totally Tail* describes the distinct qualities of a number of animals with short two-word alliterative phrases. Students can try making these short alliterative lists of characteristics for anything they might be studying.

Alphabets

Aylesworth, Jim. *The Folks in the Valley: A Pennsylvania Dutch ABC.* Illus. by Stefano Vitale. HarperCollins, 1992.

———. *Little Bitty Mousie.* Illus. by Michael Hague. Walker, 2007.

———. *Old Black Fly.* Illus. by Stephen Gammell. Holt, 1992.

Base, Graeme. *Animalia.* Abrams, 1987. (Alliteration)

Bayer, Jane. *A My Name Is Alice.* Illus. by Steven Kellogg. Dial, 1984. (Alliteration)

Bunting, Eve. *Girls A to Z.* Illus. by Suzanne Bloom. Boyds Mills, 2002.

Cline-Ransome, Lesa. *Quilt Alphabet.* Illus. by James E. Ransome. Holiday, 2001.

Dragonwagon, Crescent. *Alligator Arrived with Apples.* Illus. by José Aruego & Ariane Dewey. Macmillan, 1987. (Alliteration)

Eichenberg, Fritz. *Ape in a Cape.* Harcourt, 1952.

Elya, Susan Middleton. *F Is for Fiesta.* Illus. by G. Brian Karas. Putnam, 2006.

Elya, Susan Middleton & Merry Banks. *N Is for Navidad.* Illus. by Joe Cepeda. Chronicle, 2007.

Gag, Wanda. *The ABC Bunny.* Penguin, 1978,

Gaiman, Neil. *The Dangerous Alphabet.* Illus. by Gris Grimly. HarperCollins, 2008.

Gardner, Beau. *Have You Ever Seen?* Putnam, 1986, (Alliteration)

Gerstein, Mordicai. *The Absolutely Awful Alphabet.* Harcourt, 1999. (Alliteration)

Grimes, Nikki. *C Is For City.* Illus. by Pat Cummings. Boyds Mills, 1995.

Hague, Kathleen. *Alphabears: An ABC Book.* Illus. by Michael Hague. Holt, 1984.

Hobbie, Holly. *Toot and Puddle's ABC.* Little, 2000.

Lobel, Anita. *Alison's Zinnia.* Greenwillow, 1990. (Alliteration)

———. *Animal Antics: A to Z.* Greenwillow, 2005. (Alliteration)

———. *Away From Home*. Greenwillow, 1994. (Alliteration)
Martin, Bill, Jr. & John Archambault. *Chicka Chicka Boom Boom*. Illus. by Lois Ehlert. S & S, 1989.
Merriam, Eve. *Goodnight to Annie*. Illus. by Carol Schwartz. Hyperion, 1992. (Alliteration)
———. *Where Is Everybody? An Animal Alphabet*. Illus. by Diane de Groat. S & S, 1989. (Alliteration)
Ruurs, Margriet. *A Mountain Alphabet*. Illus. by Andrew Kiss. Tundra, 1996. (Alliteration)
Schnur, Steven. *Autumn: An Alphabet Acrostic*. Illus. by Leslie Evans. Clarion, 1997.
———. *Spring: An Alphabet Acrostic*. Illus. by Leslie Evans. Clarion, 1998.
———. *Summer: An Alphabet Acrostic*. Illus. by Leslie Evans. Clarion, 2001.
———. *Winter: An Alphabet Acrostic*. Illus. by Leslie Evans. Clarion, 2002.
Sendak, Maurice. *Alligators All Around*. HarperCollins, 1962. (Alliteration)
Seuss, Dr. *Dr. Seuss's ABC*. Random, 1963. (Alliteration)
Shahan, Sherry. *The Jazzy Alphabet*. Illus. by Mary Thelan. Philomel, 2002.
Thornhill, Jan. *The Wildlife ABC and 123*. S & S, 1988.
Van Allsburg, Chris. *The Z Was Zapped*. Houghton, 1987.
Viorst, Judith. *The Alphabet From Z to A: With Much Confusion on the Way*. Illus. by Richard Hull. Atheneum, 1994.
Yolen, Jane. *All in the Woodland Early*. Illus. by Jane Breskin Zalben. Boyds Mills, 1979.
———. *Elfabet*. Illus. by Lauren Mills. Little, 1990. (Alliteration)

Alphabet Books of Poems

Ada, Alma Flor. *Gathering the Sun*. Illus. by Simon Silva. HarperCollins, 1997.
Ashman, Linda. *M Is for Mischief*. Illus. by Nancy Carpenter. Dutton, 2008.
Bryan, Ashley. *Ashley Bryan's ABC of African American Poetry*. S & S, 1997.
Harley, Avis. *Fly with Poetry*. Boyds Mills, 2000.
Hopkins, Lee Bennett. *Alphathoughts*. Illus. by Marla Baggetta. Boyds Mills, 2003.
Johnston, Tony. *P Is for Piñata*. Illus. by John Parra. Sleeping Bear, 2008.
Marsalis, Wynton. *Jazz A B Z*. Illus. by Paul Rogers. Candlewick, 2005.
Merriam, Eve. *Halloween ABC*. Macmillan, 1987.
Steig, Jeanne. *Alpha Beta Chowder*. Illus. by William Steig. HarperCollins, 1992.
Wilbur, Richard. *The Disappearing Alphabet*. Illus. by David Diaz. Harcourt, 1997.

Alphabet/Abecedarian Poems

Harley, Avis. "Forgotten Giants" & "Ants To Zorillas." *Fly with Poetry*. Boyds Mills, 2000.
Lewis, J. Patrick. "The Alphabet Gang." *The Bookworm's Feast*. Illus. by John O'Brien. Dial, 1999.
Yolen, Jane. "Alphabet." In Hopkins, Lee Bennett. *America at War*. Illus. by Stephen Alcorn. McElderry, 2008.

Tongue Twisters

Alliteration is similar to the childhood game of "tongue twisters," but not all tongue twisters are alliterative. Jon Agee's collection *Orangutan Tongs* is filled with tongue twisters of many kinds. Morris Bishop's "Song of the Pop-Bottlers" is a modern tongue twister to try out loud. John Ciardi gives directions in his poem title: "The Rover: To Be Recited Aloud and With Gestures." His poem "Widgeonry: And Why *Shouldn't* You Use Your Dictionary?" is also a tongue twister. JonArno Lawson offers two: "Try Saying This Out Loud With Any Name You Know, And Say It Quickly" and "Try to Say These Over and Over Quickly." Pamela Duncan Edwards has a great fun with alliteration in her prose picture books, and an attempt to read them leads to tangled tongues. Ann Jonas' *Watch William Walk* uses only words that begin with "W" to tell a small story. Eloise Greenfield has written a poem about trying to say tongue twisters, "Twister."

Agee, Jon. *Orangutan Tongs: Poems to Tangle Your Tongue*. Hyperion, 2009.
Barrett, Judi. *A Snake Is Totally Tail*. Illus. by L. S. Johnson. Macmillan, 1983.
Bishop, Morris. "Song of the Pop-Bottlers." In Cole, William. *Poem Stew*. Illus. by Karen Ann Weinhaus. Lippincott, 1981.
Brown, Calef. "Tongue Tester." *Soup for Breakfast*. Houghton, 2008.
Chwast, Seymour. *She Sells Sea Shells: World Class Tongue Twisters*. S & S, 2008. (Prose)
Ciardi, John. "The Rover . . ." & "Widgeonry . . ." *Someone Could Win a Polar Bear*. Illus. by Edward Gorey. Boyds Mills, 2002.
Edwards, Pamela Duncan. *Clara Caterpillar*. Illus. by Henry Cole. HarperCollins, 2001. (Prose)
———. *Four Famished Foxes and Fosdyke*. Illus. by Henry Cole. HarperCollins, 1995. (Prose)
———. *Some Smug Slug*. Illus. by Henry Cole. HarperCollins, 1996. (Prose)
———. *The Worrywarts*. Illus. by Henry Cole. HarperCollins, 1999. (Prose)
Greenfield, Eloise. "Twister." *In the Land of Words*. Illus. by Jan Spivey Gilchrist. HarperCollins, 2004.
Jonas, Ann. *Watch William Walk*. Greenwillow, 1997.
Kuskin, Karla. "Thistles." *Dogs and Dragons, Trees and Dreams*. HarperCollins, 1980.
Lawson, JonArno. "Try Saying This With Any Name You Know, and Say It Quickly." & "Try To Say These Over and Over Quickly." *Black Stars in a White Night Sky*. Illus. by Sherwin Tjia. Boyds Mills, 2006.

Onomatopoeia (Sound Effect Words)

The crashing, banging, and zipping sound effects that children create when they play may owe a dept to cartoons and action comics, but they are onomatopoeia to poets. The first sound effect words many children learn are animal sounds. *Old MacDonald Had a Farm* and *Fiddle-I-Fee* contain these sound effect words for young children. One can tell by the title that Julie Stiegemeyer's *Gobble, Gobble Crash! A Barnyard Counting Bash* is full of animal sounds. It can be paired with Susan Pearson's poem "Barnyard Talk." Ann Jonas' *Bird Talk* and Lois Ehlert's *Top Cat* both include birdcalls.

Weather elicits lots of onomatopoetic words. David A. Johnson's *Snow Sounds: An Onomatopoeic Story* recreates a snowy morning with just onomatopoetic words and snowy pictures. Lezlie Evans' picture book *Rain Song* and Cynthia Cotten's *Rain Play* capture the sounds of rainstorms. Eve Merriam and Rebecca Kai Dotlich have each replicated the sounds of a car's windshield wipers on a rainy day.

Poems about marching bands, machinery, grumpy moods, and eerie poems often use sound effects. David McCord has captured two classic sound effects—the sound of a stick moving across a fence in "The Pickety Fence," and the sound of a train moving across the tracks in "Song of the Train." Two picture books, Jeanne Willis' *Shhh!* and Catherine Falwell's *Scoot*, use onomatopoetic words to make a point about quiet.

Baer, Gene. *Thump, Thump, Rat-A-Tat-Tat*. Illus. by Lois Ehlert. HarperCollins, 1989.
Boswell, Addie. *The Rain Stomper*. Illus. by Eric Velasquez. Cavendish, 2008.
Cotten, Cynthia. *Rain Play*. Illus. by Javaka Steptoe. Holt, 2008.
Crow, Kristyn. *Bedtime at the Swamp*. Illus. by Macky Pamintuan. HarperCollins, 2008.
Dotlich, Rebecca Kai. "Windshield Wipers." In Hopkins, Lee Bennett. *Days to Celebrate*. Illus. by Stephen Alcorn. HarperCollins, 2005.
Edwards, Pamela Duncan. *Slop Goes the Soup: A Noisy Warthog Word Book*. Illus. by Henry Cole. Hyperion, 2001.
Ehlert, Lois. *Top Cat*. Harcourt, 1998.
Esbensen, Barbara Juster. *Words with Wrinkled Knees*. Illus. by John Stadler. HarperCollins, 1987.
Evans, Lezlie. *Rain Song*. Illus. by Cynthia Jabar. Houghton, 1996.
Falwell, Cathryn. *Scoot!* HarperCollins, 2008.
Fiddle-I-Fee. Illus. by Melissa Sweet. Little, 1992.

Fleming, Denise. *In the Tall, Tall Grass*. Holt, 1991.
hooks, bell. *Grump, Groan, Growl*. Illus. by Chris Raschka. Illus. by Chris Raschka. Hyperion, 2008.
Johnson, David A. *Snow Sounds: An Onomatopoeic Story*. Houghton, 2006.
Jonas, Ann. *Bird Talk*. Greenwillow, 1999.
Katz, Bobbi. "Washing Machine." In Janeczko, Paul B. *Dirty Laundry Pile*. Illus. by Melissa Sweet. Harper Collins, 2001.
Lundgren, Mary Beth. *Seven Scary Monsters*. Illus. by Howard Fine. Clarion, 2003.
Merriam, Eve. *Bam, Bam, Bam*. Illus. by Dan Yaccarino. Holt, 1995.
———. "Mean Song." *The Singing Green*. Illus. by Kathleen Collins Howell. Morrow, 1992.
———. "Windshield Wipers." In Cullinan, Bernice E. *A Jar of Tiny Stars*. NCTE/Boyds Mills, 1996.
Old MacDonald Had a Farm. Illus. by Carol Jones. Houghton, 1989.
O'Neill, Mary. *The Sound of Day, the Sound of Night*. Illus. by Cynthia Jabar. Farrar, 2003.
Pearson, Susan. "Barnyard Talk." *Squeal and Squawk: Barnyard Talk*. Illus. by David Slonim. Cavendish, 2004.
Peters, Polly. *The Ding-Dong Bag*. Illus. by Jess Stockham. Child's Play, 2006.
Stiegemeyer, Julie. *Gobble Gobble Crash! A Barnyard Counting Bash*. Dutton, 2008.
Swados, Elizabeth. *Hey You! C'Mere: A Poetry Slam*. Illus. by Joe Cepeta. Scholastic, 2002.
Willis, Jeanne. *Shhh!* Illus. by Tony Ross. Hyperion, 2004.

Standard Seven: Students conduct research on issues and interests by generating ideas and questions, and by posing problems. They gather, evaluate and synthesize data from a variety of sources (e.g., prints and non-print texts, artifacts, people) to communicate their discoveries in ways that suit their purpose and audience.

Standard Eight: Students use a variety of technological and information resources (e.g., libraries, databases, computer networks, video) to gather and synthesize information and to create and communicate knowledge.

These two standards cross all curriculum areas. Any of the poems indexed in this collection can be paired with material found through research. When students present, write, and find poems to include with assignments they can communicate further insights about any subject under study.

Standard Nine: Students develop an understanding of and respect for diversity in language use, patterns, and dialects across cultures, ethnic groups, geographic regions, and social roles.
See also Chapter Five: Social Studies Theme One (Cultures)
See also Standard Ten (Poetry in Languages Other than English)

STANDARD NINE: LANGUAGE DIVERSITY

Human language is alive. Language diversity—how people speak and write our language—depends upon where people live. Within the United States, people use differing vocabulary, dialects, and pronunciation. Students quickly learn that the English spoken in Shakespeare's England or in Mark Twain's nineteenth-century America sound radically different from English spoken today. Poets try to capture these nuances of language in their poems. Bobbi Katz , for example, uses hints of differing languages and dialects for each character in *Trailblazers: Poems of Exploration*. People may speak with the accents or vocabularies of their country of origin. Janet S. Wong celebrates her grandfather's Chinese inflections in "My Bird Day" and "Poetry." Ilan Stavans' *¡Wachale!* celebrates Spanglish, a melding of English and Spanish. Langston Hughes and other poets relish the beauty of African American dialects and showcase them in their poetry. The examples here show some of the variations of English.

Agard, John & Grace Nichols, eds. *Under the Moon and Over the Sea*. Illus. by Cathie Felstead, et al. Candlewick, 2002. (Caribbean)

Cumbayah. Illus. by Floyd Cooper. Morrow, 1998. (Gullah)

Downing, Johnette, adapt. *My Aunt Came Back from Louisiane*. Pelican, 2008. (Cajun)

Forman, Ruth. *Young Cornrows Callin Out the Moon*. Illus. by Cbabi Bayoc. Children's, 2007. (African American)

Giovanni, Nikki, ed. *Hip Hop Speaks to Children*. Sourcebooks, 2008. (With CD) (Several)

Hughes, Langston. *The Dream Keeper*. Illus. by Brian Pinkney. Knopf, 1993. (African American)

Katz, Bobbi. *Trailblazers: Poems of Exploration*. Illus. by Carin Berger. Greenwillow, 2007.

Lewis, J. Patrick. *The Brothers' War: Civil War Voices in Verse*. National Geographic, 2007. (19th-century speech)

Moss, Jenny Jackson & Amy Dixon. *Cajun Night After Christmas*. Illus. by James Rice. Pelican, 2000. (Cajun)

Myers, Walter Dean. *Brown Angels*. HarperCollins, 1993. (African American)

Riley, James Whitcomb. "Little Orphant Annie." In Ferris, Helen. *Favorite Poems Old and New*. Illus. by Leonard Weisgard. Random, 1957, 2009. (19th-century "Hoosier")

———. *When the Frost in on the Punkin'*. Illus. by Glenna Long. Godine, 1991. (19th-century "Hoosier")

Shakespeare, William. "All the World's A Stage" & "Be Not Afeard; The Isle Is Full of Noises." In Rosen, Michael. *Classic Poetry*. Illus. by Paul Howard. Candlewick, 2009.

Shields, Carol Diggory. *Wombat Walkabout*. Illus. by Sophie Blackall. Dutton, 2009. (Australian)

Stavans, Ilan, ed. *¡Wachale!*. Cricket, 2001.

Trosclair. *Cajun Night Before Christmas*. Illus. by James Rice. Pelican, 1973.

Wong, Janet S. "My Bird Day. "*Good Luck Gold*. McElderry, 1994.

———. "Poetry." *A Suitcase of Seaweed*. Booksurge, 2008.

Standard Ten: Students whose first language is not English make use of their first language to develop competency in the English language and to develop understanding of content across the curriculum.
See also Chapter Five: Social Studies Theme One (Culture)

STANDARD TEN: POETRY IN LANGUAGES OTHER THAN ENGLISH

Some poems invite students to reflect on language variety by including several languages. Charlotte Pomerantz includes the word "thunder" in 10 languages in *Thunderboom!* Pat Mora includes the word "cheese" in 17 languages in "Ode to Pizza." While Spanish is the predominant language in books of poetry for young people, a few other languages featured in poems are included here.

Gollub, Matthew. *Cool Melons Turn to Frogs!* Illus. by Kazuko G. Stone. Lee & Low, 1998. (Japanese)

Greenberg, Jan, ed. *Heart to Heart*. Abrams, 2001. (many languages)

Harley, Avis. "Ways to Greet a Friend." In Heard, Georgia. *Falling Down the Page*. Roaring Brook, 2009.

Kimmelman. Leslie. *Everybody Bonjours*. Illus. by Sarah McMenemy. Knopf, 2008. (French)

Liu, Siyu & Orel Protopescu. *A Thousand Peaks*. Pacific View, 2002. (Chinese)

Mora, Pat. "Ode to Pizza." *My Own True Name*. Arté Público, 2000.

Pomerantz, Charlotte. *Thunderboom!* Illus. by Rob Shepperson. Front, 2005.

Spinelli, Eileen. *Summerhouse Time*. Illus. by Joanne Lew-Vriethoff. Knopf, 2007. (Novel in Verse) (Italian)

Stojic, Manya. *Hello World!* Scholastic, 2002. (42 languages)

Yolen, Jane, ed. *Street Rhymes Around the World*. Boyds Mills, 1992. (17 languages)

Young, Ed. *Beyond the Great Mountains*. Chronicle, 2005. (Chinese)

Poetry in Spanish and English

Spanish is the second most commonly spoken language in this country. Gary Soto's "Spanish" talks about how naturally it rolls off your tongue if you are born speaking it, and how "the world is twice the size" when you speak two languages. Pat Mora rejoices in her two languages, with "Words as Free as Confetti." Rane Arroyo describes his two languages, writing, "My Tongue Is Like a Map."

Some books use matched translations of Spanish and English language poems. Others feature different poems in each language. Still others include Spanish words in the course of spoken English poems. Some of the Spanish comes from countries in Latin America, some from Mexico, and some comes from within the United States. As with all languages, Spanish is constantly changing and differs somewhat from region to region.

Ada, Alma Flor. *Gathering the Sun*. Illus. by Simon Silva. English Translation by Rosa Zubizarreta. Harper Collins, 1997.

Ada, Alma Flor & F. Isabel Campoy. *Mamá Goose*. Illus. by Maribel Suárez. Hyperion, 2004.

———. *Pío Peep!* Illus. by Viví Escrivá. HarperCollins, 2003.

Alarcón, Francisco X. *Angels Ride Bikes = Los Ángeles Andan en Bicicleta*. Illus. by Maya Christina Gonzalez. Children's, 1998.

———. *Animal Poems of the Iguazu = Anmalario del Iguazú*. Illus. by Maya Christina Gonzalez. Children's, 2008.

———. *From the Bellybutton of the Moon = Del Ombligo de la Luna*. Illus. by Maya Christina Gonzalez. Children's, 1998.

———. *Iguanas in the Snow = Iguanas en la Nieve*. Illus. by Maya Christina Gonzalez. Children's, 2001.

———. *Laughing Tomatoes = Jitomates Risueños*. Illus. by Maya Christina Gonzalez. Children's, 1997.

———. *Poems to Dream Together = Poemas Para Sonar Juntos*. Illus. by Paula Barragán. Lee & Low, 2005.

Argueta, Jorge. *A Movie in My Pillow (Poems) = Una Pelicula en mi Almohada (Poemas)*. Illus. by Elizabeth Gómez. Childrens, 2001.

———. *Sopa de Frijoles = Bean Soup*. Illus. by Rafael Yockteng. Groundwood, 2009.

Bernier-Grand, Carmen T. *César: ¡Sí Se Puede! = Yes, We Can!* Illus. by David Diaz. Cavendish, 2004.

———. *Diego: Bigger than Life*. Illus. by David Diaz. Cavendish, 2009.

———. *Frida: ¡Viva la Vida! = Long Live Life!* Cavendish, 2007.

Bertrand, Diane Gonzales. *Sip, Slurp, Soup, Soup = Caldo, Caldo, Caldo*. Illus. by Alex Pardo DeLange. Arté Público, 1997.

Caraballo, Samuel. *Mis Abuelos y Yo = My Grandparents and I*. Illus. by D. Nina Cruz. Arté Público, 2004.

Carlson, Lori Marie, ed. *Cool Salsa*. Holt, 1994.

———. *Sol a Sol*. Holt, 1998.

Cisneros, Sandra. *Hairs = Pelitos*. Illus. by Terry Ybañez. Knopf, 1994.

De Colores = Bright with Colors. Illus. by David Diaz. Cavendish, 2008.

Delacre, Lulu, sel. *Arroz con Leche*. Scholastic, 1989.

Hall, Nancy Abraham & Jill Syverson-Stork, col. *Los Pollitos Dicen = The Little Chicks Sing*. Illus. by Kay Chorao. Little, 1994.

Herrera, Juan Felipe. *Calling the Doves = El Canto de las Palomas*. Illus. by Elly Simmons. Children's, 1995.

———. *Laughing Out Loud, I Fly*. Illus. by Karen Barbour. HarperCollins, 1998.

———. *The Upside Down Boy = El Niño de Cabeza*. Illus. by Elizabeth Gómez. Children's, 2000.

Jaramillo, Nelly Palacio. *Las Nanas de Abuelita = Grandmother's Nursery Rhymes*. Illus. by Elivia Savadier. Holt, 1994.

Johnston, Tony. *My Mexico = México Mío*. Illus. by F. John Sierra. Putnam, 1996.

Medina, Jane. *The Dream on Blanca's Wall = El Suenõ Pegado en la Pared de Blanca*. Illus. by Robert Casilla. Boyds Mills, 2004.
———. *My Name Is Jorge: On Both Sides of the River.* Illus. by Fabricio Vanden Broeck. Boyds Mills, 1999.
Montalvo, Margarita. *Zoológico de Poemas = Poetry Zoo*. Scholastic, 2004.
Mora, Pat. *Book Fiesta!* Illus. by Rafael López. HarperCollins, 2009.
———. *Delicious Hullabaloo = Pachanga Deliciosa*. Illus. by Francisco X. Mora. Arté Público, 1998.
———. *The Desert Is My Mother = El Desierto Es Mi Madre*. Illus. by Daniel Léchon. Lorito, 2008.
———. *My Own True Name*. Arté Público, 2000.
Nye, Naomi Shihab. *The Tree Is Older Than You Are*. S & S, 1995.
Orozco, José-Luis. *Diez Deditos = Ten Little Fingers*. Illus. by Elisa Kleven. Dutton, 1997.
———. *Rin, Rin, Rin = Do, Re, Mi*. Illus. by David Diaz. Scholastic, 2005.
Soto, Gary. "Spanish." In Carlson, Lori Marie. *Red Hot Salsa*. Holt. 2005.

English with Some Spanish

Arroyo, Rane. "My Tongue Is Like a Map." In Mora, Pat. *Love to Mamá*. Illus. by Paula S. Barragán M. Lee & Low, 2001.
Elya, Susan Middleton. *Bebé Goes Shopping*. Illus. by Steven Salerno. Harcourt, 2006.
———. *Eight Animals Bake a Cake*. Illus. by Lee Chapman. Putnam, 2002.
———. *Eight Animals on the Town*. Illus. by Lee Chapman. Putnam, 2000.
———. *Eight Animals Play Ball*. Illus. by Lee Chapman. Putnam, 2003.
———. *F Is for Fiesta*. Illus. by G. Brian Karas. Putnam, 2006,
———. *Fairy Trails*. Illus. by Mercedes MacDonald. Bloomsburg, 2005.
———. *Tooth on the Loose*. Illus. by Jenny Mattheson. Putnam, 2008.
Elya, Susan Middleton & Merry Banks. *N Is for Navidad*. Illus. by Joe Cepeda. Chronicle, 2007.
Gershator, Phillis. *Zoo Day Olé!* Illus. by Santiago Cohen. Cavendish, 2009.
Harris, Jay M. *The Moon is La Luna: Silly Rhymes in English and Spanish*. Illus. by Matthew Cordell. Houghton, 2007.
Herrera, Juan Felipe. *Downtown Boy*. Scholastic, 2005. (Novel in Verse)
Mora, Pat. *Confetti*. Illus. by Enrique O. Sanchez. Lee & Low, 1996.
———. *Join Hands!* Illus. by George Ancona. Charlesbridge, 2008.
———. *Love to Mamá*. Illus. by Paula S. Barragán M. Lee & Low, 2001.
———. *This Big Sky*. Illus. by Steve Jenkins. Scholastic, 1998.
———. *Uno, Dos, Tres = One, Two, Three*. Illus. by Barbara Lavallee. Clarion, 1996.
———. "Words as Free as Confetti." In *Confetti*. Illus. by Enrique O. Sanchez. Lee & Low, 1996. (Also in *Wonderful Words*)
Soto, Gary. *Canto Familiar*. Illus. by Annika Nelson. Harcourt, 1995.
———. *Neighborhood Odes*. Illus. by David Diaz. Harcourt, 1992.
Stavans, Ilan, ed. *¡Wachale!* Cricket, 2001.

Standard Eleven: Students participate as knowledgeable, reflective, creative, and critical members of a variety of literacy communities.

Standard Twelve: Students use spoken, written, and visual language to accomplish their own purposes (e.g., for learning, enjoyment, persuasion, and the exchange of information.

These two standards cross all curriculum areas. Standard Twelve reinforces the importance of learning to use language effectively in several different modes and for a variety of purposes.

REFERENCES

Dyson, A. H. & C. Genishi, eds. (1994). *The Need for Story: Cultural Diversity in Classroom and Community.* Urbana, IL: National Council of Teachers of English.

Standards for the English Language Arts. National Council of Teachers of English/International Reading Association. 1996. http://www.ncte.org/standards.

CHAPTER 3

Poetry and the Science Standards

Scientists and poets are close observers and chroniclers of the world around them. Scientists investigate and describe phenomena as they work to identify, experiment, and come to conclusions about how they function. Poets investigate and interpret these same phenomena, but with a slightly different eye. Both start their work with curiosity and questions. The scientist methodically lays out data so that others can follow the same trail to understanding. The poet uses imagery, figurative language, sound, and phrasing to excite wonder. Students who are free to carefully explore the natural world and to ask questions about it, and who are given time and methods to answer these questions, are learning good science. Poets can enrich this experience because they ask similar questions, and carefully describe what they see.

Standard One: Unifying Concepts and Processes of Science.
Conceptual and procedural schemes unify science disciplines and provide students with powerful ideas to help them understand the natural world. Because of the underlying principles embodied in this standard, the understanding and abilities described here are repeated in the other content areas. Unifying concepts and processes include 1) Systems, order, and organization 2) Evidence, models, and explanation 3) Change, constancy, and measurement 4) Evolution and equilibrium 5) Form and function.

STANDARD ONE: SCIENCE

Because these major concepts cross the content areas, poems about them will appear in every standard. A few examples of poems that characterize these processes are included here, along with collections of poems about the sciences.

Dotlich, Rebecca Kai. "What Is Science?" In Hopkins, Lee Bennett. *Spectacular Science*. Illus. by Virginia Halstead. S & S, 1999.

Fisher, Aileen. *The Story Goes On*. Illus. by Mique Moriuchi. Roaring Brook, 2002.

Hopkins, Lee Bennett, sel. *Spectacular Science*. Illus. by Virginia Halstead. S & S, 2004.

Lewis, J. Patrick. *Scien-trickery: Riddles in Science*. Illus. by Frank Remkiewicz. Harcourt, 2004.

Scieszka, Jon. *Science Verse*. Illus. by Lane Smith. Viking, 2004. (With CD)
Shields, Carol Diggory. *Science, Fresh Squeezed*. Illus. by Richard Thompson. Handprint, 2003.
Zolotow, Charlotte. "Beginnings." *Snippets*. Illus. by Melissa Sweet. HarperCollins, 1993.
———. *When the Wind Stops*. Illus. by Stefano Vitale. HarperCollins, 1995.

Standard Two: Science as Inquiry. Engages students in identifying questions that can be answered through scientific investigations, helps students formulate questions that are relevant and meaningful, begins to build a community of learners as students collaborate, engages students in questioning and querying other students, and raises awareness that ideas are to be presented in oral and/or written reports.

See also Chapter One : Poetry and the National Standards (Poetic Language)

See also Chapter Two: Language Arts Standard Five (Questions)

STANDARD TWO: INQUIRY

Standard Two crosses all of the science standards. Curiosity and imagination are crucial to pursuing answers to one's questions in science. Walt Whitman's *When I Heard the Learn'd Astronomer* points out that it is no good having many dry facts about something if they are not enlivened by imagination. Aileen Fisher's poetry for young children is full of the curiosity and questions about nature that are necessary for young scientists to begin. John Frank's *Keepers: Treasure-Hunt Poems* and Rebecca Kai Dotlich's *When Riddles Come Rumbling: Poems to Ponder* provide this kind of questioning and close observation for older students. J. Patrick Lewis' *Scien-trickery: Riddles in Science* invites curiosity about science.

Appelt, Kathi. "Science Fair." *Poems from Homeroom*. Holt, 2002.
Dotlich, Rebecca Kai. *When Riddles Come Rumbling: Poems to Ponder*. Boyds Mills, 2001.
Esbensen, Barbara Juster. "Discovery" & "Prediction." *Swing Around the Sun*. Illus. by Cheng-Khee Chee, et al. Carolrhoda, 2003.
Fisher, Aileen. *I Heard a Bluebird Sing*. Illus. by Jennifer Emery. Boyds Mills, 2002.
Frank, John. *Keepers: Treasure-Hunt Poems*. Illus. by Ken Robbins. Roaring Brook, 2008.
George, Kristine O'Connell. *Hummingbird Nest: A Journal of Poems*. Illus. by Barry Moser. Harcourt, 2004.
———. "Science Projects." *Swimming Upstream*. Illus. by Debbie Tilley. Clarion, 2002.
Lawson, JonArno. "I've Always Liked This Planet." *Black Stars in a White Night Sky*. Illus. by Sherwin Tjia. Boyds Mills, 2006.
Lewis, J. Patrick. *Scien-trickery: Riddles in Science*. Illus. by Frank Remkiewicz. Harcourt, 2004.
Liatsos, Sandra. "Outer Space Wondering." In Hopkins, Lee Bennett. *Blast Off!* Illus. by Melissa Sweet. HarperCollins, 1995.
Nye, Naomi Shihab. "Observer." *Come with Me*. Illus. by Dan Yaccarino. HarperCollins, 2000.
———. "People I Admire." *A Maze Me*. HarperCollins, 2005. (Curiosity)
Scieszka, Jon. "Scientific Method at the Bat." *Science Verse*. Illus. by Lane Smith. Viking, 2004. (With CD)
Singer, Marilyn. "Patience." *Footprints on the Roof*. Illus. by Meilo So. Knopf, 2002.
Whitman, Walt. *When I Heard the Learn'd Astronomer*. Illus. by Loren Long. S & S, 2004.

Tools of the Scientist

Dotlich, Rebecca Kai. "A Small Magic Funnel..." *When Riddles Come Rumbling*. Boyds Mills, 2001. (Telescope)

Fleming, Maria. "Compass." In Hopkins, Lee Bennett. *Got Geography!* Illus. by Philip Stanton. HarperCollins, 2006.

Harley, Avis. "Wondrous Wings." *The Monarch's Progress*. Boyds Mills, 2008. (Magnifying Glass)

Hopkins, Lee Bennett. "Under the Microscope." *Spectacular Science*. Illus. by Virginia Halstead. S & S, 1999. (Also in *The Bill Martin Jr. Big Book of Poetry*)

Lewis, J. Patrick. "Push Me, Pull Me" & "White-Hot Needle." *Scien-trickery*. Illus. by Frank Remkiewicz. Harcourt, 2004.

Merriam, Eve. "Points of the Compass." *The Singing Green*. Illus. by Kathleen Collins Howell. Morrow, 1992.

Silverstein, Shel. "Nope." *Falling Up*. HarperCollins, 1996. (Microscope)

Vargo, Sharon. "Looking Through the Microscope." In Hopkins, Lee Bennett. *Hamsters, Shells, and Spelling Bees*. Illus. by Sachiko Yoshikawa. HarperCollins, 2008.

Worth, Valerie. "Magnifying Glass," "Magnet," & "Compass." *All the Small Poems and Fourteen More*. Illus. by Natalie Babbitt. Farrar, 1994.

Standard Three: Physical Sciences. These include the properties of and changes to objects and materials; position and motion of objects; understanding of light, heat, electricity, magnetism, and transfer of energy.

STANDARD THREE: PHYSICAL SCIENCES

Bang, Molly. *Living Sunlight*. Scholastic, 2009.

———. *My Light*. Scholastic, 2004.

Coatsworth, Elizabeth. "Swift Things are Beautiful." In Dunning, Stephen, et al. *Reflections on a Gift of Watermelon Pickle*. HarperCollins, 1967.

Dotlich, Rebecca Kai. *In the Spin of Things: Poetry of Motion*. Illus. by Karen Dugan. Boyds Mills, 2003.

Fisher, Aileen. "The Spinning Earth." *I Heard a Bluebird Sing*. Illus. by Jennifer Emery. Boyds Mills, 2002.

George, Kristine O'Connell. "Sleeping Outside." *Toasting Marshmallows*. Illus. by Kate Kiesler. Clarion, 2001. (Earth's rotation)

Holbrook, Sara. "Basic Physics." *By Definition*. Illus. by Scott Mattern. Boyds Mills, 2003. (Gravity)

———. "Stuck Here." *The Dog Ate My Homework*. Boyds Mills, 1996. (Gravity)

Lawson, JonArno. "The Old Man's Lie." *Black Stars in a White Night Sky*. Illus. by Shewin Tjia. Boyds Mills, 2006. (Electricity)

Levy, Constance. "Power Failure." *A Tree Place*. Illus. by Robert Sabuda. McElderry, 1994.

Lewis, J. Patrick. "Push Me, Pull Me," "Gee," "There's Something in the Water," & "The Old Switcheroo." *Scien-trickery*. Illus. by Frank Remkiewicz. Harcourt, 2004. (Magnet, Gravity, Oxygen, & Electricity)

Prelutsky, Jack. "I Made Something Strange with My Chemistry Set." *A Pizza the Size of the Sun*. Illus. by James Stevenson. HarperCollins, 1996.

Sandburg, Carl. "From 'Lines Written for Gene Kelly to Dance to.'" In Hopkins, Lee Bennett. *Rainbows Are Made*. Illus. by Fritz Eichenberg. Harcourt, 1982. (Gravity) (Also in *Got Geography*!)

Scieszka, Jon. "Mini Ha Ha (Or, the Atomic Joke Is on You)" & "What's the Matter?" *Science Verse*. Illus. by Lane Smith. Viking, 2004. (Chemistry) (With CD)

Shields, Carol Diggory. Sections: "Chemistry" & "Physics." *Science, Fresh Squeezed*. Illus. by Richard Thompson. Handprint, 2003.

Silverstein, Shel. "Plugging In." *Falling Up*. HarperCollins, 1996. (Electricity)

Singer, Marilyn. *Central Heating: Poems About Fire and Warmth*. Illus. Meilo So. Knopf, 2005.

———. "Spinner." In Heard, Georgia. *Falling Down the Page*. Roaring Brook, 2009.

Weisburd, Stefi. "Shocking." *Barefoot*. Illus. by Lori McElrath-Eslick. Boyds Mills, 2008. (Static electricity)

Worth, Valerie. "Garbage." *All the Small Poems and Fourteen More*. Illus. by Natalie Babbitt. Farrar, 1994. (Chemistry)

Yolen, Jane. *A Mirror to Nature: Poems About Reflection*. Illus. by Jason Stemple. Boyds Mills, 2009.

Liquids and Solids: Water and Ice

See also Standard Five (The Water Cycle)

Dotlich, Rebecca Kai. "Ice Cubes." *In the Spin of Things*. Illus. by Karen Dugan. Boyds Mills, 2003.

Graham, Joan Bransfield. *Splish, Splash*. Illus. by Steve Scott. Houghton, 1994.

Moore, Lilian. "Waterfall." In Janeczko, Paul B. *Seeing the Blue Between*. Candlewick, 2002.

Sandburg, Carl. "Metamorphosis." In Hopkins, Lee Bennett. *Rainbows Are Made*. Illus. by Fritz Eichenberg. Harcourt, 1982. (Also in *Spectacular Science*)

Worth, Valerie. "Frost." *All the Small Poems and Fourteen More*. Illus. by Natalie Babbitt. Farrar, 1994.

Yolen, Jane, sel. *Once Upon Ice: And Other Frozen Poems*. Illus. by Jason Stemple. Boyds Mills, 1997.

———. *Water Music*. Illus. by Jason Stemple. Boyds Mills, 1995.

Light and Shadow

Poetry about light includes light from the sun, starlight, lightning, fire, and electricity. Poets write about prisms, the light spectrum, and rainbows. Poems about light and shadow generally have emotional connections. Why do shadows and shade so often evoke feelings of sadness, fear, or cold? Are there times when shadows are beautiful and safe? When is the light dangerous? These questions and their answers sometimes appear in poetry.

Argueta, Jorge. "Shadow." *A Movie in My Pillow = Una Pelicula en Mi Almohada*. Illus. by Elizabeth Gómez. Children's 2001.

Baird, Audrey. "Our Sponsor Is . . . " *Storm Coming!* Illus. by Patrick O'Brien. Boyds Mills, 2003. (Rainbow)

Bang, Molly. *Living Sunlight*. Scholastic, 2009.

Brown, Margaret Wise. "So Many Nights." In Martin, Bill, Jr. & Michael Sampson. *The Bill Martin Jr. Big Book of Poetry*. S & S, 2008.

Cendrars, Blaise. *Shadow*. Trans. and Illus. by Marcia Brown. Scribners, 1982.

Chandra, Deborah. "Porch Light." In Kennedy, X. J. & Dorothy M. Kennedy. *Knock at a Star*. Illus. by Karen Lee Baker. Little, 1999.

Dakos, Kalli. "I Am a Shadow by the Classroom Wall." *Put Your Eyes Up Here*. Illus. by G. Brian Karas. S & S, 2003.

Dotlich, Rebecca Kai. "Fireworks" & "Backyard Bubbles." *Lemonade Sun*. Illus. by Jan Spivey Gilchrist. Boyds Mills, 1998.

———. "New England Lighthouse." In Hopkins, Lee Bennett. *My America*. Illus. by Stephen Alcorn. S & S, 2000.

———. "S." *When Riddles Come Rumbling*. Boyds Mills, 2001.

Esbensen, Barbara Juster. "Four Poems for Roy G. Biv" & "Rainbow Making." *Who Shrank My Grandmother's House?* Illus. by Eric Beddows. HarperCollins, 1992.

———. "Nightfall." In Pearson, Susan. *The Drowsy Hours*. Illus. by Peter Malone. Harper Collins, 2002.

Fisher, Aileen. "Until We Built a Cabin." In Martin, Bill, Jr. & Michael Sampson. *The Bill Martin Jr. Big Book of Poetry*. S & S, 2008.

George, Kristine O'Connell. "Flashlight." *Toasting Marshmallows*. Illus. by Kate Kiesler. Clarion, 2001.

———. "Plowed Fields." *The Great Frog Race*. Illus. by Kate Kiesler. Clarion, 1997.

Giovanni, Nikki. "Rainbows." *Spin a Soft Black Song*. Illus. by George Martins. Farrar, 1985.

Graham, Joan Bransfield. *Flicker Flash*. Illus. by Nancy Davis. Houghton, 1999.

Harley, Avis. "Phosphorescence." *Fly with Poetry*. Boyds Mills, 2000.

Hines, Anna Grossnickle. *Winter Lights*.Greenwillow, 2005.

———. "Shadows." *Pieces*. HarperCollins, 2001.

Hollander, John. "Swan and Shadow." In Janeczko, Paul B. *A Poke in the I.* Illus. by Chris Raschka. Candlewick, 2001.

Hubbell, Patricia. "8 A. M. Shadows." In De Regniers, Beatrice Schenk. *Sing a Song of Popcorn.* Scholastic, 1988.

Kennedy, X. J. "Flashlight." In Paschen, Elise. *Poetry Speaks to Children.* Sourcebooks, 2005. (With CD)

Levy, Constance. "Rainbow Making." *Splash!* Illus. by David Soman. Orchard, 2002.

Moore, Lilian. "Winter Dark Comes Early." *Mural on Second Avenue.* Illus. by Roma Karas. Candlewick, 2005.

Paul, Ann Whitford. *Shadows Are About.* Scholastic, 1992.

Prelutsky, Jack. "I Spied My Shadow Slinking." *The New Kid on the Block.* Illus. by James Stevenson. Green willow, 1984.

———. "Shadow Thought." *It's Snowing, It's Snowing!* Illus. by Yossi Abolafia. HarperCollins, 2006.

———. "What Happens to the Colors?" *My Parents Think I'm Sleeping.* Illus. by Yossi Abolafia. Greenwillow, 1985.

Rossetti, Christina. "The Rainbow." In Martin, Bill, Jr. & Sampson, Michael. *The Bill Martin Jr. Big Book of Poetry.* S & S, 2008.

Sandburg, Carl. "Sketch," "Bubbles," & "Window." In Hopkins, Lee Bennett. *Rainbows Are Made.* Harcourt, 1982

Sayre, April Pulley. *Shadows.* Illus. by Harvey Stevenson. Holt, 2002.

Schertle, Alice. "Walk Softly." *Keepers.* Illus. by Ted Rand. Lothrop, 1996.

Schimel, Lawrence. "Crystal Vision." In Hopkins, Lee Bennett. *Spectacular Science.* Illus. by Virginia Halstead. S&S, 1999.

Singer, Marilyn. "Turquoise, Teal, Aquamarine." *How to Cross a Pond.* Illus. by Meilo So. Knopf, 2003.

Stevenson, Robert Louis. *My Shadow.* Illus. by Glenna Lang. Godine, 1989.

———. "My Shadow" & "Shadow March." *A Child's Garden of Verses.* Illus. by Diane Goode. Morrow, 1998.

Swanson, Susan Marie. *The House in the Night.* Illus. by Beth Krommes. Houghton, 2008.

Thurman, Judith. "Zebra." In Prelutsky, Jack. *The Random House Book of Poetry for Children.* Random, 1983.

Worth, Valerie. "Hose," "Soap Bubble," "Door," & "Kaleidoscope." *All the Small Poems and Fourteen More.* Illus. by Natalie Babbitt. Farrar, 1994.

———. "Prism" & "Cellar." *Peacock.* Illus. by Natalie Babbitt. Farrar, 2002.

Yolen, Jane. "Dragonfly." *Least Things.* Illus. by Jason Stemple. Boyds Mills, 2003.

Zolotow, Charlotte. "Look!" *Everything Glistens and Everything Sings.* Illus. by Margot Tomes. Harcourt, 1987.

Standard Four: Life Sciences. These include the characteristics, structure and function of organisms and living systems; life cycles, reproduction of organisms, and heredity; populations and ecosystems; and diversity and adaptation of organisms.

See also Chapter Five: Social Studies Theme Three (People, Places and Environments)

STANDARD FOUR: LIFE SCIENCES

Not surprisingly, poets explore and write about the natural world more than any other subject. Some poems are celebrations of nature's beauty and complexity. Others focus in on tiny worlds. To show the range of these poems, Carol Diggory Shields' poems in the life sciences, for example, include light-hearted but accurate poems on amoebas, cells, genes, fungus, ecosystems, and evolution.

Shields, Carol Diggory. Section: "Life Sciences." *Science, Fresh Squeezed.* Illus. by Richard Thompson. Handprint, 2003.

Nature

Chaikin, Miriam. *Don't Step on the Sky.* Illus. by Hiroe Nakata. Holt, 2002.
Fisher, Aileen. *I Heard a Bluebird Sing.* Illus. by Jennifer Emery. Boyds Mills, 2002.
Frasier, Deborah L. *On the Day You Were Born.* Harcourt, 1991.
George, Kristine O'Connell. *The Great Frog Race.* Illus. by Kate Kiesler. Clarion, 1997.
Harrison, David. *Wild Country.* Boyds Mills, 1999.
Ho, Mingfong. *Maples in the Mist.* Illus. by Jean and Mou-Sien Tseng. Lothrop, 1996.
Levy, Constance. *A Tree Place.* Illus. by Robert Sabuda. McElderry, 1994.
Lindbergh, Reeve. *The Circle of Days: From Canticle of the Sun by St. Francis of Assisi.* Illus. by Cathie Felstead. Candlewick, 1998.
Martin, Bill, Jr. & Michael Sampson. *I Love Our Earth.* Illus. by Dan Lipow. Charlesbridge, 2006.
———. Section: "The World of Nature." *The Bill Martin Jr. Big Book of Poetry.* S & S, 2008.
Michael, Pamela, ed. *River of Words: Young Poets and Artists on the Nature of Things.* Milkweed, 2008.
Mordhorst, Heidi. *Pumpkin Butterfly: Poems from the Other Side of Nature.* Illus. by Jenny Reynish. Boyds Mills, 2009.
Noda, Takayo. *Dear World.* Dial, 2003.
Nicholls, Judith, comp. *The Sun in Me.* Illus. by Beth Krommes. Barefoot, 2003.
Nye, Naomi Shihab, sel. Section: "Earth and Animals." *The Tree Is Older Than You Are.* S & S, 1995.
———. Section: "This Earth and Sky in Which We Live: Water That Used to Be a Cloud." *This Same Sky.* Macmillan, 1992.
Paolillo, Paul & Dan Brewer. *Silver Seeds.* Illus. by Steve Johnson & Lou Fancher. Viking, 2001.
Prelutsky, Jack, sel. Section: "Nature Is." *The Random House Book of Poetry for Children.* Illus. by Arnold Lobel. Random, 1983.
Reibstein, Mark. *Wabi Sabi.* Illus. by Ed Young. Little, 2008.
Ryder, Joanne. *Each Living Thing.* Illus. by Ashley Wolff. Harcourt, 2000.
Schertle, Alice. *A Lucky Thing.* Illus. by Wendell Minor. Harcourt, 1999.
Whitman, Walt. *Nothing but Miracles.* Illus. by Susan L. Roth. National Geographic, 2003.
Yolen, Jane. *Color Me a Rhyme.* Illus. by Jason Stemple. Boyds Mills, 2000.
———. *Least Things.* Illus. by Jason Stemple. Boyds Mills, 2003.
———, sel. *Mother Earth, Father Sky.* Illus. by Jennifer Hewitson. Boyds Mills, 1996.

Poetry about Ecosystems

An ecosystem can be large, or small and unique. Poetry about ecosystems enriches science study, and can enhance students' literary understanding of setting. Jean Craighead George's *Talking Earth* and *Missing 'Gator of Gumbo Limbo*, for example, take place in the Everglades. Two poetry collections about the Everglades, *The Seldom-Ever-Shady Glades* and *Welcome to the River of Grass*, would could be used to enhance both the science and the literary study of these novels.

Harrison, David. *Wild Country: Outdoor Poems for Young People.* Boyds Mills, 1999.
Hopkins, Lee Bennett, sel. *My America: A Poetry Atlas of the United States.* Illus. by Stephen Alcorn. S & S, 2000.
Locker, Thomas & Candace Christiansen, eds. *Home: A Journey Through America.* Harcourt, 2000.

Rivers and Wetlands

Arnosky, Jim. *Deer at the Brook.* Scholastic, 1986.
Bateman, Donna M. *Deep in the Swamp.* Illus. by Brian Lies. Charlesbridge, 2007.
Falwell, Cathryn. *Scoot!* Greenwillow, 2008. (Ponds)
Hughes, Langston. *The Negro Speaks of Rivers.* Illus. by E. B. Lewis. Disney, 2009.
Lithgow, John. *I'm a Manatee.* Illus. by Ard Hoyt. S & S, 2003. (Everglades) (With CD)

Roberts, Elizabeth Maddox. "Water Noises." In Smith, William Jay. *Up the Hill and Down*. Illus. by Allan Eitzen. Boyds Mills, 2003.

Schertle, Alice. "Pond." *A Lucky Thing*. Illus. by Wendell Minor. Harcourt, 1999.

Sidman, Joyce. *Song of the Water Boatman*. Illus. by Beckie Prange. Houghton, 2005.

Singer, Marilyn. *How to Cross a Pond*. Illus. by Meilo So. Knopf, 2003.

Stevenson, Robert Louis. "Where Go the Boats?" *A Child's Garden of Verses*. Illus. by Diane Goode. Morrow, 1998. (Also in *Talking Like the Rain*)

Van Wassenhove, Sue. *The Seldom-Ever Shady Glades*. Boyds Mills, 2008.

Yolen, Jane. *Welcome to the River of Grass*. Illus. by Laura Regan. Putnam, 2001.

Deserts

Baylor, Byrd. *The Desert Is Theirs*. Illus. by Peter Parnall. Macmillan, 1975.

———. *Desert Voices*. Illus. by Peter Parnall. Macmillan, 1981.

———. *I'm in Charge of Celebrations*. Illus. by Peter Parnall. Scribners, 1986.

Bruchac, Joseph. "Far from Here . . . " *Between Earth and Sky*. Illus. by Thomas Locker. Harcourt, 1996.

Buchanan, Ken & Debbie Buchanan. *It Rained on the Desert Today*. Illus. by Libba Tracy. Northland, 1994.

Fisher, Lillian M. "Child of the Sun." In Martin, Bill, Jr. & Michael Sampson. *The Bill Martin Jr. Big Book of Poetry*. S & S, 2008.

Larios, Julie. "Turquoise Lizard." *Yellow Elephant*. Illus. by Julie Paschkis. Harcourt, 2006.

Lewis, J. Patrick. "Knockabout and Knockaboom." *A World of Wonders*. Illus. by Alison Jay. Dial, 2002.

Mora, Pat. *Delicious Hullabaloo = Pachanga Deliciosa*. Illus. by Francisco X. Mora. Arté Público, 1998.

———. *The Desert Is My Mother = El Desierto Es Mi Madre*. Illus. by Daniel Léchon. Lorito, 2008. (Also in *My Own True Name*)

———. "Gold." In Locker, Thomas & Candace Christiansen. *Home*. Harcourt, 2000.

———. "River Voice." *Confetti*. Illus. by Enrique O. Sanchez. Lee & Low, 1996.

———. *This Big Sky*. Illus. by Steve Jenkins. Scholastic, 1998.

Siebert, Diane. *Mohave*. Illus. by Wendell Minor. Crowell, 1988.

Singer, Marilyn. "Desert Day." *Central Heating*. Illus. by Meilo So. Knopf, 2005.

Yolen, Jane. "Brown." *Color Me a Rhyme*. Illus. by Jason Stemple. Boyds Mills, 2000.

———. "Sand, Sun, Stone." *Horizons*. Illus. by Jason Stemple. Boyds Mills, 2002.

Oceans and Coastal Ecosystems

Agard, John & Grace Nichols, eds. *Under the Moon and Over the Sea*. Illus. by Cathie Felstead, et al. Candlewick, 2002.

Cyrus, Kurt. *Hotel Deep*. Harcourt, 2005.

Frank, John. Section: "At the Beach." *Keepers*. Illus. by Ken Robbins. Roaring Brook, 2008.

Frasier, Debra. *Out of the Ocean*. Harcourt, 1998.

Harley, Avis. *Sea Stars*. Illus. by Margaret Butschler. Boyds Mills, 2006.

Harrison, David. Section: "Sea." *Wild Country.*Boyds Mills, 1999.

Rose, Deborah Lee. *One Nighttime Sea*. Illus. by Steve Jenkins. Scholastic, 2003.

Ruurs, Margriet. *A Pacific Alphabet*. Illus. by Dianna Bonder. Whitecap, 2004.

Ryan, Pam Muñoz. *Hello Ocean*. Illus. by Mark Astrella. Charlesbridge, 2002.

Schertle, Alice. *All You Need for a Beach*. Illus. by Barbara Lavallee. Harcourt, 2004.

Shaw, Alison, comp. *Until I Saw the Sea*. Holt, 1995.

Zolotow, Charlotte. Section: "The Sea." *Everything Glistens and Everything Sings*. Illus. by Margot Tomes. Harcourt, 1987.

———. *The Seashore Book*. Illus. by Wendell Minor. HarperCollins, 1992.

Meadows and Prairies

Bouchard, David. *If You're Not from the Prairie*. Illus. by Henry Ripplinger. Atheneum, 1995.
Goble, Paul. *Song of Creation*. Eerdmans, 2004.
Jackson, Kathryn & Byron Jackson. "Open Range." In Pearson, Susan. *The Drowsy Hours*. Illus. by Peter Malone. HarperCollins, 2002.
Sidman, Joyce. *Butterfly Eyes*. Illus. by Beth Krommes. Houghton, 2003.
Siebert, Diane. *Heartland*. Illus. by Wendell Minor. HarperCollins, 1989.

Mountains and Forests

Cotten, Cynthia. *At the Edge of the Woods*. Illus. by Reg Cartwright. Holt, 2002.
Harrison, David. *Farmer's Dog Goes to the Forest*. Illus. by Arden Johnson-Petrov. Boyds Mills, 2005.
———. Sections: "Mountains," "High Country," & "Forest." *Wild Country*. Boyds Mills, 1999.
Locker, Thomas. *Mountain Dance*. Harcourt, 2001.
Ruddell, Deborah. *A Whiff of Pine, A Hint of Skunk: A Forest of Poems*. Illus. by Joan Rankin. S & S, 2009.
Ruurs, Margriet. *A Mountain Alphabet*. Illus. by Andrew Kiss. Tundra, 1996.
Siebert, Diane. *Cave*. Illus. by Wayne McLoughlin. HarperCollins, 2000.
———. *Sierra*. Illus. by Wendell Minor. HarperCollins, 1991.

Rainforests

Alarcón, Francisco X. *Animal Poems of the Iguazu = Animalaria del Iguazú*. Illus. by Maya Christina Gonzales. Children's 2008.
Berkes, Marianne. *Over In the Jungle*. Illus. by Jeannette Canyon. Dawn, 2007.
Katz, Susan. *Looking for Jaguar*. Illus. by Lee Christiansen. Greenwillow, 2005.
Nichols, Grace. "For Forest." In Hopkins, Lee Bennett. *Got Geography!* Illus. by Philip Stanton. HarperCollins, 2006.
Olaleye, Isaac. "Forest Farm Melody" & "A Walk Through My Rain Forest." *The Distant Talking Drum*. Illus. by Frané Lessac. Boyds Mills, 1995.
Ryder, Joanne. *Jaguar in the Rain Forest*. Illus. by Michael Rothman. Morrow, 1996.
Salas, Laura Purdie. *Chatter, Sing, Roar, Buzz*.Capstone, 2008.
Singer, Marilyn. "Rain Forest." *How to Cross a Pond*. Illus. by Meilo So. Knopf, 2003.

Polar Ecosystems

Appelt, Kathi. "The Research Paper: A Sestina." *Poems from Homeroom*. Holt, 2002.
Minor, Wendell & Florence Minor. *If You Were a Penguin*. HarperCollins, 2009.
Sierra, Judy. *Antarctic Antics*. Illus. by José Aruego & Ariane Dewey. Harcourt, 1998.
Singer, Marilyn. "Early Explorers." *Footprints on the Roof*. Illus. by Meilo So. Knopf, 2002.
Spinelli, Eileen. *Polar Bear, Arctic Hare*. Illus. by Eugenie Fernandes. Boyds Mills, 2007.

Animals

Some poems about animals are serious explorations of the qualities of the animal, while others are humorous or fantastic. Young scientists can compare what they are learning about the lives and behavior of each creature with what the poets say. General collections of poems are listed first, followed by poems and collections about one or two specific creatures. Students may want to make collections of poems about their own favorite animals, using the general collections below as resources and adding the poems they have written.

Barbe, Walter B. sel. Section: "Animals." *A School Year of Poems*. Illus. by Dennis Hockerman. Boyds Mills, 2005.
Belle, Jennifer. *Animal Stackers*. Illus. by David McPhail. Hyperion, 2005.
De Regniers. Beatrice Schenk, sel. Section: "Mostly Animals." *Sing a Song of Popcorn*. Scholastic, 1988.
———. *It Does Not Say Meow*. Illus. by Paul Galdone. Houghton, 1979.
Dotlich, Rebecca Kai. *Sweet Dreams of the Wild*. Illus. by Katherine Dodge. Boyds Mills, 1996.
Ehlert, Lois. *Oodles of Animals*. Harcourt, 2008.
Elliott, David. *On the Farm*. Illus. by Holly Meade. Candlewick, 2008.
Esbensen, Barbara Juster. *Words with Wrinkled Knees*. Illus. by John Stadler. HarperCollins, 1987.
Fisher, Aileen. *The House of a Mouse*. Illus. by Joan Sandin. HarperCollins, 1988.
———. *Know What I Saw?* Illus. by Deborah Durland DeSaix. Roaring Brook, 2004.
———. *Rabbits, Rabbits*. Illus. by Gail Niemann. HarperCollins, 1983.
Florian, Douglas. *Beast Feast*. Harcourt, 1994.
———. *Mammalabilia*. Harcourt, 2000.
———. *Omnibeasts*. Harcourt, 2004.
———. *Zoo's Who*. Harcourt, 2005.
Hague, Michael, comp. *Animal Friends*. Holt, 2007.
Harley, Avis. *African Acrostics*. Illus. by Deborah Noyes. Candlewick, 2009.
Heard, Georgia. *Creatures of Earth, Sea, and Sky*. Illus. by Jennifer Owings Dewey. Boyds Mills, 1992.
Hoberman, Mary Ann. *A Fine, Fat Pig*. Illus. by Malcah Zeldis. HarperCollins, 1991.
Hopkins, Lee Bennett, sel. *A Pet for Me*. Illus. by Jane Manning. HarperCollins, 2003.
Hubbell, Patricia. *Earthmates*. Illus. by Jean Cassels. Cavendish, 2000.
Kennedy, Caroline, sel. Section: "Animals." *A Family of Poems*. Illus. by Jon J. Muth. Hyperion, 2005.
Kumin, Maxine. *Mites to Mastodons*. Illus. by Pamela Zagarenski. Houghton, 2006.
Larios, Julie. *Yellow Elephant*. Illus. by Julie Paschkis. Harcourt, 2006.
Larrick, Nancy. Section: "I'd Take the Hound with the Drooping Ears." *Piping Down the Valleys Wild*. Illus. by Ellen Raskin. Topeka, 1968.
Lewis, J. Patrick. *A Hippopotamusn't*. Illus. by Victoria Chess. Dial, 1990.
———. *Two-Legged, Four-Legged, No-Legged Rhymes*. Illus. by Pamela Paparone. Knopf, 1991.
Livingston, Myra Cohn. *If You Ever Meet a Whale*. Illus. by Leonard Everett Fisher. Holiday, 1992
Maddox, Marjorie. *A Crossing of Zebras: Animal Packs in Poetry*. Illus. by Philip Huber. Boyds Mills, 2008.
Martin, Bill, Jr. & Michael Sampson. Section: "Animals." *The Bill Martin Jr. Big Book of Poetry*. S & S, 2008.
Merriam, Eve. *Where Is Everybody?* Illus. by Diane de Groat. S & S, 1989.
Montalvo, Margarita. *Zoológico de Poemas = Poetry Zoo*. Scholastic, 2004.
Pearson, Susan. *Squeal and Squawk*. Illus. by David Slonim. Cavendish, 2004.
Prelutsky, Jack, sel. *The Beauty of the Beast*. Illus. by Meilo So. Knopf, 1997.
———. Sections: "Dogs and Cats and Bears and Bats" & "The Ways of Living Things." *The Random House Book of Poetry for Children*. Illus. by Arnold Lobel. Random, 1983.
Ruddell, Deborah. *A Whiff of Pine, A Hint of Skunk*. Illus. by Joan Rankin. S & S, 2009.
Ryder, Joanne. *Without Words*. Illus. by Barbara Sonneborn. Sierra Club, 1995.
Schertle, Alice. *Advice for a Frog*. Illus. by Norman Green. Lothrop, 1995.
———. *How Now Brown Cow?* Illus. by Amanda Schaffer. Harcourt, 1994.
Sierra, Judy. *Beastly Rhymes to Read After Dark*. Illus. by Brian Biggs. Knopf, 2008.
———. *There's a Zoo in Room 22*. Illus. by Barney Saltzberg. Harcourt, 2000.
Spinelli, Eileen. *Polar Bear, Arctic Hare*. Illus. by Eugenie Fernandes. Boyds Mills, 2007.
Whipple, Laura, sel. *Animals, Animals*. Illus. by Eric Carle. Putnam, 1989.
Wise, William. *Zany Zoo*. Illus. by Lynn Munsinger. Houghton, 2007.
Worth, Valerie. *Animal Poems*. Illus. by Steve Jenkins. Farrar, 2007.

Yolen, Jane. *Count Me a Rhyme.* Illus. by Jason Stemple. Boyds Mills, 2006.

Zolotow, Charlotte. Section: "Animals." *Everything Glistens and Everything Sings* Illus. by Margot Tomes. Harcourt, 1987.

Cats and Dogs

Because so many American children have cats and dogs as pets, they are often familiar with and interested in the qualities of these animals. It appears that poets for children agree. Some children don't or can't have cats or dogs, but they know famous pets from movies and television shows, and the pets of their friends and neighbors. Students might want to find out about when cats and dogs first became attached to humans. They might look at "The Irish Student and his Cat" from an anonymous illuminated manuscript of the eighth or ninth century, as an example of a person long ago who treasured his pet.

"For I Will Consider my Cat Jeoffry" by Christopher Smart describes all of the qualities of his cat. This poem might be used as a model for describing the qualities of a cat or dog, Gary Soto's "Ode to Mi Perrito" and "Ode to Mi Gato"' might encourage students to try writing an ode in honor of an animal. Students might want to make their own books of pet poems by collecting poems that reflect the qualities they see in dogs and cats.

Florian, Douglas. *Bow Wow Meow Meow: It's Rhyming Cats and Dogs.* Harcourt, 2003.

Hopkins, Lee Bennett, sel. *A Pet for Me.* Illus. by Jane Manning. HarperCollins, 2003.

Pearson, Susan. *Who Swallowed Harold? And Other Poems About Pets.* Illus. by David Slonim. Cavendish, 2005.

Salas, Laura Purdie. *A Fuzzy-Fast Blur.* Capstone, 2008.

Sidman, Joyce. *Meow Ruff.* Illus. by Michelle Berg. Houghton, 2006.

Soto, Gary. "Ode to Mi Perito" & "Ode to Mi Gato." *Neighborhood Odes.* Illus. by David Diaz. Harcourt, 1992.

Cats

Bartoletti, Susan Campbell. *Nobody's Nosier Than a Cat.* Illus. by Beppe Giacobbe. Hyperion, 2003.

Beard, Henry. *Poetry For Cats: The Definitive Anthology of Distinguished Feline Verse.* Illus. by Gary Zamchick. Villard, 1994.

Cameron, Alice. *The Cat Sat on the Mat.* Illus. by Carol Jones. Houghton, 1994.

Creech, Sharon. *Hate That Cat.* HarperCollins, 2008. (Novel in Verse)

De Regniers, Beatrice Schenk. *So Many Cats!* Illus. by Ellen Weiss. Houghton, 1985.

Duncan, Lois. *I Walk at Night.* Illus. by Steve Johnson and Lou Fancher. Viking, 2000.

Ehlert, Lois. *Feathers for Lunch.* Harcourt, 1990.

———. *Top Cat.* Harcourt, 1998.

Farjeon, Eleanor. *Cats Sleep Anywhere.* Illus. by Anne Mortimer. HarperCollins, 1996.

Franco, Betsy. *A Curious Collection of Cats.* Illus. by Michael Wertz. Tricycle, 2008.

Grimes, Nikki. *When Gorilla Goes Walking.* Illus. by Shane Evans. Scholastic, 2007.

"The Irish Student and His Cat." In Krull, Kathleen. *A Pot O' Gold.* Illus. by David McPhail. Hyperion, 2004.

Johnston, Tony. *Cat, What Is That?* Illus. by Wendell Minor. HarperCollins, 2001.

Kirk, Daniel. *Cat Power!* Hyperion, 2007. (With CD)

Kuskin, Karla. Section: "I Do Not Wish I Were a Cat." *Moon, Have You Met My Mother?* Illus. by Sergio Ruzzier. HarperCollins, 2003.

———. *So What's It Like to be a Cat?* Illus. by Betsy Lewin. Atheneum, 2005.

———. *The Upstairs Cat.* Illus. by Howard Fine. Clarion, 1997.

Lach, William, ed. *Curious Cats: In Art and Poetry.* Atheneum, 1999.

Lewin, Betsy. *Cat Count*. Holt, 2003.
Myers, Christopher. *Black Cat*. Scholastic, 1999.
Reibstein, Mark. *Wabi Sabi*. Illus. by Ed Young. Little, 2008.
Rylant, Cynthia. *Boris*. Harcourt, 2005. (Novel in Verse)
———. *Cat Heaven*. Scholastic, 1997.
Saul, Carol P. *Barn Cat: A Counting Book*. Illus. by Mary Azarian. Little, 1998.
Schoenherr, Ian. *Cat and Mouse*. HarperCollins, 2008.
Smart, Christopher. "For I Will Consider My Cat Jeoffry." In Willard, Nancy, col. *Step Lightly*. Harcourt, 1998.
Swenson, May. "Five Cat Poems." *The Complete Poems to Solve*. Illus. by Christy Hale. Macmillan, 1993.
Thompson, Lauren. *How Many Cats?* Illus. by Robin Eley. Disney, 2009.

Dogs

Bartoletti, Susan Campbell. *Nobody's Diggier Than a Dog*. Illus. by Beppe Giacobbe. Hyperion, 2005.
Beaumont, Karen. *Doggone Dogs!* Dial, 2008.
———. *Move Over, Rover!* Illus. by Jane Dyer. Harcourt, 2006.
Creech, Sharon. *Love That Dog*.HarperCollins, 2001. (Novel in Verse)
Dewdney, Anna. *Grumpy Gloria*. Viking, 2006.
Ehlert, Lois. *Wag a Tail*. Harcourt, 2007.
Frost, Helen. *Diamond Willow*. Farrar, 2008. (Novel in Verse)
George, Kristine O'Connell. *Little Dog and Duncan*. Illus. by June Otani. Clarion, 2002.
———. *Little Dog Poems*. Illus. by June Otani. Clarion, 1999.
Gottfried, Maya. *Good Dog*. Illus. by Robert Rahway Zakanitch. Knopf, 2005.
Johnston, Tony. *It's About Dogs*. Raintree, 2000.
Kirk, Daniel. *Dogs Rule!* Disney, 2003. (With CD)
Kuskin, Karla. *City Dog*. Clarion, 1994.
MacLachlan, Patricia & Emily MacLachlan Charest. *Once I Ate a Pie*. Illus. by Katy Schneider. HarperCollins, 2006.
O'Hair, Margaret. *My Pup*. Illus. by Tammie Lyon. Cavendish, 2008.
Sidman, Joyce. *The World According to Dog*. Illus. by Doug Mindell. Houghton, 2003.
Singer, Marilyn. *It's Hard To Read a Map With a Beagle on Your Lap*. Illus. by Clement Oubrerie. Holt, 1993.
Sklansky, Amy E. *From the Doghouse*. Illus. by Karla Firehammer, et al. Holt, 2002.
Wood, Audrey. *A Dog Needs a Bone*. Scholastic, 2007.

Camels

People have a hard time taking camels seriously because of their unusual looks. Mark Twain said of the camel: "When he is down on all his knees, flat on his breast to receive his load, he looks something like a goose swimming; and when he is upright he looks like an ostrich with an extra set of legs." (Geismar, 1976). An anonymous quotation says, "A camel is a horse designed by a committee." (*Oxford Dictionary of Modern Quotations*, 1991). Students who have loved Mithoo in Suzanne Fisher Staples' *Shabanu* will have seen another side of the camel and understand the importance of this seemingly aloof creature in desert climates. Students might want to study more about the camel, why it is uniquely adapted to the desert in which it lives, and then write a poem in praise of the camel. Or, they can select a favorite animal of their own, look for the science, stories, and poems about it and create their own unit of study.

Belloc, Hilaire. "Camel." *The Bad Child's Book of Beasts; More Beasts for Worse Children*. Dover, 1961.
Carryl, Charles Edward. *The Camel's Lament*. Illus. by Charles Santore. Random, 2004.

Cassedy, Sylvia. "Camel." In Prelutsky, Jack. *The Beauty of the Beast*. Illus. by Meilo So. Knopf, 1997.

Esbensen, Barbara Juster. "Tonk, Tonk! Do You Hear Bells?" *Words with Wrinkled Knees*. Illus. by John Stadler. HarperCollins, 1987.

Farber, Norma. "Camel." *When It Snowed That Night*. Illus. by Petra Mathers. HarperCollins, 1993.

Florian, Douglas. "The Bactrian Camel." *Mammalabilia*. Harcourt, 2000.

Hoberman, Mary Ann. "Camel." *The Llama Who Had No Pajama*. Illus. by Betty Fraser. Harcourt, 1998.

Katz, Bobbi. "Camel Question." In Janeczko, Paul B. *Hey You!* Illus. by Robert Rayevsky. HarperCollins, 2007.

Kipling, Rudyard. "Commissariat Camels." In Whipple, Laura. *Animals, Animals*. Putnam, 1989.

———. 'How the Camel Got His Hump." *The Just So Stories*. Illus. by Barry Moser. HarperCollins, 1996. (Prose)

Kumin, Maxine. "Camel." *Mites to Mastodons*. Illus. by Pamela Zagarenski. Houghton, 2006.

Lewis, J. Patrick. "How Many Humps?" *Doodle Dandies*. Illus. by Lisa Desimini. S & S, 1998.

———. "How to Tell a Camel." *A Hippopotamusn't*. Illus. by Victoria Chess. Dial, 1990.

Lobel, Arnold. "The Camel Dances." *Fables*. HarperCollins, 1980. (Prose)

Lutz, Gertrude May. "African Sunrise." In Dunning, Stephen, et al. *Reflections on a Gift of Watermelon Pickle*. HarperCollins, 1967.

Nash, Ogden. "The Camel." In De Regniers, Beatrice Schenk. *Sing a Song of Popcorn*. Scholastic, 1988.

Norris, Leslie. "The Camels, The Kings' Camels." In Duncan, Beverly K. *Christmas in the Stable*. Harcourt, 1990.

Prelutsky, Jack. "The Camelberta Peaches." *Scranimals*. Illus. by Peter Sis. Greenwillow, 2002.

Shakespeare, William. "Song of the Camels." In Ferris, Helen. *Favorite Poems Old and New*. Random, 1957, 2009.

Silverstein, Shel. "They've Put a Brassiere on the Camel." *A Light in the Attic*. HarperCollins, 1981.

Soto, Gary. "The Last Camel of Aswan." *Worlds Apart*. Illus. by Greg Clarke. Putnam, 2005.

Staples, Suzanne Fisher. *Shabanu*. Knopf, 1989. (prose)

Unobagha, Uzo. "Drinking, Drinking" & "Down Along the Camel's Hump." *Off to the Sweet Shores of Africa*. Illus. by Julia Cairns. Chronicle, 2000.

Worth, Valerie. "Camels." *Animal Poems*. Illus. by Steve Jenkins. Farrar, 2007.

Bats

Bats have the characteristics of several different types of creatures. They look somewhat like mice, fly like birds, and use sonar to guide them as some underwater creatures do. Anyone who spends times outdoors can appreciate bats, which can eat more than half their weight in insects in one night of hunting. Science teachers in upper elementary grades have begun creating units on bats that culminate in the building of bat houses that will attract bats to areas with lots of mosquitoes such as parks and riverbanks.

Bats struggle with disease. Scientists are working to discover why White Nose Syndrome is killing many bats in New England. Bats are also susceptible to rabies. Because of several recent scares involving bats, teachers should caution students against picking up dead or dying bats. If a bat can be caught, chances are good that it is sick.

Randall Jarrell's novel *The Bat-Poet* shows the bat in a kindly light. Unlike his brothers and sisters, the young bat poet wants to stay awake during the day so that he can closely observe the world around him for details to put in his poems. His poems, including a lovely poem about mother bats tenderly enfolding their sleeping children with their wings, are included in the novel. The bat poet's image of the bat, which links it to other mammals who care for their young, can also be found in Alice Schertle's "Fruit Bats," illustrated by Norman Green so that you must turn the book to the side in order to see the bats hanging upside down to sleep. Theodore Roethke's poem, "The Bat" suggests that what makes us uncomfortable is that "mice with wings can wear a human face."

Ackerman, Diane. "Bats, When They Are on the Wing . . . " *Animal Sense*. Illus. by Peter Sis. Knopf, 2003.
Dotlich, Rebecca Kai. "Black Bat." *Sweet Dreams of the Wild*. Illus. by Katharine Dodge. Boyds Mills, 1996.
Esbensen, Barbara Juster. "Every night . . . " *Words With Wrinkled Knees*. Illus. by John Stadler. Crowell, 1986.
"Five Batty Bats." *Scared Silly!* Illus. and comp. by Marc Brown. Little, 1994.
Florian, Douglas. "The Bat." *Beast Feast*. Harcourt, 1994.
———. "The Bats." *Zoo's Who*. Harcourt, 2005.
Heard, Georgia. "Bat Patrol." *Creatures of Earth, Sea and Sky*. Illus. by Jennifer Owings Dewey. Boyds Mills, 1992.
Herschberger, Ruth. "The Bat." Dunning, Stephen, et al. *Reflections on a Gift of Watermelon Pickle*. Harper Collins, 1967.
Hubbell, Patricia. "Flittermice." *Earthmates*. Illus. by Jean Cassels. Cavendish, 2000.
Hughes, Ted. "The Beggarly Bat." *Collected Poems for Children*. Illus. by Raymond Briggs. Farrar, 2005.
Jarrell, Randall. *The Bat-Poet*. Illus. by Maurice Sendak. Macmillan, 1964.
Levy, Constance. "Sleepytime." *I'm Going To Pet a Worm Today*. Illus. by Ronald Himler. McElderry, 1991.
Lewis, J, Patrick. "The Nose." In Janeczko, Paul B. *A Foot in the Mouth*. Illus. by Chris Raschka. Candlewick, 2009.
Lies, Brian. *Bats at the Beach*. Houghton, 2006.
———. *Bats at the Library*. Houghton, 2008.
Merriam, Eve. "Bat." *Halloween ABC*. Illus. by Lane Smith. S & S, 1987.
Peavy, Linda. "Suspended." In Duncan, Beverly K. *Christmas in the Stable*. Harcourt, 1990.
Roethke, Theodore. "The Bat." Dunning, Stephen, et al. *Reflections on a Gift of Watermelon Pickle*. HarperCollins, 1967.
Schertle, Alice. "Fruit Bats." *Advice For a Frog*. Illus. by Norman Green. Lothrop, 1995.
Sierra, Judy. "Mary Had a Vampire Bat." *Monster Goose*. Illus. by Jack E. Davis. Harcourt, 2001.
Singer, Marilyn. "Bat." *Fireflies at Midnight*. Illus. by Ken Robbins. Atheneum, 2003.
Sklansky, Amy E. "The Bat" & "Night Flight." *Skeleton Bones and Goblin Groans*. Illus. by Karen Dismukes. Holt, 2004.
Worth, Valerie. "Bat." *All the Small Poems and Fourteen More*. Illus. by Natalie Babbitt. Farrar, 1994.

Birds

Bird study and bird watching encourage close observation, data collection, use of reference materials, and other aspects of science. Poets sing the praises of birds for their beauty and their song. They may sing the praises of soaring eagles and hawks, or the glorious song of meadowlarks. They also find beauty in the least-loved birds. Karla Kuskin writes a poem to the pigeon. April Pulley Sayre's poetic picture book *Vulture View* invites readers to consider these birds with new eyes.

Adoff, Arnold. *Birds: Poems*. Illus. by Troy Howell. HarperCollins, 1982.
Baylor, Byrd. *Hawk, I'm Your Brother*. Illus. by Peter Parnall. Scribners, 1976.
Ehlert, Lois. *Feathers for Lunch*. Harcourt, 1990.
Ferris, Helen, ed. Section: "Bird-Watcher." *Favorite Poems Old and New*. Random, 1957, 2009.
Fleischman, Paul. *I Am Phoenix*. Illus. by Ken Nutt. HarperCollins, 1985.
Florian, Douglas. *On the Wing*. Harcourt, 1996.
Jonas, Ann. *Bird Talk*. Greenwillow, 1999.
Kiesler, Kate. *Wings on the Wind*. Clarion, 2002.
Kuskin, Karla. Section: "Pigeon Is a Pretty Word." *Moon, Have You Met My Mother?* Illus. by Sergio Ruzzier. HarperCollins, 2003.
Larrick, Nancy, ed. Section" I Heard a Bird Sing." *Piping Down the Valleys Wild*. Illus. by Ellen Raskin. Topeka, 1968.
McMillan, Bruce. *Puffins Climb, Penguins Rhyme*. Harcourt, 1995.

Minor, Wendell & Florence Minor. *If You Were a Penguin*. HarperCollins, 2009.

Prelutsky, Jack. Section "Hollow-Boned Singers." *The Beauty of the Beast*. Illus. by Meilo So. Knopf, 1997.

Rosen, Michael. *The Cuckoo's Haiku*. Illus. by Stan Fellows. Candlewick, 2009.

Ryder, Joanne. *Wild Birds*. Illus. by Susan Estelle Kwas. HarperCollins, 2003.

Sayre, April Pulley. *Bird, Bird, Bird: A Chirping Chant*. Northword, 2007.

———. *Vulture View*. Illus. by Steve Jenkins. Holt, 2007.

Sierra, Judy. *Antarctic Antics*. Illus. by José Aruego & Ariane Dewey. Harcourt, 1998.

Swinburne, Stephen R. *Unbeatable Beaks*. Illus. by Joan Paley. Holt, 1999.

Van Wassenhove, Sue. *The Seldom-Ever-Shady Glades*. Boyds Mills, 2008.

Yolen, Jane. *Fine Feathered Friends*. Illus. by Jason Stemple. Boyds Mills, 2004.

———. *Wild Wings*. Illus. by Jason Stemple. Boyds Mills, 2002.

———. *Bird Watch*. Illus. by Ted Lewin. Philomel, 1990.

Hummingbirds

Hummingbirds are not only beautiful, changing colors as they catch the light in different ways, but their distinctive movements and humming sound are appealing. But these tiny creatures are also ferocious with one another as they defend the flowers and feeders near their nests. The roar of two tiny bright missiles as they zoom inches from your garden hat is exhilarating, amusing, and just a bit frightening. Keith Baker's *Little Green* captures the color and movements of the hummingbird for younger students. Joanne Ryder's *Dancers In the Garden* and Kristine O'Connell George's notebook of hummingbird observations, *Hummingbird Nest*, beautifully mix science with poetry for older students.

Baker, Keith. *Little Green*. Harcourt, 2001.

Dotlich, Rebecca Kai. "Hummingbird, Hummingbird . . .?" *Sweet Dreams of the Wild*. Illus. by Katherine Dodge. Boyds Mills, 1996.

Florian, Douglas. "The Hummingbird." *On the Wing*. Harcourt, 1996.

George, Kristine O'Connell. *Hummingbird Nest*. Illus. by Barry Moser. Harcourt, 2004.

Groves, Paul. "Humming Bird." In Prelutsky, Jack. *The Beauty of the Beast*. Illus. by Meilo So. Knopf, 1997.

Heard, Georgia. "Hummingbird." *Creatures of Earth, Sea, and Sky*. Illus. by Jennifer Owings Dewey. Boyds Mills, 1992.

Kemp, Harry Hibbard. "The Humming Bird." In Ferris, Helen. *Favorite Poems Old and New*. Random, 1957, 2009.

Lawson, JonArno. "Hummingbird." *Black Stars in a White Night Sky*. Illus. by Sherwin Tjia. Boyds Mills, 2006.

Levy, Constance. "The Guys and I and the Hummingbird." *I'm Going to Pet a Worm Today*. Illus. by Ronald Himler. McElderry, 1991.

———. "Hummingbird with Red (Archilochus Colubris.)" *A Tree Place*. Illus. by Robert Sabuda. McElderry, 1994.

Lewis, J. Patrick. "Yummy Hummingbird." *A Hippopotamusn't*. Illus. by Victoria Chess. Dial, 1990.

Merriam, Eve. "Ruby-Throated Hummingbird." *The Singing Green*. Illus. by Kathleen Collins Howell. Morrow, 1992.

Ryder, Joanne. *Dancers in the Garden*. Illus. by Judith Lopez. Sierra Club, 1992.

Worth, Valerie. "Hummingbird." *All the Small Poems and Fourteen More*. Illus. by Natalie Babbitt. Farrar, 1994. (Also in *Peacock*)

Yolen, Jane. "Hummingbird." *Least Things*. Illus. by Jason Stemple. Boyds Mills, 2003.

———. "Hummer." *Wild Wings*. Illus. by Jason Stemple. Boyds Mills, 2002.

———. "Time Piece." *Bird Watch*. Illus. by Ted Lewin. Philomel, 1990.

Crows

Crows are not well-loved birds, perhaps because they seem unfazed by humans' attempts to get rid of them. Poets find crows fascinating. I call crows the "loyal" birds because they don't abandon Wyoming in the cold winters. Their black sheen against the snow and their raucous calls are good company. Joanne Ryder refers to crows as the "stay-at-home" birds, a cozy way to name them. Marilyn Singer has written collection of poems about them, *The Company of Crows*. As students look at various poems about these birds, they can watch for the ways poets use imagery, word arrangement, and sound qualities to capture their natures.

Bodecker, N. M. "Footprints of a Sparrow." In Bauer, Caroline Feller. *Snowy Day*. Illus. by Margot Tomes. HarperCollins, 1986.

Brown, Margaret Wise. "Wild Black Crows" & "Those Crazy Crows." *Nibble, Nibble*. Illus. by Leonard Weisgard. HarperCollins, 1959.

Coatsworth, Elizabeth. "March." In Larrick, Nancy. *Piping Down the Valleys Wild*. Illus. by Ellen Raskin. Topeka, 1968.

Cunningham, Julia. "Crows on a Certain Evening." *The Stable Rat*. Illus. by Anita Lobel. Greenwillow, 2001.

Drake, Leah Bodine. "The Crows." In Dunning, Stephen, et al. *Reflections on a Gift of Watermelon Pickle*. HarperCollins, 1967.

Florian, Douglas. "The Common Crow." *On the Wing*. Harcourt, 1996.

Froman, Robert. "Sky Day Dream." In Janeczko, Paul B. *A Poke in the I*. Illus. by Chris Raschka. Candlewick, 2001.

Frost, Robert. "Dust of Snow." *You Come Too*. Illus. by Thomas W. Nason. Holt, 1959. (Also in *The Beauty of the Beast*)

———."The Last Word of a Bluebird As Told to a Child." In Kennedy, Caroline. *A Family of Poems*. Illus. by Jon J. Muth. Hyperion, 2005. (Also in *The Bill Martin Jr. Big Book of Poetry*)

Harrison, David L. "Corn." *Farmer's Garden*. Illus. by Arden Johnson-Petrov. Boyds Mills, 2000.

Hines, Anna Grossnickle. "Ballet." *Pieces*.HarperCollins, 2001.

Hubbell, Patricia. "Crows." *Earthmates*. Illus. by Jean Cassels. Cavendish, 2000.

Hughes, Ted. "Crow" & "Horrible Song." *Collected Poems for Children*. Illus. by Raymond Briggs. Farrar, 2005.

Kennedy, X. J. "Ten Billion Crows." In Prelutsky, Jack. *The Beauty of the Beast*. Illus. by Meilo So. Knopf, 1997.

Keyser, Gustave. "Absolutes." In Dunning, Stephen, et al. *Reflections on a Gift of Watermelon Pickle*. Harper Collins, 1967.

Levy, Constance. "Crow Tree." *I'm Going to Pet a Worm Today*. Illus. by Ronald Himler. McElderry, 1991.

———. "Ice Talk." *A Tree Place*. Illus. by Robert Sabuda. McElderry, 1994.

Maddox, Marjorie. "A Murder of Crows." *A Crossing of Zebras*. Illus. by Philip Huber. Boyds Mills, 2008.

McCord, David. "Crows" & "Many Crows, Any Owl." *One at a Time*. Illus. by Henry B. Kane. Little, 1986.

Medina, Jane. "Mrs. Farley's Crows." *The Dream on Blanca's Wall = El Sueño Pegado en la Pared De Blanca*. Illus. by Robert Casilla. Boyds Mills, 2004.

Miller, Kate. "King Crow." *Poems in Black and White*. Boyds Mills, 2007.

Moore, Lilian. "Scarecrow Complains." In Prelutsky, Jack . *The 20th Century Children's Poetry Treasury*. Illus. by Meilo So. Knopf, 1999.

Mora, Pat. "One Blue Door." *This Big Sky*. Illus. by Steve Jenkins. Scholastic, 1998.

Nyhart, Nina. "Scarecrow's Dream." In Janeczko, Paul B. *Dirty Laundry Pile*. Illus. by Melissa Sweet. Harper Collins, 2001.

Prelutsky, Jack. "Oh Farmer . . . " *Beneath a Blue Umbrella*. Illus. by Garth Williams. Greenwillow, 1987.

———. "Raucously . . . " *If Not for the Cat*. Illus. by Ted Rand. HarperCollins, 2004.

———. "Today Is a Day To Crow About." *The New Kid on the Block*. Illus. by James Stevenson. Greenwillow, 1984.

Roemer, Heidi B. "I Like Crows." *Come to My Party*. Illus. by Hideo Takahashi. Holt, 2004.

Ryder, Joanne. *Wild Birds*. Illus. by Susan Estelle Kwas. HarperCollins, 2003.
Schertle, Alice. "Showing the Wind." *A Lucky Thing*. Illus. by Wendell Minor. Harcourt, 1999.
Singer, Marilyn. *The Company of Crows.*. Illus. by Linda Saport. Clarion, 2002.
Spires, Elizabeth. "Three Crows." *I Heard God Talking to Me*. Farrar, 2009.
Thurman, Judith. "New Notebook." In Prelutsky, Jack. *The 20th Century Children's Poetry Treasury*. Illus. by Meilo So. Knopf, 1999.
Wong, Janet. "Low Crow." *Twist: Yoga Poems*. Illus. by Julie Paschkis. McElderry, 2007.
Worth, Valerie. "Crows." *All the Small Poems and Fourteen More*. Illus. by Natalie Babbitt. Farrar, 1994.
Yolen, Jane. "Crow Call." *Bird Watch*. Illus. by Ted Lewin. Philomel, 1990.

Eggs and Hatching

Eggs cross the groups of animals, being common to birds, reptiles and amphibians, and insects. Ruth Heller's *Chickens Aren't the Only Ones* introduces all of the egg layers in rollicking rhyme. Dianna Aston's *An Egg Is Quiet* describes the qualities of many types of eggs. Karla Kuskin's "My Home Is a White Dome," asks readers to imagine themselves inside that egg and awaking as it cracks open. Aileen Fisher wonders how the chick knows how to get out of the egg. Valerie Worth's poem "Egg" compares the "quirk and freak and whim" of the hen with the solid calm of the egg.

Aston, Dianna. *An Egg Is Quiet*. Illus. by Sylvia Long. Chronicle, 2006.
Crotty, K. M. "Birth of Sue." *Dinosongs: Poems to Celebrate a T. Rex Named Sue*. Illus. by Kurt Vargö. Scholastic, 2000. (With CD)
Finney, Eric. "Chicks." In Yolen, Jane & Andrew Fusek Peters. *Here's a Little Poem*. Illus. by Polly Dunbar. Candlewick, 2007.
Fisher, Aileen L. "Baby Chick." In Martin, Bill, Jr. & Sampson, Michael. *The Bill Martin Jr. Big Book of Poetry*. S & S, 2008.
George, Kristine O'Connell. "Egg." *The Great Frog Race*. Illus. by Kate Kiesler. Clarion, 1997. (Also in *The 20th Century Children's Poetry Treasury*)
Heller, Ruth. *Chickens Aren't the Only Ones*. Grosset, 1981.
Hoberman, Mary Ann. "Eggs." *The Llama Who Had No Pajama*. Illus. by Betty Frasier. Harcourt, 1998.
Kuskin, Kara. "My Home Is a White Dome." *Moon, Have You Met My Mother?* Illus. by Sergio Ruzzier. Harper Collins, 2003.
Lawson, JonArno. "Humpty Dumpty." *Black Stars in a White Night Sky*. Illus. by Sherwin Tjia. Boyds Mills, 2006.
McCord, David. "The Importance of Eggs." *One at a Time*. Illus. by Henry B. Kane. Little, 1986.
Prelutsky, Jack. "I Am Waiting . . . " *The Dragons Are Singing Tonight*. Illus. by Peter Sis. Greenwillow, 1993.
———. "I'm Trapped in an Egg." *My Dog May Be a Genius*. Illus. by James Stevenson. HarperCollins, 2008.
Sandburg, Carl. "Look at Six Eggs." In Kiesler, Kate. *Wings on the Wind*. Clarion, 2002.
Steig, Jeanne. "The Enigmatic Egg." *Alpha Beta Chowder*. Illus. by William Steig. HarperCollins, 1992.
Worth, Valerie. "Egg." *All the Small Poems and Fourteen More*. Illus. by Natalie Babbitt. Farrar, 1994.

Reptiles and Amphibians

Florian, Douglas. *Lizards, Frogs, and Polliwogs*. Harcourt, 2001.
Prelutsky, Jack: Section "Dragons In Miniature." *The Beauty of the Beast*. Illus. by Meilo So. Knopf, 1997.

Life Cycles: Frogs and Toads

Cyrus, Kurt. "Used to Be a Pollywog . . . " *Oddhopper Opera*. Harcourt, 2001.

Florian, Douglas. "The Polliwogs." *Lizards, Frogs, and Polliwogs*. Harcourt, 2001
George, Kristine O'Connell. "Polliwogs" & "The Great Frog Race." *The Great Frog Race*. Illus. by Kate Kiesler. Clarion, 1997.
Harley, Avis. "Explode Into Song." *Fly with Poetry*.Boyds Mills, 2000.
Hoberman, Mary Ann. "Frog." *The Llama Who Had No Pajama*. Illus. by Betty Frasier. Harcourt, 1998.
Kumin, Maxine. "Polliwogs." *Mites to Mastodons*. Illus. by Pamela Zagarenski. Houghton, 2006.
Kuskin, Karla. "A Frog's Dream" & "Over a Stone." *Moon, Have You Met My Mother?* Illus. by Sergio Ruzzier. HarperCollins, 2003.
Larios, Julie. "Green Frog." *Yellow Elephant*. Illus. by Julie Paschkis. Harcourt, 2006.
Levy, Constance. "Camouflaged Amphibian." *A Tree Place*. Illus. by Robert Sabuda. McElderry, 1994.
Park, Linda Sue. "Frog." *Tap Dancing on the Roof*. Illus. by Istvan Banyai. Clarion, 2007.
Ryder, Joanne. *Toad by the Road*. Illus. by Maggie Kneen. Holt, 2007.
Schertle, Alice. "One" & "A Traditional Frog's Curse." *A Lucky Thing*. Illus. by Wendell Minor. Harcourt, 1999.
Sidman, Joyce. "Don't I Look Delicious?" *Butterfly Eyes*. Illus. by Beth Krommes. Houghton, 2006.
Singer, Marilyn. "Frog." *Fireflies at Midnight*. Illus. by Ken Robbins. Atheneum, 2003.
Worth, Valerie. "Frog" & "Toad." *All the Small Poems and Fourteen More*. Illus. by Natalie Babbitt. Farrar, 1994.

Insects

Bulion, Leslie. *Hey There, Stink Bug!* Illus. by Leslie Evans. Charlesbridge, 2006.
Cyrus, Kurt. *Oddhopper Opera*. Harcourt, 2007.
Fisher, Aileen. *When It Comes to Bugs*. Illus. by Chris Degen & Bruce Degen. HarperCollins, 1986.
Fleischman, Paul. *Joyful Noise*. Illus. by Eric Beddows. HarperCollins, 1988.
Fleming, Denise. *Beetle Bop*. Harcourt, 2007.
Florian, Douglas. *Insectlopedia*. Harcourt, 1998.
Hanson, Warren. *Bugtown Boogie*. Illus. by Steve Johnson & Lou Fancher. HarperCollins, 2008.
Harley, Avis. *The Monarch's Progress*. Boyds Mills, 2008.
Hopkins, Lee Bennett, sel. *Flit, Flutter, Fly!* Illus. by Peter Palagonia. Doubleday, 1992.
Krebs, Laurie. *The Beeman*. Illus. by Melissa Iwai. National Geographic, 2002.
Morrow, Barbara Olenyik. *Mr. Mosquito Put on His Tuxedo*. Illus. by Ponder Goembel. Holiday, 2009.
Pinczes, Elinor. *A Remainder of One*. Illus. by Bonnie MacKain. Houghton, 1995.
Prelutsky, Jack. Section "In Trillions We Thrive." *The Beauty of the Beast*. Illus. by Meilo So. Knopf, 1997.
Sayre, April Pulley. *Ant, Ant, Ant! An Insect Chant*. Illus, by Trip Park. Northwords, 2005.
———. *Army Ant Parade*. Illus. by Rick Chrustowski. Holt, 2002.

Life Cycles: Butterflies

Adoff, Arnold. "On May Day." *In for Winter, Out for Spring*. Illus. by Jerry Pinkney. Harcourt, 1991.
Bagert, Brod. "Caterpillars." In Prelutsky, Jack. *The Beauty of the Beast*. Illus. by Meilo So. Knopf, 1997.
Dotlich, Rebecca Kai. "Caterpillar, Caterpillar . . . " *Sweet Dreams of the Wild*. Illus. by Katharine Dodge. Boyds Mills, 1996.
———. "I'm Fastened Firm Upon This Limb . . . ." *When Riddles Come Rumbling*. Boyds Mills, 2001.
Ehlert, Lois. *Waiting for Wings*. Harcourt, 2001.
Fisher, Aileen. "Caterpillars." In Martin, Bill, Jr. & Michael Sampson. *The Bill Martin Jr. Big Book of Poetry*. S & S, 2008. (Also in *Surprises*)
———. "Twice Born" & "Butterfly Wings." *I Heard a Bluebird Sing*. Illus. by Jennifer Emery. Boyds Mills, 2002.
Florian, Douglas. "Caterpillar" & "The Monarch Butterfly." *Insectlopedia*. Harcourt, 1998.

Franklin, Benjamin. "Butterfly." In Hopkins, Lee Bennett. *Flit, Flutter, Fly.* Illus. by Peter Palagonia. Doubleday, 1992.

Harley, Avis. "Editing the Chrysalis." *Fly with Poetry.* Boyds Mills, 2000.

———. *The Monarch's Progress.* Boyds Mills, 2008

———. "Orange Flame Butterfly," "Viceroy," & "Zebra Butterfly." *Leap Into Poetry.* Boyds Mills, 2002.

Johnston, Tony. "Caterpillar." In Hopkins, Lee Bennett. *Small Talk.* Illus. by Susan Gaber. Harcourt, 1995.

Katz, Susan. "Live Butterflies." *Mrs. Brown on Exhibit: And Other Museum Poems.* Illus. by R. W. Alley. S & S, 2002.

Lewis, J. Patrick. "The Butterfly Is . . . " *Doodle Dandies.* Illus. by Lisa Desimini. S & S, 1998.

———. "Conversation on a Leaf." *Please Bury Me in the Library.* Illus. by Kyle M. Stone. Harcourt, 2005.

McCord, David. "Cocoon." *One at a Time.* Illus. by Henry B. Kane. Little, 1986. (Also in *The Beauty of the Beast*)

Rosenblatt, Joe. "I Get High on Butterflies." In Booth, David, sel. *'Til All the Stars Have Fallen.* Illus. by Kady MacDonald Denton. Viking, 1990.

Rossetti, Christina. "The Caterpillar." In De Regniers, Beatrice Schenk. *Sing A Song of Popcorn.* Scholastic, 1988. (Also in *Tomie De Paola's Rhyme Time*)

Ryder, Joanne. *Where Butterflies Grow.* Illus. by Lynne Cherry. Dutton, 1989.

Sayre, April Pulley. "Question Mark Butterfly" & "Comma Butterfly." *Ant, Ant, Ant! An Insect Chant.* Illus. by Trip Park. Northwords, 2005.

Sidman, Joyce. "Ultraviolet." *Butterfly Eyes.* Illus. by Beth Krommes. Houghton, 2006.

Singer, Marilyn. "Monarch Butterfly." *Fireflies at Midnight.* Illus. by Ken Robbins. Atheneum, 2003.

Swenson, May. "Was Worm." *The Complete Poems to Solve.* Illus. by Christy Hale. Macmillan, 1993.

Worth, Valerie. "Caterpillar." *All the Small Poems and Fourteen More.* Illus. by Natalie Babbitt. Farrar, 1994.

Yolen, Jane. "Caterpillar" & "Butterfly." *Least Things.* Illus. by Jason Stemple. Boyds Mills, 2003.

———. "Caterpillar's Lullaby." In Hopkins, Lee Bennett. *Small Talk.* Illus. by Susan Gaber. Harcourt, 1995.

Spiders

Spiders are not insects, but poems about them are often found in this area of animal poetry collections. Many people dread and fear spiders. Learning more about them, and looking at the ways they are portrayed in poetry may help students (and their teachers) to overcome these feelings. Naomi Shihab Nye writes lovingly of a spider "Rose," who "keeps spinning her elegant web inside us . . . " long after she has disappeared. Others love the spider for its patience, its persistence, and for eating bothersome insects. Kate Hovey's *Arachne Speaks* ties spider science to the myth from which Arachnids get their name, and makes a tremendous read-aloud or performance piece. In a lighter mood, Judy Sierra creates a parody of "The Itsy Bitsy Spider" that might be a model for other spider poems.

Dakos, Kalli. "Something Splendid." *Don't Read This Book, Whatever You Do!* Illus. by G. Brian Karas. S & S, 1993.

Dotlich, Rebecca Kai. "Black Spider, Black Spider, Where Do You Sleep?" *Sweet Dreams of the Wild.* Illus. by Katharine Dodge. Boyds Mills, 1996.

———. "You Spin a Zillion . . . " & "Web." *When Riddles Come Rumbling.* Boyds Mills, 2001.

Florian, Douglas. "The Black Widow Spider." *Insectlopedia.* Harcourt, 1998.

Haraway, Fran. "Tarantula." In Hopkins, Lee Bennett. *A Pet for Me.* Illus. by Jane Manning. HarperCollins, 2003.

Heard, Georgia. "The Orb Weaver." *Creatures of Earth, Sea and Sky.* Illus. by Jennifer Owings Dewey. Boyds Mills, 1992.

Hoberman, Mary Ann. "The Spider's Web." *A Fine Fat Pig.* Illus. by Malcah Zeldis. HarperCollins, 1991.

Hubbell, Patricia. "Night." In Larrick, Nancy. *Piping Down the Valleys Wild.* Illus. by Ellen Raskin. Topeka, 1968.

Kuskin, Karla. "Spiders Are All Right, I Guess." *Moon, Have You Met My Mother?* Illus. by Sergio Ruzzier. HarperCollins, 2003. (Also in *The Sky Is Always the Sky*)
Nye, Naomi Shihab. "Rose." *A Maze Me*. Greenwillow, 2005.
Schertle, Alice. "Spider." *Keepers*. Illus. by Ted Rand. Lothrop, 1996.
Sierra, Judy. "The Itsy Bitsy Spider." *Monster Goose*. Illus. by Jack E. Davis. Harcourt, 2001.
Silverstein, Shel. "The Weavers." *Falling Up*. HarperCollins, 1996.
Singer, Marilyn. "Spider." *Fireflies at Midnight*. Illus. by Ken Robbins. Atheneum, 2003.
Swenson, Mae. "Geometrid." *The Complete Poems to Solve*. Illus. by Christy Hale. Macmillan, 1993.
Worth, Valerie. "Spider." *Animal Poems*. Illus. by Steve Jenkins. Farrar, 2007.
———. "Web." *All the Small Poems and Fourteen More*. Illus. by Natalie Babbitt. Farrar, 1994.
Yolen, Jane. "Six Spiders Spinning." *Count Me a Rhyme*. Illus. by Jason Stemple. Boyds Mills, 2006.
———. "Spider." *Least Things*. Illus. by Jason Stemple. Boyds Mills, 2003.

Fish and Other Water Creatures

Cyrus, Kurt. *Hotel Deep*. Harcourt, 2005.
Florian, Douglas. *In the Swim*. Harcourt, 1997.
Harley, Avis. *Sea Stars*. Illus. by Margaret Butschler. Boyds Mills, 2006.
Prelutsky, Jack. Section: "Jubilant, We Swim." *The Beauty of the Beast*. Illus. by Meilo So. Knopf, 1997.
Rose, Deborah Lee. *One Nighttime Sea*. Illus. by Steve Jenkins. Scholastic, 2003.
Ryder, Joanne. *Winter Whale*. Illus. by Michael Rothman. Morrow, 1991.
Sayre, April Pulley. *Trout Are Made of Trees*. Illus. by Kate Endle. Charlesbridge, 2008.
———. *Trout, Trout, Trout! A Fish Chant*. Illus. by Trip Park. Northwords, 2004.
Wood, Audrey. *Ten Little Fish*. Scholastic, 2004.

Life Cycles: Salmon

Fletcher, Ralph. "Ma." *A Writing Kind of Day*. Illus. by April Ward. Boyds Mills, 2005.
Florian, Douglas. "The Salmon." *In the Swim*. Harcourt, 1997. (Also in *A Poke in the I*)
Harley, Avis. "Birthstones." *Fly with Poetry*. Boyds Mills, 2000.
Harrison, David. "Salmon." *Wild Country*. Boyds Mills, 1999.
Levy, Constance. "To a Salmon at the Falls." *Splash!* Illus. by Robert Sabuda. Orchard, 2002

Plants and Trees

Poems about seeds and acorns represent the beginning of new lives, and show the continuing cycles of nature. Plants are praised both for food and for their beauty. Trees represent longevity, strength, growth, and change. Tony Johnston's picture book, *Yonder*, shows a tree changing over the seasons, growing as time passes, and sheltering the memories of family. Because of the idiom "family tree," poets sometimes use trees to make this point.

Seeds and Plants

Aston, Diana Hutts. *A Seed Is Sleepy*. Illus. by Sylvia Long. Chronicle, 2007.
Bang, Molly & Penny Chisholm. *Living Sunlight: How Plants Bring Earth to Life*. Scholastic, 2008.
Bunting, Eve. *Flower Garden*. Illus. by Kathryn Hewitt. Harcourt, 1994.
Fisher, Aileen. "The Seed." *Always Wondering*. Illus. by Joan Sandin. HarperCollins, 1991.
Havill, Juanita. "When I Grow Up" & "Seedlings." *I Heard It from Alice Zucchini*. Illus. by Christine Davenier. Chronicle, 2006.

Johnston, Tony. *The Whole Green World*. Illus. by Elisa Kleven. Farrar, 2005.
Levy, Constance. "Seed Secrets." *A Tree Place*. Illus. by Robert Sabuda. McElderry, 1994.
Lobel, Anita. *Alison's Zinnia*. Greenwillow, 1990.
Lobel, Arnold. *The Rose in My Garden*. Illus. by Anita Lobel. Greenwillow, 1984.
Worth, Valerie. "Acorn." *All the Small Poems and Fourteen More*. Illus. by Natalie Babbitt. Farrar, 1994.
Yolen, Jane. "Recipe for Green." *Here's a Little Poem*. Illus. by Polly Dunbar. Candlewick, 2007.
Zolotow, Charlotte. "The Little Seed." *Seasons*. Illus. by Eric Blegvad. HarperCollins, 2002.

Food Plants and Gardening

Ada, Alma Flor. *Gathering the Sun*. Illus. by Simon Silva. HarperCollins, 1997.
Barbe, Walter, sel. Section: "Gardens and Flowers." *A School Year of Poems*. Illus. by Dennis Hockerman. Boyds Mills, 2005.
Florian, Douglas. *Vegetable Garden*. Harcourt, 1996.
Harrison, David L. *Farmer's Garden*. Illus. by Arden Johnson-Petrov. Boyds Mills, 2000.
Havill, Juanita. *Grow*. Illus. by Stanislawa Kodman. Peachtree, 2008. (Novel in Verse)
———. *I Heard It from Alice Zucchini: Poems About the Garden*. Illus. by Christine Davenier. Chronicle, 2006.
Hubbell, Patricia. *Black Earth, Gold Sun*. Illus. by Mary Newell DePalma. Cavendish, 2001.
Mallett, David. *Inch by Inch: The Garden Song*. Illus. by Ora Eitan. HarperCollins, 1975.
Mora, Pat. *¡Yum! Mm Mm! Que Rico! America's Sproutings*. Illus. by Rafael López. Lee & Low, 2007.
Rylant, Cynthia. *This Year's Garden*. Illus. by Mary Szilagi. Macmillan, 1985.
Shannon, George. *Busy in the Garden*. Illus. by Sam Williams. HarperCollins, 2006.
Spinelli, Eileen. *In Our Backyard Garden*. Illus. by Marcy Ramsey. S & S, 2004.
Swanson, Susan Marie. *To Be Like the Sun*. Illus. by Margaret Chodos-Irvine. Harcourt, 2008.

Pumpkins

Adoff, Arnold. "It Is Late." *In for Winter, Out for Spring*. Illus. by Jerry Pinkney. Harcourt, 1991.
Fleming, Denise. *Pumpkin Eye*. Holt, 2001.
Florian, Douglas. "Plump Pumpkin!" *Autumnblings*. Greenwillow, 2003.
Graves, Robert. "The Pumpkin." In Larrick, Nancy. *Piping Down the Valleys Wild*. Illus. by Ellen Raskin. Topeka, 1962.
Grimes, Nikki. "Pumpkin." *A Pocketful of Poems*. Illus. by Javaka Steptoe. Clarion, 2001.
Havill, Juanita. "The Pumpkin's Revenge." *I Heard It from Alice Zucchini*. Illus. by Christine Davenier. Chronicle, 2006.
Hopkins, Lee Bennett. "Autumn's Beginning." *Good Rhymes, Good Times*. Illus. by Frané Lessac. Harper Collins, 1995.
Horowitz, Dave. *The Ugly Pumpkin*. Putnam, 2005.
Kennedy, X. J. "Roasting Pumpkin Seeds." In Rosen, Michael J. ed. *Food Fight*. Harcourt, 1996.
Lewis, J. Patrick. "The Biggest Pumpkin." *The World's Greatest*. Illus. by Keith Graves. Chronicle, 2008.
Liatsos, Sandra Olson. "Pumpkin Picking." In Prelutsky, Jack. *The 20th Century Children's Poetry Treasury*. Illus. by Meilo So. Knopf, 1999.
McCord, David. "Pumpkins." *One at a Time*. Illus. by Henry B. Kane. Little, 1986.
Merriam, Eve. "Jack-O-Lantern." *Halloween ABC*. Illus. by Lane Smith. S & S, 1987.
Mora, Pat. "Pumpkin." *¡Yum! Mm Mm! Que Rico! America's Sproutings*. Illus. by Rafael López. Lee & Low, 2007.
Nye, Naomi Shihab. "Day After Halloween, Jack-O-Lantern Candle All Burned Out." *A Maze Me*. Harper Collins, 2005.

Prelutsky, Jack. "The Time Has Come." *It's Raining Pigs and Noodles.* Illus. by James Stevenson. Greenwillow, 2000.

Roemer, Heidi B. "Pumpkins for Sale" & "Harvest Slice." *Come to My Party.* Illus. by Hideko Takahashi. Holt, 2004.

Schnur, Steven. "Pumpkin." *Autumn.* Illus. by Leslie Evans. Clarion, 1977.

Shannon, George. "A Bright Idea." *Busy in the Garden.* Illus. by Sam Williams. Greenwillow, 2006.

Spinelli, Eileen. "Jack-O-Lantern." *In Our Backyard Garden.* Illus. by Marcy Ramsey. S & S, 2004.

Tall, Grace Cornell. "To Pumpkins at Pumpkin Time." In Bauer, Caroline Feller. *Halloween Stories and Poems.* Illus. by Peter Sis. HarperCollins, 1989.

Whitehead, Jenny. "At the Pumpkin Patch." *Holiday Stew.* Holt, 2007.

Worth, Valerie. "Pumpkins." *All the Small Poems and Fourteen Others.* Illus. by Natalie Babbitt. Farrar, 1994. (Also in *The Earth Is Painted Green*)

Trees

Alarcón, Francisco X. "Giant Sequoias." *Iguanas in the Snow = Iguanas en la Nieve.* Illus. by Maya Christina Gonzalez. Children's, 2001.

Argueta, Jorge. *Trees Are Hanging from the Sky.* Illus. by Rafael Yockteng. Groundwood, 2003.

Behn, Harry. *Trees.* Illus. by James Endicott. Holt, 1992.

Brenner, Barbara, ed. Sections: "Tree Green" & "Last Green." *The Earth Is Painted Green.* Illus. by S. D. Schindler. Scholastic, 1994.

Clement, Jennifer. "Lemon Tree." In Nye, Naomi Shihab. *The Tree Is Older Than You Are.* S & S, 1995.

Esbensen, Barbara Juster. "Tell Me." *Who Shrank My Grandmother's House?* Illus. by Eric Beddows. Harper Collins, 1992.

Fisher, Aileen. "Windy Tree." *Always Wondering.* Illus. by Joan Sandin. HarperCollins, 1991.

Frost, Robert. *Birches.* Illus. by Ed Young. Holt, 1988.

George, Kristine O'Connell. *Old Elm Speaks.* Illus. by Kate Kiesler. Clarion, 1998.

Gerber, Carole. *Leaf Jumpers.* Illus. by Leslie Evans. Charlesbridge, 2004.

———. *Winter Trees.* Illus. by Leslie Evans. Charlesbridge, 2008.

Greenfield, Eloise. "The Tree" & "Under the Sunday Tree." *Under the Sunday Tree.* Illus. by Amos Ferguson. HarperCollins, 1988.

Harley, Avis. "Tree Dancers." *Fly with Poetry.* Boyds Mills, 2000.

Harris, Wilson, "Tell Me Trees! What Are You Whispering?" In Agard, John & Grace Nichols. *Under the Moon and Over the Sea.* Illus. by Cathie Felstead, et al. Candlewick, 2002.

Heard, Georgia. "Oak Tree." *Falling Down the Page.* Roaring Brook, 2009.

Johnston, Tony. *Yonder.* Illus. by Lloyd Bloom. Dial, 1988.

Kuskin, Karla. "If You Stood with Your Feet in the Earth . . . " *Moon, Have You Met My Mother?* Illus. by Sergio Ruzzier. HarperCollins, 2003.

Levy, Constance. "Tree Coming Up." *I'm Going to Pet a Worm Today.* Illus. by Ronald Himler. Macmillan, 1991.

Lewis, J. Patrick. "First Recorded 6000-Year-Old Tree in America." *A Burst of Firsts.* Illus. by Brian Ajhar. Dial, 2001.

Lyon, George Ella. "Tree Song." In Heard, Georgia. *Falling Down the Page.* Roaring Brook, 2009.

Sandburg, Carl. "Proud Torsos." In Hopkins, Lee Bennett. *Rainbows Are Made.* Illus. by Fritz Eichenberg. Harcourt, 1982.

Sidman Joyce. "We Are Waiting (A Pantoum.)" *Butterfly Eyes.* Illus. by Beth Krommes. Houghton, 2006.

Sneve, Virginia Driving Hawk, adapt. "Mother We Are Cold." *Dancing Teepees.* Illus. by Stephen Gammell. Holiday, 1989.

Soto, Gary. "Pepper Tree." *A Fire in My Hands.* Harcourt, 2006.

Spinelli, Eileen. "On the Day My Baby Brother Is Born, We Plant a Tree in His Honor." & "Planting a Tree for Granddad's Birthday." *In Our Backyard Garden*. Illus. by Marcy Ramsey. S & S, 2004.

Udry, Janice May. *A Tree Is Nice*. Illus. by Marc Simont. HarperCollins, 1956.

Wong, Janet. "Tree." *Twist: Yoga Poems*. Illus. by Julie Paschkis. McElderry, 2007.

Arbor Day

Fisher, Aileen. "Arbor Day: Let's Plant a Tree." In Hopkins, Lee Bennett. *Ring Out Wild Bells*. Harcourt, 1992.

George, Kristine O'Connell. "Celebration." *Old Elm Speaks*. Illus. by Kate Kiesler. Clarion, 1998.

Hales, Barbara M. "Grandpa's Trees (Planted for Arbor Day.)" In Hopkins, Lee Bennett. *My America*. Illus. by Stephen Alcorn. S & S, 2000.

Hayford, James. "Time to Plant Trees." In Kennedy, X. J. & Dorothy M. Kennedy. *Knock at a Star*. Illus. by Karen Lee Baker. Little, 1999.

Livingston, Myra Cohn. "Arbor Day." *Festivals*. Illus. by Leonard Everett Fisher. Holiday, 1996.

Moore, Lilian. "Maple Talk." In Janeczko, Paul B. *Dirty Laundry Pile*. Illus. by Melissa Sweet. HarperCollins, 2001.

Whitehead, Jenny. "Plant Some Trees for Arbor Day" *Holiday Stew*. Holt, 2007.

Standard Five: Earth and Space Science. These include an understanding of atmospheric processes and the water cycle; understanding of the earth's composition and structure; and an understanding of the composition and structure of the universe and the earth's place within it.

See also Chapter Five: Social Studies Theme Three (People, Places, and Environments)

STANDARD FIVE: EARTH AND SPACE SCIENCE

This category includes geology and astronomy. In some of these poems, aspects of geology are compared to human feelings and struggles. "Ode To Stone: Amy Moscowitz," for example, in Nikki Grimes' *Bronx Masquerade*, compares the young narrator's numb feelings to stone. Objects in space, from the brilliance of the sun, the reflected light of the moon, and the fleeting brilliance of a shooting star are also compared to the human condition.

Shields, Carole Diggory. Section: "Earth and Space Sciences." *Science, Fresh Squeezed*. Illus. by Richard Thompson. Handprint, 2003.

Geology

Baylor, Byrd. *Everybody Needs a Rock*. Illus. by Peter Parnall. Macmillan, 1974.

Christian, Peggy. *If You Find a Rock*. Illus. by Barbara Hirsch Lember. Harcourt, 2000.

Esbensen, Barbara Juster. "Geode." *Who Shrank My Grandmother's House?* Illus. by Eric Beddows. Harper Collins, 1992.

Fisher, Aileen. *Sing of the Earth and Sky: Poems About Our Planet and the Wonders Beyond*. Illus. by Karmen Thompson. Boyds Mills, 2001.

Frank, John. "Geode," "Desert Rose," "Prospecting," & Tourmalines." *Keepers: Treasure Hunt Poems*. Illus. by Ken Robbins. Roaring Brook, 2008.

Graham, Joan Bransfield. "Awesome Forces." In Hopkins, Lee Bennett. *Got Geography*. Illus. by Philip Stanton. HarperCollins, 2006.

Grimes, Nikki. "Ode to Stone: Amy Moscowitz." *Bronx Masquerade*. Dial, 2002.

Harley, Avis. "A Rock Acrostic." *Fly with Poetry*. Boyds Mills, 2000.

Harrison, David. "Glacier" & "The Pond." *Wild Country*. Boyds Mills, 1999.

Harshman, Terry Webb. "Show-and-Tell Rocks." In Heard, Georgia. *Falling Down the Page*. Roaring Brook, 2009.

Heide, Florence Parry. "Rocks." In Hopkins, Lee Bennett. *Small Talk*. Illus. by Susan Gaber. Harcourt, 1995. (Also in *Sing a Song of Popcorn*)

Hoban, Russell. "Stupid Old Myself." In Prelutsky, Jack. *The Random House Book of Poetry for Children*. Illus. by Arnold Lobel. Random, 1983.

Katz, Susan. "Earthquake." *Mrs. Brown on Exhibit*. Illus. by R. W. Alley. S & S, 2002.

Kim, Kwang-Kyu. "The Birth of a Stone." In Nye, Naomi Shihab. *This Same Sky*. Macmillan, 1992.

Kuskin, Karla. "Unaccountable Billions . . . " *Moon, Have You Met My Mother?* Illus. by Sergio Ruzzier. HarperCollins, 2003.

Levy, Constance. "Volcano" & "Rock Tumbler." *A Tree Place*. Illus. by Robert Sabuda. McElderry, 1994.

Lewis, J. Patrick. "The Stone Skipping Record." *The World's Greatest*. Illus. by Keith Graves. Chronicle, 2008.

———. "Who Could Somersault the San Andreas Fault" & "How Will a Cave Behave?" *A World of Wonders*. Illus. by Alison Jay. Dial, 2004.

Merriam, Eve. "I Found a Little Stone." *You Be Good and I'll Be Night*. Illus. by Karen Lee Schmidt. Morrow, 1988.

Mitton, Tony. "The Histon Boulder." *Plum*. Illus. by Mary GrandPré. Scholastic, 2003.

Mordhorst, Heidi. "What I Wanted and What I Got." *Squeeze*. Illus. by Jesse Torrey. Boyds Mills, 2005.

Newman, Joseph S. "Geology." In Thomas, Marlo & Christopher Cerf. *Thanks and Giving*. S & S, 2004.

Olofsson, Tommy. "Old Mountains Want to Turn into Sand." In Nye, Naomi Shihab. *This Same Sky*. Macmillan, 1992.

Patterson, Ray. "I've Got a Home in That Rock." In Adoff, Arnold. *My Black Me*. Dutton, 1974.

Peters, Lisa Westberg. *Earthshake: Poems from the Ground Up*. Illus. by Cathie Felstead. HarperCollins, 2003.

Pomerantz, Charlotte. "Stem and Stone." *Thunderboom!* Illus. by Rob Shepperson. Front Street, 2005.

Prelutsky, Jack. "Grubby Grebbles Eat Rocks." *Baby Uggs Are Hatching*. Illus. by James Stevenson. Greenwillow, 1982.

Ryder, Joanne. *Earthdance*. Illus. by Norman Gorbaty. Holt, 1996.

Schaefer, Lola M. *An Island Grows*. Illus. by Cathie Felstead. HarperCollins, 2006.

Schertle, Alice. *All You Need for a Beach*. Illus. by Barbara Lavallee. Harcourt, 2004.

Siebert, Diane. *Cave*. Illus. by Wayne McLoughlin. HarperCollins, 2000.

Singer, Marilyn. "Center of the Earth." *Central Heating*. Illus. by Meilo So. Knopf, 2005.

———. *Footprints on the Roof: Poems About the Earth*. Illus. by Meilo So. Knopf, 2002.

———. "Sophie: Science Class . . . " *All We Needed to Say*. Illus. by Lorna Clark. Atheneum, 1996.

Worth, Valerie. "Pebbles," "Rocks," & "Mud." *All the Small Poems and Fourteen More*. Illus. by Natalie Babbitt. Farrar, 1994.

Yolen, Jane. "Boss Rock." *Horizons*. Illus. by Jason Stemple. Boyds Mills, 2002.

Dinosaurs and Fossils

Dinosaurs are as popular in poetry as they are in other forms of literature. Valerie Worth and J. Patrick Lewis have written short poems about how dinosaurs seem to stay alive and well in our imaginations although they have been gone for millennia. Some of the poetry written for children is funny; other poems carefully describe types of dinosaurs from what we know of them. Jack Prelutsky's fourteen poems about dinosaurs in *Tyrannosaurus Was A Beast* use stylistic devices that echo the qualities of the dinosaurs. Joanne Ryder asks readers to imagine themselves as dinosaurs, with all of the hazards of prehistoric life in *Tyrannosaurus Time*. Because of their size, young children may think of dinosaurs as dragons. Both seem large, distant, and a bit frightening. Poet Judy Sierra diminishes these fears with her *Good Night Dinosaurs*, simple, light-hearted rhymes about dinosaurs sleeping. Jon Scieszka points out one of the hazards of dinosaur study in his parody of Poe's *The Raven*,

"Dino-sore." Alas, dinosaurs may be part of so many units in school over the grades that children stop caring about them at all.

Some poets describe the living dinosaur, and others the fossilized bones. Jeff Moss' *Bone Poems* came from observing fossil bones in the American Museum of Natural History. Bobbi Katz has written a biographical poem about Mary Anning, an eleven-year-old who discovered dinosaur fossils in Lyme Regis, England. Interestingly, three picture book biographies about her were published in 1999. Students might want to compare and contrast the information presented about her in the books and the poem.

Anholt, Laurence. *Stone Girl, Bone Girl: The Story of Mary Anning*. Illus. by Sheila Moxley. Orchard, 1999. (Prose)

Armour, Richard. "Pachycephalosaurus (Pak-i-sef-a-lo-saw-rus)." In De Regniers, Beatrice Schenk, et al. *Sing a Song of Popcorn*. Scholastic, 1988.

Atkins, Jeannine. *Mary Anning and the Sea Dragon*. Illus. by Michael Dooling. Farrar, 1999. (Prose)

Barton, Byron. *Bones, Bones, Dinosaur Bones*. Crowell, 1990.

Baylor, Byrd. *If You Are a Hunter of Fossils*. Illus. by Peter Parnall. Scribners, 1980.

Brown, Don. *Rare Treasure: Mary Anning and Her Remarkable Discoveries*. Houghton, 1999. (Prose)

Crotty, K. M. *Dinosongs: Poems to Celebrate a T. Rex Named Sue*. Illus. by Kurt Vargö. The Field Museum/Scholastic, 2000.

Dakos, Kalli. "Sleeping Beside a Stegosaurus on an Overnight Class Trip to the Museum." *Put Your Eyes up Here*. Illus. by G. Brian Karas. S & S, 2003.

Dotlich, Rebecca Kai. "Fossil Finds." In Hopkins, Lee Bennett. *Days to Celebrate*. Illus. by Stephen Alcorn. Greenwillow, 2005.

Fletcher, Ralph. "Poem Fossil." *A Writing Kind of Day*. Illus. by April Ward. Boyds Mills, 2005.

Florian, Douglas. "Destinations." *Bing Bang Boing*. Harcourt, 1994. (Fossil)

Frank, John. "Fossil." *Keepers*. Illus. by Ken Robbins. Roaring Brook, 2008.

Glaser, Isabel Joshlin. "What If . . . " In Hopkins, Lee Bennett. *Good Books, Good Times!* Illus. by Harvey Stevenson. HarperCollins, 1990.

Harley, Avis. "Forgotten Giants," "Perhaps" & "Dinosaur Bones." *Fly with Poetry*. Boyds Mills, 2000.

Heide, Florence Parry. "Absolutely Nothing." In Brown, Marc. *Scared Silly!* Little, 1994.

Hoberman, Mary Ann. "The Dinosaur." *You Read to Me, I'll Read to You: Very Short Scary Tales to Read Together*. Illus. by Michael Emberley. Little, 2007.

Katz, Bobbi. "Mary Anning." *Trailblazers*. Illus. by Carin Berger. Greenwillow, 2007.

Katz, Susan. "Dinosaur TV." *Mrs. Brown on Exhibit*. Illus. by R. W. Alley. S & S, 2002.

Lewis, J. Patrick. "The Dumbest Dinosaur (Stegosaurus)." *The World's Greatest*. Illus. by Keith Graves. Chronicle, 2008.

———. "T-bones." *Scien-trickery*. Illus. by Frank Remkiewicz. Harcourt, 2004.

Mitton, Tony. *Dinosaurumpus*. Illus. by Guy Parker-Rees. Orchard, 2003.

Moore, Lilian. "To the Skeleton of the Dinosaur in the Museum." In Hopkins, Lee Bennett. *Behind the Museum Door*. Illus. by Stacey Dressen-McQueen. Abrams, 2007.

Moss, Jeff. *Bone Poems*. Illus. by Tom Leigh. Workman, 1997.

Prelutsky, Jack. *Tyrannosaurus Was a Beast*. Illus. by Arnold Lobel. Greenwillow, 1988.

Ryder, Joanne. *Tyrannosaurus Time*. Illus. by Michael Rothman. Morrow, 1999.

Schertle, Alice. "Dinosaur Bone." In Hopkins, Lee Bennett. *Spectacular Science*. Illus. by Virginia Halstead. S & S, 1999.

———. "O Trilobite." In Hopkins, Lee Bennett. *Behind the Museum Door*. Illus. by Stacey Dressen-McQueen. Abrams, 2007.

Scieszka, Jon. "Dino-sore." *Science Verse*. Illus. by Lane Smith. Viking, 2004.

Shields, Carol Diggory. "The First." *American History, Fresh-Squeezed*. Illus. by Richard Thompson. Handprint, 2002.

Sierra, Judy. *Good Night Dinosaurs*. Illus. by Victoria Chess. Clarion, 1996.

Singer, Marilyn. "Prehistoric Praise." *Footprints on the Roof*. Illus. by Meilo So. Knopf, 2002.

Worth, Valerie. "Dinosaurs." *All the Small Poems and Fourteen More*. Illus. by Natalie Babbitt. Farrar, 1994.

Yolen, Jane. "The Fossilot." In Brown, Marc. *Scared Silly!* Little, 1994.

Weather

Barbe, Walter B. sel. Section: "Weather." *A School Year of Poems*. Illus. by Dennis Hockerman. Boyds Mills, 2005.

Brown, Calef. "Weatherbee's Diner." *Flamingos on the Roof*. Houghton, 2006.

De Regniers, Beatrice Schenk, sel. Section: "Mostly Weather." *Sing a Song of Popcorn*. Scholastic, 1988.

Fisher, Aileen. "Weather Is Full of the Nicest Sounds." In *I Heard a Bluebird Sing*. Illus. by Jennifer Emery. Boyds Mills, 2002.

Hopkins, Lee Bennett. *Weather*. Illus. by Melanie Hall. HarperCollins, 1994.

Kennedy, X. J. & Dorothy M. Kennedy. Section: "Wind and Weather." *Talking Like the Rain*. Illus. by Jane Dyer. Little, 1992.

Larrick, Nancy, ed. Section "I Like It When It's Mizzly and Just a Little Drizzly." *Piping Down the Valleys Wild*. Illus. by Ellen Raskin. Topeka, 1968.

Locker, Thomas. *Cloud Dance*. Harcourt, 2000.

Schwartz, Alvin. Section: "Rain and Shine." *And the Green Grass Grew All Around*. Illus. by Sue Truesdell. HarperCollins, 1999.

Singer, Marilyn. *On the Same Day in March*. Illus. by Frané Lessac. HarperCollins, 2000.

"Weather." In Martin, Bill, Jr. & Michael Sampson. *The Bill Martin Jr. Big Book of Poetry*. S & S, 2008.

Rain

Aardema, Verna. *Bringing the Rain to Kapiti Plain*. Illus. by Beatriz Vidal. Dial, 1981.

Adoff, Arnold. "So Dry This July." *In for Winter, Out for Spring*. Illus. by Jerry Pinkney, Harcourt, 1991.

———. "Outside." *Outside, Inside Poems*. Illus. by John Steptoe. Harcourt, 1981.

Bauer, Caroline Feller. *Rainy Day*. Illus. by Michele Chessare. HarperCollins, 1986.

Boswell, Addie. *The Rain Stomper*. Illus. by Eric Velasquez. Cavendish, 2008.

Bryan, Ashley. "Rain Coming." *Sing to the Sun*. HarperCollins, 1992.

Buchanan, Ken & Debby Buchanan. *It Rained on the Desert Today*. Illus. by Libba Tracy. Northland, 1994.

Cotten, Cynthia. *Rain Play*. Illus. by Javaka Steptoe. Holt, 2008.

Dotlich, Rebecca Kai. "Rainy Morning" & "Wet City." *When Riddles Come Rumbling*. Boyds Mills, 2001.

Evans, Lezlie. *Rain Song*. Illus. by Cynthia Jabar. Houghton, 1995.

Florian, Douglas. "Rain Song" & "Rain Reign." *Handsprings*. HarperCollins, 2006.

Hesse, Karen. *Come on, Rain!* Illus. by John J. Muth. Scholastic, 1999.

Hughes, Langston. "April Rain Song" & "In Time of Silver Rain." *The Dream Keeper*. Illus. by Brian Pinkney. Knopf, 1993.

Martin, Bill, Jr. & John Archambault. *Listen to the Rain*. Illus. by James Endicott. Holt, 1988.

Moore, Lilian. "Rain Pools" & "Summer Rain." *Mural on Second Avenue*. Illus. by Roma Karas. Candlewick, 2005.

Olaleye, Isaac. "Tropical Rainstorm!" & "Rainy Season." *The Distant Talking Drum*. Illus. by Frané Lessac. Boyds Mills, 1995.

Snow

See also Science Standard Five (Seasons: Winter)

Bauer, Caroline Feller, sel. *Snowy Day.* Illus. by Margot Tomes. HarperCollins, 1986.

Dotlich, Rebecca Kai. "Snowy Morning" & "Zipper." *When Riddles Come Rumbling.* Boyds Mills, 2001.

Hillert, Margaret. "Listen." In Hopkins, Lee Bennett. *Weather.* Illus. by Melanie Hall. HarperCollins, 1994.

Johnson, David A. *Snow Sounds: An Onomatopoeic Story.* Houghton, 2006.

McCord, David. "Snowflakes." *One at a Time.* Illus. by Henry B. Kane. Little, 1986. (Also in *Spectacular Science*)

Merriam, Eve. "It Fell in the City." *Blackberry Ink.* Illus. by Hans Wilhelm. Morrow, 1985.

Nash, Ogden. "Winter Morning." In Hopkins, Lee Bennett. *Weather.* Illus. by Melanie Hall. HarperCollins, 1994.

Prelutsky, Jack. *It's Snowing, It's Snowing!* Illus. by Yossi Abolafia. HarperCollins, 2006.

Rylant, Cynthia. *Snow.* Illus. by Lauren Stringer. Harcourt, 2008.

Schertle, Alice. *All You Need for a Snowman.* Illus. by Barbara Lavallee. Harcourt, 2002.

Wind

Adoff, Arnold. "The Morning Wind." *In for Winter, Out for Spring.* Illus. by Jerry Pinkney. Harcourt, 1991.

Baird, Audrey B. "The Traveler" & "No Autographs." *A Cold Snap!* Illus. by Patrick O'Brien. Boyds Mills, 2002.

Bauer, Carline Feller, sel. *Windy Day.* Illus. Dirk Zimmer. Lippincott, 1988.

Dotlich, Rebecca Kai. "Lady Wind" & "Wind Chimes." *In the Spin of Things.* Illus. by Karen Dugan. Boyds Mills, 2003.

———. "Pinwheels." *Lemonade Sun.* Illus. by Jan Spivey Gilchrist. Boyds Mills, 1998.

Eastwick, Ivy O. "The Wind Comes Running." In James, Simon. *Days Like This.* Candlewick, 1999.

Florian, Douglas. "The Wind." *Autumnblings.* HarperCollins, 2003.

George, Kristine O'Connell. "Spring Wind." *The Great Frog Race.* Illus. by Kate Kiesler. Clarion, 1997.

Ghigna, Charles. "Air Force" & "Racing the Wind." *A Fury of Motion.* Boyds Mills, 2003.

Kuskin, Karla. "Days That the Wind Takes Over." *Moon, Have You Met My Mother?* Illus. by Sergio Ruzzier. HarperCollins, 2003.

Moore, Lilian. *While You Were Chasing a Hat.* Illus. by Rosanne Litzinger. HarperCollins, 2001.

———. "To a Red Kite." *Mural on Second Avenue.* Illus. by Roma Karas. Candlewick, 2005.

Mora, Pat. "Can I, Can I Catch the Wind?" *Confetti.* Illus. by Enrique O. Sanchez. Lee & Low, 1996.

O'Neill, Mary. "What Are You, Wind?" In Hopkins, Lee Bennett. *Spectacular Science.* Illus. by Virginia Halstead. S & S, 1999.

Schertle, Alice. "Showing the Wind." *A Lucky Thing.* Illus. by Wendell Minor. Harcourt, 1999.

Stevenson, Robert Louis. "The Wind" & "Windy Nights." *A Child's Garden of Verses.* Illus. by Diane Goode. Morrow, 1998.

Unobagha, Uzo. "Harmattan Is in the Air," "The Whirlwind Is Whirling," "Up the Iroko," & "Rush! Says the Tradewind." *Off to the Sweet Shores of Africa.* Illus. by Julia Carins. Chronicle, 2000.

Storms

Adoff, Arnold. "My Brother Aaron . . . " & "Clouds Are Black . . . " *In for Winter, Out for Spring.* Illus. by Jerry Pinkney. Harcourt, 1991.

Baird, Audrey. "Approaching Storm." *A Cold Snap!* Illus. by Patrick O'Brien. Boyds Mills, 2002.

———. *Storm Coming!* Illus. by Patrick O'Brien. Boyds Mills, 2003.

Brand, Dionne. "Hurricane." *Earth Magic.* Illus. by Eugenie Fernandes. Kids Can, 2006. (Also in *'Til All the Stars Have Fallen*)

Bryan, Ashley. "Hurricane." *Sing to the Sun.* HarperCollins, 1992.

Dotlich, Rebecca Kai. "Storm." *When Riddles Come Rumbling.* Boyds Mills, 2001.

George, Kristine O'Connell. "Storm." *Old Elm Speaks.* Illus. by Kate Kiesler. Clarion, 1998.

———. "Storm." *Toasting Marshmallows.* Illus. by Kate Kiesler. Clarion, 2001.

Graves, Donald. "Thunderstorm." *Baseball, Snakes, and Summer Squash*. Boyds Mills, 1996.

Gunning, Monica. "Tropical Hurricane." *Not a Copper Penny in Me House*. Illus. by Frané Lessac. Boyds Mills, 1993.

Havill, Juanita. "Summer Storm." *I Heard It from Alice Zucchini*. Illus. by Christine Davenier. Chronicle, 2006.

Kuskin, Karla. "Where Would You Be on a Night Like This?" *Moon, Have You Met My Mother?* Illus. by Sergio Ruzzier. HarperCollins, 2003.

Lawson, JonArno. "Tsunami." *Black Stars in a White Night Sky*. Illus. by Sherwin Tjia. Boyds Mills, 2006.

Levy, Constance. "Windstorm." *I'm Going to Pet a Worm Today*. Illus. by Ronald Himler. McElderry, 1991.

Lewis, J. Patrick. "Her-I-Cane." *The Bookworm's Feast*. Illus. by John O'Brien. Dial, 1999.

Mora, Pat. "Suspense." *This Big Sky*. Illus. by Steve Jenkins. Scholastic, 1998.

Mortensen, Denise Dowling. *Ohio Thunder*. Illus. by Kate Kiesler. Clarion, 2006.

Prelutsky, Jack. "What a Glorious Day for an Ogre." *Awful Ogre's Awful Day*. Illus. by Paul O. Zelinsky. Harper Collins, 2001.

Smith, Alan. "Emily Hurricane." In Agard, John & Grace Nichols. *Under the Moon and Over the Sea*. Illus. by Cathie Felstead, et al. Candlewick, 2002.

Starbird, Kaye. "The Snowstorm." In Bauer, Caroline Feller. *Snowy Day*. Illus. by Margot Tomes. HarperCollins, 1986.

Swados, Elizabeth. "Storm." *Hey You! C'Mere*. Illus. by Joe Cepeda. Scholastic, 2002.

Turner, Ann. *Rainflowers*. Illus. by Robert J. Blake. HarperCollins, 1992.

Water and the Water Cycle

See also Standard Three (Liquids and Solids)

See also Standard Five (Weather)

Graham, Joan Bransfield. *Splish, Splash*. Illus. by Steve Scott. Houghton, 1994.

Kerley, Barbara. *A Cool Drink of Water*. National Geographic, 2002.

Levy, Constance. *Splash! Poems of Our Watery World*. Illus. by David Soman.Orchard, 2002.

———. "What Water Wishes." *I'm Going to Pet a Worm Today*. Illus. by Ronald Himler. McElderry, 1991.

Michael, Pamela, ed. *River of Words: Images and Poetry in Praise of Water*. Heydey Books, 2003.

Schaeffer, Lola M. *This Is the Rain*. Illus. by Jane Wattenberg. HarperCollins, 2001.

Scieszka, Jon. "Water Cycle." *Science Verse*. Illus. by Lane Smith. Viking, 2004.

Shields, Carol Diggory. "The Itsy-Bitsy Spider and the Water Cycle." *Science, Fresh Squeezed*. Illus. by Richard Thompson. Handprint, 2003.

Singer, Marilyn. *How to Cross a Pond: Poems About Water*. Illus. by Meilo So. Knopf, 2003.

Stafford, Kim R. *We Got Here Together*. Illus. by Debra Frasier. Harcourt, 1994.

Swenson, May. Section: "Water Poems." *The Complete Poems to Solve*. Illus. by Christy Hale. Macmillan, 1993.

Yolen, Jane. *A Mirror to Nature*. Illus. by Jason Stemple. Boyds Mills, 2009.

———. *Water Music*. Illus. by Jason Stemple. Boyds Mills, 1995.

———. *Welcome to the River of Grass*. Illus. by Laura Regan. Putnam, 2001.

Astronomy

Burleigh, Robert. *One Giant Leap*. Illus. by Mike Wimmer. Philomel, 2009.

Esbensen, Barbara Juster. *The Night Rainbow*. Illus. by Helen K. Davie. Scholastic, 2000. (Aurora Borealis)

Fisher, Aileen. *Sing of the Earth and Sky*. Illus. by Karmen Thompson. Boyds Mills, 2001.

Florian, Douglas. *Comets, Stars, the Moon, and Mars*. Harcourt, 2007.

———. "Styropoem." *Bing Bang Boing*. Harcourt, 1994. (Star)

Frasier, Deborah. *A Birthday Cake Is No Ordinary Cake*. Harcourt, 2006.
Harley, Avis. "Shooting Star." In Heard, Georgia. *Falling Down the Page*. Roaring Brook, 2009.
Hemp, Christine. "Connecting Cord." In Janeczko, Paul B. *Seeing the Blue Between*. Candlewick, 2002.
Hopkins, Lee Bennett, sel. *Blast Off!* Illus. by Melissa Sweet. HarperCollins, 1995.
———. *Sky Magic*. Illus. by Mariusz Stawarski. Dutton, 2009.
Hubbell, Patricia. "Hello, Moon." In Janeczko, Paul B. *Hey You!* Illus. by Robert Rayevsky. HarperCollins, 2007.
Katz, Bobbi. "Dawn at the Cosmodrome," "John Glenn, the First American in Orbit," "Valentina Teresh . . . What?" "The Landing," "On the Space Shuttle Discovery," & "A Science Mission Specialist." *Trailblazers*. Illus. by Carin Berger. Greenwillow, 2007.
Lewis, J. Patrick. "Aurora Borealis." *A World of Wonders*. Illus. by Alison Jay. Dial, 2002.
———. "Hello, Black Hole." In Janeczko, Paul B. *Hey You!* Illus. by Robert Rayevsky. HarperCollins, 2007.
———. "First Men on the Moon" & "First American Woman In Space." *A Burst of Firsts*. Illus. by Brian Ajhar. Dial, 2001.
———. "First Moon Landing." In Hopkins, Lee Bennett. *Blast Off!* Illus. by Melissa Sweet. HarperCollins, 1995.
Marzollo, Jean. *Sun Song*. Illus. by Laura Regan. HarperCollins, 1995.
McCord, David. "Orion." *One at a Time*. Illus. by Henry B. Kane. Little, 1986.
McLoughland, Beverly. "To An Astronaut." In Janeczko, Paul B. *Hey You!* Illus. by Robert Rayevsky. Harper Collins, 2007.
Nye, Naomi Shihab. "Meteor Watch." *A Maze Me*.Greenwillow, 2005.
Singer, Marilyn. "Distance From the Sun." *Central Heating*. Illus. by Meilo So. Knopf, 2005. (Planets)
———. "The Moon's Gravity." *How To Cross a Pond*. Illus. by Meilo So. Knopf, 2003.
———. "Tanya: There Is No Sound In Space . . . " *All We Needed To Say*. Illus. by Lorna Clark. Atheneum, 1996.
Soto, Gary. "The Boy's First Flight." *A Fire in My Hands*. Harcourt, 2006.
Stevenson, Robert Louis. *The Moon*. Illus. by Tracey Campbell Pearson. Farrar, 2006.
Swenson, May. Section: "Space and Flight Poems." *The Complete Poems To Solve*. Illus. by Christy Hale. Macmillan, 1993.
Untermeyer, Louis. "Questions at Night." In Pearson, Susan. *The Drowsy Hours*. Illus. by Peter Malone. Harper Collins, 2002.
Wallace, Nancy Elizabeth, col. *The Sun, the Moon, and the Stars*. Houghton, 2003.
Whitman, Walt. *When I Heard the Learn'd Astronomer*. Illus. by Loren Long. S & S, 2004.
Worth, Valerie. "Stars" & "Sun." *All the Small Poems and Fourteen More*. Illus. by Natalie Babbitt. Farrar, 1994.

The Seasons

Adoff, Arnold. *In for Winter, Out for Spring*. Illus. by Jerry Pinkney. Harcourt, 1991.
Barbe, Walter B. sel. "Seasons." *A School Year of Poems*. Illus. by Dennis Hockerman. Boyds Mills, 2005.
Brenner, Barbara, ed. *The Earth Is Painted Green*. Illus. by S. D. Schindler. Scholastic, 1994.
Bruchac, Joseph & Jonathan London. *Thirteen Moons on Turtle's Back: A Native American Year of Moons*. Illus. by Thomas Locker. Philomel, 1992.
Carberry, H. D. "Nature." In Agard, John & Grace Nichols. *Under the Moon and Over the Sea*. Illus. by Cathie Felstead, et al. Candlewick, 2002.
Carlstrom, Nancy White. *Who Gets the Sun Out of Bed?* Illus. by David McPhail. Little, 1992.
Dotlich, Rebecca Kai. *In the Spin of Things*. Illus. by Karen Dugan. Boyds Mills, 2003.
Eastwick, Ivy. Section: "Seasons and Weather." *Some Folks Like Cats*. Illus. by Mary Kurnick Maass. Boyds Mills, 2002.
Esbensen, Barbara Juster. *Swing Around the Sun*. Illus. by Cheng-khee Chee, et al. Carolrhoda Books, 2003.

Franco, Betsy. *Mathematickles!* Illus. by Steven Salerno. S & S, 2003.
Giovanni, Nikki. *The Sun Is So Quiet*. Illus. by Ashley Bryan. Holt, 1996.
Hines, Anna Grossnickle. *Pieces: A Year in Quilts*. HarperCollins, 2001.
Hopkins, Lee Bennett, sel. *Ring Out Wild Bells*. Illus. by Karen Bauman. Harcourt, 1992.
———. *Weather: Poems for All Seasons*. Illus. by Melanie Hall. HarperCollins, 1994.
Hovey, Kate. "Siren Song II: Persephone's Abduction," "Hades Speaks," "Persephone Speaks," "Demeter Speaks," & "Spring Round (Nymphs' Song.)." *Ancient Voices*. Illus. by Murray Kimber. S & S, 2004.
Johnston, Tony. *Yonder*. Illus. by Lloyd Bloom. Dial, 1988.
Katz, Bobbi. *Once Around the Sun*. Illus. by LeUyen Pham. Harcourt, 2006.
Kennedy, Caroline, sel. Section: "The Seasons." *A Family of Poems*. Illus. by Jon J. Muth. Hyperion, 2005.
Kobayashi, Issa. *Today and Today*. Illus. by G. Brian Karas. Scholastic, 2007.
Larrick, Nancy, ed. Section: "I Wonder What the Spring Will Shout." *Piping Down the Valleys Wild*. Illus. by Ellen Raskin, Topeka , 1999.
Lin, Grace & Ranida T. McKneally. *Our Seasons*. Charlesbridge, 2006.
Livingston, Myra Cohn. *A Circle of Seasons*. Illus. by Leonard Everett Fisher. Holiday, 1982.
Maher, Ramona. *Alice Yazzie's Year*. Illus. by Shonto Begay. Ten Speed, 2004.
Mak, Kam. *My Chinatown*. HarperCollins, 2002
Martin, Bill, Jr. *The Turning of the Year*. Illus. by Greg Shed. Harcourt, 1998.
Martin, Bill, Jr. & Michael Sampson. Section: "Around the Year." *The Bill Martin Jr. Big Book of Poetry*. S & S, 2008.
Prelutsky, Jack, sel. Section: "The Four Seasons." *The Random House Book of Poetry for Children*. Illus. by Arnold Lobel. Random, 1983.
Roemer, Heidi. B. *Come To My Party*. Illus. by Hideko Takahashi. Holt, 2004.
Sidman, Joyce. *Red Sings from Treetops: A Year in Colors*. Illus. by Pamela Zagarenski. Houghton, 2009.
Singer, Marilyn. "Summer Solstice" & "Winter Solstice." *Footprints on the Roof*. Illus. by Meilo So. Knopf, 2002.
Updike, John. *A Child's Calendar*. Illus. by Trina Schart Hyman. Holiday, 1999.
Whitehead, Jenny, sel. *Holiday Stew*. Holt, 2007.
Zolotow, Charlotte. *Seasons*. Illus. by Eric Blegvad. HarperCollins, 2002.

Seasons and Seasonal Metaphors

See also Chapter Two: Language Arts Standard Six (Metaphors)

Sometimes a particular animal or bird is used as a metaphor to represent a season and its qualities. Wild geese, with their distinctive calls and the constantly moving "V" shape as their fly over, are featured in many autumn poems. Geese seem to take away the summer as they fly south. Rachel Field's classic poem, "Something Told the Wild Geese" is an early example of this image. In "Wild Goose" Curtis Heath wonders why we call them "silly geese" when these birds fly south to warmth while human stay in the cold. Barbara Juster Esbensen's "The Return" speaks of the geese coming back north in the spring.

Bears are the metaphor representing winter's cold, with its large and sleepy silence. William Stafford's *The Animal That Drank Up Sound* moves readers from the end of autumn through winter into spring, as does Alice Schertle's *Very Hairy Bear* and Ani Rucki's *When the Earth Wakes*. William Stafford's book ends the silence of winter with the song of the cricket. Jane Yolen suggests winter ends with the cries of the red-winged blackbird. Others suggest Spring Peepers, butterflies, and robins, as all of nature seems to come to life again. Students could search for animals in poems that represent spring and summer.

Autumn

Alarcón, Francisco X. *Angels Ride Bikes: And Other Fall poems = Los Ángeles Andan en Bicicleta: Y Otros Poemas de Otono*. Illus. by Maya Christina Gonzalez. Children's, 1999.

Andresen, Sally. "Fall." In Dunning, Stephen, et al. *Reflections on a Gift of Watermelon Pickle*. HarperCollins, 1967.

Coatsworth, Elizabeth. "And Stands there Sighing." In Kennedy, X. J. and Dorothy M. Kennedy. *Knock at a Star*. Illus. by Karen Lee Baker. Little, 1999.

Corkett, Anne. "November." In Booth, David, sel. *'Til All the Stars Have Fallen*. Illus. by Kady MacDonald Denton. Viking, 1990.

Ehlert, Lois. *Leaf Man*. Harcourt, 2005.

———. *Red Leaf, Yellow Leaf*. Harcourt, 1991.

Evatt, Harriet. "Wild Geese." In Barbe, Walter B. *A School Year of Poems*. Illus. by Dennis Hockerman. Boyds Mills, 2005,

Field, Rachel. "Something Told the Wild Geese." In Hall, Donald. *The Oxford Illustrated Book of American Children's Poems*. Oxford 1999.

Florian, Douglas. *Autumnblings*. Greenwillow, 2003.

George, Kristine O'Connell. "Canada Geese." *The Great Frog Race*. Illus. by Kate Kiesler. Clarion, 1997.

Gerber, Carole. *Leaf Jumpers*. Illus. by Leslie Evans. Charlesbridge, 2004.

Heard, Georgia. "Recipe for Writing an Autumn Poem." *Falling Down the Page*. Roaring Brook, 2009.

Heath, Curtis. "Wild Goose." In Rogasky, Barbara. *Leaf By Leaf*. Illus. by Marc Tauss. Scholastic, 2001. (Also in *Reflections on a Gift of Watermelon Pickle & The Beauty of the Beast*).

Hughes, Ted. "Goose." *Collected Poems for Children*. Illus. by Raymond Briggs. Farrar, 2005.

Kunimoto, Tsumori. "The Wild Geese Returning." In Prelutsky, Jack. *The Beauty of the Beast*. Illus. by Meilo So. Knopf, 1997.

McCord, David. "V." *One at a Time*. Illus. by Henry B. Kane. Little, 1986.

Riley, James Whitcomb. *When the Frost Is on the Punkin'*. Illus. by Glenna Lang. Godine, 1991.

Roemer, Heide B. "Evening View." *Come to My Party*. Illus. by Hideo Takahashi. Holt, 2004.

Rogasky, Barbara, sel. *Leaf by Leaf: Autumn Poems*. Illus. by Marc Tauss. Scholastic, 2001.

Ryder, Joanne. "A Long Flapping V." In Prelutsky, Jack. *The Beauty of the Beast*. Illus. by Meilo So. Knopf, 1997.

Rylant, Cynthia. *In November*. Illus. by Jill Kastner. Harcourt, 2000.

Salas, Laura. *Shrinking Days, Frosty Nights: Poems about Fall*. Capstone, 2008.

Schnur, Steven. *Autumn: An Alphabet Acrostic*. Illus. by Leslie Evans. Clarion, 1997.

Worth, Valerie. "Autumn Geese." *All the Small Poems and Fourteen More*. Illus. by Natalie Babbitt. Farrar, 1994.

Yolen, Jane. "Bird Watcher." *Bird Watch*. Illus. by Ted Lewin. Philomel, 1990.

———. "Five Geese Five." *Count Me a Rhyme*. Illus. by Jason Stemple. Boyds Mills, 2006.

Zolotow, Charlotte. *Say It!* Illus. by James Stevenson. Greenwillow, 1980.

Winter

See also Standard Five (Snow)

Alarcón, Francisco X. *Iguanas in the Snow: And Other Winter Poems = Iguanas en la Nieve: y Otras Poemas de Invierno*. Illus. by Maya Christina Gonzalez. Children's, 2001.

Baird, Audrey B. *A Cold Snap: Frosty Poems*. Illus. by Patrick O'Brien. Boyds Mills, 2002.

Booth, David, sel. Section: "In Silent Snow." *'Til All the Stars Have Fallen*. Illus. by Kady MacDonald Denton. Viking, 1990.

Fisher, Aileen. *Do Rabbits Have Christmas?* Illus. by Sarah Fox-Davies. Holt, 2007.

Florian, Douglas. *Winter Eyes*. Greenwillow, 1999.

Frost, Robert. *Stopping by Woods on a Snowy Evening*. Illus. by Susan Jeffers. Dutton, 2001.
George, Kristine O'Connell. *One Mitten*. Illus. by Maggie Smith. Clarion, 2004.
Gerber, Carole. *Winter Trees*. Illus. by Leslie Evans. Charlesbridge, 2008.
Hayford, James. *Knee-Deep in Blazing Snow: Growing Up in Vermont*. Illus. by Michael McCurdy. Boyds Mills, 2005.
Hines, Anna Grossnickle. *Winter Lights*. HarperCollins, 2005.
Johnson, David A. *Snow Sounds: An Onomatopoeic Story*. Houghton, 2006.
Kuskin, Karla. *Under My Hood I Have a Hat*. Illus. by Fumi Kosaka. HarperCollins, 2004.
Neitzel, Shirley. *The Jacket I Wear in the Snow*. Illus. by Nancy Winslow Parker. Greenwillow, 1989.
Prelutsky, Jack. *It's Snowing! It's Snowing! Winter Poems*. Illus. by Yossi Abolafia. HarperCollins, 2006.
Rogasky, Barbara, sel. *Winter Poems*. Illus. by Trina Schart Hyman. Scholastic, 1994.
Rucki, Ani. *When the Earth Wakes*. Scholastic, 1998.
Schertle, Alice. *All You Need for a Snowman*. Illus. by Barbara Lavallee. Harcourt, 2002.
———. *Very Hairy Bear*. Harcourt, 2007.
Schnur, Steven. *Winter: An Alphabet Acrostic*. Illus. by Leslie Evans. Clarion, 2002.
Seuling, Barbara. *Winter Lullaby*. Illus. by Greg Newbold. Harcourt, 1998.
Shakespeare, William. *Winter Song*. Illus. by Melanie Hall. Boyds Mills, 2006.
Stafford, William. *The Animal That Drank Up Sound*. Illus. by Debra Frasier. Harcourt, 1992.
Thomas, Patricia. *Red Sled*. Illus. by Chris L. Demarest. Boyds Mills, 2008.
Van Laan, Nancy. *When Winter Comes*. Illus. by Susan Gaber. Atheneum, 2000.
Yolen, Jane. *Once Upon Ice and Other Frozen Poems*. Illus. by Jason Stemple. Boyds Mills, 1997.
———. *Snow, Snow: Winter Poems for Children*. Illus. by Jason Stemple. Boyds Mills, 1998.
Zolotow, Charlotte. *Something Is Going to Happen*. Illus. by Catherine Stock. HarperCollins, 1988.

Spring

Alarcón, Francisco X. *Laughing Tomatoes: And Other Spring Poems = Jitomates Risueños: Y Otras Poemas de Primavera*. Illus. by Maya Christina Gonzales. Children's, 1997.
Brenner, Barbara, ed. Section: "First Green." *The Earth Is Painted Green*. Illus. by S. D. Schindler. Scholastic, 1994.
Bunting, Eve. *Flower Garden*. Illus. by Kathryn Hewitt. Harcourt, 1994.
De Colores = Bright with Colors. Illus. by David Diaz. Cavendish, 2008.
Esbensen, Barbara Juster. "The Return." *Swing Around the Sun*. Illus. by Cheng-khee Chee, et al. Carolrhoda, 2003.
Florian, Douglas. *Handsprings*. HarperCollins, 2006.
Kuskin, Karla. Section: "Spring Again, Spring Again, Spring . . ." *Moon, Have You Met My Mother?* Illus. by Sergio Ruzzier. HarperCollins, 2003.
Maddox, Marjorie. "A Charm of Butterflies." *A Crossing of Zebras*. Illus. by Philip Huber. Boyds Mills, 2008
Schnur, Steven. *Spring: An Alphabet Acrostic*. Illus. by Leslie Evans. Clarion, 1998.
Shannon, George, sel. *Spring: A Haiku Story*. Illus. by Malcah Zeldis. Greenwillow, 1996.
Stafford, William. *The Animal That Drank Up Sound*. Illus. by Debra Frasier. Harcourt, 1992.
Yolen, Jane. "Why Does?" *Fine Feathered Friends*. Illus. by Jason Stemple. Boyds Mills, 2004.

Summer

Alarcón, Francisco X. *From the Bellybutton of the Moon: And Other Summer Poems = Del Ombligo de la Luna: y Otras Poemas de Verano*. Illus. by Maya Christina Gonzales. Children's, 1998.
Berry, Lynne. *Duck Dunks*. Illus. by Hiroe Nakata. Holt, 2008.

Dotlich, Rebecca Kai. *Lemonade Sun*. Illus. by Jan Spivey Gilchrist. Boyds Mills, 1998.

Florian, Douglas. *Summersaults*. HarperCollins, 2002.

———. *Vegetable Garden*. Harcourt, 1996.

George, Kristine O'Connell. *Toasting Marshmallows: Camping Poems*. Illus. by Kate Kiesler. Clarion, 2001.

Gershwin, George. *Summertime*. Illus. by Mike Wimmer. S & S, 1999.

Greenfield, Eloise. *The Friendly Four*. Illus. by Jan Spivey Gilchrist. HarperCollins, 2006.

Harrison, David L. *Farmer's Garden*. Illus. by Arden Johnson-Petrov. Boyds Mills, 2000.

Payne, Nina. *Summertime Waltz*. Illus. by Gabi Swiatkowska. Farrar, 2005.

Schertle, Alice. *All You Need for a Beach*. Illus. by Barbara Lavallee. Harcourt, 2004.

Schnur, Steven. *Summer: An Alphabet Acrostic*. Illus. by Leslie Evans. Clarion, 2001.

Spinelli, Eileen. *Summerhouse Time*. Illus. by Joanne Lew-Vriethoff. Knopf, 2007. (Novel in verse)

Worth, Valerie. "Crickets." *All the Small Poems and Fourteen More*. Illus. by Natalie Babbitt. Farrar, 1994.

Standard Six: Science and Technology. These standards establish connections between the natural and designed worlds and provide students with opportunities to develop decision-making abilities. They are not standards for technology education; rather, these standards emphasize abilities associated with the process of design and fundamental understandings about the enterprise of science and its various linkages with technology.
Link with Chapter Five: Social Studies Theme Two (Time, Continuity, and Change)
Link with Chapter Five: Social Studies Theme Eight (Technology and Society)

STANDARD SIX: SCIENCE AND TECHNOLOGY

Innovations in technology cross the disciplines. Mathematics, for example, has been greatly changed by the advent of increasingly sophisticated computers. Those of us who write with word processors or use email, twitter, or social networks can attest that these increases in the speed of communication have changed social systems. Social studies materials reveal how inventions have affected social and historical change.

Inventors and Inventions

Florian, Douglas. "Inventions I'd Like to See." *Laugh-eteria*. Harcourt, 1999.

Holbrook, Sara. "Leave-Behinds." *Nothing's the End of the World*. Illus. by J. J. Smith-Moore. Boyds Mills, 1995.

Hopkins, Lee Bennett, sel. *Incredible Inventions*. Illus. by Julia Sarcone-Roach. Harper Collins, 2009.

Katz, Bobbi. "The Story of the Cotton Gin," "A Useless Gadget," (Telephone) "Thomas Alva Edison: Our Visit," "The Assembly Line," "Skyscraper," & "Imagine!" *We The People*. Illus. by Nina Crews. Greenwillow, 2000.

Nelson, Marilyn. *Carver: A Life in Poems*. Front, 2001. (George Washington Carver)

Perry, Andrea. *Here's What You Do When You Can't find Your Shoe (Ingenious Inventions for Pesky Problems)*. Illus. by Alan Snow. Atheneum, 2003. (Humorous Inventions)

Prelutsky, Jack. "Eureka! Hooray!" *My Dog May Be A Genius*. Illus. by James Stevenson. HarperCollins, 2008. (Humorous invention)

Schimel, Lawrence. "American Wizard." In Hopkins, Lee Bennett. *Lives*. Illus. by Leslie Staub. HarperCollins, 1999. (Thomas Alva Edison)

Sidman, Joyce. *Eureka! Poems About Inventions*. Illus. by K. Bennett Chavez. Millbrook, 2002.

Silverstein, Shel. "Invention." *Where the Sidewalk Ends*. HarperCollins, 1974.

Stoutenberg, Adrien. "Assembly Line." In Panzer, Nora. *Celebrate America*. Smithsonian/ Hyperion, 1994.

Machines

See also Chapter Five: Social Studies Theme Eight (Transportation)

Florian, Douglas. "My Robot." *Bing Bang Boing*. Harcourt, 1994.

Harley, Avis. "Jargon." *Leap into Poetry*. Boyds Mills, 2001. (Computer language)

Herrero Pinto, Floria. "Coils the Robot." *This Same Sky*. Macmillan, 1992.

Hubbell, Patricia. "Concrete Mixers." In Prelutsky, Jack. *The Random House Book of Poetry for Children*. Illus. by Arnold Lobel. Random, 1983.

Katz, Bobbi. "Washing Machine." In Janeczko, Paul B. *Dirty Laundry Pile*. Illus. Melissa Sweet. Harper Collins, 2001.

Merriam, Eve. "Umbilical." In Cullinan, Bernice E. *A Jar of Tiny Stars*. Illus. by Andi MacLeod. NCTE/ Boyds Mills, 1996.

Moore, Lilian. "Construction." In Cullinan, Bernice E. *A Jar of Tiny Stars*. Illus. by Andi MacLeod. NCTE/ Boyds Mills, 1996.

Morrison, Lillian. "At Times." *Guess Again!* Illus. by Christy Hale. August, 2006.

Pape, Donna Lugg. "The Click Clacker Machine." In Prelutsky, Jack. *The 20th Century Children's Poetry Treasury*. Illus. by Meilo So. Knopf, 1999.

Pender, Lydia. "Ditchdiggers." In Prelutsky, Jack. *The 20th Century Children's Poetry Treasury*. Illus. by Meilo So. Knopf, 1999.

Prelutsky, Jack. "A Dragon Is in My Computer." *The Dragons Are Singing Tonight*. Illus. by Peter Sis. Greenwillow, 1993.

———. "I Made a Perpetual Motion Machine" & "I Think My Computer Is Crazy." *A Pizza the Size of the Sun*. Illus. by James Stevenson. HarperCollins, 1996.

———. "My Brother Built a Robot." *Something Big Has Been Here*. Illus. by James Stevenson. Greenwillow, 1990.

Salas, Laura. *Move it! Work It! A Song About Simple Machines*. Illus. by Viviana Garafoli. Picture Window, 2009.

Shields, Carol Diggory. "All-New Eniac!" *American History, Fresh Squeezed!* Illus. by Richard Thompson. Handprint, 2002.

———. "Who Needs School?" *Lunch Money*. Illus. by Paul Meisel. Dutton, 1995.

Silverstein, Shel. "Homework Machine" & "Channels." *A Light in the Attic*. HarperCollins, 1981.

———. "Jimmy Jet and His TV Set." *Where the Sidewalk Ends*. HarperCollins, 1974.

———. "My Robot," "Writer Waiting," & "Remote-A-Dad." *Falling Up*. HarperCollins, 1996.

Soto, Gary. "The Function of Two E-Mail Accounts." *A Fire in My Hands*. Harcourt, 2006.

Worth, Valerie. "Lawnmower." *All the Small Poems and Fourteen More*. Illus. by Natalie Babbitt. Farrar, 1994.

Zimmer, Tracie Vaughan. "Programmer." *Steady Hands*. Illus. by Megan Halsey and Sean Addy. Clarion, 2009.

Buildings

See also Chapter Five: Social Studies Theme Three (Houses)

Brooks, Geraldine. "Building." In Janeczko, Paul B. *Poetry from A to Z*. Illus. by Cathy Boback. S & S, 1994. (Also in *Celebrate America*)

Lee, Dennis. "Skyscraper." In Janeczko, Paul B. *Hey, You!* Illus. by Robert Rayevsky. HarperCollins, 2007.

Lewis, J. Patrick. "Empire State Building" & "The Eiffel Tower." *Monumental Verses*. National Geographic, 2005.

Moore, Lilian. "Construction." *Mural on Second Avenue*. Illus. by Roma Karas. Candlewick, 2005.

Murton, Jessie Wilmore. "Song of the Builders." In Panzer, Nora. *Celebrate America*. Smithsonian/Hyperion, 1994.

Sandburg, Carl. "Skyscraper." In Rosen, Michael. *Classic Poetry*. Illus. by Paul Howard. Candlewick, 2009.

Tippet, James S. "Building a Skyscraper." In Prelutsky, Jack. *The 20th Century Children's Poetry Treasury.* Illus. by Meilo So. Knopf, 1999.

Standard Seven: Science in Personal and Social Perspectives. An important purpose of science education is to give students a means to understand and act on personal and social issues. The science in personal and social perspectives standards help students develop decision-making skills, understandings associated with personal health, populations, resources, and environments, changes in environments, and challenges for science and technology.
See also Chapter Four: Mathematics Standard Six (Problem Solving)
See also Chapter Seven: Health Standards One (Health Promotion) and Eight (Race)

STANDARD SEVEN: SCIENCE IN PERSONAL AND SOCIAL PERSPECTIVES

Poetry in any of the science standards may address these standards. Poets who write about ecosystems, for example, often mention their fragility and complexity. Poems in this section will focus on the environment. A poet may mourn the passing of a species, the destruction of a beautiful place, or sing praises for all of creation. The standards and the poets encourage students to not only think about their role in taking care of the world, but to act upon it.

Environmental Issues

Alarcón Francisco X. "Angels Ride Bikes = Los Ángeles Andan en Bicicleta." *Angels Ride Bikes = Los Ángeles Andan en Bicicleta.* Illus. by Maya Christina Gonzales. Children's, 1999. (Air Pollution)

Bang, Molly. *Nobody Particular: One Woman's Fight to Save the Bays.* Holt, 2000.

Berger, Carin. *OK Go.* HarperCollins, 2009. (Air Pollution)

Brenner, Barbara. Section: "Forever Green." *The Earth Is Painted Green.* Illus. by S. D. Schindler. Scholastic, 1994.

Brown, Calef. "The Mark." *Soup for Breakfast.* Houghton, 2008. (Treatment of Animals)

Eliot, T. S. "The Yellow Fog . . . " In Pearson, Susan. *The Drowsy Hours.* Illus. by Peter Malone. HarperCollins, 2002.

Fleischman, Paul. "The Passenger Pigeon." *I Am Phoenix.* Illus. by Ken Nutt. HarperCollins, 1985.

Goble, Paul. *Song of Creation.* Eerdmans, 2004.

Heard, Georgia. "Will We Ever See?" *Creatures of Earth, Sea and Sky.* Illus. by Jennifer Owings Dewey. Boyds Mills, 1992.

Hoberman, Mary Ann. *A House Is a House for Me.* Illus. by Betty Fraser. Viking, 1978.

Johnston, Tony. *The Whole Green World.* Illus. by Elisa Kleven. Farrar, 2005.

Katz, Bobbi. "For the Earth Day Essay Contest." *We the People.* Illus. by Nina Crews. Greenwillow, 2000.

Kumin, Maxine. "Extinct." *Mites to Mastodons.* Illus. by Pamela Zagarenski. Houghton, 2006.

Lewis, J. Patrick. "Two Animals Talking" & "Walk Lightly." *A World of Wonders.* Illus. by Alison Jay. Dial, 2002.

Lithgow, John. *I'm a Manatee.* Illus. by Ard Hoyt. S & S, 2003. (Includes CD)

London, Jonathon. *Giving Thanks.* Illus. by Gregory Manchess. Candlewick, 2003.

Martin, Bill, Jr. & Michael Sampson. *I Love Our Earth.* Illus. by Dan Lipow. Charlesbridge, 2006.

Ryder, Joanne. *Each Living Thing.* Illus. by Ashley Wolff. Harcourt, 2000.

———. *Earthdance.* Illus. by Norman Gorbaty. Holt, 1996.

Sandburg, Carl. "Buffalo Dusk." In Hopkins, Lee Bennett. *Rainbows Are Made.* Illus. by Fritz Eichenberg. Harcourt, 1982.

Schertle, Alice. "Black Rhino" & "Secretary Bird." *Advice for a Frog.* Illus. by Norman Green. Lothrop, 1995.

Seuss, Dr. *The Lorax.* Random, 1971.

Silken, Jon. "Caring for the Animals." In Nye, Naomi Shihab. *This Same Sky*. Macmillan, 1992.

Singer, Marilyn. "Home." *Footprints on the Roof*. Illus. by Meilo So. Knopf, 2002.

Staines, Bill. *All God's Critters*. Illus. by Kadir Nelson. S & S, 2009.

Swamp, Chief Jake. *Giving Thanks: A Native American Good Morning Message*. Illus. by Erwin Printup Jr. Lee & Low, 1995.

Thom the World Poet. "Praise to That Which." In Nye, Naomi Shihab. *Is This Forever or What?* HarperCollins, 2004.

Turner, Ann. *Heron Street*. Illus. by Lisa Desimini. HarperCollins, 1989.

Viorst, Judith. "Prayer of the Good Green Boy." *Sad Underwear*. Illus. by Richard Hull. Atheneum, 1995.

Webb, Charles. "The Animals Are Leaving." In Janeczko, Paul B. *Poetry from A to Z*. Illus. by Cathy Boback. S & S, 1994.

Weeks, Sarah. *Crocodile Smile: 10 Songs of the Earth as the Animals See It*. Illus. by Lois Ehlert. HarperCollins, 2003. (Includes CD)

Whitehead, Jenny. "Mother Earth" & "A Little Litter Poem." *Holiday Stew*. Holt, 2007.

Yolen, Jane. *Where Have All the Unicorns Gone?* Illus. by Ruth Sanderson. S & S, 2000.

———, sel. *Mother Earth, Father Sky: Poems of Our Planet*. Illus. by Jennifer Hewitson. Boyds Mills, 1996.

Standard Eight: History and Nature of Science. In learning science, students need to understand that science reflects its history and is an ongoing, changing enterprise. The standards . . . recommend the use of history in school science programs to clarify different aspects of scientific enquiry, the human aspects of science, and the role that science has played in the development of various cultures.

See also Chapter Five: Social Studies Theme Two (History and Biography)
See also Standard Six (Science and Technology)
See also Standard Five (Astronomy)

STANDARD EIGHT: HISTORY AND NATURE OF SCIENCE

This standard has obvious connections to the study of history. As with innovations in technology, innovations in scientific understanding have greatly affected the way historians have made sense of the past. Students should be aware of these ties as they study such innovators as Galileo, Copernicus, and Darwin.

Scientists

Bryant, Jen. *Ringside, 1925: Views from the Scopes Trial*. Knopf, 2008. (Darwin and the Teaching of Evolution) (Novel in Verse)

Katz, Bobbi. "Journal Jottings, Charles Darwin, 1831–1836," "I Love My Work: Richard Spruce," "Herakleion," & "Sylvia Earle: Deep Ocean Explorer." *Trailblazers*. Illus. by Carin Berger. Greenwillow, 2007.

Lewis, J. Patrick. "AE=VIP." *Scien-trickery*. Illus. by Frank Remkiewicz. Harcourt, 2004.

———. "I Was Trying to Save the Beauty of the Living World" & "Notes from a Day in the Bush." *Vherses*. Illus. by Mark Summers. Creative, 2005. (Rachel Carson & Jane Goodall)

McCord, David. "Smart Mr. Doppler." *One at a Time*. Illus. by Henry B. Kane. Little, 1986.

Museums

Hoberman, Mary Ann. "Anthropoids." *The Llama Who Had No Pajama*. Illus. by Betty Fraser. Harcourt, 1998.

Hopkins, Lee Bennett, sel. *Behind the Museum Door: Poems to Celebrate the Wonders of Museums*. Illus. by Stacey Dressen-McQueen. Abrams, 2007.

Katz, Susan. *Mrs. Brown on Exhibit: And Other Museum Poems.* Illus. by R. W. Alley. S & S, 2002.
Lithgow, John. *Carnival of the Animals.* Illus. by Boris Kulikov. S & S, 2004. (Natural History Museum)
Moss, Jeff. *Bone Poems.* Illus. by Tom Leigh. Workman, 1997. (American Museum of Natural History)

Zoos

De Regniers, Beatrice Schenk. *May I Bring a Friend?* Illus. by Beni Montresor, Atheneum, 1964
Gershator, Phillis. *Zoo Day Olé!* Illus. by Santiago Cohen. Cavendish, 2009.
Milne, A. A. "At the Zoo." *When We Were Very Young.* Illus. by Ernest Shepard. Penguin, 2008.
Nietzel, Shirley. *Our Class Took a Trip to the Zoo.* Illus. by Nancy Winslow Parker. Greenwillow, 2002.
Seuss, Dr. *If I Ran the Zoo.* Random, 1950.
Sierra, Judy. *Wild About Books.* Illus. by Marc Brown. Knopf, 2004.
Whitehead, Jenny. "My View at the Zoo." *Lunch Box Mail.* Holt, 2001.

REFERENCES

Chatton, B. (2006). "Uncommon Crows: A Unit of Study for Upper Elementary and Middle School Students." *The Dragon Lode* 24 (Spring): 29–36.
Geismer, M. *The Higher Animals: A Mark Twain Bestiary.* Illus. by Jean-Claude Suares. Crowell, 1976.
National Science Education Standards. National Science Teachers Association. 1996. http://www.nsta.org/standards
Oxford Dictionary of Modern Quotations. Oxford University Press, 1991: 5.

CHAPTER 4

Poetry and the Mathematics Standards

Standard One: Number and Operations. Programs should enable students to understand numbers, ways of representing numbers, relationships among numbers, and number systems; understand meanings of operations and how they relate to one another; compute fluently and make reasonable estimates.

STANDARD ONE: NUMBERS

Numbers are basic to the operations of mathematics. Poets explore the way numbers sound, how they look, and how they are used. May Swenson describes what the numbers from one to ten look like in poetic terms in "Cardinal Ideograms." Students might want to try creating word pictures of higher numbers. Loreen Leedy's whimsical picture book *Missing Math: A Number Mystery* lists all the situations in which readers would be lost without numbers. She asks how you could have a birthday if you don't know how old you were or on what day you were born, among other situations that require numbers. Jane Yolen's *Count Me a Rhyme* includes the roman numerals for the numbers one to ten, words that are formed from the name of each number, and a poem featuring that number of objects.

Giovanni, Nikki. "Two Friends." *Spin a Soft Black Song*. Illus. by George Martins. Farrar, 1985.

Harshman, Marc & Barbara Garrison. *Only One*. Dutton, 1993.

———. *Only One Neighborhood*. Dutton, 2007.

Hoberman, Mary Ann. "Centipede." *The Llama Who Had No Pajama*. Illus. by Betty Fraser. Harcourt, 1998.

Leedy, Loreen. *Missing Math: A Number Mystery*. Cavendish, 2008.

Lesynski, Loris. "Zero." *Zigzag*. Annick, 2004.

Lewis, J. Patrick. "Nothing Doing." *Scien-trickery*. Illus. by Frank Remkiewicz. Harcourt, 2004. (Zero)

Merriam, Eve. "Arithmetrix." *The Singing Green*. Illus. by Kathleen Collins Howell. Morrow, 1992.

———. "Zero." *Halloween ABC*. Illus. by Lane Smith. Macmillan, 1987.

Silverstein, Shel. "The Monkey." *Falling Up*. HarperCollins, 1996.

Soto, Gary. "Teaching the Numbers." *A Fire In My Hands*. Illus. by James M. Cardillo. Scholastic, 1991.

Swenson, May. "Cardinal Ideograms." *The Complete Poems to Solve*. Illus. by Christy Hale. Macmillan, 1993. (Also in *Oxford Illustrated Book of American Children's Poems*)

Yolen, Jane. *Count Me a Rhyme*. Illus. by Jason Stemple. Boyds Mills, 2006.

STANDARD ONE: COUNTING

The rhymed, predictable texts of counting books and rhymes provide an obvious link between poetry and mathematics. In counting books, a number sequence is used as a framework for a simple story, and the mnemonic device of a rhyme helps children to remember the counting scheme. The books typically represent numbers as numerals and as words, relating numbers to one another in a sequence. Counting out rhymes are used in play to decide turn-taking or for games such as jump rope. Poets have used the rhyme and number sequence of these traditional rhymes to create their own.

Counting Books

Children are exposed to counting rhymes through nursery rhymes. Some of these have been illustrated as picture books. Keith Baker's picture book, *Big Fat Hen* and Anna Grossnickle Hines' *1, 2, Buckle My Shoe* provide illustrations for the classic rhyme. Older children enjoy Shel Silverstein's parody of this rhyme, "One, two," in which someone yells back, "Buckle your own shoe!"

Most counting books feature a subject or theme. Olive Wadsworth's classic *Over in the Meadow*, available in several illustrated editions, counts animals. The rhyme and rhythm are so well known that a number of modern versions with differing settings and creatures have been published. They include Jennifer Ward's *Over in the Garden* and Marianne Berkes' *Over in the Jungle*. The classic counting song "This Old Man" has been recreated in Karen Ehrhardt's *This Jazz Man*, which tells a counting out story about jazz.

Sometimes counting books provide insight into another culture or language. Pat Mora's *Uno, Dos, Tres = One, Two, Three* and Susan Middleton Elya's *Eight Animals on the Town* introduce Spanish-language vocabulary and Mexican culture. These books can be used with older students for language or social studies instruction. Celeste Davidson Mannis' *One Leaf Rides the Wind* and Jan Thornhill's wildlife books can be used in science lessons for older students.

Children might want to look at a variety of counting books to compare how various authors use the number system. Some books, but not all, show the numbers one to ten, following our decimal system. Some books count from one to seven. Students may notice that seven is also an important number in our culture; there are seven dwarves, seven days of the week, and seven seas. Some books jump to large numbers after counting to ten. In *Chicka Chicka 1, 2, 3*, Bill Martin Jr. and Michael Sampson count rhythmically from one to 20, and then by tens. They also spend some time on zero: "0's hero of the number tree." Some books show a "countdown" as in Molly Bang's *Ten, Nine, Eight* and Aileen Fisher's *Know What I Saw?* Three poets have counted cats, each in a different way, in their books. Students might want to compare the picture book cat poems of Beatrice Schenk De Regniers, Betsy Lewin, and Lauren Thompson.

Some poets look at the ways we may count in the course of a day or night. Philip Booth's *Crossing* describes the way we have to skip numbers while counting train cars as they get faster and faster. Mary Ann Hoberman provides a little insight into the nighttime cliché of "Counting Sheep." Felice Holman tries "Counting Birds." And Karla Kuskin lists a number of different ways we might count, from counting noses to attempts to count birds or leaves. She finishes her poem "Counting" with her feeling that no matter how hard she tries, she cannot count all of the stars.

Adams, Pam, ret. *This Old Man*. Child's Play, 2000.
Andreasen, Dan. *The Baker's Dozen*.Holt, 2007.
Baker, Keith. *Potato Joe*. Harcourt, 2008.
———. *Quack and Count*. Harcourt, 1999.
———. *Big Fat Hen*. Harcourt, 1994.
Bang, Molly. *Ten, Nine, Eight*. Greenwillow, 1983.
Becker, John. *Seven Little Rabbits*. Illus. by Barbara Cooney. Walker, 2007. (Also in *Juba This and Juba That*)
Berkes, Marianne. *Over in the Jungle: A Rainforest Rhyme*. Illus. by Jeannette Canyon. Dawn, 2007.
Bond, Felicia. *Tumble Bumble*. HarperCollins, 1996.
Booth, Philip. *Crossing*. Illus. by Bagram Ibatoulline. Viking, 2001.
Calmenson, Stephanie. *Dinner at the Panda Palace*. Illus. by Nadine Bernard Westcott. HarperCollins, 1992.
Christelow, Eileen. *Five Little Monkeys Sitting in a Tree*. Houghton, 1991.
———. *Five Little Monkeys Jumping on the Bed*. Houghton, 1989.
Cotten, Cynthia. *At the Edge of the Woods*. Illus. by Reg Cartwright. Holt, 2002.
Crews, Donald. *Ten Black Dots*. HarperCollins, 1986.
De Regniers, Beatrice Schenk. *So Many Cats!* Illus. by Ellen Weiss. Houghton, 1988.
Edwards, Pamela Duncan. *Roar! A Noisy Counting Book*. Illus. by Henry Cole. HarperCollins, 2000.
Ehrhardt, Karen. *This Jazz Man*. Illus. by R. G. Roth. Harcourt, 2006.
Elliott, David. *One Little Chicken*. Illus. by Ethan Long. Holiday, 2007.
Elya, Susan Middleton. *Eight Animals on the Town*. Illus. by Lee Chapman. Putnam, 2000.
Enderle, Judith Ross & Stepanie Gordon Tessler. *Six Creepy Sheep*. Illus. by John O'Brien. Boyds Mills, 1992.
Gershator, Phillis. *Zoo Day Olé!* Illus. by Santiago Cohen. Cavendish, 2009.
Hines, Anna Grossnickle, Anna. *1, 2, Buckle My Shoe*. Harcourt, 2008.
Huck, Charlotte. *A Creepy Countdown*. Illus. by Jos. A. Smith. Greenwillow, 1998.
Koller, Jackie French. *Seven Spunky Monkeys*. Illus. by Lynn Munsinger. Harcourt, 2005.
———. *One Monkey Too Many*. Illus. by Lynn Munsinger. Harcourt, 1999.
LeSieg, Theo. *Ten Apples up on Top!* Illus. by Ray McKie. Random, 1961.
Leuck, Laura. *One Witch*. Illus. by S. D. Schindler. Walker, 2003.
Lewin, Betsy. *Cat Count*. Holt, 2003.
Loveless, Liz. *1, 2, Buckle My Shoe*. Hyperion, 1993.
Lundgren, Mary Beth. *Seven Scary Monsters*. Illus. by Howard Fine. Clarion, 2003.
Mannis, Celeste Davidson. *One Leaf Rides the Wind*. Illus. by Susan Kathleen Hartung. Viking, 2002.
Martin, Bill, Jr. & Michael Sampson. *Chicka, Chicka 1, 2, 3*. Illus. by Lois Ehlert. S & S, 2004.
———. *Rock It, Sock It, Number Line*. Illus. by Heather Cahoon. Holt, 2001.
Mora, Pat. *Uno, Dos, Tres = One, Two, Three*. Illus. by Barbara Lavallee. Clarion, 1996.
Rose, Deborah Lee. *One Nighttime Sea*. Illus. by Steve Jenkins. Scholastic, 2003.
Saul, Carol P. *Barn Cat*. Illus. by Mary Azarian. Little, 1998.
Schulman, Janet. *10 Trick-or-Treaters*. Illus. by Linda Davick. Knopf, 2005.
Sendak, Maurice. *One Was Johnny*.HarperCollins, 1962.
Stiegemeyer, Julie. *Gobble Gobble Crash!* Illus. by Valeri Gorbachev. Dutton, 2008.
Ten in the Bed. Illus. by Jane Cabrera. Holiday, 2006.
Thompson, Lauren. *How Many Cats?* Illus. by Robin Eley. Disney, 2009.
Thornhill, Jan. *The Wildlife ABC & 123*. MapleTree, 2004.
Tudor, Tasha. *1 Is One*. S & S, 2000.
The Twelve Days of Christmas. Illus. by Jan Brett. Putnam, 1989.
Wadsworth, Olive. *Over in the Meadow*. Illus. by Jan Thornhill. Maple Tree, 2004.
———. *Over in the Meadow*. Illus. by Anno Vojtech. North-South, 2003.
———. *Over in the Meadow*. Illus. by Ezra Jack Keats. Scholastic, 1985.

Ward, Jennifer. *Over in the Garden*. Illus. by Kenneth J. Spengler. Northland, 2002.
Williams, Suzanne. *Ten Naughty Little Monkeys*. Illus. by Suzanne Watts. HarperCollins, 2007.
Wood, Audrey. *Ten Little Fish*. Illus. by Bruce Wood. Scholastic, 2004.
Yolen, Jane. *An Invitation to the Butterfly Ball*. Illus. by Jane Breskin Zalben. Boyds Mills, 1992.

Counting-Out Rhymes

Some traditional counting-out rhymes have been published as the text for picture books, but many more are printed in nursery rhyme collections. Leo and Diane Dillon collect 24 counting-out rhymes in *Mother Goose: Numbers on the Loose*. Counting-out rhymes are used in children's play all over the world. Jane Yolen's *Street Rhymes Around the World*, and Joanna Cole and Stephanie Calmenson's *Miss Mary Mack: And Other Children's Street Rhymes* include international examples.

Some contemporary counting-out rhymes are included here, along with collections that feature traditional rhymes. Students might want to look through poetry collections for other examples, or to create their own counting out rhymes.

Brown, Calef. "One to Ten (And Back Again.)" *Soup for Breakfast*. Houghton, 2008.
Cole, Joanna & Stephanie Calmenson. *The Eentsy, Weentsy Spider: Fingerplays and Action Rhymes*. Illus. by Alan Tiegreen. HarperCollins, 1991.
———. *Miss Mary Mack, And Other Children's Children's Street Rhymes*. Illus. by Alan Tiegreen. Morrow, 1990.
Dillon, Leo & Diane Dillon, eds. *Mother Goose: Numbers on the Loose*. Harcourt, 2007.
Dove, Rita. "Count to Ten and We'll Be There." In Paschen, Elise. *Poetry Speaks to Children*. Sourcebooks, 2005. (With CD)
"Five Little Chickens." In Larrick, Nancy. *Piping Down the Valleys Wild*. Illus. by Ellen Raskin. Topeka, 1968.
"Five Little Squirrels." In De Regniers, Beatrice Schenk. *Sing a Song of Popcorn*. Scholastic, 1988.
Fleischman, Paul. "Morning." *I Am Phoenix*. Illus. by Ken Nutt. HarperCollins, 1985.
Florian, Douglas. "Tree-Tice." *Autumnblings*. HarperCollins, 2003.
Franco, Betsy. *Counting Our Way to the Hundredth Day!* Illus. by Steven Salerno. S & S, 2004.
"The Graceful Elephant = Un Elefante se Balanceaba." In Delacre, Lulu. *Arroz con Leche: Popular Songs and Rhymes from Latin America*. Scholastic, 1989. (Also in *Los Pollitos Dicen*)
Hoberman, Mary Ann. "Counting-Out Rhyme." *The Llama Who Had No Pajama*. Illus. by Betty Fraser. Harcourt, 1998.
———. "Sheep Counting. *A Fine Fat Pig*. Illus. by Malcah Zeldis. HarperCollins, 1991.
Holman, Felice. "Counting Birds." In Hopkins, Lee Bennett. *Marvelous Math*. Illus. by Karen Barbour. S & S, 1997.
Kiesler, Kate. "To the Magpie." *Wings on the Wind*. Clarion, 2002.
Kuskin, Karla. "Counting." *Dogs and Dragons, Trees and Dreams*. HarperCollins, 1980.
McCord, David. "Five Little Bats" & "Alphabet (Eta Z.)" *One at a Time*. Illus. by Henry B. Kane. Little, 1986.
Merriam, Eve. "Ten Little Apples." *You Be Good and I'll Be Night*. Illus. by Karen Lee Schmidt. Morrow, 1988.
Millay, Edna St. Vincent. "Counting-Out Rhyme." In Dunning, Stephen, et al. *Reflections on a Gift of Watermelon Pickle*. HarperCollins, 1967.
Mora, Pat. "Castanet Clicks." *Confetti*. Illus. by Enrique O. Sanchez. Lee & Low, 1996. (Also in *Oxford Illustrated Book of American Children's Poetry*)
O'Keefe, Susan Heyboer. "One Hungry Monster." In Brown, Marc. *Scared Silly!* Little, 1994.
"Oliver Twist." In Rosen, Michael. *Poems for the Very Young*. Illus. by Bob Graham. Houghton, 1993.
"One, Two, Three, Four, Five . . . " In Shaw, Alison. *Until I Saw the Sea*. Holt, 1995.
Prelutsky, Jack. "Countdown." In Brown, Marc. *Scared Silly!* Little, 1994.
Ryder, Joanne. "The Pond's Chorus" & "Yummy Bugs." *Toad by the Road*. Illus. by Maggie Kneen. Holt, 2007.

Salas, Laurie Purdie. "Counting on Me." *Stampede!* Illus. by Steven Salerno. Clarion, 2009.
Sierra, Judy. "Penguins' First Swim." *Antarctic Antics.* Illus. by José Aruego & Ariane Dewey. Harcourt, 1998.
Silverstein, Shel. "One, Two." *A Light in the Attic.* HarperCollins, 1981.
Soto, Gary. "Teaching Numbers." *A Fire in My Hands.* Harcourt, 2006.
Wong, Janet. "One to Ten." *Good Luck Gold.* McElderry, 1994. (Also in *Marvelous Math*)
Yolen, Jane. *Street Rhymes Around the World.* Illus. by Jeanette Winter, et al. Boyds Mills, 1992.

Counting by Groups

Dakos, Kalli. "Ten Ants in the Classroom." *The Bug in Teacher's Coffee.* Illus. by Mike Reed. HarperCollins, 1999. (Counting by Tens)
Manning, Maurie J. *The Aunts Go Marching.* Boyds Mills, 2003.
Martin, Bill, Jr. & Michael Sampson. *Chicka, Chicka 1, 2, 3.* Illus. by Lois Ehlert. S & S, 2004.

STANDARD ONE: ARITHMETIC

When poets write about arithmetic operations, they tend to put them together, pairing addition and subtraction, for example, in the same poem. Poems about arithmetic or that pair two operations are included in the first section. Poems that feature only one operation are listed under that subject.

Poets play with the language of arithmetic and the ways we use it idiomatically in a number of these poems. When people talk about something being a "plus" or that people are "divided" on an issue, they transfer math talk to other subjects. Students might try to write a poem using one of these idioms.

"Arithmetic." In Kennedy, Dorothy M. sel. *I Thought I'd Take My Rat to School.* Illus. by Abby Carter. Little, 1993.
Berry, Lynne. *Duck Dunks.* Illus. by Hiroe Nakota.
Graham, Joan Bransfield. "Nature Knows Its Math." In Hopkins, Lee Bennett. *Marvelous Math.* Illus. by Karen Barbour. S & S, 1997.
McCord, David. "Dividing," "Rhyme," & "Who Hasn't Played Gazinta?" *One at a Time.* Illus. by Henry B. Kane. Little, 1986. (Multiplication & Division) (Also in *Marvelous Math*)
Prelutsky, Jack. "A Microscopic Topic." *The New Kid on the Block.* Illus. by James Stevenson. Greenwillow, 1984.
Sandburg, Carl. "Arithmetic." In Hopkins, Lee Bennett. *Rainbows Are Made.* Illus. by Fritz Eichenberg. Harcourt, 1982.
Shannon, George. "Garden Math" & "Supper Math." *Busy in the Garden.* Illus. by Sam Williams, Houghton, 2006.
Watson, Clyde. "How Many Miles to Old Norfolk?" & "Mister Lister." *Father Fox's Pennyrhymes.* Illus. by Wendy Watson. HarperCollins, 1971.

Addition

Baird, Audrey B. "Add It Up." *A Cold Snap!* Illus. by Patrick O'Brien. Boyds Mills, 2002.
Baker, Keith. *Quack and Count.* Harcourt, 1999.
Dakos, Kalli. "Math Test." *The Bug in Teacher's Coffee.* Illus. by Mike Reed. HarperCollins, 1999.
De Regniers, Beatrice Schenk. *So Many Cats!* Illus. by Ellen Weiss. Clarion, 1988.
Florian, Douglas. "The Sum of Summer." *Summersaults.* HarperCollins, 2002.
Lee, Dennis. "Nine Black Cats." *The Ice Cream Store.* Illus. by David McPhail. Scholastic, 1992.
Lewin, Betsy. *Cat Count.* Holt, 2003.
Shields, Carol Diggory. "Math My Way." *Lunch Money.* Illus. by Paul Meisel. Dutton, 1995.

Subtraction

Ciardi, John. "About Being Very Good and Far Better Than Most But Still Not Quite Good Enough to Take on the Atlantic Ocean." *Doodle Soup*. Illus. by Merle Nacht. Houghton, 1985.

———. "Little Bits." *You Read to Me, I'll Read to You*. Illus. by Edward Gorey. HarperCollins, 1961.

Dakos, Kalli. "Why Must It Be Minus 3?" *Don't Read This Book, Whatever You Do!* Illus. by G. Brian Karas. S & S, 1993.

Reeves, James. "A Pig Tale." In De Regniers, Beatrice Schenk. *Sing a Song of Popcorn*. Scholastic, 1988.

Multiplication

Graves, Donald. "Multiplication." *Baseball, Snakes, and Summer Squash*. Boyds Mills, 1996.

Horton, Joan. *Math Attack!* Illus. by Krysten Brooker. Farrar, 2009.

Hulme, Joy. *Sea Squares*. Illus. by Carol Schwartz. Hyperion, 1991.

Kuskin, Karla. "Is Six Times One a Lot of Fun?" *Moon, Have You Met My Mother?* Illus. by Sergio Ruzzier. HarperCollins, 2003. (Also in *Marvelous Math*)

Michelson, Richard. *Ten Times Better*. Illus. by Leonard Baskin. Cavendish, 2000.

Pomerantz, Charlotte. "Twenty-Nine Girls." *Thunderboom!* Illus. by Rob Shepperson. Front, 2005.

Settimo, Janet. "Hamster Math." In Hopkins, Lee Bennett. *Hamsters, Shells, and Spelling Bees*. Illus. by Sachiko Yoshikawa. HarperCollins, 2008.

Division

Dodds, Dayle Ann. *The Great Divide: A Mathematical Marathon*. Illus. by Tracy Mitchell. Candlewick, 1999.

Hoberman, Mary Ann. "How Many?" *The Llama Who Had No Pajama*. Illus. by Betty Fraser. Harcourt, 1998.

———. *One of Each*. Illus. by Marjorie Priceman. Little, 1997.

Holbrook, Sara. "Divided." *I Never Said I Wasn't Difficult*. Boyds Mills, 1996.

McLoughland, Beverly. "SOS." In Martin, Bill, Jr. & Michael Sampson. *The Bill Martin Jr. Big Book of Poetry*. S & S, 2008. (Also in *Marvelous Math*)

Park, Linda Sue. "Long Division." *Tap Dancing on the Roof*. Illus. by Istvan Banyai. Clarion, 2007.

Pinczes, Elinor. *A Remainder of One*. Illus. by Bonnie MacKain. Houghton, 1995.

———. *One Hundred Hungry Ants*. Illus. by Bonnie MacKain. Houghton, 1993.

Yolen, Jane. "Horizon." *Horizons*. Illus. by Jason Stemple. Boyds Mills, 2002. (Also in *Got Geography!*)

Fractions and Decimals

Ciardi, John. "There's Nothing to It." *Doodle Soup*. Illus. by Merle Nacht. Houghton, 1985.

———. "Chang McTang McQuarter Cat." *You Read to Me, I'll Read to You*. Illus. by Edward Gorey. Harper Collins, 1961.

Hoberman, Mary Ann. "One Half of a Giraffe." *A Fine Fat Pig*. Illus. by Malcah Zeldis. HarperCollins, 1991.

Hopkins, Lee Bennett. "Fractions." *Marvelous Math*. Illus. by Karen Barbour. S & S, 1997.

Livingston, Myra Cohn. "Math Class." In Kennedy, Dorothy M. *I Thought I'd Take My Rat to School*. Illus. by Abby Carter. Little, 1993.

Prelutsky, Jack. "I Know How to Add." *What a Day It Was at School!* Illus. by Doug Cushman. HarperCollins, 2006.

———. "I Sailed on Half a Ship." *A Pizza the Size of the Sun*. Illus. by James Stevenson. HarperCollins, 1996.

STANDARD ONE: MONEY

Link from Chapter Five: Social Studies Theme Seven (Production, Distribution, and Consumption)

Link with Chapter Seven: Health Standard Five (Decision-Making to Enhance Health)

Poets sometimes write about the feel and sound of coins, as Valerie Worth does in "Coins." Sometimes money is used symbolically. Carl Sandburg ruminates on the idea that "money is power" in a section of his poem "The People, Yes." Gary Soto worries about economics in "How Things Work."

Some poems are about not spending money wisely. Shel Silverstein's "Smart," in which the young narrator doesn't know he's being shortchanged, makes a point about knowing how money works. It can be paired with Judith Viorst's prose work, *Alexander, Who Used to Be Rich Last Sunday.*

Cheng, Andrea. "Dawn: Sorting Change." *Where the Steps Were.* Boyds Mills, 2008.

Fletcher, Ralph. "Writer's Notebook." *A Writing Kind of Day.* Illus. by April Wood. Boyds Mills, 2005.

Greenfield, Eloise. "Keepsake." *In the Land of Words.* Illus. by Jan Spivey Gilchrist. HarperCollins, 2004.

Hoberman, Mary Ann. "The Dime." *You Read to Me, I'll Read to You: Very Short Stories to Read Together.* Illus. by Michael Emberley. Little, 2001.

———. "Money." *The Llama Who Had No Pajama.* Illus. by Betty Fraser. Harcourt, 1998.

Lewis, J. Patrick. "Gas: $1.00 A Gallon." *Arithme-tickle.* Illus. by Frank Remkiewicz. Harcourt, 2002.

Milne, A. A. "Market Square." *When We Were Very Young.* Illus. by Ernest H. Shepard. Dutton, 1988.

Sandburg, Carl. "The People, Yes." In Hopkins, Lee Bennett. *Rainbows Are Made.* Illus. by Fritz Eichenberg. Harcourt, 1982.

Silverstein, Shel. "Smart." *Where the Sidewalk Ends.* HarperCollins, 1974.

Soto, Gary. "How Things Work." *A Fire In My Hands.* Scholastic, 1991.

Worth, Bonnie. *One Cent, Two Cent, Old Cent, New Cent: All About Money.* Illus. by Aristides Ruiz & Joe Matheiu. Random, 2008.

Worth, Valerie. "Coins." *All the Small Poems and Fourteen More.* Illus. by Natalie Babbitt. Farrar, 1987.

Shopping

Units on shopping help students to understand the use and value of money. Typically, shopping units occur in primary grades as part of units on neighborhoods and community helpers. In the modern world, shopping is more global, with products arriving in American stories from all over the world. In upper elementary grades and middle school classrooms, students can study shopping while working on units of production, distribution, and consumption of goods.

The poetry and books about shopping show processes in this country and around the world. These works show the differences in the way food and other merchandise is produced and distributed in various cultures. Not all of the poems are serious, but all can add to understanding about aspects of shopping and trade. Reading a few poems set in the past and a few from different cultures can give students insights into differences between wants and needs. Students are struck when reading Donald Hall's *Ox-Cat Man*, for example, with how little the family needs to purchase to survive, and how few luxuries they require.

Vera B. Williams' *A Chair for My Mother* is a prose work that shows the value of saving up for a goal, delayed gratification in order to get something you really want, and working together to purchase something important. The big pickle jar in this book gradually fills with coins saved from grocery shopping, tips for waitressing, and other small sources. Similarly, in Tolowa Mollel's prose story *My Rows and Piles of Coins*, a young boy in Tanzania is saving all of his coins to buy a bicycle. In Carol Boston Weatherford's poem "One Red Cent" the child narrator comments on how people don't bother to pick up pennies, but the child does and puts them in a jar to save.

In the sequel to Williams' book, *Something Special for Me*, when the money jar fills for a second time, Rosa is allowed to use the money for a birthday present for herself. Rosa wants to purchase something like the chair that her whole family can enjoy. The story emphasizes that shared pleasure in something you have earned is more important than wealth. Byrd Baylor's *The Table Where Rich People Sit* echoes the warm family feeling of Williams' story and suggests that being rich does not necessarily mean having money.

Alarcón, Francisco X. "Earthly Paradise." *Angels Ride Bikes = Los Ángeles Andan En Bicicleta*. Illus. by Maya Christina Gonzalez. Children's, 1999.

Baylor, Byrd. *The Table Where Rich People Sit*. Illus. by Peter Parnall. Scribner's, 1994.

Brenner, Barbara. "Market Day." *The Earth Is Painted Green*. Illus. by S. D. Schindler. Scholastic, 2000. (Caribbean)

Cheng, Andrea. "Marketplace." *Shanghai Messenger*. Illus. by Ed Young. Lee & Low, 2005.

Dewdney, Anna. *Llama Llama Mad at Mama*. Viking, 2007.

Elya, Susan Middleton. *Bebé Goes Shopping*. Illus. by Steven Salerno. Harcourt, 2006.

———. *Eight Animals on the Town*. Illus. by Lee Chapman. Putnam, 2000.

Florian, Douglas. "Self Serve." *Bing Bang Boing*. Harcourt, 1994.

Gunning, Monica. "The Corner Shop." *Not a Copper Penny in Me House*. Illus. by Frané Lessac. Boyds Mills, 1993. (Caribbean)

Hall, Donald. *Ox-Cart Man*. Illus. by Barbara Cooney. Viking, 1979. (Early 19th Century)

Hopkins, Lee Bennett. "Woolworth: Downtown Newark." *Been to Yesterdays*. Illus. by Charlene Rendero. Boyds Mills, 1995. (1950's)

Katz, Bobbi. "Shopping; Liza Charlesworth." *We the People*. Illus. by Nina Crews. Greenwillow, 2000. (1940's)

Miranda, Anne. *To Market, To Market*. Illus. by Janet Stevens. Harcourt, 1997.

Mollel, Tololwa M. *My Rows and Piles of Coins*. Illus. by E. B. Lewis. Clarion, 1999. (Prose)

Mora, Pat. *Uno, Dos, Tres = One , Two, Three*. Illus. by Barbara Lavallee. Clarion, 1996. (Mexico)

Olaleye, Isaac. "Village Market." *The Distant Talking Drum*. Illus. by Frané Lessac. Boyds Mills, 1995. (Africa)

Prelutsky, Jack. "I Went to the Store." *The Frogs Wore Red Suspenders*. Illus. by Petra Mathers. HarperCollins, 2002.

Shaw, Nancy. *Sheep in a Shop*. Illus. by Margot Apple. Houghton , 1991.

Singer, Marilyn. *Shoe Bop*. Illus. by Hiroe Nakata. Dutton, 2008.

Soto, Gary. "My Teacher in the Market." *Canto Familiar*. Illus. by Annika Nelson. Harcourt, 1995.

Spinelli, Eileen. "Market Day" & "Shopping for Tea." *Tea Party Today*. Illus. by Karen Dugan. Boyds Mills, 1999.

Unobagha, Uzo. "I'm Off to the Market to See My Yam." *Off to the Sweet Shores of Africa*. Illus. by Julia Cairns. Chronicle, 2000.

Weatherford, Carole B. "One Red Cent" & "The City Market." *Sidewalk Chalk*. Illus. by Dimitrea Tokunbo. Boyds Mills, 2006.

Wong, Janet. "Dinner." *Good Luck Gold*. McElderry, 1994.

Worth, Valerie. "Garage Sale." *All the Small Poems and Fourteen More*. Illus. by Natalie Babbitt. Farrar, 1994.

Prose Works about Money

Anderson, Jon R. *Money: A Rich History*. Illus. by Thor Wickstrom. Grosset, 2003.

Leedy, Loreen. *Follow the Money!* Holiday, 2002.

Viorst, Judith. *Alexander, Who Used to be Rich Last Sunday*. Illus. by Ray Cruz. S & S, 1978.

Williams, Rozanne Lanczak. *Learning about Coins*. Illus. by Michael Jarrett. Gareth Stevens, 2004.

———. *The Coin Counting Book*. Charlesbridge, 2001.

Williams, Vera B. *A Chair for My Mother*. HarperCollins, 1982.

———. *Something Special for Me*. HarperCollins, 1986.

Standard Two: Algebra. Programs should enable students to understand patterns, relations, and functions; represent and analyze mathematical situations and structures using algebraic symbols; use mathematical models to represent and understand quantitative relationships; analyze change in various contexts.

STANDARD TWO: ALGEBRA

Holbrook, Sara. "The Search." *The Dog Ate My Homework*. Boyds Mills, 1996.

Hubbell, Patricia. "Equations." In Kennedy, Dorothy M. *I Thought I'd Take My Rat to School*. Illus. by Abby Carter. Little, 1993.

McCord, David. "Exit X." *One at a Time*. Illus. by Henry B. Kane. Little, 1986.

Soto, Gary. "American School in India." *Worlds Apart*. Illus. by Greg Clarke. Putnam, 2005.

Yolen, Jane. "One Hundred Percent." *Water Music*. Illus. by Jason Stemple. Boyds Mills, 1995.

Relationships

Barrett, Judi. *Things That Are Most in the World*. Illus. by John Nickle. Atheneum, 1998.

Behn, Harry. "Growing Up." In Prelutsky, Jack. *The Random House Book of Poetry for Children*. Illus. by Arnold Lobel. Random, 1983.

Eastwick, Ivy. "Very Tall." *Some Folks Like Cats*. Illus. by Mary Kurnick Maass. Boyds Mills, 2002.

Esbensen, Barbara Juster. "The Visit." *Who Shrank My Grandmother's House?* Illus. by Eric Beddows. Harper Collins, 1992.

Fisher, Aileen. "Little Talk." *Always Wondering*. Illus. by Joan Sandin. HarperCollins, 1991.

Florian, Douglas. *A Pig Is Big*. HarperCollins, 2000.

Frost, Robert. "Fireflies in the Garden." *You Come Too*. Illus. by Thomas W. Nason. Holt, 1959.

Harrison, David. "Beyond Measure." *Wild Country*. Boyds Mills, 1999.

Hoberman, Mary Ann. "Comparisons." *The Llama Who Had No Pajama*. Illus. by Betty Fraser. Harcourt, 1998.

Kumin, Maxine. "Mites," "Inchworm," & "Giraffe." *Mites to Mastodons*. Illus. by Pamela Zagarenski. Houghton, 2006.

Levy, Constance. "Big" & "Little." *I'm Going to Pet a Worm Today*. McElderry, 1991.

Lewis, J. Patrick. *Big Is Big (And Little, Little): A Book of Contrasts*. Illus. by Bob Barner. Holiday, 2007.

———. *The World's Greatest*. Illus. by Keith Graves. Chronicle, 2008.

Merriam, Eve. "Big Little Boy." In De Regniers, Beatrice Schenk. *Sing a Song of Popcorn*. Scholastic, 1988.

Milne, A. A. "The Four Friends." *When We Were Very Young*. Illus. by Ernest H. Shepard. Dutton, 1988.

Prelutsky, Jack. "I Am Tired of Being Little" & "Something Big Has Been Here." *Something Big Has Been Here*. Illus. by James Stevenson. Greenwillow, 1990.

———. "A Microscopic Topic." *The New Kid on the Block*. Illus. by James Stevenson. Greenwillow, 1984.

Richards, Laura E. "The Snail and the Mouse." In Prelutsky, Jack. *Read-Aloud Rhymes for the Very Young*. Illus. by Marc Brown. Knopf, 1986.

Swanson, Susan Marie. *To Be Like the Sun*. Illus. by Margaret Chodos-Irvine. Harcourt, 2008.

Patterns

Students need to recognize patterns to understand the complexities of numerical systems. Each of the disciplines uses patterns to order the world. The social studies arrange events chronologically and our world by mapping. Scientists use taxonomies and systems. Patterns that appear in nature often overlap; poets write about these "likenesses" across species. The language arts are arranged by genres, forms, and rules. Learning in the disciplines includes understanding that humans strive to see order in the universe, and that different disciplines arrange knowledge using different patterns. As they explore each of the subject areas, students may begin to see patterns that link mathematics with other subject areas.

One simple mathematical pattern is a series in which objects are placed in some kind of order. This might be from smallest to largest, as with the Russian nesting dolls, or a series arranged by heights, lengths, or widths. It might be a series from light to heavy or from narrow to wide. This pattern is also found in poetry and stories. "This Is the Key," a nursery rhyme in which a kingdom contains a city, which contains a town, and so on down to the smallest element uses this pattern. Susan Marie Swanson's picture book, *The House in the Night* is a modern version of this same pattern. Karla Kuskin's "Around and Around" starts with the smallest element, a bee on a flower, and takes it out to the largest-the earth spinning around the sun.

Another pattern that mathematicians and poets use is cumulative; the number of objects increases or diminishes. Counting rhymes use the natural progression to numbers in this way, sometimes reversing them as Molly Bang does in *Ten, Nine, Eight.* In Karen Beaumont's *Move Over Rover*, all of the animals cram one by one into the doghouse in a rainstorm until they discover the skunk who was in there first. All of them leave except the skunk, but not in a neat patterned order!

Poets describe patterns in nature. Avis Harley describes the small, intricate patterns on a butterfly's wing in "Viceroy." Ruth Heller's series of rhymed picture books on camouflage describe the ways animals hide themselves by matching their patterns to those of something else. Constance Levy compares a toad to a stone in "Camouflaged Amphibian." Mary Ann Hoberman humorously looks at the striped pattern of the zebra in "Abracadabra."

Poets and artists see familiar patterns and forms in the world around them. Jane Yolen asked poets to respond to Jason Stemple's photographs in *Once Upon Ice*. The poets saw teeth, fingers, and Munch's "The Scream" in the ice formations. Betsy Franco's collection of poems *Bees, Snails, and Peacock Tails: Patterns and Shapes Naturally* explores patterns in the natural world around us.

Scientists name aspects of nature because they remind them of something else. Pansies, for example, come from the French word "penser" for "to think" because the small thoughtful "face" of the pansy looks almost human. The Weeping Willow reminds us of a mourning human form. Poets describe this tendency to see human forms and emotions reflected in the patterns of nature as *personification*.

Different cultures may see different patterns in the same objects. Tony Johnston's "Rabbit in the Moon" harks back to the ancient Aztecs, who saw a rabbit rather than a "man in the moon." Judith Wright, a poet from Australia, sees that rabbit as well. Different cultures see the patterns of stars differently. Some will see The Big Dipper, others Ursa Major or The Plough in the same grouping of stars.

Bang, Molly. *Ten, Nine, Eight*. Greenwillow, 1983.

Beaumont, Karen. *Move Over, Rover!* Illus. by Jane Dyer. Harcourt, 2006.

Bond, Felicia. *Tumble Bumble*. HarperCollins, 1996. (Cumulative)

De Regniers, Beatrice Schenk. *May I Bring a Friend?* Illus. by Beni Montresor. Atheneum, 1964. (Cumulative)

Ehlert, Lois. *Leaf Man*. Harcourt, 2005.

Esbensen, Barbara Juster. "You Must Read This Word Underwater." *Words with Wrinkled Knees*. Illus. by John Stadler. HarperCollins, 1987.

Florian, Douglas. 'Winter Wear." *Winter Eyes*. Greenwillow, 1999.

Franco, Betsy. *Bees, Snails, and Peacock Tails: Patterns and Shapes Naturally*. Illus. by Steven Jenkins. S & S, 2008.

Harley, Avis. "Viceroy." *Leap into Poetry*. Boyds Mills, 2001.

Heller, Ruth. *How to Hide a Butterfly: And Other Insects*. Spoken Arts, 2001.

———. *How to Hide a Crocodile: And Other Reptiles*. Spoken Arts, 2001.

———. *How to Hide a Meadow Frog: And Other Amphibians*. Spoken Arts, 2001.
———. *How to Hide an Octopus: And Other Sea Creatures*. Spoken Arts, 2001.
———. *How to Hide a Parakeet: And Other Birds*. Spoken Arts, 2001.
———. *How to Hide a Polar Bear: And Other Mammals*. Spoken Arts, 2001.
Hoberman, Mary Ann. "Abracadabra." *A Fine Fat Pig*. Illus. by Malcah Zeldis. HarperCollins, 1991.
Hubbell, Patricia. "The Phantom Fawn." *Earthmates*. Illus. by Jean Cassels. Cavendish, 2000.
Johnston, Tony. "Rabbit in the Moon." *The Ancestors are Singing*. Illus. by Karen Barbour. Farrar, 2003.
Kuskin, Karla. "Around and Around." *Dogs and Dragons, Trees and Dreams*. HarperCollins, 1980.
Levy, Constance. "Camouflaged Amphibian." *A Tree Place*. Illus. by Robert Sabuda. McElderry, 1994.
Swanson, Susan Marie. *The House in the Night*. Illus. by Beth Krommes. Houghton, 2008.
"This Is the Key." In Kennedy, Caroline. *A Family of Poems*. Illus. by Jon J. Muth. Hyperion, 2005.
Van Laan, Nancy. *Possum Come a-Knockin.'* Illus. by George Booth. Knopf, 1990. (Cumulative)
Wright, Judith. "Full Moon Rhyme." In Rosen, Michael. *Classic Poetry*. Illus. by Paul Howard. Candlewick, 2009.
Yolen, Jane, sel. *Once Upon Ice*. Illus. by Jason Stemple. Boyds Mills, 1997.

Standard Three: Geometry. Programs should enable students to analyze characteristics and properties of two- and three-dimensional geometric shapes and develop mathematical arguments about geographic relationships; specify locations and describe spatial relationships using coordinate geometry and other representational systems; apply transformations and use symmetry to analyze mathematical situations; use visualization, special reasoning, and geometric modeling to solve problems.

STANDARD THREE: GEOMETRY

Poets use shapes, lines, dots, and angles to describe the world around them. These descriptions cross the subject line between mathematics and art. The poet applies geometry in new situations. The circle is a symbol of completion in many cultures. Two poems discuss its significance in Native American cultures.

Bernier-Grand, Carmen T. "Mexican Cubism." *Diego*. Illus. by David Diaz. Cavendish, 2009.
Black Elk. "The Life of a Man Is a Circle." In Sneve, Virginia Driving Hawk. *Dancing Teepees*. Illus. by Stephen Gammell. Holiday, 1989.
Crews, Donald. *Ten Black Dots*. Greenwillow, 1986.
Fisher, Aileen. "Earth Meets Sky." *Sing of the Earth and Sky*. Illus. by Karmen Thompson. Boyds Mills, 2001. (Line)
———. "Wind Circles." In Kennedy, Dorothy M. *I Thought I'd Take My Rat to School*. Illus. by Abby Carter. Little, 1993.
Florian, Douglas. "The Moon." *Comets, Stars, the Moon, and Mars*. Harcourt, 2007.
Franco, Betsy. *Bees, Snails, and Peacock Tails: Patterns and Shapes Naturally*. Illus. by Steve Jenkins. S & S, 2008.
Greene, Rhonda Gowler. *When a Line Bends . . . A Shape Begins*. Illus. by James Kaczman. Houghton, 1997.
Khamis, Dhabiya. "Unoccupied Chairs." In Nye, Naomi Shihab. *The Space Between Our Footsteps*. S & S, 1998.
Kuskin, Karla. "Square as a House." *Dogs and Dragons, Trees and Dreams*. HarperCollins, 1980.
Lewis, J. Patrick. "The Circle and the Poles." *A World of Wonders*. Illus. by Alison Jay. Dial, 2002.
Milne, A. A. "Lines and Squares." *When We Were Very Young*. Illus. by Ernest H. Shepard. Dutton, 1988.
Sandburg, Carl. "Circles." In Hopkins, Lee Bennett. *Hand in Hand*. Illus. by Peter M. Fiore. S & S, 1994. (Also in *Rainbows Are Made*)
Silverstein, Shel. "Shapes." *A Light in the Attic*. HarperCollins, 1981.

Wong, Janet. "Triangle." *Twist: Yoga Poems*. Illus. by Julie Paschkis. McElderry, 2007.
Yolen, Jane. "Horizon." *Horizons*. Illus. by Jason Stemple. Boyds Mills, 2002.

Standard Four: Measurement. Programs should enable students to understand measurable attributes of objects and the units, systems, and processes of measurement; apply appropriate techniques, tools, and formulas to determine measurements.

STANDARD FOUR: MEASUREMENT

Poets tend to use abstract measuring systems as they try on different ways of viewing the world. Because of its name, the inchworm seems an obvious subject for measurement, but Maxine Kumin reflects on the relatively short distance the worm can travel in her poem, "Inchworm." Students might consider ways of measuring the world from an animal's perspective. How would an ant measure distance? An elephant? What might they call their units of measurement?

Poets use phrases and terms of measurement in different ways. Eloise Greenfield's "Weights" considers the expression "weight of the world on your shoulders." John Ciardi asks, "How Much Is a Gross?" Upon looking at the picture book version of the song, *I Love You! A Bushel and a Peck*, students might want to investigate these measures. Students might look at other idioms for measurement, such as "an arm's length," "keeping your distance," or "pound for pound." They might discover that "Mark Twain" is not just a name—it's a measurement.

Aldis, Dorothy. "Inchworm." In Hopkins, Lee Bennett. *Flit, Flutter, Fly*. Illus. by Peter Palagonia. Delacorte, 1992.
Baird, Audrey B. "What Temperatures." *A Cold Snap!* Illus. by Patrick O'Brian. Boyds Mills, 2002.
Ciardi, John. "How Much Is a Gross?" *Doodle Soup*. Illus. by Merle Nacht. Houghton, 1986.
Dotlich, Rebecca Kai. "In Grandpa's House." In Micklos, John, Jr. *Grandparent Poems*. Illus. by Layne Johnson. Boyds Mills, 2004.
Greenfield, Eloise. "Weights." *Nathaniel Talking*. Illus. by Jan Spivey Gilchrist. Black Butterfly, 1988.
Kumin, Maxine. "Inchworm." *Mites to Mastodons*. Illus. by Pamela Zagarenski. Houghton, 2006.
Lewis, J. Patrick. "Pardon My Yardstick." *Arithme-tickle*. Illus. by Frank Remkiewicz. Harcourt, 2002.
Loesser, Frank. *I Love You! A Bushel and a Peck*. Illus. by Rosemary Wells. HarperCollins, 2005.
Mallett, David. *Inch by Inch: The Garden Song*. Illus. by Ora Eitan. HarperCollins, 1975.
McCord, David. "How Tall?" *One at a Time*. Illus. by Henry B. Kane. Little, 1986.
Milne, A. A. "Halfway Down." *When We Were Very Young*. Illus. by Ernest H. Shepard. Sutton, 1988.
Prelutsky, Jack. "I Went to a Yard Sale." *It's Raining Pigs and Noodles*. Illus. by James Stevenson. Greenwillow, 2000.

STANDARD FOUR UNIT: TIME

Time is a complex subject with rich poetic implications. We make time, take time, are on time, behind the times, just in time, or about time, and sometimes we need time-outs. Florence Parry Heide and Judith Heide Pierce play with these phrases in their collection of poems titled *It's About Time*. This large vocabulary of time words indicates how significant it is to humans in western cultures. If we begin to list the "time" words we know, they might include "clock" and "watch," instruments for telling time. We might think of "day," "week," and "year" as units of time. Other terms are more complicated. Why does the word "quarters" mean—a fraction, a period of time, a school term, and also a piece of money? What is a fortnight? What is a score, as in Lincoln's *Gettysburg Address*? What is a bicentennial? An octogenarian? Is biweekly twice a week or every two weeks? Kimberly Olson

Fakih's *Off the Clock: A Lexicon of Time Words and Expressions* is out of print, but if available provides an extensive list of time words for study as part of units on time. Part of the study of time should include the ways that different cultures throughout history have marked the passing of time, including by the seasons and different forms of calendars. Several books that feature the use of a lunar calendar are listed here. Martin Jenkins' prose work *The Time Book: A Brief History from Lunar Calendars to Atomic Clocks* is a useful history of how humans have made sense of and kept time.

Time can be relative. For mayflies, a whole life is fit into a single day. Two poets, Paul Fleischman and Mary Ann Hoberman have chronicled these short lives. Hoberman also describes the very short life of the shrew. For humans, time can feel relative too. Sometimes minutes and days fly by; other times, as Kali Dakos notes in "The School Bell" the last few seconds of the school day can be the longest.

Time is everywhere in stories and poems. Nursery rhymes about time include *Hickory Dickory Dock*. Keith Baker has created a picture book version of this rhyme, and Jim Aylesworth adds new verses in his picture book. Other nursery rhymes feature days of the week, as in "Monday's Child Is Fair of Face" or "Solomon Grundy, Born on a Monday." A number of books and poems are arranged as days of the week or months of the year, as Maurice Sendak does in *Chicken Soup with Rice*. Lee Bennett Hopkins' *Days to Celebrate* is a helpful yearlong calendar of poems that fit holidays and occasions, both well known and obscure.

Aylesworth, Jim. *The Completed Hickory Dickory Dock*. Illus. by Eileen Christelow. Atheneum, 1990.

Baker, Keith. *Hickory Dickory Dock*. Harcourt, 2007.

Brooks, Gwendolyn. "Marie Lucille." *Bronzeville Boys and Girls*. Illus. by Faith Ringgold. HarperCollins, 2007.

Brown, Jason Robert. *Tickety-Tock*. Illus. by Mary GrandPré. HarperCollins, 2009.

Ciardi, John "At Night" (Minutes) & "How Time Goes" (Years). *Doodle Soup*. Illus. by Merle Nacht. Houghton, 1986.

Dakos, Kalli. "The School Bell." *The Bug in Teacher's Coffee*. Illus. by Mike Reed. HarperCollins, 1999.

Esbensen, Barbara Juster. "Time." *Who Shrank My Grandmother's House?* Illus. by Eric Beddows. Harper Collins, 1992.

Fakih, Kimberly Olson. *Off the Clock: A Lexicon of Time Words and Expressions*. Ticknor and Fields, 1995. (Prose)

Fisher, Aileen. "On Time." *Always Wondering*. Illus. by Joan Sandin. HarperCollins, 1991.

Fleischman, Paul. "Mayflies." *Joyful Noise*. Illus. by Eric Beddows. HarperCollins, 1988.

Ghigna, Charles. "Loco Motion." *A Fury of Motion*. Boyds Mills, 2003.

Grandits, John. "Allergic to Time." *Blue Lipstick*. Clarion, 2006.

———. "My Stupid Day." *Technically, It's Not My Fault*. Clarion, 2004.

Heide, Florence Parry, Judith Heide Gilliland, & Roxanne Heide Pierce. *It's About Time!* Illus. by Cathryn Falwell. Houghton, 1999.

Hoberman, Mary Ann. "May Fly," "Shrew," & "Time." *The Llama Who Had No Pajama*. Illus. by Betty Fraser. Harcourt, 1998.

Hopkins, Lee Bennett, sel. *Days to Celebrate*. Illus. by Stephen Alcorn. HarperCollins, 2005.

Jenkins, Martin. *The Time Book: A Brief History from Lunar Calendars to Atomic Clocks*. Illus. by Richard Holland. Candlewick, 2009. (Prose)

Kennedy, X. J. & Dorothy M. Kennedy. Section: "Calendars and Clocks." *Talking Like the Rain*. Illus. by Jane Dyer. Little, 1992.

Marzollo, Jean. *Sun Song*. Illus. by Laura Regan. HarperCollins, 1995.

McCord, David. "No Present Like the Time" & "Tick Tock Talk." *One at a Time*. Illus. by Henry B. Kane. Little, 1986.

McGinley, Phyllis. "Daylight Saving Time." In Prelutsky, Jack. *The Random House Book of Poetry for Children*. Illus. by Arnold Lobel. Random, 1983.

———. "Lengths of Time." In De Regniers, Beatrice Schenk. *Sing a Song of Popcorn*. Scholastic, 1988.

Merriam, Eve. "Is It Robin O'Clock?" *Blackberry Ink*. Illus. by Hans Wilhelm. Morrow, 1985.

———. "Train Leaves the Station . . . " *You Be Good and I'll Be Night*. Illus. by Karen Lee Schmidt. Morrow, 1988.

Nims, Bonnie. "How to Get There." In Prelutsky, Jack. *The Random House Book of Poetry for Children*. Illus. by Arnold Lobel. Random, 1983.

Orleons, Ilo. "Time Passes." In Hopkins, Lee Bennett. *Marvelous Math*. Illus. by Karen Barbour. S & S, 1997.

Prelutsky, Jack. *Awful Ogre's Awful Day*. Illus. by Paul O. Zelinsky. HarperCollins, 2001.

———. "Turtle Time." *The Beauty of the Beast*. Illus. by Meilo So. Knopf, 1997.

Shields, Carol Diggory. "Clock Watching." *Lunch Money*. Illus. by Paul Meisel. Dutton, 1995.

Singer, Marilyn. *Nine O'Clock Lullaby*. Illus. by Frané Lessac. HarperCollins, 1991.

Soto, Gary. "Que Hora Es?" *Canto Familiar*. Illus. by Annika Nelson. Harcourt, 1995.

———. "Some Words About Time." *A Fire in My Hands*. Harcourt, 2006.

Stevenson, Robert Louis. "The Sun's Travel." *A Child's Garden of Verses*. Illus. by Diane Goode. Morrow, 1998.

Sullivan, A. M. "Measurement." In Prelutsky, Jack. *The Random House Book of Poetry for Children*. Illus. by Arnold Lobel. Random, 1983.

Yolen, Jane. "Time Piece." *Bird Watch*. Illus. by Ted Lewin. Philomel, 1990.

Clocks and Watches

Hoberman, Mary Ann. "Clock Chime." *The Llama Who Had No Pajama*. Illus. by Betty Fraser. Harcourt, 1998.

Katz, Susan. "Raymond in the Clock Museum." *Mrs. Brown on Exhibit*. Illus. by R. W. Alley. S & S, 2002.

Kimmel, Robert. "Clock." In Nye, Naomi Shihab. *Salting the Ocean*. Illus. by Ashley Bryan. Greenwillow, 2000.

Little, Lessie Jones. "Mama's Grandpa Clock." *Children of Long Ago*. Illus. by Jan Spivey Gilchrist. Lee & Low, 2000.

Prelutsky, Jack. "I Gave My Friend a Cuckoo Clock." *It's Raining Pigs and Noodles*. Illus. by James Stevenson. Greenwillow, 2000.

Sparough, J. Thomas. "Hourglass." In Hopkins, Lee Bennett. *Marvelous Math*. Illus. by Karen Barbour. S & S, 1997.

Swenson, May. "The Watch." *The Complete Poems to Solve*. Illus. by Christy Hale. Macmillan, 1993.

Winters, Kay. "The Clockmaker." *Colonial Voices*. Illus. by Larry Day. Dutton, 2008.

Worth, Valerie. "Clock." *All the Small Poems and Fourteen More*. Illus. by Natalie Babbitt. Farrar, 1994.

Days of the Week and Months of the Year

Bruchac, Joseph & Jonathan London. *Thirteen Moons on Turtle's Back*. Illus. by Thomas Locker. Putnam, 1992. (Months in American Indian year)

De Regniers, Beatrice Schenk. "The Churlish Child's Week/The Cheerful Child's Week." *The Way I Feel . . . Sometimes*. Illus. by Susan Meddaugh. Clarion, 1988.

Dotlich, Rebecca Kai. "If It's Monday." *Over in the Pink House*. Illus. by Melanie Hall. Boyds Mills, 2004.

Dragonwagon, Crescent. *Alligators and Others All Year Long*. Illus. by José Aruego & Ariane Dewey. S & S, 1997. (Months)

Katz, Bobbi. *Once Around the Sun*. Illus. by LeUyen Pham. Harcourt, 2006. (Months)

Kitching, John. "Ways of the Week." In Foster, John. *A Very First Poetry Book*. Oxford, 1987.

Lewis, J. Patrick. "Promises, Promises." *The Bookworm's Feast*. Illus. by John O'Brien. Dial, 1999. (Days of the Week)

Livingston, Myra Cohn. *Calendar.* Illus. by Will Hillenbrand. Holiday, 2007. (Months)
Martin, Bill, Jr. *The Turning of the Year.* Illus. by Greg Shed. Harcourt, 1998. (Months)
McNaughton, Colin. "Monday's Child Is Red and Spotty." In Prelutsky, Jack. *For Laughing Out Loud.* Knopf, 1991.
Nikola-Lisa, W. *Till Year's Good End: A Calendar of Medieval Labors.* Illus. by Christopher Manson. Atheneum, 1997.
Rossetti, Christina. "The Months." In Ferris, Helen. *Favorite Poems Old and New.* Illus. by Leonard Weisgard. Random, 1957, 2009.
Rylant, Cynthia. *Bless Us All.* S & S, 1998. (Months)
———. *Long Night Moon.* Illus. by Mark Siegel. S & S, 2004. (Months by moons)
Sendak, Maurice. *Chicken Soup with Rice.* HarperCollins, 1962.
Updike, John. *A Child's Calendar.* Illus. by Trina Schart Hyman. Holiday, 1999. (Months)

Very Long Periods of Time

Baylor, Byrd. *If You Are a Hunter of Fossils.* Illus. by Peter Parnall. Macmillan, 1980.
Crotty, K. M. "Twilight of the Dinosaurs." *Dinosongs.* Illus. by Kurt Vargö. Scholastic, 2000. (With CD)
Mitchell, Adrian. "A Speck Speaks." In Harrison, Michael & Christopher Stuart-Clark. *Oxford Book of Story Poems.* Oxford, 1990.
Moss, Jeff. "America, the Beautiful Home of the Dinosaurs" & "A Long Time (Or Sometimes You're Not as Important as You Think.)" *Bone Poems.* Illus. by Tom Leigh. Workman, 1997.
Nicholls, Judith. "Journey." In Harrison, Michael & Christopher Stuart-Clark, *The Oxford Book of Story Poems.* Oxford, 1990.
Prelutsky, Jack. "I'm Caught Up in Infinity." *It's Raining Pigs and Noodles.* Illus. by James Stevenson. Greenwillow, 2000.
———. "Long Gone." In Prelutsky, Jack. *The Random House Book of Poetry for Children.* Illus. by Arnold Lobel. Random, 1983.
Schertle, Alice. "Bristlecone." *Keepers.* Illus. by Ted Rand. Lothrop, 1996.
———. "Galapagos Tortoise." *Advice for a Frog.* Illus. by Norman Green. Lothrop, 1995.

Standard Five: Data Analysis and Probability. Instructional programs should enable students to formulate questions that can be addressed with data and collect, organize, and display relevant data to answer them; select and use appropriate statistical methods to analyze data; develop and evaluate inferences and predictions that are based on data; understand and apply basic concepts of probability.

Standard Six: Problem Solving. Instructional programs should enable students to build new mathematical knowledge through problem solving; solve problems that arise in mathematics and in other contexts; apply and adapt a variety of appropriate strategies to solve problems; monitor and reflect on the process of mathematical problem solving.

Links with Chapter Two: Language Arts Standard Seven
Links with Chapter Three: Science Standards Two and Seven
Links with Chapter Five: Social Studies Theme Ten
Links with Chapter Six: Dance Standard Four; Theatre Standards Six and Seven; Art Standards Five and Six; Music Standards Six and Seven
Links with Chapter Seven: Physical Education Standard Five; Health Standard Five

STANDARD SIX: PROBLEM SOLVING

Problem solving and decision-making are included in all of the discipline Standards. The mathematic standards allude to this when they say "solve problems that arise in mathematics and in other contexts." In fact, to make sense of poems and to write poetry, students must use problem-solving techniques.

The story or word problem is well known to mathematics students. In Jon Scieszka's *Math Curse*, the young heroine finds that once she begins to think about it, everything can turn into a story problem. Carl Sandburg's "Arithmetic" comments on the difficulties of word problems. Some poets have created new and entertaining math problems in the form of poetry. Betsy Franco uses the forms of arithmetic to tell small stories about nature in *Mathematickles!* John Grandits creates concrete poems in the form of graphs and charts.

Franco, Betsy. *Mathematickles!* Illus. by Steven Salerno. S & S, 2003.

Grandits, John. "A Chart of My Emotional Day" & "My Absolutely Bad . . . " *Blue Lipstick.* Clarion, 2006.

Sandburg, Carl. "Arithmetic." In Hopkins, Lee Bennett. *Rainbows are Made.* Illus. by Fritz Eichenberg. Harcourt, 1982.

Scieszka, Jon. *Math Curse.* Illus. by Lane Smith. Viking, 1995. (Prose)

Riddles

Riddles are defined as "conundrums" or "enigmas, " both words for statements requiring thought to be understood. They require logic and an understanding of the complexities of language. Riddles are small story problems to solve. Eloise Greenfield makes the connection between riddles and problem solving with "Riddles," saying she likes riddles that make you really think. Riddles can involve language similarities such as homonyms (What's black and white and read all over?) They can be humorous. *Simms Taback's Great Big Book of Spacey, Snakey, Buggy Riddles* collects silly riddles featuring animal characteristics. Children may recognize the nursery rhyme riddle, "As I was going to St. Ives." "Riddle Song," ("I Gave My Love a Cherry") from folk traditions is another.

Riddles can also be serious. One of the world's oldest riddles is the riddle of the sphinx, who killed anyone who tried and failed to answer its question. Adam Rex spoofs the riddle while also giving readers a chance to solve it in "The Sphinx Ain't All That—Yeah, You Heard Me." Julie Larios' "Sphinx" alludes to the riddle but does not share it.

Poets write individual riddles, and also entire collections of riddle poems. Some poems are clearly title "Riddle" while others are small metaphors that the reader must guess. Riddle poems can be posted in classrooms and libraries with invitations for students to try to solve them. Students might try to write their own riddle poems about subjects they are studying.

"As I Was Going to St. Ives." In Schwartz, Alvin. *And the Green Grass Grew All Around.* Illus. by Sue Truesdell. HarperCollins, 1992.

Dotlich, Rebecca Kai. *When Riddles Come Rumbling: Poems to Ponder.* Boyds Mills, 2001.

"Folk Riddles." In Krull, Kathleen. *A Pot O' Gold.* Illus. by David McPhail. Hyperion, 2004.

Franco, Betsy. *Riddle Poem of the Day.* Scholastic, 2005.

———. *Thematic Riddle Poems.* Scholastic, 2000.

Frost, Robert. "One Guess." *You Come Too.* Illus. by Thomas Nason. Holt, 1975.

Greenfield, Eloise. "Riddles." *In the Land of Words.* Illus. by Jan Spivey Gilchrist. HarperCollins, 2004.

Harley, Avis. "Rhinocerous Beetle." *Leap into Poetry.* Boyds Mills, 2001.

Hoberman, Mary Ann. "Riddle." *The Llama Who Had No Pajama.* Illus. by Betty Fraser. Harcourt, 1998.

———. "One Two." *A Fine Fat Pig.* Illus. by Malcah Zeldis. HarperCollins, 1991.

Larios, Julie. "Sphinx." *Imaginary Menagerie.* Illus. by Julie Paschkis. Harcourt, 2008.

———. "White Owl." *Yellow Elephant.* Illus. by Julie Paschkis. Harcourt, 2006.

Lewis, J. Patrick. *Scien-trickery: Riddles in Science*. Illus. by Frank Remkiewicz. Harcourt, 2004.

———. *Arithme-tickle: An Even Number of Odd Riddle Rhymes*. Illus. by Frank Remkiewicz. Harcourt, 2002.

———. "City Riddles." *A World of Wonders*. Illus. by Alison Jay. Dial, 2002.

Maestro, Marco & Giulio Maestro. *Geese Find the Missing Piece: School Time Riddle Rhymes*. HarperCollins, 1999.

McCord, David. "Look: What Am I?" *One at a Time*. Illus. by Henry B. Kane. Little, 1986.

Merriam, Eve. "Fiddle-Faddle." *The Singing Green*. Illus. by Kathleen Collins Howell. Morrow, 1992.

———. "What In the World?" In De Regniers, Beatrice Schenk. *Sing a Song of Popcorn*. Scholastic, 1988.

Morrison, Lillian. *Guess Again! Riddle Poems*. Illus. by Christy Hale. August, 2006.

Rex, Adam. "The Sphinx Ain't All That—Yeah, You Heard Me." *Frankenstein Takes the Cake*. Harcourt, 2008.

"Riddle Me Day." In Nicholls, Judith. *The Sun in Me*. Illus. by Beth Krommes. Barefoot, 2003.

"Riddle Song." In Kennedy, X. J. & Dorothy M. Kennedy. *Knock At a Star*.Little, 1999.

"Riddles = Adivinanzas." In Jaramillo, Nelly Palacio. *Grandmother's Nursery Rhymes = Las Nanas de Abuelita*. Illus. by Elivia. Holt, 1994.

Schertle, Alice. "I, Alone: Riddle." *Keepers*. Illus. by Ted Rand. Lothrop, 1996.

Schwartz, Alvin, sel. Section: "Riddles." *And the Green Grass Grew All Around*. Illus. by Sue Truesdell. Harper Collins, 1992.

Scieszka, Jon. "Hey Diddle, Diddle." *Science Verse*. Illus. by Lane Smith. Viking, 2004.

Shannon, George. "A Riddle Garden" & "A Riddle Picnic." *Busy in the Garden*. Illus. by Sam Williams. Greenwillow, 2006.

Sidman, Joyce. *Butterfly Eyes*. Illus. by Beth Krommes. Houghton, 2006.

———. "A Small Green Riddle." *Song of the Water Boatman*. Illus. by Becky Prange. Houghton, 2005.

Sierra, Judy. "Predator Riddles." *Antarctic Antics*. Illus. by José Aruego & Ariane Dewey. Harcourt, 1998.

Singer, Marilyn. "Tanya: Who Is First, Last, and In the Middle?" *All We Needed to Say*. Illus. by Lorna Clark. Atheneum, 1996.

Spires, Elizabeth. "Riddle." In Rosen, Michael. *Food Fight*. Harcourt, 1996.

Swenson, May. *The Complete Poems to Solve*. Illus. by Christy Hale. Macmillan, 1993.

Swift, Jonathan. "A Riddle." In Krull, Kathleen. *A Pot O' Gold*. Illus. by David McPhail. Hyperion, 2004.

Taback, Simms. *Simms Taback's Great Big Book of Spacey, Snakey, Buggy Riddles*. Riddles by Katy Hall and Lisa Eisenbery. Viking, 2008. (Prose)

Standard Seven: Reasoning and Proof. Instructional programs should enable all students to recognize reasoning and proof as fundamental aspects of mathematics; make and investigate mathematical conjectures; develop and evaluate mathematical arguments and proofs; select and use various types of reasoning and methods of proof.

Standard Eight: Communication. Instructional programs should enable all students to organize and consolidate their mathematical thinking through communication; communicate their mathematical thinking coherently and clearly to peers, teachers, and others; analyze and evaluate the mathematical thinking and strategies of others; use the language of mathematics to express mathematical ideas precisely.

Link with Chapter Two: Language Arts Standards Four,Five, and Eleven

Link with Chapter Six: Dance Standard Three; Theatre Standard One

Standard Nine: Connections. Instructional programs should enable all students to recognize and use connections among mathematical ideas; understand how mathematical ideas interconnect

and build on one another to produce a coherent whole; recognize and apply mathematics in contexts outside of mathematics.

Link with Chapter Two: Language Arts Standards Eleven and Twelve

STANDARD NINE: CONNECTING MATHEMATICS AND POETRY

The National Standards in Mathematics are interrelated. It is not possible to consider algebra without number and operations; it is not possible to communicate understanding of mathematics without being able to use math in differing contexts. Teacher Shari Griffin shared Betsy Franco's *Mathematickles!* with her fourth and fifth grade students to encourage them to see how math and language arts can be linked. In her author's note Franco, who has written several books linking mathematics and poetry, states "... words are written in place of numbers in all sorts of math problems ... Once you've read this book, I bet you won't be able to resist writing a few math problems of your own." (Franco, 2003) Shari's students began coming up with ideas for these interesting math problems after she had shared only a few of Franco's poems with them. The students not only decided to try writing a poems on their own, they also thought this would be a great lesson they could teach their parents. A number of the students went home and did just that, coming to school the next day with lists of their own ideas, and also some their parents created. The parents seemed to enjoy this "homework" and came up with amusing problems about cell phones, food, and family members. One dad even created his problems as rebuses, creating a new dimension to these poems. Daniel, grade 4, an English language learner (ELL) student, created "Kids divided by cake = No remainder." Jack, grade 4, suggested "Kid + Dodgeball = Nurse's Office" and "Jack + Computer = That's a long story." Melissa, grade 5, created a play on words: "Monkey × ½ = Key."

Shari's students and their parents enjoyed expressing what they knew about mathematics and language in these brief poems. Shari also wanted her fourth and fifth graders to try creating word problems/riddles in the form of persona poems. The class came up with the name "mathiddles" to parallel Betsy Franco's *Mathematickles!* Shari described the process to me in a May email in this way:

> I talked about my vague idea that we could look for relationships between fractional parts and what they represent. Then ... I said something scholarly like "Right. So I'm not exactly sure how I'd do it, but go ahead and figure it out!"

And some of her students did just that. Here is Liam's "mathiddle":

I am more than one half,
And less than one whole.
I am equivalent to a fraction
With a prime number
As a numerator
And a denominator
That is the
First square number
I am a percent
I am 75%

Liam
Grade 5

Allowing students to find the pleasure in mathematics is critical. As with other standards, the standards in mathematics don't mention how teachers and librarians can help students to enjoy and appreciate the subject. Some poets, like Franco, enjoy mathematics and allow students to express their own pleasure at understanding math. Lee Bennett Hopkins' *Marvelous Math* is an upbeat collection of poems on all aspects of mathematics. The title poem, by Rebecca Kai Dotlich, is a celebration of all of the things mathematics can do. J. Patrick Lewis' *Arithme-tickle*, a collection of humorous poetic story problems that cover many aspects of mathematics, makes a nice pairing with Franco's *Mathematickles!*

All too often students are frustrated with mathematics instruction and that frustration sometimes turns up in poetry. Carl Sandburg's "Arithmetic" includes nine attempts to define arithmetic, and satirizes the story problem. Nikki Grimes' "Dear Teacher" is a letter written in the form of a story problem signed by a boy who, thanks to the teacher's help, doesn't hate math "1/2 as much as he used to." Giving students opportunities to both read and write math poetry provides methods for discovering what students understand and enjoy about mathematics, and where their difficulties lie.

Math Delights

Appelt, Kathi. "Dreaming in Haiku." *Poems from Homeroom*. Holt, 2002.

Franco, Betsy. *Mathematickles!* Illus. by Steven Salerno. S & S, 2003.

Frost, Helen. "The Answer: Andrew." *Spinning Through the Universe*.Farrar, 2004.

George, Kristine O'Connell. "Math." *Swimming Upstream*. Illus. by Debbie Tilley. Clarion, 2002.

Grimes, Nikki. "Dear Teacher." *Thanks a Million*. Illus. by Cozbi A. Cabrera. HarperCollins, 2006.

———. "Math Score." *Danitra Brown, Class Clown*. Illus. by E. B. Lewis. HarperCollins, 2005.

Hopkins, Lee Bennett, sel. *Marvelous Math*. Illus. by Karen Barbour. S & S, 1997.

Leedy, Loreen. *Missing Math: A Number Mystery*. Cavendish, 2008.

Lewis, J. Patrick. *Arithme-tickle: An Even Number of Odd Riddle-Rhymes*. Illus. by Frank Remkiewicz. Harcourt, 2002.

Zolotow, Charlotte. "Possibilities." *Snippets*. Illus. by Melissa Sweet. HarperCollins, 1992.

Math Frustrations

Dakos, Kalli. "Math Is Brewing and I'm in Trouble," "They Don't Do Math in Texas," & "The Wind Is Calling Me Away." *If You're Not Here, Please Raise Your Hand*. Illus. by G. Brian Karas. Macmillan, 1990.

Florian, Douglas. "Arithmetickle." *Laugh-eteria*. Harcourt, 1999.

Ghigna, Charles. "School Doze." *A Fury of Motion*. Boyds Mills, 2003.

Graves, Donald. "Faking It." *Baseball, Snakes & Summer Squash*. Boyds Mills, 1996.

Grimes, Nikki. "Homework." *Danitra Brown, Class Clown*. Illus. by E. B. Lewis. HarperCollins, 2005.

Holbrook, Sara. "The Search." *The Dog Ate My Homework*. Boyds Mills, 1996.

Horton, Joan. *Math Attack!* Illus. by Kyrsten Brooker. Farr, 2009.

Lee, Dennis. "Nine Black Cats." *The Ice Cream Store*. Illus. by David McPhail. Scholastic, 1991.

McCord, David. "Exit X." *One at a Time*. Illus. by Henry B. Kane. Little, 1986.

Prelutsky, Jack. "A Group of Moose." *It's Raining Pigs and Noodles*. Illus. by James Stevenson. Greenwillow, 2000.

Sandburg, Carl. "Arithmetic." In Hopkins, Lee Bennett. *Rainbows Are Made*. Illus. by Fritz Eichenberg. Harcourt, 1982.

Soto, Gary. "Eraser and School Clock." *Canto Familiar*. Illus. by Annika Nelson. Harcourt, 1995.

Weatherford, Carole Boston. "Lucky Numbers." *Sidewalk Chalk*. Illus. by Dimitrea Tokunbo. Boyds Mills, 2006.

Wong, Janet. "Math." *Good Luck Gold*. McElderry, 1994.

REFERENCES

Principles and Standards for School Mathematics . National Council of Teachers of Mathematics. http://standards.nctm.org/document

Franco, Betsy. *Mathematickles!* Illus. by Steven Salerno. S & S, 2003.

CHAPTER 5

Poetry and the Social Studies Standards

Theme One: Culture. The study of culture prepares students to answer such questions as: What are the common characteristics of different cultures? How do belief systems, such as religion or political ideals, influence other parts of the culture? How does the culture change to accommodate different ideas and beliefs? What does language tell us about culture?
See also Chapter Two: Language Arts Standards Nine and Ten (Language Diversity)
See also Chapter Seven: Health Standard Eight (Race)

THEME ONE: WORLD CULTURES

Culture encompasses the knowledge, beliefs, political ideals, values, and traditions of societies. The social studies seek to help students understand how cultures differ from one another, how they change over time, and what cultures may have in common. While there is more poetry in English representing cultures from around the world, it still does not reflect all countries or all cultures. Teachers and librarians may want to collect poems in works for adults that might introduce less-well represented cultural groups.

A number of books give glimpses of how people around the world do things differently and yet are, in many ways, the same. Naomi Shihab Nye's collection *This Same Sky* is a collection of contemporary poems from around the world. In the introduction, Nye quotes a Turkish poet who talks about a worm who only knows the world of an apple. She then says "From over on the next tree, voices are calling to us—from the next orchard even! How are our branches different and our stories similar? And what lovely, larger life becomes ours when we listen to one another?" (p. xii)

Around the World

Baer, Edith. *This Is the Way We Go to School*. Illus. by Steve Björkman. Scholastic, 1990.

Baylor, Byrd. *The Way to Start a Day*. Illus. by Peter Parnall. Macmillan, 1978.

Frank, John. *How to Catch a Fish*. Illus. by Peter Sylvada. Roaring Brook, 2007.

Gordon, Ruth. *Time Is the Longest Distance*. HarperCollins, 1991.

Greenberg, Jan, ed. *Side by Side*. Abrams, 2008.

Hoberman, Mary Ann, sel. *My Song Is Beautiful*. Little, 1994.
Hopkins, Lee Bennett. *City I Love*. Illus. by Marcellus Hall, 2009.
Kerley, Barbara. *A Cool Drink of Water*. National Geographic, 2002.
———. *A Little Peace*. National Geographic, 2007.
———. *You and Me Together*. National Geographic, 2005.
Koch, Kenneth & Kate Farrell, sel. *Talking to the Sun*. Holt, 1985.
Livingston, Myra Cohn. *Festivals*. Illus. by Leonard Everett Fisher. Holiday, 1996.
Lowe, Ayana, ed. *Come and Play*. Bloomsbury, 2008.
Nye, Naomi Shihab, sel. *This Same Sky*. Macmillan, 1992.
Philip, Neil, ed. *It's a Woman's World*. Dutton, 2000.
Yolen, Jane. *Sacred Places*. Illus. by David Shannon. Harcourt, 1996.
———, ed. *Street Rhymes Around the World*. Boyds Mills, 1992.

Africa

Aardema, Verna. *Bringing the Rain to Kapiti Plain*. Illus. by Beatriz Vidal. Dial, 1981.
Cendrars, Blaise. *Shadow*. Trans and illus. by Marcia Brown. Scribners, 1982.
Greenfield, Eloise. *Africa Dream*. Illus. by Carole Byard. HarperCollins, 1977.
Grimes, Nikki. *Is It Far to Zanzibar?* Illus. by Betsy Lewin. Lothrop, 2000.
Harley, Avis. *African Acrostics*. Illus. by Deborah Noyes. Candlewick, 2009.
Olaleye, Isaac. *The Distant Talking Drum*. Illus. by Frané Lessac. Boyds Mills, 1995.
Slier, Deborah, ed. *Make a Joyful Sound*. Illus. by Cornelious Van Wright & Ying-Hwa Hu. Checkerboard, 1991.
To Everything There Is a Season. Illus. by Jude Daly. Eerdmans, 2006.
Unobagha, Uzo. *Off to the Sweet Shores of Africa*. Illus. by Julia Cairns. Chronicle, 2000.
Wilson, Anna. *Over in the Grassland*. Illus. by Alison Bartlett. Little, 1999.

Asia and the Middle East

Cheng, Andrea. *Shanghai Messenger*. Illus. by Ed Young. Lee & Low, 2005. (Novel in Verse)
Demi, ed. & illus. *In the Eyes of the Cat: Japanese Poetry for All Seasons*. Trans. by Tze-si Huang. Holt, 1992.
Gollub, Matthew. *Cool Melons Turn to Frogs!* Illus. by Kazuko G. Stone. Lee & Low, 1998.
Ho, Minfong. *Maples in the Mist*. Illus. by Jean & Mou-sien Tseng. Lothrop, 1996.
———. *Peek! A Thai Hide-and-Seek*. Illus. by Holly Meade. Candlewick, 2004.
Liu, Siyu & Orel Protopopescu, sels. *A Thousand Peaks: Poems from China*. Pacific View, 2002.
Mannis, Celeste Davidson. *One Leaf Rides the Wind*. Illus. by Susan Kathleen Hartung. Viking, 2002.
Nye, Naomi Shihab, sel. *The Flag of Childhood*. Aladdin, 1998. (Abridged version of *The Space Between Our Footsteps*)
———. *19 Varieties of Gazelle*. Greenwillow, 2002.
———, sel. *The Space Between Our Footsteps*. S & S, 1998.
Reibstein, Mark. *Wabi Sabi*. Illus. by Ed Young. Little, 2008.
Spivak, Dawnine. *Grass Sandals*. Illus. by Demi. Atheneum, 1997.
Wyndham, Robert, sel. *Chinese Mother Goose Rhymes*. Illus. by Ed Young. Putnam, 1989.
Young, Ed. *Beyond the Great Mountains*. Chronicle, 2005.

Caribbean

Agard, John & Grace Nichols, eds. *Under the Moon and Over the Sea*. Illus. by Cathie Felstead. Candlewick, 2002.

Berry, James. *A Nest Full of Stars*. Illus. by Ashley Bryan. Greenwillow, 2004.
Brand, Dionne. *Earth Magic*. Illus. by Eugenie Fernandes. Kids Can, 2006.
Bryan, Ashley. *Sing to the Sun*. HarperCollins, 1992.
Caraballo, Samuel. *Mis Abuelos y Yo = My Grandparents and I*. Illus. by D. Nina Cruz. Arté Público, 2004.
Engle, Margarita. *The Poet Slave of Cuba: A Biography of Juan Francisco Manzano*. Holt, 2006.
———. *The Surrender Tree*. Holt, 2008.
———. *Tropical Secrets: Holocaust Refugees in Cuba*. Holt, 2009. (Novel in Verse)
Greenfield, Eloise. *Under the Sunday Tree*. Illus. by Amos Ferguson. HarperCollins, 1988.
Gunning, Monica. *Not a Copper Penny in Me House*. Illus. by Frané Lessac. Boyds Mills, 1993.
Joseph, Lynn. *An Island Christmas*. Illus. by Catherine Stock. Houghton, 1996.
Lessac, Frané, sel. *Caribbean Canvas*. HarperCollins, 1989.
Nichols, Grace. *Come on into My Tropical Garden*. HarperCollins, 1990.

Europe (See Also World History)

Anderson, M. T. *Strange Mr. Satie*. Illus. by Petra Mathers. Viking, 2003.
Bemelmans, Ludwig. *Madeline*. Viking, 1939, 1962.
Collins, Judy. *My Father*. Illus. by Jane Dyer. Little, 1989.
Kimmelman, Leslie. *Everybody Bonjours!* Illus. by Sarah McMenemy. Knopf, 2008.
Krull, Kathleen, sel. *A Pot O' Gold*. Illus. by David McPhail. Hyperion, 2004.
Marciano, John Bemelmans. *Madeline and the Cats of Rome*. Viking, 2008.

Australia

Herrick, Steven. *By the River*. Boyds Mills, 2006. (Novel in Verse)
———. *Naked Bunyip Dancing*. Illus. by Beth Norling. Front, 2005. (Novel in Verse)
Paterson, A. B. "Waltzing Matilda" & "Mulga Bill's Bicycle." In Rosen, Michael. *Classic Poetry*. Illus. by Paul Howard. Candlewick, 2009.
Shields, Carol Diggory. *Wombat Walkabout*. Illus. by Sophie Blackall. Dutton, 2009.

Mexico and Latin America

Alarcón, Francisco X. *From the Bellybutton of the Moon = Del Ombligo de la Luna*. Illus. by Maya Christina Gonzalez. Children's, 1998.
Andrews-Goebel, Nancy. *The Pot That Juan Built*. Illus. by David Diaz. Lee & Low, 2002.
Bernier-Grand, Carmen T. *Diego: Bigger Than Life*. Illus. by David Diaz. Cavendish, 2009.
———. *Frida: ¡Viva la Vida! = Long Live Life*. Cavendish, 2007.
Delacre, Lulu, sel. *Arroz con Leche*. Scholastic, 1989.
Franklin, Kristine L. & Nancy McGirr, eds. *Out of the Dump*. Lothrop, 1995.
Griego, Margot C., Betsy L. Bucks, & Laurel H. Kimball, sels. *Tortillitas para Mamá*. Illus. by Barbara Cooney. Holt, 1981.
Jaramillo, Nelly Palacio. *Las Nanas de Abuelita = Grandmother's Nursery Rhymes*. Illus. by Elivia Savadier. Holt, 1994.
Johnston, Tony. *The Ancestors Are Singing*. Illus. by Karen Barbour. Farrar, 2003.
———. *My Mexico = México Mío*. Illus. by F. John Sierra. Putnam, 1996.
———. *P Is for Piñata*. Illus. by John Parra. Sleeping Bear, 2008.
Mora, Pat. Section: "Thorns." *My Own True Name*. Arté Público, 2000.
———. *Uno, Dos, Tres = One, Two, Three*. Illus. by Barbara Lavallee. Clarion, 1996.

Nye, Naomi Shihab, sel. *The Tree Is Older Than You Are.* S & S, 1995.

Orozco, José-Luis, sel. *Fiestas.* Illus. by Elisa Kleven. Dutton, 2002.

Ray, Deborah Kogan. *To Go Singing Through the World.* Farrar, 2006.

Sayre, April Pulley. *Army Ant Parade.* Illus. by Rick Chrustowski. Holt, 2002.

Serrano, Francisco. *The Poet King of Tezcoco.* Illus. by Pablo Serrano. Groundwood, 2007.

THEME ONE: CULTURAL DIVERSITY IN THE UNITED STATES

American Indians

Baylor, Byrd. *The Desert Is Theirs.* Illus. by Peter Parnall. Macmillan, 1975. (Papago)

Begay, Shonto. "Grandmother." In Hittleman, Carol G. & Daniel R. Hittleman. *A Grand Celebration.* Illus. by Kay Life. Boyds Mills, 2002. (Navajo)

Belting, Natalia. *Whirlwind Is a Spirit Dancing: Poems Based on Traditional American Indian Songs and Stories.* Illus. by Leo & Diane Dillon. Milk & Cookie, 2006.

Bierhorst, John. *In the Trail of the Wind: American Indian Poems and Ritual Orations.* Farrar, 1971.

Brandon, William, sel. *The Magic World: American Indian Songs and Poems.* Morrow, 1971.

Bruchac, Joseph. *Between Earth and Sky: Legends of Native American Sacred Places.* Illus. by Thomas Locker. Harcourt, 1996.

———. "Song to the Firefly" & "Longhouse Song." In Janeczko, Paul B. *Seeing the Blue Between.* Candlewick, 2002.

———. *Thirteen Moons on Turtle's Back: A Native American Year of Moons.* Illus. by Thomas Locker. Philomel, 1992.

Clark, Ann Nolan. *In My Mother's House.* Illus. by Velino Herrara. Viking, 1991. (Tewa)

Clements, Susan. "The Reservation." In Meltzer, Milton. *Hour of Freedom.* Boyds Mills, 2003.

Daniels, Shirley. "Drums of My Fathers." In Booth, David. *'Til All the Stars Have Fallen.* Illus. by Kady MacDonald Denton. Viking, 1990.

Freneau, Philip. "The Indian Burying Ground." In Meltzer, Milton. *Hour of Freedom.* Boyds Mills, 2003.

Frost, Helen. *Diamond Willow.* Farrar, 2008. (Novel in Verse) (Athapascan people)

———. "My People: Jack." *Spinning Through the Universe.* Farrar, 1998. (Novel in Verse)

George, Chief Dan. "And My Heart Soars." In Booth, David. *'Til All the Stars Have Fallen.* Illus. by Kady McDonald Denton. Viking, 1990.

Harjo, Joy. "Naming, or There Is No Such Thing as an Indian." In Greenberg, Jan. *Heart to Heart.* Abrams, 2001.

Hirschfelder, Arlene B. & Beverly R. Singer, ed. *Rising Voices.* Scribner's, 1992.

Katz, Bobbi. "The First Americans," "A Message for the Settlers: Chief Wahunsonacock (Powhatan)," & "The Trail of Tears: Barbara Wank." *We the People.* Illus. by Nina Crews. HarperCollins, 2000.

Kenny, Maurice. "Legacy." In Panzer, Nora. *Celebrate America.* Hyperion, 1994.

Livingston, Myra Cohn. "Creek Indian Busk or New Year: The Old Men's Dance." *Festivals.* Illus. by Leonard Everett Fisher, 1996.

Louis, Adrian C. "Petroglyphs of Serena." In Meltzer, Milton. *Hour of Freedom.* Boyds Mills, 2003. (Pine Ridge)

Maher, Ramona. *Alice Yazzie's Year.* Illus. by Shonto Begay. Ten Speed, 2004. (Navaho)

———. "September = Bini'ant'aatsoh." In Kennedy, Dorothy M. *I Thought I'd Take My Rat to School.* Illus. by Abby Carter. Little, 1993. (Navaho)

Mederis, Angela Shelf. *Dancing with the Indians.* Illus. by Samuel Byrd. Holiday, 1991. (Seminole)

Mora, Pat. "Tall Walking Woman." *This Big Sky.* Illus. by Steve Jenkins. Scholastic, 1998.

———. "Tigua Elder." *My Own True Name.* Arté Público, 2000.

Ochoa, Annette Piña, Betsy Franco, & Traci L. Gourdine, eds. *Night Is Gone, Day Is Still Coming.* Candlewick, 2003.

Pomerantz, Charlotte. "Where Do These Words Come From?" In De Regniers, Beatrice Schenk. *Sing a Song of Popcorn.* Scholastic, 1988.

Sandburg, Carl. "Circles." In Meltzer, Milton. *Hour of Freedom*. Boyds Mills, 2003. (Also in *Rainbows Are Made*)
Shields, Carol Diggory. "Trail of Tears." *American History, Fresh Squeezed!* Illus. by Richard Thompson. Handprint, 2002.
Silko, Leslie Marmon. "In Cold Storm Light." In Clinton, Catherine. *A Poem of Her Own*. Illus. by Stephen Alcorn. Abrams, 2003.
Sneve, Virginia Driving Hawk, sel. *Dancing Teepees*. Illus. by Stephen Gammell. Holiday, 1989.
———. *Enduring Wisdom*. Illus. by Synthia Saint James. Holiday, 2003.
Swamp, Chief Jake. *Giving Thanks*. Illus. by Erwin Printup Jr. Lee & Low, 1995.
Turner, Ann. *Sitting Bull Remembers*. Illus. by Wendell Minor. HarperCollins, 2007.
"White Floating Clouds," "The Grass on the Mountain" (Paiute), "Is It Raining Up There?" (Papago), "The Corn Grows Up" (Navaho), & "Nicely, Nicely" (Zuni). In Brenner, Barbara. *The Earth Is Painted Green*. Illus. by S. D. Schindler. Scholastic, 1994.
Yolen, Jane. "Four Corners." *Sacred Places*. Illus. by David Shannon. Harcourt, 1996.

Immigrants

America is a nation of immigrants, and yet those whose families have been in this country have lost of sense of their origins over time. Donald Graves captures this feeling in his poem "Not from Anywhere." Emma Lazarus' "The New Colossus" posted on the Statue of Liberty has come to represent America's opportunities for immigrants. What the poetry reveals is that the sadness of leaving a known language, culture, family, and friends is as strong as the pull toward a better life. Allen Say's picture book *Grandfather's Journey* describes it this way: "The funny thing is, the moment I am in one country, I am homesick for the other." (p. 31) Many students are born in this country, but their immigrant parents struggle with language and cultural changes. Jane Medina's "The Parent-Teacher Conference = La Conferencia" captures the role many children play as go-betweens for their parents who now live in a culture and language they don't understand.

Ada, Alma Flor. "Mexico." *Gathering the Sun*. Illus. by Simon Silva. HarperCollins, 1994.
Adoff, Arnold. "Great Grandma Ida," "Borders," & "Four Foot Feat." *All the Colors of the Race*. Illus. by John Steptoe. Morrow, 1982.
Applegate, Katherine. *Home of the Brave*. Feiwel, 2007. (Novel in Verse)
Baca, Jimmy Santiago. "Immigrants in Our Own Land." In Meltzer, Milton. *Hour of Freedom*. Illus. by Marc Nadel. Boyds Mills, 2003.
Citino, David. "Steerage." In Greenberg, Jan. *Heart to Heart*. Abrams, 2001.
Graves, Donald. "Not from Anywhere." *Baseball, Snakes, and Summer Squash*. Boyds Mills, 1996.
Gunning, Monica. *America, My New Home*. Illus. by Ken Condon. Boyds Mills, 2004.
Hoffman, Martin & Woody Guthrie. "Deportee: Plane Wreck at Los Gatos." In Stavens, Ilan. *¡Wachale!* Cricket, 2001.
Katz, Bobbi. "Letter to China." *We the People*. Illus. by Nina Crews. Greenwillow, 2000.
Lai, Him Mark, Genny Lim, and Judy Yung. *Island: Poetry and History of Chinese Immigrants on Angel Island, 1910–1940*. University of Washington, 2003.
Lazarus, Emma. "The New Colossus." In Clinton, Catherine. *A Poem of Her Own*. Illus. by Stephen Alcorn. Abrams, 2003. (Also in *Days to Celebrate*)
Lee, Li-Young. "I Ask My Mother to Sing." In Panzer, Nora. *Celebrate America*. Smithsonian/Hyperion, 1994.
Lewis, J. Patrick. "The Immigrants." *Heroes and She-roes*. Illus. by Jim Cooke. Dial, 2005.
———. "Statue of Liberty." *Monumental Verses*. National Geographic, 2005.
Medina, Jane. "The Parent-Teacher Conference = La Conferencia." *The Dream on Blanca's Wall = El Sueño Pegado en la Pared de Blanca*. Illus. by Robert Casilla. Boyds Mills, 2004.

Mora, Pat. "Immigrants = Los Immigrantes," "Elena," "Two Worlds," & "Learning English: Chorus in Many Voices." *My Own True Name.* Arté Público, 2000.

———. "A Voice." In Nye, Naomi Shihab. *Is This Forever or What?* HarperCollins, 2004.

Mura, David. "Fresh from the Island Angel." In Greenberg, Jan. *Heart to Heart.* Abrams, 2001.

Nye, Naomi Shihab. "My Father and the Fig Tree" & "What Kind of Fool Am I?" *19 Varieties of Gazelle.* HarperCollins, 2002.

Say, Allen. *Grandfather's Journey.* Houghton, 1993. (Prose)

Song, Cathy. "Lost Sister." In Clinton, Catherine. *A Poem of Her Own.* Illus. by Stephen Alcorn. Abrams, 2003.

Suárez-Baez, Emma. "Almost Evenly Divided." In Nye, Naomi Shihab. *What Have You Lost?* Greenwillow, 1999.

Testa, Maria. *Something About America.* Candlewick, 2005. (Novel in Verse)

African Americans

A number of collections of poetry by and about African Americans have been published in the last few years, some with accompanying works of art. In addition, volumes of poetry and individual poems by Ysaye M. Barnwell, Geraldine Brooks, Ashley Bryan, Lucille Clifton, Nikki Giovanni, Eloise Greenfield, Nikki Grimes, Langston Hughes, Angela Johnson, Walter Dean Myers, Marilyn Nelson, Ntozake Shange, Joyce Carol Thomas, and Carole Boston Weatherford are included throughout this book. Poems about African American roots and cultural traditions are listed after the collections below.

Anthologies of African American Poetry

Adedjouma, Davida, ed. *The Palm of My Heart: Poetry of African-America Children.* Illus. by R. Gregory Christie. Lee & Low, 1996.

Adoff, Arnold, sel. *I Am the Darker Brother: An Anthology of Modern Poems by Black Americans.* Macmillan, 1970.

———, sel. *My Black Me: A Beginning Book of Black Poetry.* Dutton, 1974.

Bryan, Ashley. *Ashley Bryan's ABC of African-American Poetry.* S & S, 1997.

Clinton, Catherine. *I, Too, Sing America: Three Centuries of African American Poetry.* Illus. by Stephen Alcorn. Houghton, 1998.

Giovanni, Nikki. *Shimmy Shimmy Shimmy Like My Sister Kate: Looking at the Harlem Renaissance Through Poems.* Holt, 1996.

Hudson, Wade, ed. *Pass it on: African American Poetry for Children.* Illus. by Floyd Cooper. Scholastic, 1993.

Rochelle, Belinda, sel. *Words with Wings: A Treasury of African-American Poetry and Art.* HarperCollins, 2001.

Slier, Deborah, sel. *Make a Joyful Sound.* Illus. by Cornelius Van Wright & Ying-Hwa Hu. Checkerboard, 1991.

Steptoe, Javaka, sel. and illus. *In Daddy's Arms I Am Tall: African-Americans Celebrating Fathers.* Lee & Low, 1997.

Strickland, Dorothy S. & Michael R. Strickland. sel. *Families: Poems Celebrating the African-American Experience.* Illus. by John Ward. Boyds Mills, 1994.

Sullivan, Charles, sel. *Children of Promise.* Abrams, 1991.

African American Roots and Traditions

Bennett, Gwendolyn B. "Heritage." In Clinton, Catherine. *I, Too, Sing America.* Illus. by Stephen Alcorn. Houghton, 1998.

Bryan, Ashley. "Ancestry." *Sing to the Sun.* HarperCollins, 1992

Cullen, Countee. "Heritage." In Giovanni, Nikki. *Shimmy Shimmy Shimmy Like My Sister Kate.* Holt, 1996.

English, Karen. "I Come from the Ones Who Lived (Malcolm.)" *Speak to Me (and I Will Listen Between the Lines).* Illus. by Amy June Bates. Farrar, 2004.

Greenfield, Eloise. *Africa Dream.* Illus. by Carol Byard. HarperCollins, 1977.

———. "Tradition." *Under the Sunday Tree.* Illus. by Amos Ferguson. HarperCollins, 1988.

Hines, Ann Grossnickle. "Kwanzaa." *Winter Lights.* HarperCollins, 2005.

Hru, Dakari Kamau. "The Mask." In Slier, Deborah. *Make a Joyful Sound.* Illus. by Cornelius Van Wright & Ying-Hwa Hu. Checkerboard, 1991.

Hughes, Langston. "Afro-American Fragment" & "Drums." In Roessel, David & Arnold Rampersad, *Langston Hughes.* Illus. by Benny Andrews. Sterling, 2006.

———. "The Negro" & "African Dance." *The Dream Keeper.* Illus. by Bryan Pinkney. Knopf, 1994.

Igus, Toyomi. *I See the Rhythm.* Illus. by Michelle Wood. Children's, 1998.

Livingston, Myra Cohn. "Kwanzaa." *Festivals.* Illus. by Leonard Everett Fisher. Holiday, 1996.

Long, Doughtry. "#4." In Slier, Deborah. *Make a Joyful Sound.* Illus. by Cornelius Van Wright & Ying-Hwa Hu. Checkerboard, 1991.

McLester, Cedric. "Kwanzaa Is . . . " In Slier, Deborah. *Make a Joyful Sound.* Illus. by Cornelius Van Wright & Ying-Hwa Hu. Checkerboard, 1991.

Myers, Walter Dean. "Pride." *Brown Angels.* HarperCollins, 1993.

Oyewole, Abiodun. "Africa." In Slier, Deborah. *Make a Joyful Sound.* Illus. by Cornelius Van Wright & Ying-Hwa Hu. Checkerboard, 1991.

Perkins, Useni Eugene. "Ayo." In Slier, Deborah. *Make a Joyful Sound.* Illus. by Cornelius Van Wright & Ying-Hwa Hu. Checkerboard, 1991.

Sanchez, Sonia. "Haiku." In Slier, Deborah. *Make a Joyful Sound.* Illus. by Cornelius Van Wright & Ying-Hwa Hu. Checkerboard, 1991.

Latino Americans

Ada, Alma Flor. *Gathering the Sun.* HarperCollins, 1997.

Alarcón, Francisco X. *Angels Ride Bikes = Los Ángeles Andan en Bicycleta* . Illus. by Maya Christina Gonzalez. Children's, 1999.

———. *Iguanas in the Snow = Iguanas en la Nieve.* Illus. by Maya Christina Gonzalez. Children's, 2001.

———. *Laughing Tomatoes = Jitomates Risueños.* Illus. by Maya Christina Gonzalez. Children's, 1997.

———. *Poems to Dream Together = Poemas para Sonar Juntos.* Illus. by Paula Barragán. Lee & Low, 2005.

Argueta, Jorge. *A Movie in My Pillow = Una Pelicula en mi Almohada.* Illus. by Elizabeth Gómez. Children's, 2001.

Caraballo, Samuel. *Mis Abuelos y Yo = My Grandparents and I.* Illus. by D. Nina Cruz. Arté Público, 2004.

Carlson, Lori M. ed. *Cool Salsa.* Holt, 1994.

———. *Sol a Sol.* Illus. by Emily Lisker. Holt, 1998.

Cisneros, Sandra. *Hairs = Pelitos.* Illus. by Terry Ybañez. Knopf, 1994.

Elya, Susan Middleton. *F Is for Fiesta.* Illus. by G. Brian Karas. Putnam, 2006.

———. *N Is for Navidad.* Illus. by Joe Cepeda. Chronicle, 2007.

Flores-Morales, Julia. "Barrio School." In Kennedy, Dorothy M. *I Thought I'd Take My Rat to School.* Illus. by Abby Carter. Little. 1993.

Herrera, Juan Felipe. *Calling the Doves = El Canto de las Palomas.* Illus. by Elly Simons. Children's, 1995.

———. *Downtown Boy.* Scholastic, 2005. (Novel in Verse)

———. *The Upside Down Boy = El Niño de Cabeza.* Illus. by Elizabeth Gómez. Children's, 2000.

Hines, Anna Grossnickle. "Farolitos." *Winter Lights.* HarperCollins, 2005.

Johnston, Tony. "Posada, Tepotzotlan." *The Ancestors Are Singing.* Illus. by Karen Barbour. Farrar, 2003.

Livingston, Myra Cohn. "Las Posadas." *Festivals.* Illus. by Leonard Everett Fisher. Holiday, 1996.

Medina, Jane. *The Dream on Blanca's Wall = El Sueño Pegado en la Pared de Blanca.* Illus. by Robert Casilla. Boyds Mills, 2004.

———. *My Name Is Jorge.* Illus. by Fabricio Vanden Broeck. Boyds Mills, 1999.

Mora, Pat. *Confetti.* Illus. by Enrique O. Sanchez. Lee & Low, 1996.

———. *My Own True Name*. Arté Público, 2000.
Rios, Alberto. "Day of the Refugios." In Panzer, Nora. *Celebrate America*. Hyperion, 1994.
Soto, Gary. *Canto Familiar*. Illus. by Annika Nelson. Harcourt, 1995.
———. *A Fire in My Hands*. Harcourt, 2006.
———. *Neighborhood Odes*. Illus. by David Diaz. Harcourt, 1992.
Stavans, Ilan, ed. *¡Wachale!* Cricket, 2001.

Asian and Middle Eastern Americans

Cheng, Andrea. *Shanghai Messenger*. Illus. by Ed Young. Lee & Low, 2005. (Novel in Verse)
Glenn, Mel. *Split Image*. HarperCollins, 2002. (Novel in Verse)
Hom, Marlon K. *Songs of Gold Mountain*. University of California, 1987.
Katz, Bobbi. "At the Gila River Camp: Roy Kato" & "A Letter to China: Kun Yang Lin." *We the People*. Illus. by Nina Crews. HarperCollins, 2000.
Lai, Him Mark, Genny Lim, & Judy Yung. *Island: Poetry and History of Chinese Immigrants on Angel Island, 1910–1940*. University of Washington, 2003.
Lee, Li-Young. "I Ask My Mother to Sing." In Panzer, Nora. *Celebrate America*. Hyperion, 1994.
Livingston, Myra Cohn. "Chinese New Year," "Tet Nguyen-Dan," and "Cherry Blossom Festival." In *Festivals*. Illus. by Leonard Everett Fisher. Holiday, 1996.
Mak, Kam. *My Chinatown*. HarperCollins, 2002.
Nye, Naomi Shihab. *19 Varieties of Gazelle*. Greenwillow, 2002.
Okita, Dwight. "In Response to Executive Order 9066: All Americans of Japanese Descent Must Report To Relocation Centers." In Meltzer, Milton. *Hour of Freedom*. Boyds Mills, 2003. (Also in *Celebrate America*)
Park, Linda Sue. *Bee-Bim Bop!* Illus. by Ho Baek Lee. Clarion, 2005.
Wong, Janet S. *Good Luck Gold*. McElderry, 1994
———. "Prayer for the Lunar New Year." In Hopkins, Lee Bennett. *Days to Celebrate*. Illus. by Stephen Alcorn. HarperCollins, 2005.
———. *A Suitcase of Seaweed*. Booksurge, 2008.

Mixed Heritage

In *A Suitcase of Seaweed*, Janet Wong divides her poems into three sections that represent the three aspects of her heritage: Korean, Chinese, and American. She also explores the topic of mixed heritage in her two novels in verse about Minn and Jake. Arnold Adoff writes about his own loving mixed-race family in *Black Is Brown Is Tan* and *All the Colors of the Race*.

Adoff, Arnold. *All the Colors of the Race*. Illus. by John Steptoe. Morrow, 1982.
———. *Black Is Brown Is Tan*. Illus. by Emily Arnold McCully. HarperCollins, 2002.
Cheng, Andrea. *Shanghai Messenger*. Illus. by Ed Young. Lee & Low, 2005.
Grimes, Nikki. *Aneesa Lee and the Weaver's Gift*. Illus. by Ashley Bryan. Lothrop, 1999.
———. *Dark Sons*. Hyperion, 2006. (Novel in verse)
Hogan, Linda. "The Truth Is." In Philip, Neil. *It's a Woman's World*. Dutton, 2000.
McLoughland, Beverly. "Lisa." In Hollyer, Belinda. *She's All That*. Illus. by Susan Hellard. Houghton, 2006
Wong, Janet. *Minn and Jake*. Illus. by Geneviève Côté. Farrar, 2003. (Novel in Verse)
———. *Minn and Jake's Almost Terrible Summer*. Illus. by Geneviève Côté. Farrar, 2008. (Novel in Verse)

Theme Two: Time, Continuity, and Change. Human beings seek to understand their historical roots and to locate themselves in time. Knowing how to read and reconstruct the past allows

one to develop a historical perspective and to answer such questions as: Who am I? What happened in the past? How am I connected to those in the past? How has the world changed and how might it change in the future? Why does our personal sense of relatedness to the past change?

THEME TWO: WORLD HISTORY AND BIOGRAPHY

Too often studying history means memorizing names and dates—a process that kills student interest in the past. We need to feel our connections to the past. Jack Prelutsky points out in "I'm Learning Our History" that "We're all part of history—it's happening now." Reza Shirazi's "History Class" describes the difference between wading through those school experiences, and actually visiting one of the sites where history was made.

In a very short poem, "Buffalo Dusk," Carol Sandburg captures the relentless movement of history, even when much is lost. One of the hardest lessons for students to grasp is that history is not fixed. Our understanding of events changes as we see those events in different contexts or from different perspectives. History is the stories we tell ourselves about events, and those stories are modified and rethought as our experiences change. It is important to look at differing interpretations of events. Some worry that students should not learn about the mistakes of the past. A quote from John F. Kennedy on the title page of Nora Panzer's *Celebrate America* says that we must trust our citizens with "unpleasant facts, foreign ideas, alien philosophies, and competitive values," if we believe in thinking people in a democracy.

History is not made up only of big events. It occurs in the lives of all people. Poets tell the stories of women and children who lived everyday lives in the past. Poets are telling the histories of people from various cultural traditions. African American poets are telling their own history in new ways. Too often, for example, the image of dispirited slaves waiting for rescue has been recreated in history books. In Jeanette Winter's *Follow the Drinking Gourd*, an illustrated version of the well-known spiritual, a white man, Peg-Leg Joe, tells the slaves about the dipper and helps them escape. Students can compare that with Robert Hayden's powerful "Runagate, Runagate" to see a more complex picture of runaway slaves.

History and biography are presented together in the following poems, arranged by time periods. Some people are the subjects of many poems. These are grouped together after works in the historical periods.

Dakos, Kalli. "Herstory = Her Story." *Don't Read This Book, Whatever You Do!* Illus. G. Brian Karas. S & S, 1993.

Prelutsky, Jack. "I'm Learning Our History." *What a Day it Was at School!* Illus. by Doug Cushman. Harper Collins, 2006.

Sandburg. Carl. "Buffalo Dusk." *Rainbows are Made*. Illus. by Fritz Eichenberg. Harcourt, 1982. (Also in *Sing a Song of Popcorn*)

Shirazi, Reza. "History Class." In Nye, Naomi Shihab. *The Space Between Our Footsteps*. S & S, 1998. (Also in *The Flag of Childhood*)

Stoker, Austin. "History." In Nye, Naomi Shihab. *Salting the Ocean*. Illus. by Ashley Bryan. Greenwillow, 2000.

Whitman, Walt. "When I Read the Book." *Voyages*. Harcourt, 1988.

Collections of Biographical Poems

Hopkins, Lee Bennett, ed. *Lives: Poems About Famous Americans*. Illus. by Leslie Staub. HarperCollins, 1999.

Katz, Bobbi. *Trailblazers: Poems of Exploration*. Illus. by Carin Berger. HarperCollins, 2007.

———. *We the People*. Illus. by Nina Crews. Greenwillow, 2000.

Lewis, J. Patrick. *Freedom Like Sunlight: Praisesongs for Black Americans*. Illus. by John Thompson. Creative, 2000.

———. *Heroes and She-Roes: Poems of Amazing and Everyday Heroes*. Illus. by Jim Cooke. Dial, 2005.

———. *Vherses: A Celebration of Outstanding Women*. Illus. by Mark Summers. Creative, 2005.

Paul, Ann Whitford. *All by Herself*. Illus. by Michael Steirnagle. Harcourt, 1999.

Ancient History

Baylor, Byrd. *One Small Blue Bead* Illus. by Symeon Shimin. Macmillan, 1965.

Brandon, William. (Twelve poems from the Nahuatl and Maya cultures) *The Magic World*. Morrow, 1971.

Bruchac, Joseph. *Between Earth and Sky*. Illus. by Thomas Locker. Harcourt, 1996.

Bunting, Eve. *I Am the Mummy Heb-Nefert*. Illus. by David Christiana. Harcourt, 1997.

Harley, Avis. "Catching a Butterfly (2)." *The Monarch's Progress*. Boyds Mills, 2008.

Hovey, Kate. *Voices of the Trojan War*. Illus. by Leonid Gore. McElderry, 2004.

Katz, Susan. "The Mummy's Smile." *Mrs. Brown on Exhibit*. Illus. by R. W. Alley. S & S, 2002.

Lewis, J. Patrick. "Stonehenge," "Easter Island," Great Pyramid of Cheops," & "Rose City of Petra." *Monumental Verses*. National Geographic, 2005.

Livingston, Myra Cohn. "Mummy." In Hopkins, Lee Bennett. *Behind the Museum Door*. Illus. by Stacey Dressen-McQueen. Abrams, 2007.

"Love Lyric." Trans. from ancient Egyptian by Noel Stock. In Smith, William Jay. *Here Is My Heart*. Illus. by Jane Dyer. Little, 1999.

Singer, Marilyn. "Fire-Bringers." *Central Heating*. Illus. by Meilo So. Knopf, 2005.

Smith, William Jay. "The Queen of the Nile." *Here Is My Heart*. Illus. by Jane Dyer. Little, 1999.

Steig, Jeanne. "Exegesis on the Sphinx." *Alpha Beta Chowder*. Illus. by William Steig. HarperCollins, 1992.

Yolen, Jane. "Copan," "Easter Island," & "Stonehenge." *Sacred Places*. Illus. by David Shannon. Harcourt, 1996.

———. "Wheels." In Hopkins, Lee Bennett. *Behind the Museum Door*. Illus. by Stacey Dressen-McQueen. Abrams, 2007. (Mesopotamia)

The Middle Ages

Ashman, Linda. *Come to the Castle!* Illus. by S. D. Schindler. Roaring Brook, 2009.

Brug, Sondra Gilbert. "Tales in Tapestry." In Hopkins, Lee Bennett. *Behind the Museum Door*. Illus. by Stacey Dressen-McQueen. Abrams, 2007.

"The Irish Student and his Cat." From an anonymous 8th/9th century manuscript. In Krull, Kathleen, sel. *A Pot O' Gold*. Illus. by David McPhail. Hyperion, 2004.

Katz, Susan. "Middle Ages." *Mrs. Brown on Exhibit*. Illus. by R. W. Alley. S & S, 2002.

Lewis, J. Patrick. "Machu Picchu." *Monumental Verses*. National Geographic, 2005.

Lewis, J. Patrick & Rebecca Kai Dotlich. *Castles*. Illus. by Dan Burr. Boyds Mills, 2006.

Lindbergh, Reeve, ret. *The Circle of Days: From Canticle of the Sun by St. Francis of Assisi*. Illus. by Cathie Felstead. Candlewick, 1998.

McLoughland, Beverly. "Suit of Armor." In Hopkins, Lee Bennett. *Behind the Museum Door*. Illus. by Stacey Dressen-McQueen. Abrams, 2007.

Nikola-Lisa. W. *Till Year's Good End: A Calendar of Medieval Labors*. Illus. by Christopher Manson. Atheneum, 1997.

Sandell, Lisa Ann. *Song of the Sparrow*. Scholastic, 2007. (Novel in Verse) (5th-century Britain)

Schlitz, Laura Amy. *Good Masters! Sweet Ladies! Voices from a Medieval Village*. Illus. by Robert Byrd. Candlewick, 2007.

Other European History

Frost, Helen. *The Braid*. Farrar, 2006. (Novel in Verse) (Highland Clearance)
George, Kristine O'Connell. "Joan of Arc." *Swimming Upstream*. Illus. by Debbie Tilley. Clarion, 2002.
Hardy, Thomas. "At the Railway Station, Upway." In Rosen, Michael. *Classic Poetry*. Illus. by Paul Howard. Candlewick, 2009.
Lewis, J. Patrick. "Arc de Triumphe" & "The Eiffel Tower." *Monumental Verses*. National Geographic, 2005.
Lewis, J. Patrick & Rebecca Kai Dotlich. "Tower of London." *Castles*. Illus. by Dan Burr. Boyds Mills, 2006
Shakespeare, William. *Winter Song*. Illus. by Melanie Hall. Boyds Mills, 2006.
Stevenson, Robert Louis. "Keepsake Mill," "The Lamplighter," & "From a Railway Carriage." *A Child's Garden of Verses*. Illus. by Diane Goode. Morrow, 1998.

Pirates

Harrison, David L. *Pirates*. Illus. by Dan Burr. Boyds Mills, 2008.
Kiesler, Kate. "The Parrot." *Wings on the Wind*. Clarion, 2002.
Schertle, Alice. "Galleon." *Keepers*. Illus. by Ted Rand. Lothrop, 1996.
Silverstein, Shel. "Morgan's Curse." *Falling Up*. HarperCollins, 1996.
Stevenson, Robert Louis. "Pirate Story." *A Child's Garden of Verses*. Illus. by Diane Goode. Morrow, 1998.
Thomson, Sarah L. *Pirates, Ho!* Illus. by Stephen Gilpin. Cavendish, 2008.
Yolen, Jane. *The Ballad of the Pirate Queens*. Illus. by David Shannon. Harcourt, 1995.

World War I

Dunbar-Nelson, Alice. "I Sit and Sew." In Clinton, Katherine. *A Poem of Her Own*. Illus. by Stephen Alcorn. Abrams, 2003.
Lewis, Claudia. "Over There" & "Armistice Day, World War I." *Long Ago in Oregon*. Illus. by Joel Fontaine. HarperCollins, 1987.
Masefield, John. "The General." In Rosen, Michael. *Classic Poetry*. Illus. by Paul Howard. Candlewick, 2009.
McCrae, John. "In Flanders Fields." In Hopkins, Lee Bennett. *America at War*. Illus. by Stephen Alcorn. S & S, 2008.
Sandburg, Carl. "Grass." In Hopkins, Lee Bennett. *America at War*. Illus. by Stephen Alcorn. S & S, 2008.
Shields, Carol Diggory. "The Great War." *American History, Fresh Squeezed!* Illus. by Richard Thompson. Handprint, 2002.
Teasdale, Sara. "There Will Come Soft Rains." In Hopkins, Lee Bennett. *America at War*. Illus. by Stephen Alcorn. S & S, 2008.
Yeats, William Butler. "An Irish Airman Foresees His Death." In Rosen, Michael. *Classic Poetry*. Illus. by Paul Howard. Candlewick, 2009.

World War II

Borden, Louise. *Across the Blue Pacific*. Illus. by Robert Andrew Parker. Houghton, 2006.
Engle, Margarita. *Tropical Secrets: Holocaust Refugees in Cuba*. Holt, 2009. (Novel in Verse)
Hesse, Karen. *Aleutian Sparrow*. McElderry, 2003. (Novel in Verse)
Hopkins, Lee Bennett, sel. Section: "World War II." *America At War*. Illus. by Stephen Alcorn. McElderry, 2008.
Jennings, Elizabeth. "The Second World War." In Philip, Neil, *It's a Woman's World*. Dutton, 2000.
Judge, Lita. *One Thousand Tracings: Healing the Wounds of World War II*. Hyperion, 2007.
Katz, Bobbi. "On the Home Front: Gina Shaw" & "At the Gila River Camp: Roy Kato." *We the People*. Illus. by Nina Crews. Greenwillow, 2000.

———. "When Granny Made My Lunch." In Janeczko, Paul B. *Seeing the Blue Between.* Candlewick, 2002. (Holocaust Survivor)

Lewis, J. Patrick. "People Are Really Good at Heart: Anne Frank." *Vherses.* Illus. by Mark Summers. Creative Eds. 2005.

LeZotte, Ann Clare. *T4: A Novel in Verse.* Houghton, 2008.

Myers, Walter Dean. "Frank G." & "Lemuel B." *Here in Harlem.*Holiday, 2004.

Noriko, Ibaragi. "When I Was at My Most Beautiful." In Philip, Neil. *It's a Woman's World.* Dutton, 2000.

Okita, Dwight. "In Response to Executive Order 9066: All Americans of Japanese Descent Must Report to Relocation Centers." In Panzer, Nora. *Celebrate America.* Smithsonian/ Hyperion, 1994. (Also in *Hour of Freedom*)

Pickova, Eva. "Fear." In Philip, Neil. *It's a Woman's World.* Dutton, 2000.

Sadako, Kurihara. "Let Us Be Midwives." In Philip, Neil. *It's a Woman's World.* Dutton, 2000.

Testa, Maria. *Becoming Joe DiMaggio.* Candlewick, 2002. (Novel in Verse)

Volavková, Hana, ed. *I Never Saw Another Butterfly.* Knopf, 1994.

Wong, Nellie. "Can't Tell." In Philip, Neil. *It's a Woman's World.* Dutton, 2000.

Yolen Jane. *All Those Secrets of the World.* Illus. by Leslie Baker. Little, 1991.

THEME TWO: AMERICAN HISTORY AND BIOGRAPHY

Clinton, Catherine. *I, Too, Sing America.* Illus. by Stephen Alcorn. Houghton, 1998.

Hall, Donald, ed. *The Oxford Illustrated Book of American Children's Poems.* Oxford, 1999.

Hopkins, Lee Bennett, sel. *America at War.* Illus. by Stephen Alcorn. McElderry, 2008.

———. *Hand in Hand.* Illus. by Peter M. Fiore. S & S, 1994.

Johnston, Tony. *Yonder.* Illus. by Lloyd Bloom. Dial, 1988.

Katz, Bobbi. *We the People.* Illus. by Nina Crews. Greenwillow, 2000.

Meltzer, Milton, comp. *Hour of Freedom.* Boyds Mills, 2003.

Panzer, Nora, ed. *Celebrate America.* Smithsonian/Hyperion, 1994.

Rochelle, Belinda, sel. *Words with Wings.* HarperCollins, 2001.

Shields, Carol Diggory. *American History: Fresh Squeezed!* Illus. by Richard Thompson. Handprint, 2002.

Weatherford, Carole Boston. *Remember the Bridge.* Philomel, 2002.

The Earliest Americans

Bruchac, Joseph. *Between Earth and Sky: Legends of Native American Sacred Places.* Illus. by Thomas Locker. Harcourt, 1996.

Katz, Bobbi. "The First Americans." *We the People.* Illus. by Nina Cruz. HarperCollins, 2000.

Mora, Pat. *¡Yum! Mm Mm! Que Rico: America's Sproutings.* Illus. by Rafael López. Lee & Low, 2007.

Colonial Period

Freneau, Philip. "The Indian Burying Ground." In Meltzer, Milton. *Hour of Freedom.* Boyds Mills, 2003.

Katz, Bobbi. Section: "We the People." *We the People.* Illus. by Nina Cruz. HarperCollins, 2000.

Shields, Carol Diggory. "Manhattan" & "The Pilgrims." *American History, Fresh Squeezed!* Illus. by Richard Thompson. Handprint, 2002.

Sigourney, Lydia H."The Indians' Welcome to the Pilgrim Fathers." In Meltzer, Milton. *Hour of Freedom.* Boyds Mills, 2003.

Eighteenth-Century America

Aylesworth, Jim. *The Folks in the Valley.* Illus. by Stefano Vitale. HarperCollins, 1992.

Catrow, David. *We the Kids: The Preamble to the Constitution of the United States.* Dial, 2002.

Emerson, Ralph Waldo. "Concord Hymn." In Meltzer, Milton. *Hour of Freedom.* Boyds Mills, 2003.

Hopkins, Lee Bennett, sel. Section: "The American Revolution." *America at War.* Illus. by Stephen Alcorn. McElderry, 2008.

Hush, Little Baby: A Folk Song. Illus. by Marla Frazee. Harcourt, 1999.

Katz, Susan. *A Revolutionary Field Trip.* Illus. by R. W. Alley. S & S, 2004.

Kay, Verla. *Homespun Sarah.* Illus. by Ted Rand. Putnam, 2003.

Longfellow, Henry Wadsworth. *The Midnight Ride of Paul Revere.* Illus. by Jeffrey Thompson. National Geographic, 2002.

———. *The Midnight Ride of Paul Revere.* Illus. by Christopher Bing. Handprint, 2001.

———. *Paul Revere's Ride.* Illus. by Ted Rand. Dutton, 1990.

———. *Paul Revere's Ride: The Landlord's Tale.* Illus. by Charles Santore. HarperCollins, 2003.

Winters, Kay. *Colonial Voices.* Illus. by Larry Day. Dutton, 2008.

Yankee Doodle. Illus. by Steven Kellogg. S & S, 1976.

George Washington (1732–1799)

Chandra, Deborah & Madeleine Comora. *George Washington's Teeth.* Illus. by Brock Cole. Farrar, 2003.

Hopkins, Lee Bennett. "John Hancock." *Hand in Hand.* Illus. by Peter M. Fiore. S & S, 1994.

Katz, Bobbi. "Inauguration Day Thoughts" & "A Memorial Parade." *We the People.* Illus. by Nina Crews. Greenwillow, 2000.

———. "George Washington's Birthday: Wondering." In Hopkins, Lee Bennett, *Ring Out Wild Bells.* Illus. by Karen Baumann. Harcourt, 1992.

Livingston, Myra Cohn. "Paul Revere Speaks." In Hopkins, Lee Bennett. *Hand in Hand.* Illus. by Peter M. Fiore. S & S, 1994.

———. "President's Day." *Celebrations.* Illus. by Leonard Everett Fisher. Holiday, 1985.

Rowden, Justine. "Faster, Faster, Faster!" *Paint Me a Poem.* Boyds Mills, 2005.

Sandburg, Carl. "Washington Monument by Night." In Meltzer, Milton. *Hour of Freedom.* Boyds Mills, 2003.

Small, David. *George Washington's Cows.* Farrar, 1994.

Turner, Nancy Byrd. "Washington." In Ferris, Helen. *Favorite Poems Old and New.* Illus. by Leonard Weisgard. Random, 1957, 2009.

"Washington (Inscription At Mount Vernon)." In Hopkins, Lee Bennett. *Hand in Hand.* Illus. by Peter M. Fiore. S & S, 1994.

Slavery

Bontemps, Arna. "Southern Mansion." In Adoff, Arnold. *I Am the Darker Brother.* S & S, 1997.

Brand, Dionne. "Slave Ship." *Earth Magic.* Illus. by Eugenie Fernandes. Kids Can, 2006.

Clifton, Lucille. "Auction Street." In Rochelle, Belinda. *Words with Wings.* HarperCollins, 2001.

Dove, Rita. "The Abduction." In Meltzer, Milton. *Hour of Freedom.* Boyds Mills, 2003.

Engle, Margarita. *The Poet Slave of Cuba.* Illus. by Sean Qualls. Holt, 2006.

Fletcher, Ralph. "Bill of Sale." *A Writing Kind of Day.* Illus. by April Ward. Boyds Mills, 2005.

Garrison, William Lloyd. "The Hour of Freedom." In Meltzer, Milton. *Hour of Freedom.* Boyds Mills, 2003.

Hayden, Robert. "Runagate, Runagate." In Giovanni, Nikki. *Shimmy Shimmy Shimmy Like My Sister Kate.* Holt, 1996.

Hegamin, Tonya Cherie. *Most Loved in All the World.* Illus. by Cozbi A. Cabrera. Houghton, 2009.

Lewis, J. Patrick. "Down on the Plantation" & "White Nightmare." *The Brothers' War.* National Geographic, 2007.

Longfellow, Henry Wadsworth. "The Slave's Dream." In Rosen, Michael. *Classic Poetry.* Illus. by Paul Howard. Candlewick, 2009.

Nelson, Marilyn. *Fortune's Bones: The Manumission Requiem.* Front, 2004.

———. *The Freedom Business.* Illus. by Deborah Dancy. Boyds Mills, 2008.

Slate, Joseph. *I Want to Be Free.* Illus. by E. B. Lewis. Putnam, 2009.

Weatherford, Carole Boston. "On the Auction Block," "The Slave Storyteller," & "Jake's Plea." *Remember the Bridge.* Philomel, 2002.

Winter, Jeanette. *Follow the Drinking Gourd.* Knopf, 1988.

Harriet Tubman (1820–1913)

Adoff, Arnold. "I Was Harriet." *All the Colors of the Race.* Illus. by John Steptoe. Morrow, 1982.

Cornish, Sam. "Cross Over the River." In Adoff, Arnold. *My Black Me.* Dutton, 1974.

Greenfield, Eloise. "Harriet Tubman." In Hudson, Wade. *Pass It on.* Illus. by Floyd Cooper. Scholastic, 1993. (Also in *Make a Joyful Sound*)

"Harriet Tubman (On a Tablet in Auburn, New York)." In Hopkins, Lee Bennett. *Hand in Hand.* Illus. by Peter M. Fiore. S & S, 1994.

Katz, Bobbi. "Freedom!" *We the People.* Illus. by Nina Crews. Greenwillow, 2000. (Also in *Days to Celebrate*)

Lewis, J. Patrick. "Harriet Tubman Speaks." *Freedom Like Sunlight.* Illus. by John Thompson. Creative, 2000.

McLoughland, Beverly. "The Whippoorwill Calls." In Hopkins, Lee Bennett. *America at War.* Illus. by Stephen Alcorn. McElderry, 2008. (Also in *Hand in Hand*)

Weatherford, Carole Boston. "The Conductor Was a Woman (For Harriet Tubman)." *Remember the Bridge.* Philomel, 2002.

———. *Moses: When Harriet Tubman Led Her People to Freedom.* Illus. by Kadir Nelson. Hyperion, 2006.

Nineteenth-Century America

Alexander, Elizabeth & Marilyn Nelson. *Miss Crandall's School for Young Ladies of Color.* Illus. by Floyd Cooper. Boyds Mills, 2007. (1832–1834)

Anderson, M. T. *The Serpent Came to Gloucester.* Illus. by Bagram Ibatoulline. Candlewick, 2005. (1817 Massachusetts)

Child, Lydia Maria. *Over the River and Through the Wood.* Illus. by Christopher Manson. Night Sky, 2007.

———. *Over the River and Through the Wood.* Illus. by Brinton Turkle. Putnam, 1975.

Hale, Sarah Josepha. *Mary Had a Little Lamb.* Illus. by Tomie De Paola. Holiday, 1984.

Hall, Donald. *Ox-Cart Man.* Illus. by Barbara Cooney. Viking, 1979.

Hayden, Robert. "Frederick Douglass." In Giovanni, Nikki. *Shimmy Shimmy Shimmy Like My Sister Kate.* Holt, 1995.

Hughes, Langston. "Frederick Douglas: 1817–1895." In Hopkins, Lee Bennett. *Hand in Hand.* Illus. by Peter M. Fiore. S & S, 1994.

Katz, Bobbi. "Lullaby for Jean Baptiste" & "Explaining to Drouillard." *Trailblazers.* Illus. by Carin Berger. HarperCollins, 2007. (Sacagawea & York)

Kay, Verla. *Covered Wagons, Bumpy Trails.* Illus. by S. D. Schindler. Putnam, 2000.

———. *Gold Fever.* Illus. by S. D. Schindler. Putnam, 1999.

———. *Iron Horses.* Illus. by Michael McCurdy. Putnam, 1999.

———. *Orphan Train.* Illus. by Ken Stark. Putnam, 2003.

Lindbergh, Reeve. *Johnny Appleseed.* Illus. by Kathy Jakobsen. Little, 1990.

Nelson, Marilyn. *Carver: A Life in Poems.* Front, 2001. (1864–1943)

Nye, Naomi Shihab. "Full Day." *Come With Me.* Illus. by Dan Yaccarino. Greenwillow, 2000. (Westward Journey)

Paul, Ann Whitford. "Sacajawea" & "Harriet Hanson." *All by Herself.* Illus. by Michael Steirnagle. Harcourt, 1999. (Woman explorer & 1836 Mill workers' strike)

Thayer, Ernest Lawrence. *Casey at the Bat: A Ballad of the Republic Sung in the Year 1888.* Illus. by Patricia Polacco. Putnam, 1988.

Thomas, Joyce Carol. *I Have Heard of a Land.* Illus. by Floyd Cooper. HarperCollins, 1995. (Oklahoma Land Rush, 1889)

Turner, Ann. *Dakota Dugout.* Illus. by Ronald Himler. Macmillan, 1985.

———. *Sitting Bull Remembers.* Illus. by Wendell Minor. HarperCollins, 2007.

Vinz. Mark. "Lilacs." In Janeczko, Paul B. *Seeing the Blue Between.* Candlewick, 2002. (Westward Movement)

Weatherford, Carole Boston. "Bronze Cowboys." *Remember the Bridge.* Philomel, 2002.

Yolen, Jane. *Johnny Appleseed.* Illus. by Jim Burke. HarperCollins, 2008.

The Civil War (1860–1865)

Frost, Helen. "Brothers: Antoine." *Spinning Through the Universe.* Farrar, 2004. (Novel in Verse)

Hopkins, Lee Bennett, sel. Section: "The Civil War." *America at War.* Illus. by Stephen Alcorn. McElderry, 2008.

Howe, Julia Ward. "The Battle Hymn of the Republic." In Clinton, Catherine. *A Poem of Her Own.* Illus. by Stephen Alcorn. Abrams, 2003.

Kerley, Barbara. *Walt Whitman.* Illus. by Brian Selznick. Scholastic, 2004.

Lewis, J. Patrick. *The Brothers' War.* National Geographic, 2007.

Randall, Dudley. "Memorial Wreath: For the More Than 200,000 Who Served in the Union Army During the Civil War." In Adoff, Arnold. *I Am the Darker Brother.* S & S, 1996.

Weatherford, Carole Boston. "The Flag Bearer (For William Carney of Company C)." *Remember the Bridge.* Philomel, 2002.

Abraham Lincoln (1809–1865)

Aylesworth, Jim, adapt. *Our Abe Lincoln.* Illus. by Barbara McClintock. Scholastic, 2009.

Benet, Rosemary & Stephen Vincent. "Nancy Hanks." In Ferris, Helen. *Favorite Poems Old and New.* Illus. by Leonard Weisgard. Random, 1957, 2009. (Also in *Hour of Freedom*)

Hughes, Langston. "Lincoln Monument: Washington." *The Dream Keeper.* Illus. by Brian Pinkney. Knopf, 1993. (Also in *Ring Out Wild Bells*)

Johnson, James Weldon. *Lift Every Voice and Sing.* Illus. by Bryan Collier. HarperCollins, 2007. (For Lincoln's Birthday, 1900)

Katz, Bobbi. "At the Station, Part I," "A Bird's-Eye View of the Civil War," & "At the Station, Part II." *We the People.* Illus. by Nina Crews. Greenwillow, 2000.

Kennedy, X. J. "The Loneliness of Lincoln." In Hopkins, Lee Bennett. *Hand in Hand.* Illus. by Peter M. Fiore. S & S, 1994.

Lincoln, Abraham. *The Gettysburg Address.* Illus. by Michael McCurdy. Houghton, 1995.

———. "My Childhood Home." In Locker, Thomas & Candace Christiansen. *Home.* Harcourt, 2000.

Lindsay, Vachel. "Abraham Lincoln Walks at Midnight in Springfield, Illinois." In Ferris, Helen. *Favorite Poems Old and New.* Illus. by Leonard Weisgard. Random, 1957, 2009.

Livingston, Myra Cohn. "President's Day." *Celebrations.* Illus. by Leonard Everett Fisher. Holiday, 1985.

Merriam, Eve. "To Meet Mr. Lincoln." In De Regniers, Beatrice Schenk. *Sing a Song of Popcorn.* Scholastic, 1988.

Rappaport, Doreen. *Abe's Honest Words.* Illus. by Kadir Nelson. Hyperion, 2008.

Schertle, Alice. "Abe." In Hopkins, Lee Bennett. *Lives.* Illus. by Leslie Staub. HarperCollins, 1999.

Turner, Nancy Byrd. "Lincoln." In Ferris, Helen. *Favorite Poems Old and New.* Illus. by Leonard Weisgard. Random, 1957, 2009.

Whitman, Walt. "O Captain, My Captain!" In Meltzer, Milton. *Hour of Freedom.* Boyds Mills, 2003.

———. "When Lilacs Last in the Dooryard Bloom'd." In Hopkins, Lee Bennett. *Voyages*. Illus. by Charles Mikolaycak. Harcourt, 1988.

THEME TWO UNIT: THANKSGIVING

Thanksgiving did not become an official holiday until, with the urging of writer Sarah Josepha Hale, Abraham Lincoln signed it into law in 1863, during the Civil War. Thanksgiving has a complicated and rich history, as Penny Colman relates in her nonfiction book, *Thanksgiving: The True Story*. There are conflicting accounts of when and where the first thanksgiving was celebrated. The foods we serve, our assumptions about the motives of both the Pilgrims and the Wampanoag, and costume and decorations are part of a body of Thanksgiving lore that has little to do with actual historical events. Children are often startled to realize the foods they consider "traditional" could not possibly have been served at this feast. They will also be surprised to discover that for many American Indians this holiday is known as a National Day of Mourning.

In reality, cultural groups around the world celebrate days of thanksgiving, sometimes for a successful harvest (this was the purpose of the Pilgrim feast), sometimes for the birth of a healthy child, or, as in some cultures, on a daily basis, as a reminder of the many things we have to be grateful for. Francisco X. Alarcón's "Accion de Gracias = Thanksgiving" speaks to this daily ceremony of ancient people. Several books and poems take this broad approach. Nikki Grimes' *Thanks a Million*, and the poems in Marlo Thomas' collection, *Thanks and Giving: All Year Long*, give students glimpses of the many things for which they can be thankful. Jonathan London's *Giving Thanks* and Chief Jake Swamp's *Giving Thanks: A Native American Good Morning Message* encourage students to be grateful for the natural world around them.

Lydia Maria Child, an abolitionist, wrote "The New England Boy's Song About Thanksgiving Day" (We know it as *Over the River and Through the Woods*) in 1863. As the Civil War raged, this song, originally twelve verses long, was, like Abraham Lincoln's proclamation of a Thanksgiving Day, a nostalgic wish for better times. Considering Thanksgiving from the perspective of many cultural traditions, and through its history, enriches instruction in the social studies.

Alarcón, Francisco X. "Accion de Gracias = Thanksgiving." *Angels Ride Bikes = Los Ángeles Andan en Bicicleta*. Illus. by Maya Christina Gonzalez. Children's, 1999.

Anderson, Laurie Halse. *Thank You, Sarah: The Woman Who Saved Thanksgiving*. Illus. by Matt Faulkner. S & S, 2002. (Prose)

Bucchino, John. *Grateful: A Song of Giving Thanks*. Illus. by Anna-Lisa Hakkarainen. HarperCollins, 1996.

Carlstrom, Nancy White. *Thanksgiving Day at Our House: Thanksgiving Poems For the Very Young*. Illus. by R. W. Alley. S & S. 1999.

Child, Lydia Maria. "The New England Boy's Song About Thanks-Giving Day." In Clinton, Catherine. *A Poem of Her Own*. Illus. by Stephen Alcorn. Abrams, 2003.

Colman, Penny. *Thanksgiving: The True Story*. Holt, 2008. (Prose)

Dragonwagon, Crescent. *Alligator Arrived With Apples: A Potluck Alphabet Feast*. Illus. by José Aruego and Ariane Dewey. Macmillan, 1987.

Eastwick, Ivy O. "Thanksgiving." In Prelutsky, Jack, sel. *The 20th Century Children's Poetry Treasury*. Illus. by Meilo So. Knopf, 1999.

Farmiloe, Dorothy. "Recipe for Thanksgiving Day Soup." In Booth, David. *'Til All the Stars Have Fallen*. Viking, 1990.

Fisher, Aileen. "When It's Thanksgiving." *Always Wondering*. Illus. by Joan Sandin. HarperCollins, 1991.

Florian, Douglas. "Thanksgiving." *Autumnblings*. Greenwillow, 2003.

Greene, Rhonda Gowler. *The Very First Thanksgiving Day*. Illus. by Susan Gaber. Atheneum, 2002.

Grimes, Nikki. *Thanks a Million*. Illus. by Cozbi A. Cabrera. HarperCollins, 2006.

Horowitz, Dave. *The Ugly Pumpkin*. Putnam, 2005.

"Iroquois Prayer" and "Thanksgiving." In Hopkins, Lee Bennett. *Days to Celebrate*. Illus. by Stephen Alcorn. Greenwillow/HarperCollins, 2005.

Jackson, Alison. *I Know an Old Lady Who Swallowed a Pie*. Illus. by Judith Byron Schachner. Dutton, 1997.

Lewis, J. Patrick. "The Turkey's Wattle." *A Hippopotamusn't*. Illus. by Victoria Chess. Dial, 1990.

Livingston, Myra Cohn. "Thanksgiving." *Celebrations*. Illus. by Leonard Everett Fisher. Holiday, 1985.

London, Jonathan. *Giving Thanks*. Illus. by Gregory Manchess. Candlewick, 2003.

Park, Linda Sue. "November Thursday." *Tap Dancing on the Roof: Sijo (Poems)*. Illus. by Istvan Banyai. Clarion, 2007.

Prelutsky, Jack. "I Do Not Like November. "*My Dog May Be a Genius*. Illus. by James Stevenson. Greenwillow/HarperCollins, 2008.

———. *It's Thanksgiving!* Illus. by Marilyn Hafner. HarperCollins, 2007.

———. "The Turkey Shot Out of the Oven." *Something Big Has Been Here*. Illus. by James Stevenson. Greenwillow, 1990.

Shore, Diane Z. *This Is the Feast*. Illus. by Megan Lloyd. HarperCollins, 2008.

Silverstein, Shel. "Point of View." *Where the Sidewalk Ends*. Harper, 1974.

Swamp, Chief Jake. *Giving Thanks: A Native American Good Morning Message*. Illus. by Erwin Printup Jr. Lee & Low, 1995.

Thomas, Marlo and Friends. *Thanks and Giving: All Year Long*. S & S, 2004.

Updike, John. "November." *A Child's Calendar*. Illus. by Trina Schart Hyman. Holiday, 1999.

Watson, Wendy. *Thanksgiving at Our House*. Houghton, 1991.

Willey, Margaret. *Thanksgiving With Me*. Illus. by Lloyd Bloom. HarperCollins, 1998.

Yolen, Jane. "Old Tom." *Bird Watch*. Illus. by Ted Lewin. Putnam, 1990.

Twentieth-Century America

Blos, Joan. *The Heroine of the Titanic*. Illus. by Tennessee Dixon. Morrow, 1991. (Molly Brown, 1912)

Bryant, Jen. *Ringside, 1925: Views from the Scopes Trial*. Knopf, 2008. (Novel in Verse)

———. *The Trial*. Knopf, 2004. (Lindbergh Kidnapping, 1935) (Novel in Verse)

Cohan, George M. *You're a Grand Old Flag*. Illus. by Norman Rockwell. S & S, 2008.

Cormier, Robert. *Frenchtown Summer*. Delacorte, 1999. (1938)

Frampton, David. *Mr. Ferlinghetti's Poem*. Eerdmans, 2006. (1920s & 1930s Brooklyn)

Gershwin, George, DuBose Heyward, & Dorothy Heyward. *Summertime*. Illus. by Mike Wimmer. S & S, 1999. (Early 20th Century)

Glover, Denis. "Girls in a Factory." In Hollyer, Belinda. *She's All That!* Illus. by Susan Hellard. Kingfisher, 2006.

Grimes, Nikki. *Talkin' About Bessie: The Story of Aviator Elizabeth Coleman*. Illus. by E. B. Lewis. Orchard, 2002. (1892–1926)

Herrera, Juan Felipe. *Downtown Boy*. Scholastic, 2005. (1950s San Francisco) (Novel in Verse)

Hesse, Karen. *Witness*. Scholastic, 2001. (1924 Klan) (Novel in Verse)

Hughes, Langston. "Bound No'th Blues." *The Dream Keeper*. Illus. by Brian Pinkney. Knopf, 1994. (Great Migration)

Hush Little Baby. Illus. by Jerry Pinkney. Greenwillow, 2006. (Early 20th Century)

Janeczko, Paul B. *Worlds Afire*. Candlewick, 2004. (1944 Circus Fire) (Novel in Verse)

Johnson, Angela. *I Dream of Trains*. Illus. by Loren Long. S & S, 2003. (Sharecroppers, Great Migration)

Lewis, Claudia. *Long Ago in Oregon*. Illus. by Joel Fontaine. HarperCollins, 1987. (1917–1918)

Lewis, J. Patrick. "First Moon Landing." In Hopkins, Lee Bennett. *Blast Off!* Illus. by Melissa Sweet. Harper Collins, 1995.

———. "1911." *Black Cat Bone*. Illus. by Gary Kelley. Creative, 2006. (Triangle Shirtwaist Fire)

———. "Golden Gate Bridge," Empire State Building," & "Mount Rushmore." *Monumental Verses*. National Geographic, 2005.

Little, Lessie Jones. *Children of Long Ago*. Illus. by Jan Spivey Gilchrist. Lee & Low, 2000.

Livingston, Myra Cohn. "Arthur Thinks on Kennedy." In Hopkins, Lee Bennett. *Hand in Hand*. Illus. by Peter M. Fiore. S & S, 1994. (Also in *A Jar of Tiny Stars*)

Marx, Trish. *Jeanette Rankin*. New York: McElderry, 2006. (1880–1973)

Mederis, Angela Shelf. *Dancing with the Indians*. Illus. by Samuel Byrd. Holiday, 1991. (1930's)

Myers, Walter Dean. *Angel to Angel*. HarperCollins, 1998. (19th & early 20th)

———. *Brown Angels*. HarperCollins, 1993. (19th & early 20th)

Niven, Penelope. *Carl Sandburg*. Illus. by Marc Nadel. Harcourt, 2003. (1878–1967)

Norworth, Jack. *Take Me Out to the Ballgame*. Illus. by Alec Gillman. S & S, 1993. (1947 World Series, Ebbetts Field, NYC)

Oppenheim, James. "Bread and Roses." In Meltzer, Milton. *Hour of Freedom*. Boyds Mills, 2003. (Mill Workers' Strike, 1912)

Rappaport, Doreen. *Eleanor, Quiet No More*. Illus. by Gary Kelley. Hyperion, 2009.

Spires, Elizabeth. "Eleanor Roosevelt." *I Heard God Talking to Me*. Farrar, 2009.

Weatherford, Carole Boston. *Dear Mr. Rosenwald*. Illus. by R. Gregory Christie. Scholastic, 2006. (1920's)

———. *Jesse Owens*. Illus. by Eric Velasquez. Walker, 2007. (1913–1980)

The Depression and the Dust Bowl

Davis, Robert A. "Dust Bowl." In Adoff, Arnold. *I Am the Darker Brother*. S & S, 1996.

Glaser, Isabel Joshlin. "Depression." In Hopkins, Lee Bennett. *Hand in Hand*. Illus. by Peter M. Fiore. S & S, 1994. (Also in *Hour of Freedom*)

Guthrie, Woody. *This Land Is Your Land*. Illus. by Kathy Jakobsen. Little, 1998.

Hesse, Karen. *Out of the Dust*. Scholastic, 1977. (Novel in Verse)

Holiday, Billie & Arthur Herzog Jr. *God Bless the Child*. Illus. by Jerry Pinkney. HarperCollins, 2004.

Katz, Bobbi. "A New Deal: That's What This Country Needs" & "On the Way to Californ-I-A!" *We the People*. Illus. by Nina Crews. Greenwillow, 2000.

Rylant, Cynthia. *Something Permanent*. Illus. by Walker Evans. Harcourt, 1994.

"Seven-Cent Cotton and Forty-Cent Meat." In Meltzer, Milton. *Hour of Freedom*. Boyds Mills, 2003.

Wong, Janet S. "Gong Gong and Susie." *A Suitcase of Seaweed*. Booksurge, 2008.

World War II (See World History)

Civil Rights

Brooks, Gwendolyn. "A Bronzeville Mother Loiters in Mississippi. Meanwhile, a Mississippi Mother Burns Bacon." In Giovanni, Nikki. *Shimmy Shimmy Shimmy Like My Sister Kate*. Holt, 1995. (Emmett Till)

Cooper, Floyd, ret. & illus. *Cumbayah*. Morrow, 1998.

Grimes, Nikki. "Medgar and Myrlie." *Hopscotch Love*. Illus. by Melodye Benson Rosales. Lothrop, 1999.

Johnson, Bandon N. "Black Ancestors . . . " In Adedjouma, Davida. *The Palm of My Heart*. Illus. by R. Gregory Christie. Lee & Low, 1996.

Johnson, James Weldon. *Lift Every Voice and Sing*. Illus. by Bryan Collier. HarperCollins, 2007.

Katz, Bobbi. "On the Bus." *We the People*. Illus. by Nina Crews. Greenwillow, 2000.

Lewis, J. Patrick. "Fanny Lou Hamer: 'I'm Sick and Tired of Bein' Sick and Tired.' " *Vherses*. Illus. by Mark Summers. Creative, 2005.

Nelson, Marilyn. *A Wreath for Emmett Till*. Houghton, 2005.

Pinkney, Andrea Davis. *Boycott Blues*. Illus. by Brian Pinkney. Greenwillow, 2008.

Shange, Ntozake. *Coretta Scott*. Illus. by Kadir Nelson. HarperCollins, 2009.

———. *Ellington Was Not a Street*. Illus. by Kadir Nelson. S & S, 2004.

Shore, Diane Z. & Jessica Alexander. *This Is the Dream*. Illus. by James Ransome. HarperCollins, 2006.

Weatherford, Carole Boston. *Birmingham, 1963*. Boyds Mills, 2007.

Martin Luther King Jr. (1929–1968)

Brooks, Geraldine. "Martin Luther King Jr." In Clinton, Catherine. *I, Too, Sing America*. Illus. by Stephen Alcorn. Houghton, 1998. (Also in *I Am the Darker Brother*)

Cornish, Sam. "Death of Dr. King # 1." In Adoff, Arnold. *My Black Me*. Dutton, 1974.

Fisher, Aileen. "Martin Luther King." In Hopkins, Lee Bennett. *Hand in Hand*. Illus. by Peter M. Fiore. S & S, 1994. (Also in *Hour of Freedom*)

Giovanni, Nikki. "The Funeral of Martin Luther King, Jr." In Sullivan, Charles, *Children of Promise*. Abrams, 1991. (Also in *I, Too, Sing America*)

Gunning, Monica. "Washington, D. C." *America, My New Home*. Illus. by Ken Condon. Boyds Mills, 2004.

Hernandez, David. "Martin and My Father." In Carlson, Lori Marie. *Red Hot Salsa*. Holt, 2005.

Katz, Bobbi. "On the Bus." *We the People*. Illus. by Nina Crews. Greenwillow, 2000.

Kennedy, X. J. "Martin Luther King Day." In Hopkins, Lee Bennett. *Lives*. Illus. by Leslie Staub. HarperCollins, 1999.

King, Martin Luther, Jr. *I Have a Dream*. Scholastic, 1997.

Lewis, J. Patrick. "How Long? Not Long, Because No Lie Can Live Forever." *Freedom Like Sunlight*. Illus. by John Thompson. Creative, 2000.

———. "The Preachers." *Heroes and She-roes*. Illus. by Jim Cooke. Dial, 2005.

Livingston, Myra Cohn. "Martin Luther King." In Prelutsky, Jack. *The Random House Book of Poetry For Children*. Illus. by Arnold Lobel. Random, 1988. (Also in *A Jar of Tiny Stars)*

———. "Martin Luther King Day." *Celebrations*. Illus. by Leonard Everett Fisher. Holiday, 1985. (Also in *Ring Out Wild Bells)*

Perkins, Useni Eugene. "Martin Luther King, Jr." In Slier, Deborah. *Make a Joyful Sound*. Illus. by Cornelius Van Wright & Ying-Hwa Hu. Checkerboard, 1991.

Rosa Parks (1913–2005)

Cornish, Sam. "Montgomery (For Rosa Parks)." In Adoff, Arnold. *I Am the Darker Brother*. Illus. by Benny Andrews. S & S, 1997.

Giovanni, Nikki. "The Rosa Parks (A Song in Rhythm)." *Hip Hop Speaks to Children*. Sourcebooks, 2008.

Lewis, J. Patrick. "The Many and the Few." *Freedom Like Sunlight*. Illus. by John Thompson. Creative, 2000. (Also in *Lives*)

———. "The Steadfast." *Heroes and She-roes*. Illus. by Jim Cooke. Dial, 2005.

Oyewole, Abiodun. "A Protest Poem for Rosa Parks." In Slier, Deborah. *Make a Joyful Sound*. Illus. by Cornelius Van Wright & Ying-Hwa Hu. Checkerboard, 1991.

Pinkney, Andrea Davis. *Boycott Blues: How Rosa Parks Inspired a Nation*. Illus. by Brian Pinkney. Greenwillow, 2008.

Weatherford, Carole Boston. "The Mother of the Movement (For Rosa Parks)." *Remember the Bridge*. Philomel, 2002.

Malcolm X (1925–1965)

Baraka, Amiri (LeRoi Jones.) "A Poem for Black Hearts." In Giovanni, Nikki. *Shimmy Shimmy Shimmy Like My Sister Kate*. Holt, 1995.

Fields, Julia. "Aardvark." In Adoff, Arnold. *My Black Me*. Dutton, 1974

Grimes, Nikki. "Do Like Malcolm." *Hopscotch Love.* Illus. by Melodye Benson Rosales. Lothrop, 1999.

Jackson, Mae. "I Remember . . . " In Adoff, Arnold. *My Black Me.* Dutton, 1974

Knight, Etheridge. "For Malcolm, A Year After." In Meltzer, Milton. *Hour of Freedom.* Boyds Mills, 2003.

Lewis, J. Patrick. "My People." *Freedom Like Sunlight.* Illus. by John Thompson. Creative, 2000.

Thompson, Julius. "To Malcolm X." In Adoff, Arnold. *My Black Me.* Dutton, 1974.

César Chavez (1927–1993)

Ada, Alma Flor. "César Chavez." *Gathering the Sun.* Illus. by Simon Silva. HarperCollins, 1997.

Alarcón, Francisco X. "Blessed Hands" & "Dreamer of the Fields—To César Chavez." *Poems to Dream Together = Poemas Para Sonar Juntos.* Lee & Low, 2005.

———. "A Tree for César Chavez." *Laughing Tomatoes = Jitomates Risueños.* Illus. by Maya Christina Gonzalez. Children's, 1997.

Bernier-Grand, Carmen T. *César: ¡Sí, Se Puede! = Yes We Can!* Illus. by David Diaz. Cavendish, 2004.

De Colores = Bright With Colors. Illus. by David Diaz. Cavendish, 2008.

Lewis, J. Patrick. "The Organizer." *Heroes and She-roes.* Illus. by Jim Cooke. Dial, 2005.

The Vietnam War (1965–1975)

Castan, Fran. "Unveiling the Vietnam Memorial." In Nye, Naomi Shihab. *What Have You Lost?* Greenwillow, 1999.

Dotlich, Rebecca Kai. "Whispers to the Wall: Vietnam Veterans Memorial, Washington, D.C. Dedicated, 1982." In Janeczko, Paul B. *Hey You!* Illus. by Robert Rayevsky. HarperCollins, 2007.

Johnson, Angela. "War II." *The Other Side.* Orchard, 1998.

Katz, Bobbi. "Vietnam: Are We Winning?" *We the People.* Illus. by Nina Crews. Greenwillow, 2000.

Levertov, Denise. "What Were They Like?" In Meltzer, Milton. *Hour of Freedom.* Boyds Mills, 2003.

McGrath, Thomas. "Ode for the American Dead in Asia." In Meltzer, Milton. *Hour of Freedom.* Boyds Mills, 2003.

Myers, Walter Dean. *Patrol.* Illus. by Ann Grifalconi. HarperCollins, 2002.

Testa, Maria. *Almost Forever.* Candlewick, 2003. (Novel in Verse)

Twenty-first-Century America

Grimes, Nikki. *Barack Obama.* Illus. by Bryan Collier. S & S, 2009.

Heard, Georgia, sel. *This Place I Know.* Candlewick, 2002. (In memory of September 11, 2001)

Hopkins, Lee Bennett, sel. Section: "Iraq War, 2001" *America at War.* Illus. by Stephen Alcorn. McElderry, 2008.

Nye, Naomi Shihab. "Flynn on the Bus; September 11, 2001." *19 Varieties of Gazelle*: Greenwillow, 2002.

Shields, Carol Diggory. "The Lady (September 11, 2001.)" *American History, Fresh Squeezed!* Illus, by Richard Thompson. Handprint, 2002.

THEME TWO: HISTORICAL MUSEUMS, PLACES, ARTIFACTS, AND FIELD TRIPS

See also Chapter Six: Visual Arts Standard One (Quilts)

Cohen-Assif, Shlomit. "Class Pictures." In Nye, Naomi Shihab. *The Space Between Our Footsteps.* S & S, 1998. (Also in *The Flag of Childhood*)

Dor, Moshe. "Letters." In Nye, Naomi Shihab. *The Space Between Our Footsteps.* S & S, 1998. (Also in *The Flag of Childhood*)

Dumas, Gerald. "I Look at this Picture." In Hittleman, Carol G. & Daniel R. Hittleman. *A Grand Celebration.* Illus. by Kay Life. Boyds Mills, 2002.

Esbensen, Barbara Juster. "Old Photograph Album: Grandfather." *Who Shrank My Grandmother's House?* Illus. by Eric Beddows. HarperCollins, 1992. (Also in *A Grand Celebration*)

Frank, John. *Keepers.* Illus. by Ken Robbins. Roaring Brook, 2008.

George, Kristine O'Connell. "Field Trip." *Swimming Upstream.* Illus. by Debbie Tilley. Clarion, 2002.

———. "The Moccasins." In Hopkins, Lee Bennett. *Behind the Museum Door.* Illus. by Stacey Dressen-McQueen. Abrams, 2007.

Goffstein, M. B. "The Woodland Indians, circa 1890–1940." *An Artists Album.* HarperCollins, 1985.

Harrison, David L. "Guilt." *Connecting Dots.* Illus. by Kelley Cunningham Cousineau. Boyds Mills, 2004.

Hopkins, Lee Bennett, sel. *Behind the Museum Door.* Illus. by Stacey Dressen- McQueen. Abrams, 2007.

Johnston, Tony. "Grandmother's Grinding Stone" & "Museum of Anthropology." *The Ancestors Are Singing.* Illus. by Karen Barbour. Farrar, 2003.

Kan, Sau Yee. "I Keep a Photo of My Grandmother . . . ." In Micklos, John, Jr. *Grandparent Poems.* Illus. by Layne Johnson. Boyds Mills, 2004.

Katz, Susan. *Mrs. Brown on Exhibit.* Illus. by R. W. Alley. S & S, 2002.

———. *A Revolutionary Field Trip.* Illus. by R. W. Alley. S & S, 2004.

Lewis, J. Patrick. "Museum Field Trip." In Hopkins, Lee Bennett. *Behind the Museum Door.* Illus. by Stacey Dressen-McQueen. Abrams, 2007.

Medina, Jane. "The Photograph." *My Name Is Jorge.* Illus. by Fabricio Vanden Broeck. Boyds Mills, 1999.

Moss, Jeff. "The Picture." In Micklos, John, Jr. *Grandparent Poems.* Illus. by Layne Johnson. Boyds Mills, 2004.

Nye, Naomi Shihab. "Historical Marker," "Abandoned Homestead, Big Bend National Park," & "Abandoned Post Office, Big Bend." *A Maze Me.* Greenwillow, 2005.

Phillips, Robert. "My Valhalla of Lost Things." In Nye, Naomi Shihab. *What Have You Lost?* Greenwillow, 1999.

Schertle, Alice. *Keepers.* Illus. by Ted Rand. Lothrop, 1996.

Shamas, Anton. "Picture." In Nye, Naomi Shihab. *The Space Between Our Footsteps.* S & S, 1998.

Turner, Ann. "The Museum." *Street Talk.* Illus. by Catherine Stock. Houghton, 1986.

Weatherford, Carole Boston. "Aunt Lizzie's Pictures." *Sidewalk Chalk.* Illus. by Dimitrea Takunbo. Boyds Mills, 2006.

Theme Three: People, Places, and Environments. The study of people, places, and human-environment interactions assists students as they create their special views and geographic perspectives of the world beyond their personal locations. Students need the knowledge, skills, and understandings to answer such questions as: Where are things located? Why are they located there? What do we mean by "Region"? How do landforms change? What implications to these have for people?
See also Science Standards Four (Ecosystems), Five (Geology) and Seven (the Environment)

THEME THREE: GEOGRAPHY

Geography is the way we orient ourselves in the world. The first environment children learn about generally is their own home. Then a child's understanding of living environments expands to the neighborhood and community. As we learn more, our notion of our environment enlarges and becomes more complex until it encompasses both the human and natural worlds.

While some students love to look at maps, and others excel at Geography Bees, others, including some poets, do not like geography. In many cases, geography study is merely memorizing the name and locations of places, without anything to connect them to reality. When Jorge, in Jane Medina's "Was That Jorge?" corrects his teacher because the geography she talks about is his homeland, it is because he knows the places that are only words on a map to others. Poems that encourage students to think about where they might travel, such as Nikki Grimes' "Dream Places," and the poems in Gary Soto's *Worlds Apart* might help students to begin to make links geographically. Calef Brown's *Tippintown* is a guided tour of an imaginary place. This poem might encourage students to create tours of their own favorite places or places they would like to go.

Bates, Katherine Lee. *America the Beautiful*. Illus. by Wendell Minor. Putnam, 2003.

Borden, Louise. *America Is . . .* Illus. by Stacey Schuett. S & S, 2002.

Brown, Calef. *Tippintown*. Houghton, 2003.

Dotlich, Rebecca Kai. "Classroom Globe." In Hopkins, Lee Bennett. *School Supplies*. Illus. by Renée Flower. S & S, 1996.

Fletcher, Ralph. "Earth Head." *A Writing Kind of Day*. Illus. by April Ward. Boyds Mills, 2005.

Gilchrist, Jan Spivey. *My America*. Illus. by the poet & Ashley Bryan. HarperCollins, 2007.

Graves, Donald. "Geography." *Baseball, Snakes and Summer Squash*. Boyds Mills, 1996.

Grimes, Nikki. "Dream Places." *Danitra Brown Leaves Town*. Illus. by Floyd Cooper. HarperCollins, 2002.

Hopkins, Lee Bennett, sel. *Got Geography!* Illus. by Philip Stanton. HarperCollins, 2006.

———. *My America: A Poetry Atlas of the United States*. Illus. by Stephen Alcorn. S & S, 2000.

Lewis, J. Patrick. "I'm Lost Without You." *Scien-trickery*. Illus. by Frank Remkiewicz. Harcourt, 2004. (Map)

———. "Map" In Greenberg, Jan. *Heart to Heart*. Abrams, 2001.

———. *A World of Wonders: Geographic Travels in Verse and Rhyme*. Illus. by Alison Jay. Dial, 2002.

Locker, Thomas & Candace Christiansen, eds. *Home: A Journey Through America*. Harcourt, 2000.

Medina, Jane. "Was that Jorge?" *My Name Is Jorge*. Illus. by Fabricio Vanden Broeck. Boyds Mills, 1999.

Nichols, Grace. "Where I Got My Map" & "Torn Map." *Come on into My Tropical Garden*. HarperCollins, 1990.

Prelutsky, Jack. "New York Is in North Carolina." *The New Kid on the Block*. Illus. by James Stevenson. Greenwillow, 1984. (Geography Test)

Rabe, Tish. *There's a Map on My Lap!* Illus. by Aristides Ruiz. Random, 2002.

Roemer, Heidi. "Are We There Yet?" In Heard, Georgia. *Falling Down the Page*. Roaring Brook, 2009.

Schertle, Alice. "A Million Miles from Tallahassee." In Hopkins, Lee Bennett. *Oh, No! Where Are My Pants?* Illus. by Wolf Erlbruch. HarperCollins, 2005.

Siebert, Diane. *Tour America*. Illus. by Stephen Johnson. Chronicle, 2006.

Soto, Gary. "Winter Cold." *Canto Familiar*. Illus. by Annika Nelson. Harcourt, 1995. (Geography Bee)

———. *Worlds Apart*. Illus. by Greg Clarke. Putnam, 2005. (Novel in Verse)

Yolen, Jane. "Maps." In Hopkins, Lee Bennett. *Hamsters, Shells, and Spelling Bees*. Illus. by Sachiko Yoshikawa. HarperCollins, 2008.

Place Names

Place names tell stories. Sometimes names are poetic, others are quite ordinary. I live in the shadow of the Snowy Range, a rather prosaic description of the most obvious aspect of these mountains. To me, the Sierra Nevada Mountains in California, the Spanish words for snowy mountains, sound more poetic. In Colorado to the south of me, the Neversummer Range and the Mummy Range seem to have been named by more poetic souls. Students might enjoy exploring the names on the land around them, and selecting and recording those that they think are poetic. They might also like to create poetic names for nearby places, such as parks, ponds, or hills.

Poets play with place names. Sometimes they like the sound of names, as in Jack Prelutsky's four volumes of brief poems featuring places. Students might try to locate and mark on a map all of the places Prelutsky mentions. Sometimes, as in the jump rope rhyme, *A My Name Is Alice*, the names of places are used for alliteration. Sometimes, a poet wonders about the names of places, such as in Eve Merriam's "Schenectady," "Traveling," and "Geography."

Other poems are more serious. M. B. Goffstein's *School of Names* is a poem to the joys of learning the names of places. Jane Yolen and Meguido Zola write about places named by Indian people who were forced to leave them.

Bayer, Jane. *A My Name Is Alice*. Illus. by Stephen Kellogg. Dial, 1984.

Cleary, Brian P. Section: "Geography (Groan Until Ukraine Your Neck)." *Rhyme and Punishment*. Illus. by J. P. Sandy. Millbrook, 2006.

Goffstein, M. B. *School of Names*. HarperCollins, 1986.

Keenan, Sheila. *Greetings from the Fifty States: How They Got Their Names*. Illus. by Selina Alko. Scholastic, 2008. (Prose)

Lewis, J. Patrick. "If I Had Nothing Else to Do, I'd Send a Christmas Card to You." *Under the Kissletoe*. Illus. by Rob Shepperson. Boyds Mills, 2007.

Lobel, Anita. *Away from Home*. Greenwillow, 1994.

Marshak, Samuel. *Hail to Mail*. Illus. by Vladimir Radunsky. Holt, 1990.

Merriam, Eve. "Geography," "Schenectady," & "Traveling." *The Singing Green*. Illus. by Kathleen Collins Howell. Morrow, 1992.

Prelutsky, Jack. *Beneath a Blue Umbrella*. Illus. by Garth Williams. Greenwillow, 1990.

———. *The Frogs Wore Red Suspenders*. Illus. by Petra Mathers. HarperCollins, 2002.

———. *In Aunt Giraffe's Green Garden*. Illus. by Petra Mathers. HarperCollins, 2007.

———. *Ride a Purple Pelican*. Illus. by Garth Williams. Greenwillow, 1986.

Singer, Marilyn. *Nine O'Clock Lullaby*. Illus. by Frané Lessac. HarperCollins, 1991.

Viorst, Judith. "Someday . . . " *Sad Underwear*. Illus. by Richard Hull. Atheneum, 1995.

Whitman, Walt. "Mannahatta." In Hopkins, Lee Bennett. *Voyages*. Illus. by Charles Mikolaycak. Harcourt, 1988.

Yolen, Jane. "Like Ghosts of Eagles." *Mother Earth, Father Sky*. Illus. by Jennifer Hewitson. Boyds Mills, 1996.

Zola, Meguido. "Canadian Indian Place Names." In Booth, David. *'Til All the Stars Have Fallen*. Viking, 1990.

THEME THREE: HOUSES

See also Chapter Three: Standard Six (Buildings)

Primary teachers often use Mary Ann Hoberman's *A House Is a House for Me* as the centerpiece of studies of houses. The book looks at all kinds of houses, including those of people and animals. The metaphor is extended to show that everything "is either a house or it lives in a house." Houses are sometimes used as metaphors. Emily Dickinson suggests that she dwells "in possibility, a fairer house than prose . . . " in one of her poems. George Swede compares his body to a house, writing that each morning he has a chance to move in again with the new day.

Housing is an essential need for all human beings, but a house is not necessarily a home. The poems invite students to distinguish between the two. Older students will find poetry about houses can enhance their understanding of the settings of particular novels. They can be watching for poems that capture the feel of houses from different settings and time periods in fiction they are reading.

Adoff, Arnold. "This House Is the Center." *In For Winter, Out For Spring*. Illus. by Jerry Pinkney. Harcourt, 1991.

Alarcón, Francisco X. "Adobes." *Poems to Dream Together = Poemas Para Sonar Juntos*. Illus. by Paula Barragán. Lee & Low, 2005.

———. "My House = Mi Casa." *Angels Ride Bikes = Los Ángeles Andan en Bicicleta*. Illus. byMaya Christina Gonzales. Children's, 1999.

Aldis, Dorothy. "No One Heard Him Call." In Kennedy, X. J. & Dorothy M. Kennedy. *Talking Like the Rain*. Little, 1992.

Beil, Karen Magnuson. *Jack's House*. Illus. by Mike Wohnoutka. Holiday, 2008.

Brown, Calef. "Ray's House." *Flamingos on the Roof*. Houghton, 2006.

Ciardi, John. " 'I Am Home,' Said the Turtle." *Doodle Soup*. Illus. by Merle Nacht. Houghton, 1985.

Crum, Shutta. *The House in the Meadow*. Illus. by Paige Billin-Frye. Whitman, 2003.

Dickinson, Emily. "657." In Clinton, Catherine. *A Poem of Her Own*. Illus. by Stephen Alcorn. Abrams, 2003.

Eastwick, Ivy. "House for Rent." *Some Folks Like Cats*. Illus. by Mary Kurnick Maass. Boyds Mills, 2002.

Esbensen, Barbara Juster. "The Visit." *Who Shrank My Grandmother's House?* Illus. by Eric Beddows. Harper Collins, 1992.

Fisher, Aileen. "The House of a Mouse." *The House of a Mouse*. Illus. by Joan Sandin. HarperCollins, 1988.

Fisher, Lillian M. "To Build a House." In Hopkins, Lee Bennett. *Marvelous Math*. Illus. by Karen Barbour. S & S, 1997.

Fletcher, Ralph. "New House." *Moving Day*. Illus. by Jennifer Emery. Boyds Mills, 2006.

Florian, Douglas. "The Termites." *Insectlopedia*. Harcourt, 1998.

Gershator, Phillis. *Old House, New House*. Illus. by Katherine Potter. Cavendish, 2009.

Hoberman, Mary Ann. *A House Is a House for Me*. Illus. by Betty Frasier. Viking, 1978.

———. *One of Each*. Illus. by Marjorie Priceman. Little, 1997.

hooks, bell. *Homemade Love*. Illus. by Shane W. Evans. Hyperion, 2002.

Johnston, Tony. "Houses = Casitas." *My Mexico = México Mío*. Illus. by F. John Sierra. Putnam, 1996.

Krauss, Ruth. *A Very Special House*. Illus. by Maurice Sendak. HarperCollins, 1953.

Kuskin, Karla. "For You." In Smith, William Jay. *Here Is My Heart*. Illus. by Jane Dyer. Little, 1999.

Levy, Constance. "A House." *I'm Going to Pet a Worm Today*. Illus. by Ronald Himler. Macmillan, 1991.

Lewis, Claudia. "Moving to Salem." *Long Ago in Oregon*. Illus. by Joel Fontaine. HarperCollins, 1987.

Miller, Mary Britton. "Houses." In De Regniers, Beatrice Schenk. *Sing a Song of Popcorn*. Scholastic, 1988.

Milne, A. A. "Solitude." In Huck, Charlotte. *Secret Places*. Illus. by Lindsay Barrett George. Greenwillow, 1993.

Morley, Christopher. "Song for a Little House." In Ferris, Helen. *Favorite Poems Old and New*. Illus. by Leonard Weisgard. Random, 1957, 2009.

Newell, Elizabeth. "The House That I Build." In Barbe, Walter B. *A School Year of Poems*. Illus. by Dennis Hockerman. Boyds Mills, 2005.

Nye, Naomi Shihab. "Moving House." *A Maze Me*. HarperCollins, 2005.

O'John, Calvin. "Dancing Teepees." In Sneve, Virginia Driving Hawk. *Dancing Teepees*. Holiday, 1989.

Prelutsky, Jack. "Carpenter, Carpenter." *The Frogs Wore Red Suspenders*. Illus. by Petra Mathers. HarperCollins, 2002.

———, sel. Section: "Home! You're Where It's Warm Inside." *The Random House Book of Poetry for Children*. Illus. by Arnold Lobel. Random, 1983.

Robinson, Edwin Arlington. "The House on the Hill." In Ferris, Helen. *Favorite Poems Old and New*. Illus. by Leonard Weisgard. Random, 1957, 2009.

Rosen, Michael J. sel. *Home: A Collaboration of Thirty Distinguished Authors and Illustrators of Children's Books to Aid the Homeless*. HarperCollins, 1992.

Simmie, Lois. "Jeremy's House." In Huck, Charlotte. *Secret Places*. Illus. by Lindsay Barrett George. Greenwillow, 1993. (Also in *'Til All the Stars Have Fallen*)

Singer, Marilyn. "Landmark." *Central Heating*. Illus. by Meilo So. Knopf, 2005.

Swanson, Susan Marie. *The House in the Night*. Illus. by Beth Krommes. Houghton, 2008.

Swede, George. "Every Morning." In Heard, Georgia. *Songs of Myself*. Mondo, 2000.

Taback, Simms. *This Is the House That Jack Built*. Putnam, 2004.

Tippett, James. "Old Log House." In Ferris, Helen. *Favorite Poems Old and New*. Illus. by Leonard Weisgard. Random, 1957, 2009.

Turner, Ann. *Dakota Dugout*. Illus. by Ronald Himler. Macmillan, 1985.

Vega, Ed J. "Translating Grandfather's House." In Carlson, Lori, M. *Cool Salsa*. Holt, 1994.

Wong, Janet S. "Home." *Good Luck Gold*. McElderry, 1994.

———. "In the Neighborhood." *A Suitcase of Seaweed*. Booksurge, 2008.

Worth, Valerie. "Haunted House." *All the Small Poems and Fourteen More*. Illus. by Natalie Babbitt. Farrar, 1994.
Zolotow, Charlotte. "Little Girl's Dream." *Snippets*. Illus. by Melissa Sweet. HarperCollins, 1992.

THEME THREE: NEIGHBORHOODS AND COMMUNITIES

City neighborhoods appear in more poems than suburban or country neighborhoods. As students learn about their neighborhoods and communities, they might try creating poems that capture the sights, sounds, smells, and textures of their own neighborhoods. The topics and descriptions of the city poems can become models for writing about different kinds of neighborhoods. If a neighborhood has no skyscrapers, what is the tallest thing there? Perhaps it's a tree, or a grain silo. That observation might be the beginning of a poem. Eve Merriam's *Bam, Bam, Bam* is about the sounds one can hear in the city. After listening to this book, students might listen for and write down the typical sounds in their own neighborhoods. Eloise Greenfield's *The Friendly Four* provides a model for creating a neighborhood. In this book, four children create their own "town" one summer and call it "Goodsummer."

Barnwell, Ysaye M. *We Are One*. Illus. by Brian Pinkney. Harcourt, 2008.
Baylor, Byrd. *The Best Town in the World*. Illus. by Ronald Himler. Scribners, 1983.
Brooks, Geraldine. *Bronzeville Boys and Girls*. Illus. by Faith Ringgold. HarperCollins, 2007.
Bunting, Eve. *Flower Garden*. Illus. by Kathryn Hewitt. Harcourt, 1994.
Carlson, Lori Marie. Section: "Neighborhoods." *Red Hot Salsa*. Illus. by Oscar Hijuelos. Holt, 2005.
Chocolate, Debbi. *El Barrio*. Illus. by David Diaz. Holt. 2009.
Crews, Nina. *The Neighborhood Mother Goose*. Greenwillow, 2004.
De Fina, Allan. *When a City Leans Against the Sky*. Illus. by Ken Condon. Boyds Mills, 1997.
Forman, Ruth. *Young Cornrows Callin Out the Moon*. Illus. by Cbabi Bayoc. Children's 2007.
Greenfield, Eloise. *The Friendly Four*. Illus. by Jan Spivey Gilchrist. HarperCollins, 2006.
———. *Night on Neighborhood Street*. Illus. by Jan Spivey Gilchrist. Dial, 1991.
Grimes, Nikki. *C Is for City*. Illus. by Pat Cummings. Boyds Mills, 1995.
———. *My Man Blue*. Illus. by Jerome Lagarrigue. Dial, 1999.
———. *A Pocketful of Poems*. Illus. by Javaka Steptoe. Clarion, 2001.
Harshman, Marc. *Only One Neighborhood*. Illus. by Barbara Garrison. Dutton, 2007.
Havill, Juanita. *Grow*. Illus. by Stanislawa Kodman. Peachtree, 2008. (Novel in Verse)
Hesse, Karen. *Come on Rain!* Illus. by John J. Muth. Scholastic, 1999.
Hopkins, Lee Bennett. *City I Love*. Illus. by Marcellus Hall. Abrams, 2009.
———, sel. *A Song in Stone*. Illus. by Anna H. Audette. HarperCollins, 1983.
Hubbell, Pat. *City Kids*. Illus. by Teresa Flavin. Marshall Cavendish, 2001.
Larrick, Nancy, ed. Section: "The City Spreads Its Wings." *Piping Down the Valleys Wild*. Illus. by Ellen Raskin. Topeka, 1968.
Lenski, Lois. *Sing a Song of People*. Illus. by Giles LaRoche. Little, 1996.
Lewis, J. Patrick & Paul B. Janeczko. *Birds on a Wire: A Renga 'Round Town*. Illus. by Gary Lippincott. Boyds Mills, 2008.
Mak, Kam. *My Chinatown*. HarperCollins, 2002.
Merriam, Eve. *Bam, Bam, Bam*. Illus. by Dan Yaccarino. Holt, 1995.
Moore, Lilian. *Mural on Second Avenue*. Illus. by Roma Karas. Candlewick, 2005.
Myers, Christopher. *Black Cat*. Scholastic, 1999.
Prelutsky, Jack, sel. Section: "City, Oh City." *Random House Book of Poetry for Children*. Illus. by Arnold Lobel. Random, 1983.
Rosen, Michael. *Bear's Day Out*. Illus. by Adrian Reynolds. Bloomsbury, 2007.
Rylant, Cynthia. *Waiting to Waltz*. Illus. by Stephen Gammell. Bradbury, 1984.

Soto, Gary. *Neighborhood Odes*. Illus. by David Diaz. Harcourt, 1992.
Weatherford, Carole Boston. *Sidewalk Chalk*. Illus. by Dimitrea Tokunbo. Boyds Mills, 2006.
Yolen, Jane. *Sky Scrape/City Scape*. Illus. by Ken Condon. Boyds Mills, 1996.

THEME THREE UNIT: HARLEM

See also American History (The Depression and the Dust Bowl)

See also Chapter One: Poets (Langston Hughes)

See also Chapter Six: Music Standard Nine (Jazz)

Both poetry and prose have highlighted Harlem, home to a number of important African Americans. Musicians, artists, poets, and writers found a cultural home there during the Harlem Renaissance (1917–1935) and remained when the Depression made life hard for artists of all kinds. This neighborhood in New York City remains the cultural capital of African American experience.

Angelou, Maya. "Harlem Hopscotch." In Giovanni, Nikki. *Hip Hop Speaks to Children*. Jabberwocky, 2008.
Carter, Don. *Heaven's All-Star Jazz Band*. Knopf, 2002.
Collier, Brian. *Uptown*. Holt, 2000. (Prose)
Giovanni, Nikki. *Shimmy Shimmy Shimmy Like My Sister Kate: Looking at the Harlem Renaissance Through Poems*. Holt, 1996.
Grimes, Nikki. "Harlem," *A Pocketful of Poems*. Illus. by Javaka Steptoe. Clarion, 2001.
Hill, Laban Carrick. *Harlem Stomp! A Cultural History of the Harlem Renaissance* Little, 2003.
Hughes, Langston. "Good Morning." In Adoff, Arnold, ed. *My Black Me*. Dutton, 1974.
———. "Harlem." In Giovanni, Nikki. *Shimmy Shimmy Shimmy Like My Sister Kate*. Holt, 1996. (Also in *I, Too, Sing America*)
———. "Harlem Night Song." In Giovanni, Nikki. *Hip Hop Speaks to Children*. Jabberwocky, 2008.
———. "Juke Box Love Song." In Hollyer, Brenda. *She's All That*. Illus. by Susan Hellard. Kingfisher, 2006.
Isadora, Rachel. *Bring on That Beat*. Putnam, 2002.
Littlesugar, Amy. *Tree of Hope*. Illus. by Floyd Cooper. Philomel, 2001. (Prose)
McKissack, Patricia. *A Song for Harlem*. Illus. by Gordon C. James. Viking, 2007. (Prose)
Medina, Tony. "Harlem Is the Capital of My World." *Love to Langston*. Illus. by R. Gregory Christie. Lee & Low, 2002.
Muse, Daphne, sel. *The Entrance Place of Wonders: Poems of the Harlem Renaissance*. Illus. by Charlotte Riley-Webb. Abrams, 2005.
Myers, Walter Dean. *Harlem Summer*. Scholastic, 2001. (Prose)
———. *Here in Harlem: Poems in Many Voices*. Holiday, 2004.
Smith, Charles R. *Perfect Harmony: A Musical Journey with the Boys Choir of Harlem*. Hyperion, 2002.

Theme Four: Individual Development and Identity. Personal identity is shaped by one's culture, by groups, and by institutional influences. Students should consider such questions as: How to people learn? Why do people behave as they do? What influences how people learn, perceive, and grow? How do people meet their basic needs in a variety of contexts? How do individuals develop from youth to adulthood?

See also Chapter Seven: Health Standard Four (Bullying) & Standard Eight (Race)

THEME FOUR: SELF, FAMILY, AND FRIENDS

In the early grades, simple verse about getting along, balancing one's needs with those of others, and family love and friendship gives children a sense they are not alone. Older students struggle with identity and relationships in more complex ways. Most anthologies for young people contain poems about self, family, and friends. Poetry studies consistently show that young people prefer poetry about familiar experiences. Both humorous poetry and more serious examinations of self are valuable in classrooms and libraries. A newer trend is collections of poems specifically for or about girls or boys.

Poetry anthologies about the self also include poems about parents, siblings, and members of one's extended family, and friends. Poetry and picture books should reflect the diversity of families with one, two, or more parents, extended families in which grandparents, aunts and uncles play significant roles, and families from different places and with different customs and traditions.

Self

Curtis, Jamie Lee. *I'm Gonna Like Me*. Illus. by Laura Cornell. HarperCollins, 2002.

———. *It's Hard to Be Five*. HarperCollins, 2004.

———. *Today I Feel Silly*. Illus. by Laura Cornell. HarperCollins, 1998.

De Regniers, Beatrice Schenk. *The Way I Feel . . . Sometimes*. Illus. by Susan Meddaugh. Clarion, 1988.

Frasier, Debra L. *On the Day You Were Born*. Harcourt, 1991.

Grimes, Nikki. *It's Raining Laughter*. Boyds Mills, 1997.

Heard, Georgia. *Songs of Myself*. Mondo, 2000.

Heide, Florence Parry & Roxanne Heide Pierce. *Oh, Grow Up!* Illus. by Nadine Bernard Westcott. Scholastic, 1996.

Hirschfelder, Arlene B. & Beverly R. Singer, eds. Section: "Identity." *Rising Voices*. Scribners, 1992.

hooks, bell. *Grump Groan Growl*. Illus. by Chris Raschka. Hyperion, 2008.

Hopkins, Lee Bennett, ed. *Oh, No! Where Are My Pants?* Illus. by Wolf Erlbruch. HarperCollins, 2005.

Kennedy, Caroline. Section: "About Me." *A Family of Poems*. Illus. by John J, Muth. Hyperion, 2005.

Little, Jean. *Hey World, Here I Am!* Illus. by Sue Truesdell. HarperCollins, 1989.

Lyon, George Ella. "Where I'm From." In Janeczko, Paul B. *Seeing the Blue Between*. Candlewick, 2002.

Martin, Bill, Jr. & Michael Sampson, eds. Section: "Me and My Feelings." *The Bill Martin Jr. Big Book of Poetry*. S & S, 2008.

Milne, A. A. *Now We Are Six*. Illus. by Ernest H. Shepard. Dutton, 1988.

———. *When We Were Very Young*. Illus. by Ernest H Shepard. Dutton, 1988.

Prelutsky, Jack. *Me I Am*. Illus. by Christine Davenier. Farrar, 2007.

Rylant, Cynthia. *Waiting To Waltz*. Illus. by Stephen Gammell. Bradbury, 1984.

Stavans, Ilan, ed. *¡Wachale!* Cricket, 2001.

Walker, Alice. *There Is a Flower at the Tip of My Nose Smelling Me*. Illus. by Stefano Vitale. HarperCollins, 2006.

Girls and Women

Bunting, Eve. *Girls A to Z*. Illus. by Suzanne Bloom. Boyds Mills, 2002.

Clinton, Catherine, ed. *A Poem of Her Own*. Illus. by Stephen Alcorn. Abrams, 2003.

Franco, Betsy, ed. *Things I Have to Tell You: Poems and Writings by Teenage Girls*. Illus. by Nina Nickles. Candlewick, 2001.

Gaiman, Neil. *Blueberry Girl*. Illus. by Charles Vess. HarperCollins, 2009.

Hollyer, Belinda, sel. *She's All That!* Illus. by Susan Hellard. Kingfisher, 2006.

Lewis, J. Patrick. *Vherses*. Illus. by Mark Summers. Creative, 2005.

Nye, Naomi Shihab. *A Maze Me*. HarperCollins, 2005.

Paul, Ann Whitford. *All by Herself*. Illus. by Michael Sternagle. Harcourt, 1999.

Philip, Neil, ed. *It's a Woman's World*. Dutton, 2000.

Richards, Beah E. *Keep Climbing Girls*. Illus. by R. Gregory Christie. Simon and Schuster, 2006.

Boys

Franco, Betsy, ed. *You Hear Me? Poems and Writings by Teenage Boys*. Illus. by Nina Nickles. Candlewick, 2001.

Ghigna, Charles. *A Fury of Motion*. Boyds Mills, 2003.

Graves, Donald. *Baseball, Snakes, and Summer Squash*. Boyds Mills, 1996.

Lindamichellebaron. "Hugs and Kisses." In Strickland, Dorothy S. & Michael R. Strickland. *Families*. Illus. by John Ward. Boyds Mills, 1994.

Prelutsky, Jack. *Rolling Harvey Down the Hill*. Illus. by Victoria Chess. Greenwillow, 1980.

Family

Adoff, Arnold. *All the Colors of the Race*. Illus. by John Steptoe. Lothrop, 1982.

———. *In for Winter, Out for Spring*. Illus. by Jerry Pinkney. Harcourt, 1991.

Barnwell, Ysaye M. *No Mirrors in My Nana's House*. Illus. by Synthia Saint James. Harcourt, 1998.

Bertrand, Diane Gonzales. *Sip, Slurp, Soup, Soup = Caldo, Caldo, Caldo*. Illus. by Alex Pardo DeLange. Arté Público, 1997.

Brooks, Gwendolyn. *Bronzeville Boys and Girls*. Illus. by Faith Ringgold. HarperCollins, 2007.

Caraballo, Samuel. *Mis Abuelos y Yo = My Grandparents and I*. Illus. by D. Nina Cruz. Arté Público, 2004.

Collins, Judy. *My Father*. Illus. by Jane Dyer. Little, 1989.

Cooper, Melrose. *I Got a Family*. Illus. by Dale Gottlieb. Holt, 1993.

Dotlich, Rebecca Kai. *A Family Like Yours*. Illus. by Tammie Lyon. Boyds Mills, 2002.

Fletcher, Ralph. *Relatively Speaking: Poems About Family*. Illus. by Walter Lyon Krudop. Orchard, 1999.

Greenfield, Eloise. *Brothers and Sisters: Family Poems*. Illus. by Jan Spivey Gilchrist. HarperCollins, 2009.

———. *Honey I Love*. Illus. by Jan Spivey Gilchrist. HarperCollins, 2003.

———. *Nathaniel Talking*. Illus. by Jan Spivey Gilchrist. Black Butterfly, 1988.

Grimes, Nikki. *A Dime a Dozen*. Illus. by Angelo. Dial, 1998.

———. *Hopscotch Love*. Illus. by Melodye Benson Rosales. Lothrop, 1999.

———. *Oh, Brother!* Illus. by Mike Benny. Greenwillow, 2008.

———. *Stepping out with Grandma Mac*. Illus. by Angelo. Orchard, 2001.

Hamanaka, Sheila. *Grandparents Song*. HarperCollins, 2003.

Hirschfelder, Arlene B. & Beverly R. Singer, eds. Section: "Family." *Rising Voices*. Scribners, 1992.

Hittleman, Carole G. & Daniel R. Hittleman. sels. *A Grand Celebration*. Illus. by Kay Life. Boyds Mills, 2002.

Hoberman, Mary Ann. *Fathers, Mothers, Sisters, Brothers: A Collection of Family Poems*. Illus. by Marylin Hafner. Little, 1991.

———. *I'm Going to Grandma's*. Harcourt, 2007.

hooks, bell. *Homemade Love*. Illus. by Shane W. Evans. Hyperion, 2002.

Johnston, Tony. *Yonder*. Illus. by Lloyd Bloom. Dial, 1988.

Kerley, Barbara. *You and Me Together*. National Geographic, 2005.

Kobayashi, Issa. *Today and Today*. Illus. by G. Brian Karas. Scholastic, 2007.

Martin, Bill, Jr. & Michael Sampson, eds. Section: "Family and Home." *The Bill Martin Jr. Big Book of Poetry*. S & S, 2008.

Medina, Tony. *DeShawn Days*. Illus. by R. Gregory Christie. Lee & Low, 2004.

Micklos, John, Jr. comp. *Daddy Poems*. Illus. by Robert Casilla. Boyds Mills, 2000.

———. *Mommy Poems*. Illus. by Lori McElrath-Eslick. Boyds Mills, 2003.

———. *Grandparent Poems*. Illus. by Layne Johnson. Boyds Mills, 2004.
———. *No Boys Allowed: Poems About Brothers and Sisters*. Illus. by Kathleen O'Malley. Boyds Mills, 2006.
Mora, Pat. *Love to Mamá*. Illus. by Paula S. Barragán M. Lee & Low, 2001.
Myers, Walter Dean. *Angel to Angel*. HarperCollins, 1998.
Nicholls, Judith, comp. *Someone I Like: Poems About People*. Illus. by Giovanni Manna. Barefoot, 2000.
Nye, Naomi Shihab, sel. "Families: The First Tying." *This Same Sky*.Macmillan, 1992.
Philip, Neil, sel. *The Fish Is Me*. Illus. by Claire Henley. Clarion, 2002.
———. *Hot Potato*. Illus. by Claire Henley. Clarion, 2004.
Smith, Hope Anita. *Mother Poems*. Holt, 2009. (Novel in Verse)
Soto, Gary. *Canto Familiar*. Illus. by Annika Nelson. Harcourt, 1995.
———. *A Fire in My Hands*. Harcourt, 2006.
Strickland, Dorothy S. & Michael R. Strickland. sel. *Families*. Illus. by John Ward. Boyds Mills, 1994.
Thomas, Joyce Carol. *Brown Honey in Broomwheat Tea*. Illus. by Floyd Cooper. HarperCollins, 1993.
Wong, Janet. *The Rainbow Hand*. Illus. by Jennifer Hewitson. Booksurge, 2008.

Friendship

Greenfield, Eloise. *The Friendly Four*. Illus. by Jan Spivey Gilchrist. HarperCollins, 2006.
Grimes, Nikki. *Danitra Brown, Class Clown*. Illus. by E. B. Lewis. HarperCollins, 2005.
———. *Danitra Brown Leaves Town*. Illus. by Floyd Cooper. HarperCollins, 2002.
———. *Meet Danitra Brown*. Illus. by Floyd Cooper. Lothrop, 1994.
Hoberman, Mary Ann. *And to Think That We Thought That We'd Never Be Friends*. Illus. by Kevin Hawkes. Crown, 1999.
Holbrook, Sara & Allan Wolf. *More Than Friends*. Boyds Mills, 2008.
Hopkins, Lee Bennett. *Best Friends*. Illus. by James Watts. HarperCollins, 1986.
Komaiko, Leah. *Annie Bananie*. Illus. by Laura Cornell. HarperCollins, 1987.
Nikola-Lisa, W. *Bein' with You This Way*. Illus. by Michael Bryant. Lee & Low, 1994.
Raschka, Chris. *Yo! Yes?* Scholastic, 1993.
Singer, Marilyn. *All We Needed to Say*. Illus. by Lorna Clark. Atheneum, 1996.

Theme Five: Individuals, Groups, and Institutions. Institutions such as schools, churches, families, government agencies, and the courts play an integral role in people's lives. It is important that students learn how institutions are formed, what controls and influences them, how they influence individuals and culture, and how they are maintained or changed. Students may address questions such as: What is the role of institutions in this and other societies? How am I influenced by institutions? How do institutions change? What is my role in institutional change?

THEME FIVE: SCHOOL

Young people spend a sizeable part of their days in schools so this is an institution they know well. Some poems describe positive school experiences with the excitement of learning, pride in accomplishment, and admiration for a teacher. Some poems reflect on the power of education. Alice Walker's "The Women" and Carole Boston Weatherford's *Dear Mr. Rosenwald* celebrate people who worked hard to provide schooling for their children.

Poetry also describes the disappointments of schooling, from less-than-understanding teachers to homework and failing on tests. Some poems about school are humorous, and students and teachers can laugh at them together. Kalli Dakos' collections of poems about school discuss both the quirky, amusing things and the sad things that happen in classrooms. What students and teachers share in school parallels all of the feelings shared in the world around them. The poems that are difficult but important for adults to read are those that describe very unhappy experiences with teachers. César Chavez was humiliated in school for speaking Spanish, and Carmen T. Bernier-Grand describes this in "I Am a Clown." Jane Medina's Jorge struggles in school but eventually finds that his teacher is on his side.

Some poems help students learn about schoolrooms of other places and other times and, like poems about houses and neighborhoods, they can help to flesh out the setting or the feelings of characters in novels set in schools. A number of novels in verse take place in classrooms and schools.

Novels in Verse Set in Schools

Applegate, Katherine. *Home of the Brave*. Feiwel & Friends. 2007.

Cheng, Andrea. *Where the Steps Were*. Boyds Mills, 2008.

Creech, Sharon. *Hate That Cat*. HarperCollins, 2008.

———. *Love That Dog*. HarperCollins, 2001.

Frost, Helen. *Spinning through the Universe*. Farrar, 2004.

George, Kristine O'Connell. *Swimming Upstream: Middle School Poems*. Illus. by Debbie Tilley. Clarion, 2002.

Glenn, Mel. *Split Image*. HarperCollins, 2002.

Herrick, Steven. *Naked Bunyip Dancing*. Illus. by Beth Norling. Front Street, 2005.

Collections of Poems about School

Appelt, Kathi. *Poems from Homeroom*. Holt, 2002.

Carlson, Lori M. Section: "School Days." *Cool Salsa*.Holt, 1994.

Dakos, Kalli. *The Bug in Teacher's Coffee*. Illus. by Mike Reed. Harper, 1999.

———. *Don't Read This Book, Whatever You Do!* Illus. by G. Brian Karas. S & S, 1993.

———. *If You're Not Here, Please Raise Your Hand*. Illus. by G. Brian Karas. S & S, 1990.

———. *Mrs. Cole on an Onion Roll*. Illus. by JoAnn Adinolfi. S & S, 1995.

———. *Put Your Eyes Up Here*. Illus. by G. Brian Karas. S & S, 2003.

English, Karen. *Speak to Me (And I Will Listen Between the Lines)*. Illus. by Amy June Bates. Farrar, 2004.

Franco, Betsy. *Messing Around on the Monkey Bars*. Illus. by Jessie Hartland. Candlewick, 2009.

Grimes, Nikki. *Danitra Brown, Class Clown*. Illus. by E. B. Lewis. HarperCollins, 2005.

Holbrook, Sara. *The Dog Ate My Homework*. Boyds Mills, 1996.

Hopkins, Lee Bennett, ed. *Hamsters, Shells, and Spelling Bees*. Illus. by Sachiko Yoshikawa. HarperCollins, 2008.

———, sel. *School Supplies*. Illus. by Renée Flower. S & S, 1996.

Kennedy, Dorothy M. *I Thought I'd Take My Rat To School*. Illus. by Abby Carter, Little, 1993.

Lesynski, Loris. *Zigzag: Zoems for Zindergarten*. Annick, 2004.

Martin, Bill, Jr. & Michael Sampson. Section: "School Time." *The Bill Martin Jr. Big Book of Poetry*. S & S, 2008.

Medina, Jane. *The Dream on Blanca's Wall = El Sueño Pegado En la Pared de Blanca*. Illus. by Robert Casilla. Boyds Mills, 2004.

———. *My Name Is Jorge*. Illus. by Fabricio Vanden Broeck. Boyds Mills, 1999.

Prelutsky, Jack. *What a Day It Was at School!* Illus. by Doug Cushman. Greenwillow, 2006.

Salas, Laura Purdie. *Stampede! Poems to Celebrate the Wild Side of School*. Illus. by Steven Salerno. Clarion, 2009.

Shields, Carol Diggory. *Lunch Money*. Illus. by Paul Meisel. Dutton, 1995.

Sidman, Joyce. *This Is Just to Say.* Illus. by Pamela Zagarenski. Houghton, 2007.
Sierra, Judy. *There's a Zoo in Room 22.* Illus. by Barney Saltzberg. Harcourt, 2000.
Singer, Marilyn. *All We Needed to Say.* Illus. by Lorna Clark. Atheneum, 1996.
Winters, Kay. *Did You See What I Saw?* Illus. by Martha Weston. Viking, 1996.

Individual Poems about School

Alarcón, Francisco X. "Ode to Buena Vista Bilingual School." *Iguanas in the Snow = Iguanas en la Nieve.* Illus. by Maya Christina Gonzalez. Children's, 2001.
Antler. "Raising My Hand." In Panzer, Nora. *Celebrate America.* Smithsonian/ Hyperion, 1994.
Arnold, Tedd. *Super Fly Guy.* Scholastic, 2006.
Baer, Edith. *This Is the Way We Go to School.* Illus. by Steve Björkman. Scholastic, 1990.
Bernier-Grand, Carmen T. "I Am a Clown." *César: ¡Sí, Se Puede = Yes, We Can!* Illus. by David Diaz. Cavendish, 2004.
Catacalos, Rosemary. "David Talamantez on the Last Day of Second Grade." In Nye, Naomi Shihab. *Is This Forever or What?* HarperCollins, 2004.
Coffin, Robert P. Tristam. "America Was Schoolmasters." In Meltzer, Milton. *Hour of Freedom.* Boyds Mills, 2003.
Cuma, Kathryn. "We All Float in and out." In Nye, Naomi Shihab. *Salting the Ocean.* Illus. by Ashley Bryan. Greenwillow, 2000.
De Regniers, Beatrice Schenk. "Co-op-er-ate." *The Way I Feel... Sometimes.* Illus. by Susan Meddaugh. Clarion, 1988.
Fisher, Aileen. "First Day of School." *Always Wondering.* Illus. by Joan Sandin. HarperCollins, 1991.
Flores-Morales, Julia. "Barrio School." In Kennedy, Dorothy M. *I Thought I'd Take My Rat to School.* Illus. by Abby Carter. Little, 1993.
Giovanni, Nikki. "Education." *Spin a Soft Black Song.* Illus. by George Martins. Hill & Wang, 1985.
Greene. Rhonda. *This Is the Teacher.* Illus. by Mike Lester. Dutton, 2004.
Grimes, Nikki. "Dear Teacher" & 'The Lunchroom." *Thanks A Million.* Illus. by Cozbi A. Cabrera. Greenwillow, 2006.
Gunning, Monica. "Classes Under the Trees." *Not a Copper Penny in Me House.* Illus. by Frané Lessac. Boyds Mills, 1993.
Hearne, Michael. "I Can't Go Back to School." In Janeczko, Paul. *The Place My Words Are Looking For.* Bradbury, 1990.
Herrera, Juan Felipe. *The Upside-Down Boy = El Niño de Cabeza.* Illus. by Elizabeth Gómez. Children's, 2000.
Hull, Rod. "First Day at School." In James, Simon. *Days Like This.* Candlewick, 1999.
"If I Were a Pony." (Navajo Students Group Poem). In Hirschfelder, Arlene B. & Beverly R. Singer. *Rising Voices.* Scribners, 1992.
Katz, Bobbi. "June" & "September." *Once Around the Sun.* Illus. by LeUyen Pham. Harcourt, 2006.
Kirwin-Vogel, Anna. "School System Prayer." In Yolen, Jane. *Mother Earth, Father Sky.* Illus. by Jennifer Hewitson. Boyds Mills, 1996.
Lewis, Claudia. "No Dimes," and "Not in a Hundred Years." *Long Ago in Oregon.* Illus. by Joel Fontaine. HarperCollins, 1987.
Little, Jean. "Today." *Hey World, Here I Am!* Illus. by Sue Truesdell. HarperCollins, 1986.
McCord, David. "Chant II" and "The Adventures of Chris." *One at a Time.* Little, 1986.
Medina, Tony. "First Grade," "Jim Crow Row," & "In High School." *Love to Langston.* Illus. by R. Gregory Christie. Lee & Low, 2002.
Miller, Kate. "Miss Fitzgibbon's Board." *Poems in Black and White.* Boyds Mills, 2007.
Obregon, Rachel. "For My First-Grade Teacher." In Nye, Naomi Shihab. *Salting the Ocean.* Illus. by Ashley Bryan. Greenwillow, 2000.

Olaleye, Isaac. "In the Ebony Room," *The Distant Talking Drum.* Illus. by Frané Lessac. Boyds Mills, 1995.
Turner, Ann. "That's Gloria," "Read," & "Teacher Talk." *Street Talk.* Houghton, 1986.
Walker, Alice. "Women." In Clinton, Catherine. *I, Too, Sing America.* Illus. by Stephen Alcorn. Houghton, 1998. (Also *in She's All That*)
Weatherford, Carole Boston. *Dear Mr. Rosenwald.* Illus. by R. Gregory Christie. Scholastic, 2006.
Winter, Natasha. *The Night Before First Grade.* Illus. by Deborah Zemke. Grosset, 2005.
Young MC. "From ... Principal's Office." In Giovanni, Nikki. *Hip Hop Speaks to Children.* Sourcebooks, 2008.
Zimmer, Tracy Vaughan. "Teacher." *Steady Hands.* Illus. by Megan Halsey & Sean Addy. Clarion, 2009.

Homework

Dakos, Kalli. "My Writing Is ... " *Don't Read This Book, Whatever You Do.* Illus. by G. Brian Karas. S & S, 1993.
Esbensen, Barbara Juster. "Homework." *Who Shrank My Grandmother's House?* Illus. by Eric Beddows. Harper Collins, 1992. (Also in *School Supplies*)
Franco, Betsy. "Homework Blues." *Messing Around on the Monkey Bars.* Illus. by Jessie Hartland. Candlewick, 2009.
George, Kristine O'Connell. "Due Date." *Swimming Upstream.* Illus. by Debbie Tilley. Clarion, 2002.
Grimes, Nikki. "Big Plans." *Danitra Brown Leaves Town.* Illus. by Floyd Cooper. HarperCollins, 2002.
———. "Homework." *Danitra Brown, Class Clown.* Illus. by E. B. Lewis. HarperCollins, 2005.
———. "Homework." *Stepping out with Grandma Mac.* Illus. by Angelo. Orchard, 2001.
Harley, Avis. "Later." *Fly with Poetry.* Boyds Mills, 2000.
Hoban, Russell. "Homework." *Egg Thoughts.* Illus. by Lillian Hoban. HarperCollins, 1972. (Also in *I Thought I'd Take My Rat to School*)
Holbrook, Sara. "The Dog Ate My Homework," and "Kidnapped." *The Dog Ate My Homework.* Boyds Mills, 1996.
Prelutsky, Jack. "Homework! Oh, Homework!" *The New Kid on the Block.* Illus. by James Stevenson. Greenwillow, 1984. (Also in *I Thought I'd Take My Rat to School*)
———. "Homework, Sweet Homework." *My Dog May Be a Genius.* Illus. by James Stevenson. Greenwillow, 2008.
Shields, Carol Diggory. "Whew," "I'm Doing My Homework," & "Book Report." *Lunch Money.* Illus. by Paul Meisel. Dutton, 1995.
Yolen, Jane. "Homework." In Kennedy, Dorothy M. *I Thought I'd Take My Rat to School.* Illus. by Abby Carter. Little, 1993.

THEME FIVE: LIBRARIES

Libraries are an institution close to the heart of democracy. Benjamin Franklin and Thomas Jefferson fostered the idea of free access to books and reading through libraries. Poets generally write about libraries as wonderful places, but sometimes the library is less fun. Jack Prelutsky writes about an overdue book in "I'm Going to the Library." Some memories are painful. Jane Medina's poem "La Tarjeta de la Biblioteca = The Library Card," describes an insensitive staff member who doesn't believe that the boy's mother has signed his application for a card and sends him away. The young boy in Nikki Giovanni's "Ten Years Old" is rescued by a woman who says, "Give that boy what he want, he want to lead the race." These can be paired with Patricia McKissack's *Goin' Someplace Special* and Pat Mora's *Tómas and the Library Lady,* prose works that look at a library's impact on a child.

Bertram, Debbie & Susan Bloom. *The Best Book to Read.* Illus. by Michael Garland. Random, 2008.
Dakos, Kalli. "When the Librarian Reads to Us." *Put Your Eyes up Here.* Illus. by G. Brian Karas. S & S, 2003.
Esbensen, Barbara Juster. "Every Night ... " *Words with Wrinkled Knees.* Illus. by John Stadler. Crowell, 1986.

Franco, Betsy. "In the Library." *Messing Around on the Monkey Bars*. Illus. by Jessie Hartland. Candlewick, 2009.
George, Kristine O'Connell. "School Librarian." *Swimming Upstream*. Illus. by Debbie Tilley. Clarion, 2002.
Giovanni, Nikki. "Ten Years Old." *Spin a Soft Black Song*. Illus. by George Martins. Farrar, 1985. (Also in *My Black Me*)
Greenfield, Eloise. "At the Library." *The Friendly Four*. Illus. by Jan Spivey Gilchrist. HarperCollins, 2006.
Grimes, Nikki. "At the Library." *It's Raining Laughter*. Illus. by Myles C. Pinkney. Boyds Mills, 1997.
Gunning, Monica. "The Library." *America, My New Home*. Illus. by Ken Condon. Boyds Mills, 2004.
Lewis, J. Patrick. "Library." In Hopkins, Lee Bennett. *Hamsters, Shells, and Spelling Bees*. Illus. by Sachiko Yoshikawa. HarperCollins, 2008.
———. "Necessary Gardens." *Please Bury Me in the Library*. Illus. by Kyle M. Stone. Harcourt, 2005.
Lies, Brian. *Bats at the Library*. Houghton, 2008.
McKissack, Patricia. *Goin' Someplace Special*. Illus, by Jerry Pinkney. S & S, 2001. (Prose)
McLoughland, Beverly. "Surprise." In Hopkins, Lee Bennett. *Good Books, Good Times*. Illus. by Harvey Stevenson. HarperCollins, 1990.
Medina, Jane. "La Tarjeta de la Biblioteca = The Library Card." *My Name Is Jorge*. Illus. by Fabricio Vanden Broeck. Boyds Mills, 1999.
Medina, Tony. "Libraries." *Love to Langston*. Illus. by R. Gregory Christie. Lee & Low, 2002.
Mora, Pat. *A Library for Juana*. Illus. by Beatriz Vidal. Knopf, 2002.
———. *Tómas and the Library Lady*. Illus. by Raúl Colón. Random, 2000.
Prelutsky, Jack. "I'm Going to the Library." *My Dog May Be a Genius*. Illus. by James Stevenson. HarperCollins, 2008.
———. "It's Library Time." *What a Day It Was at School!* Illus. by Doug Cushman, 2006.
Schoenherr, Ian. *Read It, Don't Eat It!* HarperCollins, 2009.
Sierra, Judy. *Wild About Books*. Illus. by Marc Brown. Knopf, 2004.
Silverstein, Shel. "Overdues." *A Light in the Attic*. HarperCollins, 1981.
Singer, Marilyn. "Sophie: In the Library I Slept . . . " & "Tanya: Hot Cocoa Warm and Brown . . . " *All We Needed to Say*. Illus. by Lorna Clark. Atheneum, 1996.
Soto, Gary. "Ode to my Library." *Neighborhood Odes*. Illus. by David Diaz. Harcourt, 1992.
———. "That Girl." *A Fire in My Hands*. Harcourt, 2006.
Sturges, Philemon. *She'll Be Comin' 'Round the Mountain*. Illus. by Ashley Wolff. Little, 2004.
Wong, Janet. "The Pilot." *The Rainbow Hand*. Illus. by Jennifer Hewitson. Booksurge, 2008.
Worth, Valerie. "Library." *All the Small Poems and Fourteen More*. Illus. by Natalie Babbitt. Farrar, 1994.
Zimmer, Tracy Vaughan. "Librarian." *Steady Hands*. Illus. by Megan Halsey & Sean Addy. Clarion, 2009.

Theme Six: Power, Authority, and Governance. Understanding the historical development of structures of power, authority, and governance and their evolving functions in contemporary U.S. society and other parts of the world is essential for developing civic competence. In exploring this theme, students confront such questions as: What is power? What forms does it take? Who holds it? How is it gained, used, and justified? What is legitimate authority? How are governments created, structured, maintained, and changed? How can individual rights be protected within the context of majority rule?
See also Themes One (Culture) and Two (Time, Continuity, and Change)

THEME SIX: POWER AND GOVERNANCE

Besides looking at power and authority in history, students might consider who has power and how it functions in their families, neighborhoods and communities, and schools. One subject approached in poetry is that power is transient—it cannot last. Percy Bysshe Shelley's "Ozymandias" captures this fleeting sense with its description of a fallen statue in the desert inscribed with the power of a ruler long gone. Dr. Seuss's *Yertle the Turtle* tells this story for a much younger audience.

Seuss, Dr. *Yertle the Turtle*. Random, 1958, 2008.

Shelley, Percy Bysshe. "Ozymandias," In Rosen, Michael. *Classic Poetry*. Illus. by Paul Howard. Candlewick, 2009.

Community Helpers

See also Theme Three (Neighborhood and Community)
See also Theme Five (Schools; Libraries)

Primary grade students learn about community helpers in the course of learning about their neighborhoods. Police and firefighters, among others, appear in poems for this age group. Older students may learn about others types of workers in units on careers.

Godwin, Laura. *This Is the Firefighter*. Illus. by Julian Hector. Hyperion, 2009.

Greenfield, Eloise. "The Brave Ones" & "Traffic Cop." *Under the Sunday Tree*. Illus. by Amos Ferguson. HarperCollins, 1988.

Hamilton, Kersten. *Police Officers on Patrol*. Illus. by R. W. Alley. Viking, 2009.

Hubbell, Patricia. *Firefighters: Speeding! Spraying! Saving!* Illus. by Viviana Garofoli. Cavendish, 2008.

———. *Police: Hurrying! Helping! Saving!* Illus. by Viviana Garofoli. Cavendish, 2008.

Lewis, J. Patrick. "The Firefighter." *Heroes and She-roes*. Illus. by Jim Cooke. Dial, 2005.

Singer, Marilyn. "Fire Fighters." *Central Heating*. Illus. by Meilo So. Knopf, 2005.

Yee, Wong Herbert. *Fireman Small*. Houghton, 1994.

Zimmer, Tracy Vaughan. *Steady Hands*. Illus. by Megan Halsey & Sean Addy. Clarion, 2009.

Theme Seven: Production, Distribution, and Consumption. Because people have wants that often exceed the resources available to them, a variety of ways have evolved to answer such questions as: What is to be produced? How is production to be organized? How are goods and services to be distributed? What is the most effective allocation of the factors of production (land, labor, capital, and management)?

See Chapter Three: Science Standard Seven (Environment)

See Chapter Four: Mathematics Standard One (Money)

Theme Eight: Science, Technology, and Society. Modern life as we know it would be impossible without technology and the science that supports it. But technology brings with it many questions: Is new technology better than old? What can we learn from the past about how new technologies result in broader social change, some of which is unanticipated? How can we cope with the ever-increasing pace of change? How can we manage technology so that the greatest number of people benefit from it? How can we preserve our fundamental values and beliefs in the midst of technological change?

See also Theme Two (Time, Continuity, and Change)

See also Chapter Three: Science Standard Six (Science and Technology)

THEME EIGHT: TRANSPORTATION

Baer, Edith. *This Is the Way We Go to School*. Illus. by Steve Björkman. Scholastic, 1990.

Ferris, Helen. Section: "Transportation." *Favorite Poems Old and New.* Illus. by Leonard Weisgard. Random, 1957, 2009.

Lillegard, Dee. *Go: Poetry in Motion.* Illus. by Valeri Gorbachev. Random, 2006.

Airplanes

Green, Mary McB. "Taking Off." In Prelutsky, Jack. *The 20th Century Children's Poetry Treasury.* Illus. by Meilo So. Knopf, 1999.

Grimes, Nikki. *Talkin' About Bessie: The Story of Aviator Elizabeth Coleman.* Illus. by E. B. Lewis. Orchard, 2002.

Hubbell, Patricia. *Airplanes: Soaring! Diving! Turning!* Illus. by Megan Halsey & Sean Addy. Cavendish, 2008.

Katz, Bobbi. "The First Airplane." *We the People.* Illus. by Nina Crews. Greenwillow, 2000.

———. "My Kid Sister, Bessie." *Trailblazers.* Illus. by Carin Berger. Greenwillow, 2007. (Amelia Earhart & Bessie Colman)

Kulling, Monica. "AmeliaCramped." In Janeczko, Paul B. *A Kick in the Head.* Illus. by Chris Raschka. Candlewick, 2005. (Amelia Earhart)

Lewis, J. Patrick. "Solo" & "The Steep Ascent." *Vherses.* Illus. by Mark Summers. Creative, 2005. (Amelia Earhart & Anne Morrow Lindbergh)

McLoughland, Beverly. "Crazy Boys." In Hopkins, Lee Bennett. *Hand in Hand.* Illus. by Peter M. Fiore. S & S, 1994. (Wright Brothers)

Paul, Ann Whitford. "Amelia Earhart." *All by Herself.* Illus. by Michael Steirnagle. Harcourt, 1999.

Siebert, Diane. *Plane Song.* Illus. by Vincent Nasta. HarperCollins, 1993.

Trains

When highways were built in many places the golden age of train transportation ended, except in cities where they live on as subways and commuter transport. But with population growth and a return to more fuel-efficient transportation, high-speed trains have become more common in Europe and Japan and are being considered for or built in urban areas of the United States.

Bennett, Rowena. "A Modern Dragon." In Prelutsky, Jack. *Read-Aloud Rhymes for the Very Young.* Illus. by Marc Brown. Knopf, 1986.

Booth, Philip. *Crossing.* Illus. by Bagram Ibatoulline. Viking, 2001.

Brown, Margaret Wise. *Two Little Trains.* Illus. by Leo Dillon and Diane Dillon. HarperCollins, 2001.

Dickinson, Emily. "The Locomotive." In Ferris, Helen. *Favorite Poems Old and New.* Illus. by Leonard Weisgard. Random, 1957, 2009.

Goodman, Steve. *The Train They Call the City of New Orleans.* Illus. by Michael McCurdy. Putnam, 2003.

Hubbell, Patricia. *Trains: Steaming! Pulling! Huffing!* Illus. by Megan Halsey & Sean Addy. Cavendish, 2005.

I've Been Working on the Railroad. Illus. by Nadine Bernard Westcott. Hyperion, 1996.

Johnson, Angela. *I Dream of Trains.* Illus. by Loren Long. S & S, 2003.

Krensky, Stephen, adapt. *Casey Jones.* Illus. by Mark Schroder. Lerner, 2006.

Larrick, Nancy, ed. Section "Yet There Isn't a Train I Wouldn't Take." *Piping Down the Valleys Wild.* Illus. by Ellen Raskin. Topeka, 1968.

McCord, David. "Song of the Train." *One at a Time.* Illus. by Henry B. Kane. Little, 1986.

Merriam, Eve. "Traveling." *The Singing Green.* Illus. by Kathie Collins Howell. Morrow, 1992.

Millay, Edna St. Vincent. "Travel," In Schoonmaker, Francis. *Edna St. Vincent Millay.* Illus. by Mike Bryce. Sterling, 1999.

Mitton, Tony. "Rickety Train Ride." In Yolen, Jane & Andrew Fusik Peters. *Here's a Little Poem.* Candlewick, 2007.

Panahi, H. L. *Bebop Express*. Illus. by Steve Johnson & Lou Fancher. HarperCollins, 2005.

Sandburg, Carl. "Southern Pacific." In Hopkins, Lee Bennett. *Rainbows Are Made*. Illus. by Fritz Eichenberg. Harcourt, 1982.

Siebert, Diane. *Train Song*. Illus. by Mike Wimmer. HarperCollins, 1981.

Stevenson, Robert Louis. "From a Railway Carriage." *A Child's Garden of Verses*. Illus. by Diane Goode. Morrow, 1998.

Tippett, James S. "Trains." In Ferris, Helen. *Favorite Poems Old and New*. Illus. by Leonard Weisgard. Random, 1957, 2009.

Worth, Valerie. "Steam Engines." *Peacock*. Illus. by Natalie Babbitt. Farrar, 2002.

Zolotow, Charlotte. "The Train" & "The Train Melody." *Everything Glistens and Everything Sings*. Illus. by Margot Tomes. Harcourt, 1987.

Other Forms of Transportation

Alborough, Jez. *Duck in the Truck*. HarperCollins, 1999.

Allen, Thomas S. *The Erie Canal*. Illus. by Peter Spier. Doubleday, 2001.

Anderson, Peggy Perry. *Chuck's Truck*. Houghton, 2006.

Grandits, John. "Tyrannosaurbus Rex." *Technically, It's Not My Fault*. Clarion, 2004.

Hopkins, Lee Bennett. "Subways Are People." *Days to Celebrate*. Illus. by Stephen Alcorn. Greenwillow, 2005.

Hubbell, Patricia. *Boats: Speeding! Sailing! Cruising!* Illus. by Megan Halsey & Sean Addy. Cavendish, 2009.

———. *Cars: Rushing! Honking! Zooming!* Illus. by Megan Halsey & Sean Addy. Cavendish, 2006.

———. *Trucks: Whizz! Zoom! Rumble!* Illus. by Megan Halsey & Sean Addy. Cavendish, 2003.

Johnston, Tony. "Trucks = Camiones." *My Mexico = México Mío*. Illus. by F. John Sierra. Putnam, 1996.

Kumin, Maxine. "Buses." In Prelutsky, Jack. *The 20th Century Children's Poetry Treasury*. Illus. by Meilo So. Knopf, 1999.

Miller, Heather Lynn. *Subway Ride*. Illus. by Sue Ramá. Charlesbridge, 2009.

Schertle, Alice. *Little Blue Truck*. Illus. by Jill McElmurry. Harcourt, 2008.

Shaw, Nancy. *Sheep in a Jeep*. Illus. by Margot Apple. Houghton, 1986.

Siebert, Diane. *Motorcycle Song*. Illus. by Leonard Jenkins. HarperCollins, 2002.

———. *Truck Song*. Illus. by Byron Barton. Crowell, 1984.

Stoutenberg, Adrien. "Assembly Line." In Panzer, Nora. *Celebrate America*. Smithsonian/ Hyperion, 1994. (Henry Ford)

Theme Nine: Global Connections. The realities of global interdependence require understanding the increasingly important and diverse global connections among world societies and the frequent tension between national interests and global priorities. Students will need to address such international issues as health care, the environment, human rights, economic competition and interdependence, age-old ethnic enmities, and political and military alliances.

Theme Ten: Civic Ideals and Practices. An understanding of civic ideals and practices of citizenship is critical to full participation in society and is a central purpose of the social studies. Students confront such questions as: What is civic participation and how can I be involved? How has the meaning of citizenship evolved? What is the balance between rights and responsibilities? What is the role of the citizen in the community and the nation, and as a member of the world community? How can I make a positive difference?

See also Theme One: Cultures

See also Chapter Three: Science Standard Seven

See also Chapter Seven: Health Standard Eight

THEMES NINE AND TEN: WAR AND PEACE

See also Theme Two: Time, Continuity, and Change

In a world filled with conflict, poets and writers are increasingly writing for young people about war and peace. Audrey wrote this poem after listening to Shari Griffin read aloud the introduction to Greg Mortenson's *Three Cups of Tea*. It captures the Theme's emphasis on involvement.

We Will . . .
Find the lost
Feed the hungry.
Hear the unheard.
Teach the untaught
Enrich the poor.
Include the Friendless
Heal the wounded.

We Will . . .
Do whatever we can to help:
The lost
The hungry
The unheard
The untaught
The poor
The friendless
The wounded

Or, at least, **I** will.

Audrey
Grade 4

It is difficult to talk about war without peace, or peace without war. Tony Johnston's *Voice from Afar: Poems of Peace*, for example, has been placed with the poems on war because she approaches peace by looking at the devastation of war. Peace can be an end to armed conflict, or it can represent a state of good will, openness, and joy. Poems about the joys of connection to others have been included in the section on peace.

War

Ashrawi, Hanan Mikai'il. "From the Diary of an Almost-Four-Year-Old." In Nye, Naomi Shihab. *The Space Between Our Footsteps*. S & S, 1998. (Also in *The Flag of Childhood*)

Auden, W. H. "O What Is That Sound" In Attenborough, Liz. *Poetry by Heart*. Scholastic, 2001.

Brooke, Rupert. "The Soldier." In Attenborough, Liz. *Poetry by Heart*. Scholastic, 2001.

Cano Correa, Eugenio Alberto. "My Memories of the Nicaraguan Revolution." In Janeczko, Paul B. *A Foot in the Mouth*. Illus. by Chris Raschka. Candlewick, 2009.

Fletcher, Ralph. "The Scar." *Relatively Speaking*. Illus. by Walter Lyon Krudop. Orchard, 1999.

Greenfield, Eloise. *When the Horses Ride By*. Illus. by Jan Spivey Gilchrist. Lee & Low, 2006.

Hopkins, Lee Bennett, sel. *America at War.* Illus. by Stephen Alcorn. McElderry, 2008.
Johnston, Tony. *Voice from Afar: Poems of Peace.* Illus. by Susan Guevara. Holiday, 2008.
Kuskin, Karla. *The Upstairs Cat.* Illus. by Howard Fine. Clarion, 1997.
Myers, Walter Dean. *Patrol.* Illus. by Ann Grifalconi. HarperCollins, 2002.
Philip, Neil. *War and the Pity of War.* Illus. by Michael McCurdy. Clarion, 1998.
Sandburg, Carl. "New Feet." In Niven, Penelope. *Carl Sandburg.* Illus. by Marc Nadel. Harcourt, 2003.
Sassoon, Siegfried. "Everyone Sang." In Attenborough, Liz. *Poetry by Heart.* Scholastic, 2001.
Seuss, Dr. *The Butter Battle Book.* Random, 1984.
Testa, Maria. "Cut Short." *Something About America.* Candlewick, 2005. (Novel in Verse)
Volavková, Hana, ed. *I Never Saw Another Butterfly.* Knopf, 1994.

Peace

Alarcón, Francisco. *Poems to Dream Together = Poemas para Sonar Juntos.* Illus. by Paula Barragán. Lee & Low, 2005.
Angelou, Maya. *Amazing Peace.* Illus. by Steve Johnson & Lou Fancher. Schwartz & Wade, 2008. (With CD)
———. "Human Family." In Rochelle, Belinda. *Words with Wings.* HarperCollins, 2001.
Cumbayah. Illus. by Floyd Cooper. Morrow, 1998.
Edelman, Marion Wright. *I Can Make a Difference.* Illus. by Barry Moser. HarperCollins, 2005.
Edens, Cooper. *If You're Afraid of the Dark, Remember the Night Rainbow.* Green Tiger, 1979.
Harshman, Marc. *Only One Neighborhood.* Illus. by Barbara Garrison. Dutton, 2007.
He's Got the Whole World in His Hands. Illus. by Kadir Nelson. Dial, 2005.
Heard, Georgia. *This Place I Know.* Candlewick, 2002.
Hoberman, Mary Ann. *And to Think That We Thought That We'd Never Be Friends.* Illus. by Kevin Hawkes. Crown, 1999.
Kerley, Barbara. *A Little Peace.* National Geographic, 2007.
McClester, Cedric. "For Peace Sake." In Slier, Deborah. *Make a Joyful Sound.* Illus. by Cornelius Van Wright & Ying-Hwa Hu. Checkerboard, 1991.
Mora, Pat. *Join Hands!* Illus. by George Ancona. Charlesbridge, 2008.
Morgenstern, Susie. *I Will Make Miracles.* Illus. by Jiang Hong Chen. Bloomsbury, 2006.
Mortenson, Greg & David Oliver Relin. *Three Cups of Tea.* (Young Reader's Edition). Adapt. by Sarah Thomson. Penguin, 2009. (Prose)
Nikola-Lisa, W. *Bein' with You This Way.* Illus. by Michael Bryant. Lee & Low, 1994.
Nye, Naomi Shihab. "The Word Peace." *A Maze Me.* Greenwillow, 2005.
Ryder, Joanne. *Without Words.* Illus. by Barbara Sonneborn. Sierra Club, 1995.
Rylant, Cynthia. *The Stars Will Still Shine.* Illus. by Tiphanie Beeke. HarperCollins, 2005.
Thomas, Marlo, ed. *Free to Be . . . You and Me.* Running Press, 1987.
Thomas, Marlo & Christopher Cerf, eds. *Thanks and Giving All Year Long.* S & S, 2004.
To Every Thing There Is a Season. Illus. by Leo Dillon & Diane Dillon. Scholastic, 1998.
Walker, Alice. *Why War Is Never a Good Idea.* Illus. by Stefano Vitale. HarperCollins, 2007.
Williams, Sam. *Talk Peace.* Illus. by Mique Moriuchi. Holiday, 2005.
Willis, Jeanne. *Shhh!* Illus. by Tony Ross. Hyperion, 2004.

REFERENCES

Curriculum Standards for the Social Studies. National Council for the Social Studies. 1994. http://www.socialstudies.org/standards
Nye, Naomi Shihab, sel. *This Same Sky.* Macmillan, 1992.
Wood, J. R. *Living Voices: Multicultural Poetry in the Middle School Classroom.* Urbana, IL: National Council of Teachers of English. 2006.

CHAPTER 6

Poetry and the Fine Arts Standards

The fine arts standards include those for dance, theater, visual arts, and music. Poets describe the arts, express feelings about them, and use the language of the arts. Words can sing or dance on the page. Poets weave words, paint with words, and shape words to show their deeper meanings. Poets perform or present words dramatically. Some poems and books are filled with elements of dance, music, and celebration. Pat Mora's *Join Hands! The Ways We Celebrate Life* includes all of the arts and shows how much joy can come from movement, singing, and other interactions. Megan McDonald's "Sing Me Strong" includes elements of singing, rhythmic play, musical instruments, and dance. In many cases poetry about music is also about dance. Poetry about music is also about theater. Keep in mind that selections that fall under one of these areas of the arts may work well in other areas.

McDonald, Megan. "Sing Me Strong." In Hopkins, Lee Bennett. *Climb Into My Lap*. Illus. by Kathryn Brown. S & S, 1998.

Mora, Pat. *Join Hands! The Ways We Celebrate Life*. Illus. by George Ancona. Charlesbridge, 2008.

DANCE STANDARDS

Standard One: Identifying and demonstrating movement elements and skills in performing dance.

Links with Chapter Seven: Physical Education

Links with Music Standards

Standard One: Rhythm

While dance instruction features a number of movement elements, rhythm (meter in poetry) is the element common to poetry and dance. From birth, we create and respond to rhythm. The youngest infant shakes a rattle or bangs a spoon over and over; moves its arms and kicks its legs in rhythmic ways. Children may chant or march or sing a rhythmic song. Clapping, playing, and movement that highlight their rhythms accompany the rhythms and words of nursery rhymes. Henry's mother overheard her three-year-old enjoying the rhythms of the song "This Old Man" quietly singing new verses to himself. He added verses for colors and created rhymes, then for objects in his room, as he enjoyed the beat of the song.

Some families have their own rhythmic nonsense words created by small children as they play. In my family, the act of swinging your head rhythmically side to side was accompanied by a nonsense word, "ackenoidy." My father used the word with my small nephew who smiling participated in the rhythmic activity. Later, loving the sound of the word, he repeated it endlessly while swinging his head.

Rhythmic play and games are also part of older children's traditions. Clapping games, jump rope, and other types of games play on children's natural sense of rhythm. Songs are a good way to introduce students to rhythm as well. Rhythm is natural to human beings. Fifth grader Sarah Kate wrote in her author statement on a book of poems she created: "Sarah Kate had no problem creating poems. It was easiest to create a poem by listening to her heartbeat at night."

Poetry encourages kinetic activity, inviting children through rhythm and imagery to act out what they hear and imagine from a poem. When reading Bill Martin Jr.'s *Up and Down on the Merry-Go-Round* children can move rhythmically up and down as well. It would be difficult to read or tell *Chicka Chicka Boom Boom* without falling naturally into its rhythms. In Bill Martin Jr's introduction to his *Big Book of Poetry*, he writes that he learned to read by concentrating on the rhythms of language, which may be the reason his picture book texts are so strongly rhythmic. (Martin, 2009, p. 10)

The poems included here suggest some activities that are clearly rhythmic. Sports, music, and all types of mechanical objects can be rhythmic. The marching of musicians in a parade is highlighted in Gene Baer's *Thump, Thump, Rat-a-Tat-Tat*. Students might enjoy presenting this, Sara Holbrook's "Wham-a-Bama One Man Band," or Addie Boswell's poetic text about a girl who creates her own parade in *The Rain Stomper*.

Rhythmic Poetry

Andrews, Sylvia. *Rattlebone Rock*. Illus. by Jennifer Plecas. HarperCollins, 1995.

Baer, Gene. *Thump, Thump, Rat-a-Tat Tat*. Illus. by Lois Ehlert. HarperCollins, 1989.

Booth, Philip. *Crossing*. Illus. by Bagram Ibatoulline. Viking, 2001. (Train)

Boswell, Addie. *The Rain Stomper*. Illus. by Eric Velasquez. Cavendish, 2008.

Cotten, Cynthia. "Drummer." In Hopkins, Lee Bennett. *America at War*. Illus. by Stephen Alcorn. McElderry, 2008.

Greenfield, Eloise. "Grandma's Bones." *Nathaniel Talking*. Illus. by Jan Spivey Gilchrist. Writers and Readers, 1988. (Playing the Bones)

Hillyer, Robert. "Lullaby." In Pearson, Susan. *The Drowsy Hours*. Illus. by Peter Malone. HarperCollins, 2002. (Also in *Reflections on a Gift of Watermelon Pickle*) (Rowing a Canoe)

Hoberman, Mary Ann. "Windshield Wipers." *The Llama Who Had No Pajama*. Illus. by Betty Fraser. Harcourt, 1998.

Holbrook, Sara. "Wham-a-Bama One Man Band." *Which Way to the Dragon!* Boyds Mills, 1996.

Martin, Bill, Jr. & John Archambault. *Chicka Chicka Boom Boom*. Illus. by Lois Ehlert. S & S, 1989.

———. *Up and Down on the Merry-Go-Round*. Illus. by Ted Rand. Holt, 1988.

Martin, Bill, Jr. & Michael Sampson. *The Bill Martin Jr. Big Book of Poetry*. S & S, 2008.

———. *Rock It, Sock It, Number Line*. Illus. by Heather Cahoon. Holt, 2001.

McCord, David. "Pickety Fence" & "Song of the Train." *One at a Time*. Illus. by Henry B. Kane. Little, 1986.

Merriam, Eve. "Windshield Wiper." In Kennedy, X. J. & Dorothy M. Kennedy. *Knock at a Star*. Illus. by Karen Lee Baker. Little, 1999.

Moore, Lilian. "Sometimes." In Kennedy, X. J. & Dorothy M. Kennedy. *Talking Like the Rain*. Illus. by Jane Dyer. Little, 1992. (Heartbeat)

Prelutsky, Jack. "Dance of the Thirteen Skeletons." *Nightmares*. Illus. by Arnold Lobel. Greenwillow, 1976.
Ridlon, Marci. "Fernando." In Morrison, Lillian. *Slam Dunk*. Illus. by Bill James. Hyperion, 1995. (Basketball)

Standard Two: Understanding choreographic principles, processes, and structures.

Standard Three: Understanding dance as a way to create and communicate meaning.

Standards Two and Three: Dance

While understanding principles and techniques of choreography is less critical for elementary and middle school students, understanding that dance is a way to create and communicate meaning is vital. As bodies grow and change, the ways people use them to communicate change as well, becoming more subtle and, in many cases, more inhibited.

Young children use their bodies to communicate meaning long before they can speak. Waving, pointing, and kicking are among these early communications. As children grow older, they learn to pantomime other beings or objects. Jean Marzollo's *Pretend You're a Cat* asks young children to pretend they are various animals by taking similar positions. Jerry Pinkney's paintings of children doing this activity can encourage children to try out how they would capture the essence of other animals. Eve Merriam's "On Our Way" and "I'm a Prickly Crab" also invite children to walk like the animals. Students who have opportunities to watch or attend dance performances are introduced to the ways that professional dancers use their bodies to tell stories. Students might try improvisational dance as a response to poetry as they try to capture the meanings of poems with their bodies.

Sometimes, poets use dance as a way to describe motion in something else. Students can think about other ways we talk about dancing. What, for example, does it mean to "dance around" a subject? What does it mean to "dance attendance" on someone? What do we mean when we say someone can really "cut a rug?"

Perhaps the most powerful communication of meaning in dance is the sheer joy humans can have in movement and dancing. One type of joy comes from the memory of dancing, either alone of with someone special. In "Duet," the granddaughter in Nikki Grimes' poem comes upon her grandmother dancing alone, lost in memories that make her look young. Ana Castillo's "For Ray" describes a daddy "still cool," showing his old dance moves to a group of children. Rebecca Kai Dotlich's "Kitchen Waltz" can be paired with the exuberant prose story, *Kitchen Dance* by Maurie J. Manning. Of course, as in any endeavor, things can go wrong when we dance. Judith Viorst's "Nightmare" speaks to that.

Andrews, Sylvia. *Dancing in My Bones*. Illus. by Ellen Mueller. HarperCollins, 2001.
Bryan, Ashley. "Taste the Air." *Sing to the Sun*. Harper, 1992.
Carlson, Lori Marie. "Shuffle Jump." *Sol a Sol*. Illus. by Emily Lisker. Holt, 1998.
Carroll, Lewis. "The Mock Turtle's Song." In Rosen, Michael. *Classic Poetry*. Illus. by Paul Howard. Candlewick, 2009.
Castillo, Ana. "For Ray." In Carlson, Lori M. ed. *Cool Salsa*.Holt, 1994
Dotlich, Rebecca Kai. "Kitchen Waltz." In Miklos, John. *Mommy Poems*. Illus. by Lori McElrath-Eslick. Boyds Mills, 2003.
Esquivel, Mirian. "We Dance." In Franklin, Kristine L. & Nancy McGirr. *Out of the Dump*. Lothrop, 1996.
Giovanni, Nikki. "Dance Poem." *Spin a Soft Black Song*. Illus. by George Martins. Farrar, 1985.
———. *The Genie in the Jar*. Illus. by Chris Raschka. Holt, 1996.
Greenfield, Eloise. "Buddy's Dream." *Night on Neighborhood Street*. Illus. by Jan Spivey Gilchrist. Dial, 1991.
Grimes, Nikki. "Block Party." *Danitra Brown Leaves Town*. Illus. by Floyd Cooper. HarperCollins, 2002.
———. "Duet." *Stepping Out With Grandma Mac*. Illus. by Angelo. Orchard, 2001.
———. "Sweethearts Dance." In Janeczko, Paul B. *Seeing the Blue Between*. Candlewick, 2002.

Hines, Anna Grossnickle. "Ballet" & "Rock and Roll." *Pieces.* HarperCollins, 2001.

Hughes, Langston. "Dream Variation." *The Dream Keeper.* Illus. by Brian Pinkney. Knopf, 1994.

———. "Juke Box Love Song." In Hollyer, Belinda. *She's All That.* Illus. by Susan Hellard. Kingfisher, 2006. (Also in *Celebrate America*)

Johnson, Dinah. *Hair Dance.* Illus. by Kelly Johnson. Holt, 2007.

Kuskin, Karla. "Spring." *Dogs and Dragons, Trees and Dreams.* HarperCollins, 1980. (Also in *The 20th Century Children's Poetry Treasury*)

Lindquist, Susan Hart. "Dancing Nan." In Hopkins, Lee Bennett. *Climb into My Lap.* Illus. by Kathryn Brown. S & S, 1998.

Lowery, Linda. *Twist with a Burger, Jitter with a Bug.* Illus. by Pat Dypold. Houghton, 1995.

Manning, Maurie J. *Kitchen Dance.* Houghton, 2008. (Prose)

Marzollo, Jean. *Pretend You're a Cat.* Illus. by Jerry Pinkney. Dial, 1990.

Merriam, Eve. "I'm a Prickly Crab." *Blackberry Ink.* Illus. by Hans Wilhelm. Morrow, 1985.

———. "On Our Way." In De Regniers, Beatrice Schenk. *Sing a Song of Popcorn.* Scholastic, 1988.

Prelutsky, Jack. "Awful Ogre Dances." *Awful Ogre's Awful Day.* Illus. by Paul O. Zelinsky. Greenwillow, 2001.

Rowden, Justine. "Dancin'. " *Paint Me a Poem.* Boyds Mills, 2005.

Ryder, Joanne. *Big Bear Ball.* Illus. by Steven Kellogg. HarperCollins, 2002.

———. *Dancers in the Garden.* Illus. by Judith Lopez. Sierra Club, 1992.

Viorst, Judith. "Nightmare." *If I Were in Charge of the World.* Macmillan, 1984. (Also in *Oh, No! Where Are My Pants?*)

Specific Types of Dance

Berry, James. "Watching a Dancer." In Hollyer, Belinda. *She's All That.* Illus. by Susan Hellard. Kingfisher, 2006. (Ballet)

Berry, Wendell. "The Wheel." In Panzer, Nora. *Celebrate America.* Hyperion, 1994. (Folk dance)

Brown, Calef. "Combo Tango." *Flamingos on the Roof.* Houghton, 2006.

Cheng, Andrea. *Brushing Mom's Hair.* Illus. by Nicole Wong. Boyds Mills, 2009. (Ballet) (Novel in Verse)

Dillon, Lee & Diane Dillon. *Rap a Tap Tap: Here's Bojangles Think of That.* Scholastic, 2002.

Elliott, David. *One Little Chicken.* Illus. by Ethan Long. Holiday, 2007. (Several Types)

Fitzgerald, F. Scott. "Bingo! Bango!" In Smith, William J. *Here Is My Heart.* Illus. by Jane Dyer. Little, 1999 (Tango)

Hanson, Warren. *Bugtown Boogie.* Illus. by Steve Johnson & Lou Fancher. HarperCollins, 2008. (Several Types)

Hughes, Langston. "Negro Dancers." *The Dream Keeper.* Illus. by Brian Pinkney. Knopf, 1994. (Charleston)

Lewis, J. Patrick. "Mother of the Dance." *Vherses.* Illus. by Mark Summers. Creative, 2005. (Modern Dance)

Lithgow, John. *Carnival of the Animals.* Illus. by Boris Kulikov. S & S, 2004. (Ballet) (Includes CD)

London, Jonathan. *Who Bop?* Illus. by Henry Cole. HarperCollins, 2000. (Bebop/Swing)

Maddox, Marjorie. "A Rumba of Rattlesnakes." *A Crossing of Zebras.* Illus. by Philip Huber. Boyds Mills, 2008.

Martin, Bill, Jr. & John Archambault. *Barn Dance.* Illus. by Ted Rand. Holt, 1986.

Rowden, Justine. "Moving White Fluffs." *Paint Me a Poem.* Boyds Mills, 2005.

Ryder, Joanne. *Dance by the Light of the Moon.* Illus. by Guy Francis. Hyperion, 2007. (Barn dance)

Sandburg, Carl. "From . . . 'Lines Written for Gene Kelly to Dance to.' " In Hopkins, Lee Bennett. *Rainbows Are Made.* Harcourt, 1982.

Shannon, George. "Dancing in the Breeze." *Busy in the Garden.* Illus. by Sam Williams. Greenwillow, 2006. (Several Types)

Shulman, Lisa. *Over in the Meadow at the Big Ballet.* Illus. by Sarah Massini. Putnam, 2007.

Turner, Ann. "Breakin.' " *Street Talk.* Houghton, 1982.

Weisburd, Stefi. "If." *Barefoot.* Illus. by Lori McElrath-Eslick. Boyds Mills, 2008.

Whitehead, Jenny. "The Dance Recital." *Lunch Box Mail*. Holt, 2001. (Ballet)
Zimmer, Tracy Vaughan. "Ballet Instructor." *Steady Hands*. Illus. by Megan Halsey & Sean Addy. Clarion, 2009.

Standard Four: Applying and demonstrating critical and creative thinking skills in dance.

Standard Five: Demonstrating and understanding dance in various cultures and historical periods.

See also Chapter Four: Math Standard Six (Problem Solving)

See also Chapter Five: Social Studies Themes One and Two (Culture and History)

Standards Four and Five: Dance from Cultural Traditions

Brown, Calef. "Funky Snowman." In Giovanni, Nikki. *Hip Hop Speaks to Children*. Jabberwocky, 2008.
Dickey, R. P. "Santo Domingo Corn Dance." In Panzer, Nora. *Celebrate America*. Hyperion, 1994.
Hughes, Langston. "Danse Africaine." In Roessel, David & Arnold Rampersad. *Langston Hughes*. Illus. by Benny Andrews. Sterling, 2006.
———. "Dream Boogie" & "Dream Variations." In Giovanni, Nikki. *Hip Hop Speaks to Children*. Sourcebooks, 2008.
———. "Song for a Banjo Dance" & "African Dance." *The Dream Keeper*. Illus. by Brian Pinkney. Knopf, 1994.
Medearis, Angela Shelf. *Dancing with the Indians*. Illus. by Samuel Byrd. Holiday, 1991.
Olaleye, Isaac. "Market Square Dance." *The Distant Talking Drum*. Illus. by Frané Lessac. Boyds Mills, 1995.
Soto, Gary. "Ballet Folklorico." *Canto Familiar*. Illus. by Annika Nelson. Harcourt, 1995.
———. "Kearney Park." *A Fire in My Hands*. Harcourt, 2006.
Unobagha, Uzo. "Here We Go Dancing the Rumba Dance," "Let's Marry on the Limpopo," & "Talking Drum Rhymes." *Off to the Sweet Shores of Africa*. Illus. by Julie Cairns. Chronicle, 2000.

Standard Six: Making connections between dance and healthful living.

Standard Seven: Making connections between dance and other disciplines.
Links with Music Standards
See also Chapter Seven: Physical Education Standard Four
See also Chapter Seven: Health Standard One

THEATER STANDARDS

Standard One: Script writing by the creation of improvisations and scripted scenes based on personal experience and heritage, imagination, literature, and history
See also Chapter Two: Language Arts Standard One
See also Music Standard One (Singing: Rap and Hip Hop)

Standard One: Poetry Performance

Poetry performance is among the oldest theatrical traditions. From the recitation of epic poems by ancient storytellers to the lays and ballads shared by the bards, poetry has been an out-loud activity. If students are to experience the true power of language, they need to hear how poems sound when spoken, and they need to practice this type of performance for themselves. Sharing poetry is powerful. When we read a poem that moves us or makes us laugh, it is natural to want to share that experience with others. Many children fall in love with poems and love performing them for others. More than one child I know has not only presented Shel Silverstein's "Boa Constrictor" to me but also performed all of the appropriate body movements.

By the time they come to school children often have a large repertoire of nursery rhymes and songs, jingles from television ads, and pieces of playground verse picked up from others, all of which they eagerly share. Liz Attenborough's *Poetry by Heart: A Child's Book of Poems to Remember* provides both short and long poems that children might want to present. Any collection of poems that appeals to a student has this potential. Poetry can also be read aloud with enthusiasm and emphasis (and students often find that they have memorized poems in the process of preparation.) Teachers and librarians should create an environment in schools that encourages presentation of poetry by modeling effective presentations themselves. Several works for librarians and teachers about sharing and performing poetry are included in the references at the end of this chapter.

How do you prepare to share a poem? First, choose a poem that has affected you in some way, and that you think will affect children as well. Nothing spoils poetry for young people more than an adult sharing poetry that is inappropriate in its content or tone. Terry's poetry study and its follow-ups suggest that poems about subjects with which students are familiar (animals, family, friendship, school, sports) and poems that humorously tell stories are good places to start. (Terry, 1964) All too often, that can also be where poetry-sharing ends.

Teachers and librarians need to scaffold the reading and writing of more thoughtful, complex poetry. If a poem is relevant to what is happening in social studies or science, on the playground, or in the world at large, a powerful presentation of that poem can help students move beyond the comfortable subjects. Try to convey the experience of the poem to your listeners. Before you read aloud, read the poem several times. As you read, think about what the poet is trying to say and how the poem makes you feel. What words or groups of words can you emphasize to convey that meaning? Are there sounds that help convey the images of the poem? Does the rhythm of the poem convey its meaning? How could you use pauses and accent various words or syllables to convey meaning?

A common error many of us make in reading poetry aloud is to fall into a kind of sing-song rhythm with alternating beats accented and a hard stop at the end of each line so that every poem sounds the same. It is better to err on the side of not breaking lines when a full thought takes several lines if the meaning is clearer this way. But take time to think about the line breaks. Why did the poet break the line in a certain place? Should there be a brief pause or none at all? If students listen to poets read their own works, they will discover that poets do pay attention to these line breaks and create a kind of rhythm as they read.

Dramatic presentations reveal the richness of poems by highlighting the sounds, rhythms, and images used by the poet. We need time to read and reflect on poems in order to plan the most effective way of presenting them to others. As teachers and librarians share poems effectively with students, they should model, both in what they do and how they talk about what they do, so that students can also present poems effectively. The References list at the end of this chapter includes several useful titles about presenting poetry.

Poetry performance has taken on the aspects of theater recently through the growing interest in Poetry Slams, Poetry Jams, and Rap Sessions. Tips for writing and presenting at these events are included in Sara Holbrook's, *Wham! It's a Poetry Jam! Discovering Performance Poetry.* Nikki Giovanni's *Hip Hop Speaks to Children* includes written poems and recorded versions of poems that students can use as models for poetry performance. Elizabeth Swados' *Hey You! C'Mere: A Poetry Slam* is filled with poems that are great for performing aloud. Nikki Grimes' novel in verse and prose, *Bronx Masquerade*, introduces some students who present their own work poetry-slam style.

Attenborough, Liz. comp. *Poetry by Heart.* Scholastic, 2001.
Giovanni, Nikki, ed. *Hip Hop Speaks to Children.* Sourcebooks, 2008. (With CD)

Grimes, Nikki. *Bronx Masquerade*. Dial, 2002.
Holbrook, Sara. *Wham! It's a Poetry Jam*. Boyds Mills, 2002.
Janeczko, Paul B. sel. *A Foot in the Mouth*. Illus. by Chris Raschka. Candlewick, 2009.
Paschen, Elise, ed. *Poetry Speaks to Children*. Sourcebooks, 2005. (With CD)
Swados, Elizabeth. *Hey You! C'Mere: A Poetry Slam*. Illus. by Joe Cepeda. Scholastic, 2002.

Standard Two: Acting by developing basic acting skills to portray characters that interact in improvised and scripted scenes.

Standard Two: Acting

Only a few poems talk about theatrical performances. Not all of these are positive, as Kalli Dakos and Charles Ghigna reveal in their poems. Older students can look back on these experiences and laugh ruefully at their youthful mistakes. Myra Cohn Livingston's young "princess" and Lee Bennett Hopkins' "prince" both realize that bad moments on the stage are made up for by the sound of applause. Perhaps the best known poem about acting is William Shakespeare's "All the World's a Stage," which suggests that we are all players on the stage of life.

Adoff, Arnold. "I Was Harriet." *All the Colors of the Race*. Illus. by John Steptoe. Morrow, 1982.
Dakos, Kalli. "The Tragic Night." *Don't Read This Book, Whatever You Do!* Illus. by G. Brain Karas. S & S, 1993.
Frank, John. "Puppets." *Keepers*. Illus. by Ken Robbins. Roaring Brook, 2008.
Ghigna, Charles. "Father Time." *A Fury of Motion*. Boyds Mills, 2003.
Hopkins, Lee Bennett. "Stage Fright." *Oh, No! Where Are My Pants?* Illus. by Wolf Erlbruch. HarperCollins, 2005.
Livingston, Myra Cohn. "School Play." In Kennedy, Dorothy M. *I Thought I'd Take My Rat to School*. Illus. by Abby Carter. Little, 1993.
Shakespeare, William. "All the World's a Stage." In Rosen, Michael. *Classic Poetry*. Illus. by Paul Howard. Candlewick, 2009.
Stafford, William. "First Grade." In Paschen, Elise. *Poetry Speaks to Children*. Sourcebooks, 2005. (With CD)
VanDerwater, Amy Ludwig. "School Play." In Hopkins, Lee Bennett. *Hamsters, Shells, and Spelling Bees*. Illus. by Sachiko Yoshikawa. HarperCollins, 2008.
Wayland, April Halprin. "My Version of William Shakespeare's Sonnet Number Twelve." In Janeczko, Paul B. *A Kick in the Head*. Illus, by Chris Raschka. Candlewick, 2005.

Standard Two: Presenting Poems with Points of View

See also Music Standard One (Rhythm)

See also Chapter One: Poetry and the Standards (Novels in Verse)

See also Chapter Two: Language Arts Standard Five (Persona Poems)

While any poem can be performed effectively, poems that take points of view allow students to try an acting performance. A number of poems use first-person voice, which works well for dramatic monologues. Some poets arrange their poems as small plays, with a number of characters or objects given roles and parts. These are designed for dramatic performance. Laura Amy Schlitz's *Good Masters! Sweet Ladies! Voices from a Medieval Village*, for example, is a set of free verse monologues designed for performance as a theatrical piece along with studies of the middle ages.

Students can write their own poems for presentation, or they can find poems by others that they would like to present.

Sometimes it's fun to be a public grump. Beatrice Schenk De Regniers' "Mean Song" includes directions for reading (or singing) three times in a row on days when you are feeling mean. With mean sound effects, and some increasing volume, this would make a fine presentation. Her "The Churlish Child's Week" features alliteration for each nasty day, which could be read with suitable snarls, and then followed with her "The Cheerful Child's Week" read in an upbeat tone. Karla Kuskin's "I Woke Up This Morning," about a really bad day, includes increasing type size to show the increasing grumpiness of the narrator.

Rhythmic poems are also fun to present, because the rhythm can be expressed through movement, drumming, clapping, or other types of physical motions. Poems that include interior rhyme provide great rhythm for sharing. Because Nancy Shaw's *Raccoon Tune* combines luscious vocabulary with interior rhyme and rhythm, it cries out for an enthusiastic reading. The rhythms of April Pulley Sayre's *Ant, Ant, Ant! An Insect Chant*, *Bird, Bird, Bird! A Chirping Chant*, and *Trout, Trout, Trout! A Fish Chant* invite oral presentation.

Some poems can be presented cumulatively, with an increasing or decreasing number of voices. Counting out rhymes can be performed, adding more voices for larger numbers. Betsy Lewin's *Cat Count* involves not just counting but addition, so it's fitting that voices be added as the number of cats gets larger. Molly Bang's *Ten, Nine, Eight* can begin with ten voices and subtract one for each number, becoming softer and softer with one soft last voice as the little girl falls asleep.

Picture book poems that feature a chorus can be presented with differing numbers of voices. Each student could take one letter of the alphabet in Jim Aylesworth's *Old Black Fly*, with all chiming in on the chorus of "Shoo Fly! Shoo Fly! Shooo." Nancy Van Laan's rhythmic *Possum Come a-Knockin'* can be divided into different speakers, with all voices chiming in on the chorus.

Older students may want to look at Sara Holbrook's books of poems, most, of which are first person and lend themselves to lively performances. Mel Glenn's *My Friend's Got This Problem, Mr. Chandler* contains first person poems from the points of view of a number of high school students and could be used for monologues. Many of the poems in the novels in verse can be presented as monologues or dialogues. Arnold Adoff's "Coach Says: Listen Sonny . . . " is a great poem to perform, as the poor battered safety discovers his fate on the field.

Adoff, Arnold. "Coach Says: Listen Sonny . . . " In Cullinan, Bernice E. *A Jar of Tiny Stars*. Boyds Mills, 1996.

Aylesworth, Jim. *Old Black Fly*. Illus. by Stephen Gammell. Holt, 1992.

Bang, Molly. *Ten, Nine, Eight*. Greenwillow, 1983.

De Regniers, Beatrice Schenk. "Mean Song," "The Churlish Child's Week," & "The Cheerful Child's Week." *The Way I Feel . . . Sometimes*. Illus. by Susan Meddaugh. Clarion, 1998.

Glenn, Mel. *My Friend's Got This Problem, Mr. Chandler*. Clarion, 1992.

Holbrook, Sara. *Am I Naturally This Crazy?* Illus. by Reuban Martin. Boyds Mills, 2003.

———. *By Definition*.. Illus. by Scott Mattern. Boyds Mills, 2003.

———. *The Dog Ate My Homework*. Boyds Mills, 1996.

———. *I Never Said I Wasn't Difficult*. Boyds Mills, 1996.

———. *Nothing's the End of the World*. Illus. by J. J. Smith-Moore, Boyds Mills, 1995.

———. *Which Way to the Dragon!* Boyds Mills, 1996.

Kuskin Karla. "I Woke Up This Morning." *Dogs and Dragons, Trees and Dreams*. HarperCollins, 1980.

Lewin, Betsy. *Cat Count*. Putnam, 1981.

Sayre, April Pulley. *Ant, Ant, Ant! An Insect Chant*. Illus. by Trip Park. Northwords, 2005.

———. *Bird, Bird, Bird! A Chirping Chant*. Northwords, 2007.

———. *Trout, Trout, Trout! A Fish Chant*. Illus. by Trip Park. Northwords, 2005.

Shaw, Nancy. *Raccoon Tune*. Illus. by Howard Fine. Holt, 2003.

Van Laan, Nancy. *Possum Come a-Knockin'* Illus. by George Booth. Knopf, 1990.

Poems for More than One Voice

John Ciardi's *You Read to Me, I'll Read to You*, published in 1962, was perhaps the first poetry book that invited adult and child readers to "converse" by reading poems to one another. On one side of the page, a poem was printed in black ink ("... you read to me."), and on the other, it was in blue ("... I'll read to you"). When Paul Fleischman published *I Am Phoenix* in 1985, and *Joyful Noise* in 1988, readers were introduced to another type of shared oral reading. Each of Fleischman's poems is set up to be read by two voices, or two sets of voices, with some lines alternated and others said together. This dialogue between the two readers allows listeners to observe the unique qualities of each creature he describes. Some are dialogues that features differing points of view; others build up to a climax and then diminish; still others give a message about the bird or insect being portrayed. Fleischman has also created a book of poems for four voices designed for middle school students.

Dialogue poems are included in many collections. They are a good starting point for oral presentations of poetry, because the voices and the roles are clearly set out in the poem. Dialogue poems allow primary-grade children to practice reading aloud with one another. Poems in Mary Ann Hoberman's *You Read to Me, I'll Read to You* series retell well-known stories for younger readers. Older students enjoy Marilyn Singer's novel in verse, *All We Needed to Say* that shares school experiences through the differing perspectives of two friends, Tanya and Sophie. That could be paired with Karen English's *Speak to Me (And I Will Listen Between the Lines)*, which includes poems about school told in the voices of six children. Mel Glenn's narratives allow older readers to gain insights into students who are often reduced to "types" in middle school.

These poems all encourage students to take a familiar situation and turn it into poems that tell two sides to the story. That might even be two voices within your own head as Ciardi does in "Sometimes I Feel This Way." Joyce Sidman's *This Is Just To Say: Poems about Apology and Forgiveness* is a series of dialogues, with poems of apology in the first half and poems of forgiveness written in reply to those apologies in the second half of the book.

Some dialogue poems provide two languages or cultural perspectives in conversation. Jane Medina's "Me X 2= Yo X 2" provides for an English speaker and a Spanish speaker to share the same thought in two languages. Liz Ann Baez Aguilar uses a mixture of English and Spanish in a conversation between a mother and daughter in "Growing Up." Janet Wong's "Speak Up" is a dialogue on judging a person by her appearance. Other poems provide perspectives on history. Bobbi Katz's *We the People* includes a number of poems in two or more voices that describe people, events, or living conditions in the American past. All dialogue poems help students to understand point of view as they explore more than one perspective in these poems.

Poems for Two Voices

Aguilar, Liz Ann Baez. "Growing Up." In Mora, Pat. *Love to Mamá*. Illus. by Paula S. Barragán. Lee & Low, 2001.

Baird, Audrey. "Storm Coming! (A Poem for Two Voices)." *Storm Coming!* Illus. by Patrick O'Brien. Boyds Mills, 2003.

Ciardi, John. *You Read to Me, I'll Read to You*. Illus. by Edward Gorey. HarperCollins, 1961.

Dakos, Kalli. "There's a Cobra in the Bathroom" and "Were You Ever Fat Like Me?" *If You're Not Here, Please Raise Your Hand*. Illus. by G. Brian Karas. Macmillan, 1990.

Field, Eugene. "The Duel." In Ferris, Helen. *Favorite Poems Old and New*. Illus. by Leonard Weisgard. Random, 1957, 2009.

Fleischman, Paul. *I Am Phoenix: Poems for Two Voices*. Illus. by Ken Nutt. HarperCollins, 1985.

———. *Joyful Noise: Poems for Two Voices*. Illus. by Eric Beddows. HarperCollins, 1988.

Florian, Douglas. "Double Dutch Girls." *Summersaults*. Greenwillow, 2002.

———. "Ogre Argument." *Laugh-eteria*. Harcourt, 1999.

Franco, Betsy. *Messing Around on the Monkey Bars: And Other School Poems for Two Voices*. Illus. by Jessie Hartland. Candlewick, 2009.

George, Kristine O'Connell. "Two Voices in a Tent at Night." *Toasting Marshmallows*. Illus. by Kate Kiesler. Clarion, 2001.

Grandits, John. "Sleepover Conversation." *Technically, It's Not My Fault*. Clarion, 2004.

Greenfield, Eloise. "Poet/Poem." *In the Land of Words*. Illus. by Jan Spivey Gilchrist. HarperCollins, 2004.

Grimes, Nikki. "Unspoken." *Thanks a Million*. Illus. by Cozbi A. Cabrera. Greenwillow, 2006.

Harley, Avis. "Dialogue Poem: Dragonfly." *Leap into Poetry*. Boyds Mills, 2001.

Harrison, David L. *Farmer's Dog Goes to the Forest: Rhymes for Two Voices*. Illus. by Arden Johnson-Petrov. Boyds Mills, 2005.

———. *Farmer's Garden: Rhymes for Two Voices*. Illus. by Arden Johnson-Petrov. Boyds Mills, 2000.

Heard, Georgia. "Fishes: Poem for Two Voices," and "Frog Serenade." *Creatures of Earth, Sea and Sky*. Illus. by Jennifer Owings Dewey. Boyds Mills, 1992. (Also in *A Foot in the Mouth*)

———. "My Horse and I (Poem for Two Voices)." *Songs of Myself*. Mondo, 2000.

Hoberman, Mary Ann. "The Teapot and the Kettle." In Cole, William. *Poem Stew*. Illus. by Karen Ann Weinhaus. Lippincott, 1981.

Hoberman, Mary Ann. *You Read to Me, I'll Read to You: Very Short Fairy Tales to Read Together*. Illus. by Michael Emberley. Little, 2004.

———. *You Read to Me, I'll Read to You: Very Short Mother Goose Tales to Read Together*. Illus. by Michael Emberley. Little, 2005.

———. *You Read to Me, I'll Read to You: Very Short Scary Tales to Read Together*. Illus. by Michael Emberley. Little, 2007.

———. *You Read to Me, I'll Read to You: Very Short Stories to Read Together*. Illus. by Michael Emberley. Little, 2001.

Holbrook, Sara. "Copycat." *Which Way to the Dragon!* Boyds Mills, 1996.

Hovey, Kate. *Arachne Speaks*. Illus. by Blair Drawson. McElderry, 2001.

Katz, Bobbi. *We the People*. Illus. by Nina Cruz. Greenwillow, 2000.

Levertov, Denise. "What Were They Like?" In Hopkins, Lee Bennett. *America at War*. Illus. by Stephen Alcorn. McElderry, 2008.

Lewis, J. Patrick. "Double Doubles {A Verse Served Up by Two Booming Voices}." *Vherses*. Illus. by Mark Summers. Creative Eds. 2005.

———. "What Is Earth?" In Heard, Georgia. *Falling Down the Page*. Roaring Brook, 2009.

Lewis, J. Patrick & Paul B. Janeczko. *Birds on a Wire*. Illus. by Gary Lippincott. Boyds Mills, 2008.

Mack, Marguerite. "If You Don't Come." In Booth, David. *'Til All the Stars Have Fallen*. Viking, 1990.

MacLachlan, Patricia and Emily MacLachlan Charest. "Tilly and Maude." *Once I Ate a Pie*. Illus. by Katy Schneider. HarperCollins, 2006.

"A Man Said to Me," "What Are You?" and "What's Your Name?" In Rosen, Michael. *Poems for the Very Young*. Illus. by Bob Graham. Kingfisher, 1993.

McCord, David. "Conversation" and "Father and I in the Woods." *One at a Time* Illus. by Henry B. Kane. Little, 1977.

Medina, Jane. "Me X 2 = Yo X 2." In Hopkins, Lee Bennett. *Days to Celebrate*. Greenwillow, 2005.

Nye, Naomi Shihab. "Spring Returns To Us . . . " *Come with Me*. Illus. by Dan Yaccarino. Greenwillow, 2000.

Raschka, Chris. *Yo! Yes?* Scholastic, 1993.

Rosen, Michael. *Bear's Day Out*. Illus. by Adrian Reynolds. Bloomsbury, 2007.

Rowden, Justine. "So Close." *Paint Me a Poem*. Boyds Mills, 2005.

Shields, Carol Diggory. "Poem for Two Voices." In Hollyer, Belinda. *She's All That*. Illus. by Susan Hellard. Kingfisher, 2006.

Sidman, Joyce. "Noses" and "Dog and Squirrel." *The World According to Dog*. Illus. by Doug Mindell. Houghton, Mifflin, 2003.

Sidman, Joyce. *This Is Just to Say*. Illus. by Pamela Zagarenski. Houghton, 2007.

Singer, Marilyn. *All We Needed to Say*. Illus. by Lorna Clark. Atheneum, 1996.
Smith, William Jay. "Said Dorothy Hughes to Helen Hocking." In Kennedy, X. J. & Dorothy M. Kennedy. *Knock at a Star*. Little, 1982.
There's a Hole in the Bucket. Illus. by Nadine Bernard Westcott. Harper, 1990.
Wong, Janet. "Speak Up." *Good Luck Gold*. McElderry, 1994. (Also in *A Foot in the Mouth*)
Yolen, Jane. "Two Together: A Poem for Two Voices." *Count Me a Rhyme*. Illus. by Jason Stemple. Boyds Mills, 2006.

Poems for Multiple Voices

Dakos, Kalli. "Happy Birthday to You," & "Flying Around the Classroom." *The Bug in Teacher's Coffee*. Illus. by Mike Reed. HarperCollins, 1999.
———. "I Don't Believe in Ghosts." *Put Your Eyes Up Here*. Illus. by G. Brian Karas. S & S, 2003.
———. "If You're Not Here, Then Where Are You?" "Eric Is Allergic to Girls," "You Were Hatched in a Witch's Brew," "Are You Sleeping? Is It Clear?" "Squirt! Squirt! On the Teacher's Skirt," "There's a Cockroach Lurking Inside My Desk," & "If Kids Were Put in Charge of Schools." *Don't Read This Book, Whatever You Do!* Illus. by G. Brian Karas. S & S, 1993.
———. "It's Inside My Sister's Lunch." *If You're Not Here, Please Raise Your Hand*. Illus. by G. Brian Karas. S & S, 1990.
———. "Mrs. Cole on an Onion Roll" & "My Favorite Pencil." *Mrs. Cole on an Onion Roll*. Illus. by JoAnn Adinolfi. S & S, 1995.
English, Karen. *Speak to Me (And I Will Listen Between the Lines)*. Illus. by Amy June Bates. Farrar, 2004.
Fleischman, Paul. *Big Talk: Poems for Four Voices*. Illus. by Beppe Giacobbe. Candlewick, 2000.
Greenfield, Eloise. *The Friendly Four*. Illus. by Jan Spivey Gilchrist. HarperCollins, 2006.
Harrison, David. "Chorus of Four Frogs." In Heard, Georgia. *Falling Down the Page*. Roaring Brook, 2009.
Hovey, Kate. *Ancient Voices*. Illus. by Murray Kimber. S & S, 2004.
Schlitz, Laura Amy. *Good Masters! Sweet Ladies! Voices from a Medieval Village*. Illus. by Robert Byrd. Candlewick, 2007.

Standard Three: Designing by developing environments for improvised and scripted scenes.

Standard Four: Directing by organizing rehearsals for improvised and scripted scenes.

Standard Five: Researching by finding information to support classroom dramatizations of improvised or scripted scenes.

Standard Six: Comparing and connecting art forms by describing theatre, dramatic media (such as film, television, and electronic media), and other forms.

Standard Seven: Analyzing and explaining personal preferences and constructing meanings from classroom dramatizations and from theatre, film, television, and electronic media

Standard Eight: Understanding context by recognizing the role of theatre, film, television, and electronic media in daily life.

Standard Eight: Appreciating Theater

Standards Three through Eight are specific and technical, applying more appropriately to secondary school drama and English classes. A few poems relate experiences of attending or appreciating live theater. Performances of *Cinderella* and *Aesop's Fables* provide a significant plot thread through Andrea Cheng's novel in verse, *Where the Steps Were*. Several picture books are set up as if the work were a theatrical performance, including McClintock's illustrations for Jim Aylesworth's version of

Our Abe Lincoln, Kadir Nelson's illustrations for Bill Staines' *All God's Critters* and Chris Van Allsburg's *The Z Was Zapped: A Play In 26 Acts*.

Aylesworth, Jim. *Our Abe Lincoln: An Old Tune with New Lyrics*. Illus. by Barbara McClintock. Scholastic, 2009.
Cheng, Andrea. *Where the Steps Were*. Boyds Mills, 2008.
Grimes, Nikki. "Culture." *Meet Danitra Brown*. Illus. by Floyd Cooper. Lothrop, 1994.
Hughes, Langston. "Notes on the Broadway Theatre." In Giovanni, Nikki. *Shimmy Shimmy Shimmy Like My Sister Kate*. Holt, 1996.
Shields, Carol Diggory. "The Big Bad Wolf." *Lunch Money*. Illus. by Paul Meisel. Dutton, 1995.
Staines, Bill. *All God's Critters*. Illus. by Kadir Nelson. S & S, 2009.
Swenson, May. "To Make a Play." *The Complete Poems To Solve*. Illus. by Christy Hale. Macmillan, 1993.
Van Allsburg, Chris. *The Z Was Zapped: A Play in Twenty-Six Acts*. Houghton, 1987.

VISUAL ARTS STANDARDS

Standard One: Understanding and applying media, techniques and processes.

Standard One: Artistic Media and Processes

Poets write about both the media and the processes of art, often as metaphors for life. Charles Ghigna suggests in "Ars Longa, Vita Brevis (Art Is Long, Life Is Short)" that each of our lives is a sculpture that we alone create. Others see links between painting techniques and the ways poets create with words. David L. Harrison expresses this idea in "Wishing You Bright Paint." Still others see the techniques of the weaver as not unlike those of the poet—weaving words together to create patterns and meanings. Tony Johnston's "Let Us Weave" uses weaving as a metaphor for coming together in peace, as does Serri's "From 'Thread by Thread.' "

Andrews-Goebel, Nancy. *The Pot That Juan Built*. Illus. by David Diaz. Lee & Low, 2002. (Clay)
Baker, Keith. *Little Green*. Harcourt, 2001. (Paint)
Baylor, Byrd. *When Clay Sings*. Illus. by Tom Bahti. Macmillan, 1972.
Bernard, Robin. "Brush Dance." In Katz, Bobbi. *Pocket Poems*. Illus. by Marylin Hafner. Dutton, 2004.
Brug, Sandra Gilbert. "Tales in Tapestry." In Hopkins, Lee Bennett. *Behind the Museum Door*. Illus. by Stacey Dressen-McQueen. Abrams, 2007.
Bryan, Ashley. "The Artist" & "Pretty Is." *Sing to the Sun*. HarperCollins, 1992.
DeLeon, Joe. "Ode to Michelangelo's Bones." In Nye, Naomi Shihab. *Salting the Ocean*. Illus. by Ashley Bryan. Greenwillow, 2000.
George, Kristine O'Connell. *Fold Me a Poem*. Illus. by Lauren Stringer. Harcourt, 2005. (Origami)
———. "Clay Play." In Heard, Georgia. *Falling Down the Page*. Roaring Brook, 2009.
Ghigna, Charles. "Ars Longa, Vita Brevis (Art Is Long, Life Is Short.)" *A Fury of Motion*. Boyds Mills, 2003.
Giovanni, Nikki. *The Genie in the Jar*. Illus. by Chris Raschka. Holt, 1996.
Goffstein, M. B. *My Noah's Ark*. HarperCollins, 1978. (Wood)
Grimes, Nikki. *Aneesa Lee and the Weaver's Gift*. Illus. by Ashley Bryan. Lothrop, 1999.
Harrison, David L. "Wishing You Bright Paint." *Connecting Dots*. Illus. by Kelley Cunningham Cousineau. Boyds Mills, 2004.
Hovey, Kate. *Arachne Speaks*. Illus. by Blair Drawson. McElderry, 2001. (Weaving)
Johnston, Tony. "I Saw a Woman Weaving = Vi a una Mujer que Tejia." *My Mexico = México Mío*. Illus. by F. John Sierra. Putnam, 1996.
———. "Let Us Weave." *Voice from Afar*. Illus. by Susan Guevara. Holiday, 2008.
Katz, Susan. "Little Dancer by Degas." *Mrs. Brown on Exhibit*. Illus. by R. W. Alley. S & S, 2002. (Bronze)
Lesynski, Loris. "Paintbrush." *Zigzag*. Annick, 2004.

Lewis, J. Patrick. "Museum Field Trip. In Hopkins, Lee Bennett. *Behind the Museum Door.* Illus. by Stacey Dressen-McQueen. Abrams, 2007. (Sculpture)

Mora, Pat. "Purple Snake." *Confetti.* Illus. by Enrique O. Sanchez. Lee & Low, 1996. (Woodcarving)

Nye, Naomi Shihab. "Making a Mosaic." *A Maze Me.* Greenwillow, 2005.

Olaleye, Isaac. "Village Weavers." *The Distant Talking Drum.* Illus. by Frané Lessac. Boyds Mills, 1995.

Serri, Bracha. "From 'Thread by Thread.' " In Nye, Naomi Shihab. *The Space Between Our Footsteps.* S & S, 1998. (Also in *The Flag of Childhood*)

Sidman, Joyce. "Lucky Nose" & "To the Girl Who Rubs My Nose." *This Is Just to Say.* Illus. by Pamela Zagarenski. Houghton,2007. (Statue)

———. "Prehistory (The Discovery of Clay.)" *Eureka.* Illus. by K. Bennett Chavez.. Millbrook, 2002.

Singer, Marilyn. "Clay." In Hopkins, Lee Bennett, sel. *Behind the Museum Door.* Illus. by Stacey Dressen-McQueen. Abrams, 2007.

Spires, Elizabeth. *I Heard God Talking to Me: William Edmondson and His Stone Carvings.* Farrar, 2009.

Weatherford, Carole Boston. "The Basket Weaver." *Remember the Bridge.* Philomel, 2002.

Quilts

Quilts are frequently used as a metaphor for the diversity of the American experience, as Barack Obama did in his reference to our "patchwork heritage" in his inauguration address. Patricia McKissick's *Stitchin' and Pullin': A Gee's Bend Quilt* features poems portraying the passing down of quilting skills from grandmother to mother to child in this famous African American quilting community.

Hegamin, Tonya Cherie. *Most Loved in All the World.* Illus. by Cozbi A. Cabrera. Houghton, 2009. (Quilts)

Hines, Anna Grossnickle. *Pieces: A Year in Poems and Quilts.* HarperCollins, 2001.

Kuskin, Karla. "This Place Began." *Moon, Have You Met My Mother?* Illus. by Sergio Ruzzier. HarperCollins, 2003.

McKissack, Patricia C. *Stitchin' and Pullin': A Gee's Bend Quilt.* Illus. by Cozbi A. Cabrera. Random, 2008.

Weatherford, Carole Boston. "Miss Mae's Quilt." *Remember the Bridge.*Philomel, 2002.

Wong, Janet S. "Quilt." *A Suitcase of Seaweed.* Booksurge, 2008. (Also in *Seeing the Blue Between*)

Standard Two: Using knowledge of structures and functions.

See also Chapter Two: Language Arts Standard Six (Figurative Language)

See also Chapter Four: Mathematics Standard Three (Shape)

See also Chapter Seven: Health Standard Eight (Race)

Standard Two: Color

The structures and functions of art include sensory qualities (imagery in poetry), organizational principles, and elements of arts such as use of color, value, line, shape, and perspective. Of these, the element of color occurs most frequently in poetry. Mary O'Neill's classic *Hailstones and Halibut Bones: Poems of Color,* which uses extended metaphors to describe color, has been heavily used as a model for students' own color poems. Too often what results is simply lists of objects students can see around them as they write, or descriptions borrowed from the poems themselves. By providing a variety of poems about color from different poets, teachers give students a range of ways they can think about colors so that they can describe them in their own voices.

All colors evoke feelings. Red, for example, can represent warmth, or love, but can also stand for more threatening things like war and hatred. Blue can represent sadness, or it can be serene. As students think about colors they can think about the variety of feelings a color can evoke. Several poets have been struck by contradiction of the "blanket" of white that snow makes, covering all of the other colors. Can a person ever feel warm with that blanket of white? Most colors exist as parts of clichés: "red as a beet," "green with envy," or "white as snow," for example. Sometimes to say "white as snow" is not only clichéd but inaccurate, as Aileen Fisher suggests in her poem, "Snow Color." What color *is* snow? What color is the sky? What color is dirt? Considering the range of colors within a seemingly simple thing can help us look at it by separating, comparing, and contrasting, and exploring differences in items of the same color.

Some poets play with the names of the colors. Jack Prelutsky has written two humorous poems about "orange." He also plays with "Amarillo," the name for yellow in Spanish. J. Patrick Lewis discusses the color names for the seas in "Is the Yellow Sea Yellow?" Kalli Dakos' poem about red pencil marking of papers, "I'd Mark with the Sunshine," is a reminder of the negative emotions red ink corrections can have for students.

Color is a poet's tool. In "Rainbow Writing," Eve Merriam describes how she remembers flowers in vivid colors so that she can capture their beauty on the page. "Red" is a general name. Crimson, strawberry, paprika, and tomato are names for particular types of red. Students might chart the specific color names they can think of and then research others in books like Jeanne Heifetz's *When Blue Meant Yellow: How Colors Got Their Names* to discover other possibilities. Finding just the right red for a poem is as important for the poet as finding just the right red for a painting is for the artist. M. B. Goffstein encourages readers to move beyond the favored bright colors to consider those that help artists create shading and value. In *Artists' Helpers Enjoy the Evenings*, white, black, gray, brown, and red are shown to be essential to the artist's palette.

Edwards, Pamela Duncan. *Warthogs Paint: A Messy Color Book*. Illus. by Henry Cole. Hyperion, 2001.

Goffstein, M. B. *Artists' Helpers Enjoy the Evenings*. HarperCollins, 1987.

Heifetz, Jeanne. *When Blue Meant Yellow: How Colors Got Their Names*. Holt, 1994. (Prose)

Hubbard, Patricia. *My Crayons Talk*. Illus. by G. Brian Karas. Holt, 1996.

Larios, Julie. *Yellow Elephant: A Bright Bestiary*. Illus. by Julie Paschkis. Harcourt, 2006.

Miller, Kate. *Poems in Black and White*. Boyds Mills, 2007.

O'Neill, Mary. *Hailstones and Halibut Bones*. Illus. by John Wallner. Doubleday, 1989.

Oram, Hiawyn. *Out of the Blue: Poems about Color*. Illus. by David McKee. Hyperion, 1993.

Peek, Merle, adapt. *Mary Wore Her Red Dress and Henry Wore His Green Sneakers*. Clarion, 1985.

Rossetti, Christina. *Color*. Illus. by Mary Teichman. HarperCollins, 1992. (Also in *The Bill Martin Jr. Big Book of Poetry*)

Sidman, Joyce. *Red Sings from Treetops: A Year in Colors*. Illus. by Pamela Zagarenski. Houghton, 2009.

Wood, Audrey. *The Deep Blue Sea: A Book of Colors*. Illus. by Bruce Wood. Scholastic, 2005.

Zolotow, Charlotte. Section: "Colors." *Everything Glistens and Everything Sings*. Illus. by Margot Tomes. Harcourt, 1987.

Individual Poems About Color

Adams, Lavonne J. "Bittersweet." In Nye, Naomi Shihab. *What Have You Lost?* Greenwillow, 1999.

Beler, Zeynep. "Pink." In Nye, Naomi Shihab. *The Space Between Our Footsteps*. S & S, 1998. (Also in *The Flag of Childhood*)

Dakos, Kalli. "I'd Mark with the Sunshine." *Don't Read This Book, Whatever You Do!* Illus. by G. Brian Karas. S & S, 1993.

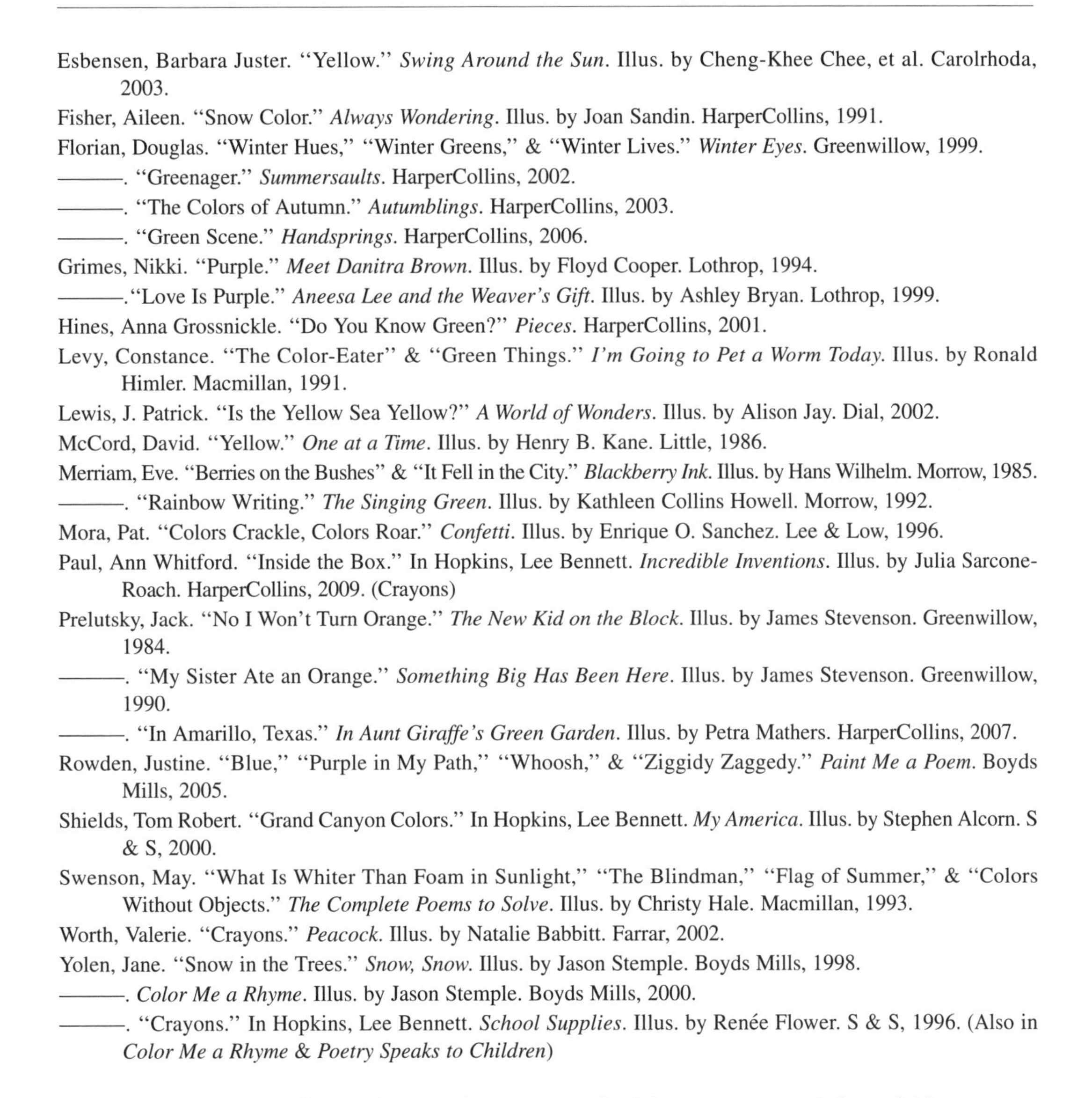

Esbensen, Barbara Juster. "Yellow." *Swing Around the Sun*. Illus. by Cheng-Khee Chee, et al. Carolrhoda, 2003.

Fisher, Aileen. "Snow Color." *Always Wondering*. Illus. by Joan Sandin. HarperCollins, 1991.

Florian, Douglas. "Winter Hues," "Winter Greens," & "Winter Lives." *Winter Eyes*. Greenwillow, 1999.

———. "Greenager." *Summersaults*. HarperCollins, 2002.

———. "The Colors of Autumn." *Autumblings*. HarperCollins, 2003.

———. "Green Scene." *Handsprings*. HarperCollins, 2006.

Grimes, Nikki. "Purple." *Meet Danitra Brown*. Illus. by Floyd Cooper. Lothrop, 1994.

———."Love Is Purple." *Aneesa Lee and the Weaver's Gift*. Illus. by Ashley Bryan. Lothrop, 1999.

Hines, Anna Grossnickle. "Do You Know Green?" *Pieces*. HarperCollins, 2001.

Levy, Constance. "The Color-Eater" & "Green Things." *I'm Going to Pet a Worm Today*. Illus. by Ronald Himler. Macmillan, 1991.

Lewis, J. Patrick. "Is the Yellow Sea Yellow?" *A World of Wonders*. Illus. by Alison Jay. Dial, 2002.

McCord, David. "Yellow." *One at a Time*. Illus. by Henry B. Kane. Little, 1986.

Merriam, Eve. "Berries on the Bushes" & "It Fell in the City." *Blackberry Ink*. Illus. by Hans Wilhelm. Morrow, 1985.

———. "Rainbow Writing." *The Singing Green*. Illus. by Kathleen Collins Howell. Morrow, 1992.

Mora, Pat. "Colors Crackle, Colors Roar." *Confetti*. Illus. by Enrique O. Sanchez. Lee & Low, 1996.

Paul, Ann Whitford. "Inside the Box." In Hopkins, Lee Bennett. *Incredible Inventions*. Illus. by Julia Sarcone-Roach. HarperCollins, 2009. (Crayons)

Prelutsky, Jack. "No I Won't Turn Orange." *The New Kid on the Block*. Illus. by James Stevenson. Greenwillow, 1984.

———. "My Sister Ate an Orange." *Something Big Has Been Here*. Illus. by James Stevenson. Greenwillow, 1990.

———. "In Amarillo, Texas." *In Aunt Giraffe's Green Garden*. Illus. by Petra Mathers. HarperCollins, 2007.

Rowden, Justine. "Blue," "Purple in My Path," "Whoosh," & "Ziggidy Zaggedy." *Paint Me a Poem*. Boyds Mills, 2005.

Shields, Tom Robert. "Grand Canyon Colors." In Hopkins, Lee Bennett. *My America*. Illus. by Stephen Alcorn. S & S, 2000.

Swenson, May. "What Is Whiter Than Foam in Sunlight," "The Blindman," "Flag of Summer," & "Colors Without Objects." *The Complete Poems to Solve*. Illus. by Christy Hale. Macmillan, 1993.

Worth, Valerie. "Crayons." *Peacock*. Illus. by Natalie Babbitt. Farrar, 2002.

Yolen, Jane. "Snow in the Trees." *Snow, Snow*. Illus. by Jason Stemple. Boyds Mills, 1998.

———. *Color Me a Rhyme*. Illus. by Jason Stemple. Boyds Mills, 2000.

———. "Crayons." In Hopkins, Lee Bennett. *School Supplies*. Illus. by Renée Flower. S & S, 1996. (Also in *Color Me a Rhyme* & *Poetry Speaks to Children*)

Standard Three: Choosing and evaluating a range of subject matter, symbols, and ideas.

Standard Four: Understanding the visual arts in relation to history and cultures.

See also Chapter Five: Social Studies Themes One and Two (Culture and History)

Standard Four: Art in History and Culture

The desire to capture beauty and to explain ourselves through art is as old as human history. Poet Avis Harley connects nature and its re-creation in two poems about butterflies. In the first, "Before," she writes that beauty existed in the wings of the butterfly before artists knew how to capture it. In "Catching a Butterfly (2)" she describes a mural in a Pharaoh's tomb that features a butterfly. The arts and architecture of different cultures, both ancient and modern, reveal how they understand and explain the world around them.

Baylor, Byrd. *When Clay Sings*. Illus. by Tom Bahti. Scribner, 1972.
Bruchac, Joseph. "There Are Also Some Places . . . " & "No One Lives Today . . . " *Between Earth and Sky: Legends of Native American Sacred Places*. Illus. by Thomas Locker. Harcourt, 1996.
Goffstein, M. B. "The Woodland Indians." *An Artists Album*. HarperCollins, 1985.
Harley, Avis. "Before" & "Catching a Butterfly (2)." *The Monarch's Progress*. Boyds Mills, 2008.
Harter, Penny. "Buffalo." In Janeczko, Paul B. *Hey, You!* Illus. by Robert Rayevsky. HarperCollins, 2007.
Johnston, Tony. "Old Powers," "Temple," & "Old Palaces." *The Ancestors Are Singing*. Illus. by Karen Barbour. Farrar, 2003.
Lewis, J. Patrick. *Monumental Verses*. National Geographic. 2005.
Lewis, J. Patrick & Rebecca Kai Dotlich. *Castles*. Illus. by Dan Burr. Boyds Mills, 2006.
Yolen, Jane. *Sacred Places*. Illus. by David Shannon. Harcourt, 1996.

Arts in Latino Cultures

A number of poems and collections describe the art and artists of Latino cultures. Students can collect poems from other cultural traditions, such as poems about quilting in African American traditions or weaving in Southwestern Indian traditions. These can be linked to social studies units when appropriate.

Andrews-Goebel, Nancy. *The Pot That Juan Built*. Illus. by David Diaz. Lee & Low, 2002.
Bernier-Grand, Carmen T. *Diego: Bigger Than Life*. Illus. by David Diaz. Cavendish, 2009.
———. *Frida: ¡Viva la Vida! = Long Live Life!* Marshall Cavendish, 2007.
Herrera, Juan Felipe. *Laughing Out Loud I Fly: Poems in English and Spanish*. Illus. by Karen Barbour. Harper Collins, 1998. (Inspired by Picasso)
Hines, Anna Grossnickle. "Christmas Path." *Winter Lights*.Greenwillow, 2005. (Farolitos)
Johnston, Tony. "Anahuacalli." *The Ancestors Are Singing*. Illus. by Karen Barbour. Farrar, 2003.
———. "I Saw a Woman Weaving." *My Mexico = México Mío*. By F. John Sierra. Putnam, 1996.
Mora, Pat. "Purple Snake" & "Dancing Paper." *Confetti*. Illus. by Enrique O. Sanchez. Lee & Low, 1996. (Carved, Painted Animals and Papel Picado)
Nye, Naomi Shihab. *The Tree Is Older Than You Are: A Bilingual Gathering of Poems and Stories from Mexico*. With paintings by Mexican Artists. S & S, 1995.

Standard Five: Reflecting upon and assessing the characteristics and merits of one's own work and the work of others.

Standard Five: Being an Artist

Many of my students have shared with me that at some point in their schooling they were criticized for not doing art "correctly," and so they gave up the pleasures of creating art. They empathize when I share Miriam Cohen's *No Good in Art*, in which a kindergarten teacher convinces young Jim that he isn't creative. Luckily for Jim, in first grade he has a very good teacher who allows her students to create art as self-expression. Alexis Rotella's poem "Purple" tells a similar story for older students.

In a number of poems, students resist criticism by teachers or peers. Brianna in Karen English's "No Such Thing as a Red Cake," declares that she paints everything the way she wants it, not what others want. In X. J. Kennedy's "Art Class," a young artist suggests that his teacher may not know as much about art as she thinks. In Naomi Shihab Nye's "How to Paint a Donkey," the speaker rejects a teacher's criticism of an artwork. But joy in the process of creating art doesn't always happen in schools. Sometimes, a person might even cheat at art in order to gain favor, as the young speaker in Janet S. Wong's "Losing Face" does.

Two poets share feelings about becoming an artist. In "When I Grow Up," Janet Wong's young speaker tries to persuade her grandfather that in America, she might grow up to be an artist. Davida Adedjouma's "Artist to Artist" tells of living out her father's dream of being an artist, a dream he sacrificed to support his family.

Art is all around us. Lilian Moore's "Mural on Second Avenue" might be an invitation to students to find art in their own neighborhoods, as are two poems in Ann Turner's *Street Talk*. Ms. Roy, the teacher in Kalli Dakos' "The Art Gallery on Penny's Back," finds artistic talent in the backpack decorations of her student, and writes a poem about it. All students need opportunities to appreciate, share, and create beauty in their classrooms and schools through works of art, poetry, music, prose writing, and classroom decoration.

Young Artists

Beaumont, Karen. *I Ain't Gonna Paint No More!* Illus. by David Catrow. Harcourt, 2005.

Cheng, Andrea. *Brushing Mom's Hair*. Illus. by Nicole Wong. Boyds Mills, 2009. (Pottery) (Novel in Verse)

Chute, Marchete. "Crayons." In Prelutsky, Jack. *Read-Aloud Rhymes for the Very Young*. Illus. by Marc Brown. Knopf, 1986. (Also in *I Thought I'd Take My Rat to School*)

Cohen, Miriam. *No Good In Art*. Illus. by Lillian Hoban. Greenwillow, 1980. (Prose)

Cook, Stanley. "Crayoning." In Foster, John. *A Very First Poetry Book*. Oxford, 1980.

Dakos, Kalli. "In Trouble." *Mrs. Cole on an Onion Roll*. Illus. by JoAnn Adinolfi. S & S, 1995.

———. "In Color," "The Art Gallery on Penny's Back," & "Special Eyeballs." *Put Your Eyes Up Here*. Illus. by G. Brian Karas. S & S, 2003.

"Dibujano un Garabato = Doodles." In Ada, Alma Flor & F. Isabel Campoy. *Mamá Goose: A Latino Nursery Treasury*. Illus. by Maribel Suárez. Hyperion, 2004.

English, Karen. "There's No Such Things As a Red Cake (Brianna.)" *Speak to Me (And I Will Listen Between the Lines)*. Illus. by Amy June Bates. Farrar, 2004.

Esbensen, Barbara Juster. "Friends." *Who Shrank My Grandmother's House?* Illus. by Erik Beddows. Harper Collins, 1992.

Fisher, Aileen. "Wind Circles." In Kennedy, Dorothy M. *I Thought I'd Take My Rat to School*. Illus. by Abby Carter, Little, 1993.

Frost, Helen. "Learning to Draw: Asha." *Spinning Through the Universe*. Farrar, 2004. (Novel in Verse)

Gelman. Rita Golden. *Doodler Doodling*. Illus. by Paul O. Zelinsky. Greenwillow, 2004.

Harley, Avis. "Catching a Butterfly (1)" *The Monarch's Progress*. Boyds Mills, 2008.

Hearn, Michael Patrick. "Rhinos Purple, Hippos Green." In Prelutsky, Jack. *The Random House Book of Poetry for Children*. Illus. by Arnold Lobel. Random, 1983.

Kennedy, X. J. "Art Class." In Kennedy, Dorothy M. *I Thought I'd Take My Rat to School*. Illus. by Abby Carter, Little, 1993. (Also in *Poetry Speaks to Children*)

Lechner, Ruth. "Drawing by Ronnie C., Grade One." In Kennedy, Dorothy M. *I Thought I'd Take My Rat to School*. Illus. by Abby Carter, Little, 1993.

Levy, Constance. "Drawing Ducks." *I'm Going to Pet a Worm Today*. Illus. by Ronald Himler. Macmillan, 1991.

McCord, David. "How to Draw a Monkey" & "Pad and Pencil." *One at a Time*. Little, 1986.

Moore, Lilian. "Mural on Second Avenue." *Mural on Second Avenue*. Illus. by Roma Karas. Candlewick, 2005.

Nye, Naomi Shihab. "How to Paint a Donkey." In Paschen, Elise. *Poetry Speaks to Children*. Sourcebooks, 2005. (With CD)

Perkins, Leslie D. "Art Class." In Hopkins, Lee Bennett. *Hamsters, Shells, and Spelling Bees*. Illus. by Sachiko Yoshikawa. HarperCollins, 2008.

———. "Popsicle Sticks and Glue." In Hopkins, Lee Bennett. *School Supplies*. Illus. by Renée Flower. S & S, 1996.

Prelutsky, Jack. "Awful Ogre Paints a Picture." *Awful Ogre Running Wild*. Illus. by Paul O. Zelinsky. Greenwillow, 2008.

———. I Drew a Yellow Unicorn." *What a Day It Was at School!* Illus. by Doug Cushman. Greenwillow, 2006.

———. "My Brother Is a Doodler." *A Pizza the Size of the Sun*. Illus. by James Stevenson. HarperCollins, 1996.

Rotella, Alexis. "Purple." In Willard, Nancy, sel. *Step Lightly*. Harcourt, 1998.

Singer, Marilyn. "Heart Art." In Hopkins, Lee Bennett. *Valentine Hearts*. Illus. by JoAnn Adinolfi. Harper Collins, 2008.

Soto, Gary. "Fernie and Me Try Art" & "Art Collectors." *Fearless Fernie*. Illus. by Regan Dunnick. Putnam, 2002. (Novel in Verse)

Turner, Ann. "Street Painting." *Street Talk*. Illus. by Catherine Stock. Houghton, 1986.

Wayland, April, Halprin. "Crayon Dance." In Janeczko, Paul B. *Dirty Laundry Pile*. Illus. by Melissa Sweet. HarperCollins, 2001.

Weatherford, Carole B. "Sidewalk Chalk" & "A Cardboard Box." *Sidewalk Chalk*. Illus. by Dimitrea Tokunbo. Boyds Mills, 2006.

Wong, Janet S. "Losing Face." *Good Luck Gold*. McElderry, 1994.

———. "When I Grow Up." *A Suitcase of Seaweed*. Booksurge, 2008. (Also in *She's All That*)

Artists and Their Work

Some poets try to capture the feeling of being an artist. Pat Lowery Collins' *I Am an Artist* describes the ways we become artists when we closely observe the beauty of the natural world. Artist Barbara Cooney's *Miss Rumphius* learns from her grandfather that each person must do something "to make the world more beautiful," and she passes that message on. Gu Cheng writes of the desire to draw a beautiful world in a sorrowful time in his metaphorical "A Headstrong Boy."

This section includes biographical poems about well-known artists as well as how artists go about their work.

Adedjouma, Davida. "Artist to Artist." In Steptoe, Javaka. *In Daddy's Arms I Am Tall*. Lee & Low, 1997.

Andrews-Goebel, Nancy. *The Pot That Juan Built*. Illus. by David Diaz. Lee & Low, 2002. (Juan Quezada)

Bernier-Grand, Carmen T. *Diego: Bigger Than Life*. Illus. by David Diaz. Cavendish, 2009. (Diego Rivera)

———. *Frida: ¡Viva la Vida! = Long Live Life!* Marshall Cavendish, 2007. (Frida Kahlo)

Bryant, Jen. *Pieces of Georgia*. Knopf, 2006. (Georgia O'Keefe)

Collins, Pat Lowery. *I Am an Artist*. Illus. by Robin Brickman. Millbrook, 1992.

Cooney, Barbara. *Miss Rumphius*. Viking, 1982. (prose)

George, Kristine O'Connell. "Sketchbook on Easel." *Old Elm Speaks*. Illus. by Kate Kiesler. Clarion, 1998.

Goffstein, M. B. *An Artist*. HarperCollins, 1980. (Monet)

———. *An Artists Album*. HarperCollins, 1985. (Five artists)

Grandits, John. "Mondrian." *Blue Lipstick*. Clarion, 2007.

Gu Cheng. "A Headstrong Boy." In Nye, Naomi Shihab. *This Same Sky*. Macmillan, 1992.

Katz, Susan. "Statues," "Little Dancer, by Degas," & "Sarah Enters a Painting." *Mrs. Brown on Exhibit*. Illus. by R. W. Alley. S & S, 2002.

Lewis, J. Patrick. "Unstill Life: Georgia O'Keefe." *Vherses*. Illus. by Mark Summers. Creative, 2005.

Lithgow, John. *Micawber*. Illus. by C. F. Payne. S & S, 2002. (Includes CD)

Livingston, Myra Cohn. "In This Picture." In Smith, William Jay. *Here Is My Heart*. Illus. by Jane Dyer. Little, 1999.

Mora, Pat. "For Georgia O'Keefe." *My Own True Name* . Arté Público, 2000.

Myers, Walter Dean. "Reuben Mills, 34, Artist." *Here in Harlem*. Holiday, 2004.
Prelutsky, Jack. "There Was a Man In Mexico." *In Aunt Giraffe's Green Garden*. Illus. by Petra Mathers. HarperCollins, 2007.
Prévert, Jacques. *How to Paint the Portrait of a Bird*. Trans. & illus. by Mordicai Gerstein. Roaring Brook, 2007.
Robinson, Lee. "Georgia O'Keefe Remembers Texas." In Nye, Naomi Shihab. *Is This Forever or What?* HarperCollins, 2004.
Singer, Marilyn. "The Painter." *The Company of Crows*. Illus. by Linda Saport. Clarion, 2002.
Spinelli, Eileen. "Creativity." In Heard, Georgia. *Falling Down the Page*. Roaring Brook, 2009.
Spires, Elizabeth. *I Heard God Talking to Me: William Edmondson and His Stone Carvings*. Farrar, 2009.
Swenson, May. "Fountain Piece" & "A Boy Looking at Big David." *The Complete Poems to Solve*. Illus. by Christy Hale. Macmillan, 1993.
Yolen, Jane. "Ice Can Scream." *Once Upon Ice*. Illus. by Jason Stemple. Boyds Mills, 1997. (Edvard Munch)
Zelk, Zoltan. "Salt and Memory: A Tribute to Marc Chagall." In Nye, Naomi Shihab, *This Same Sky*. Macmillan, 1992.
Zimmer, Tracie Vaughn. "Artist." *Steady Hands*. Illus. by Megan Halsey & Sean Addy. Clarion, 2009.

Art Museums

Gunning, Monica. "The Museum." *America, My New Home*. Illus. by Ken Condon. Boyds Mills, 2004.
Hopkins, Lee Bennett. *Behind the Museum Door: Poems to Celebrate the Wonders of Museums*. Illus. by Stacey Dressen-McQueen. Abrams, 2007.
Johnston, Tony. "Anahuacalli," *The Ancestors Are Singing*. Illus. by Karen Barbour. Farrar, 2003.
Katz, Susan. *Mrs. Brown on Exhibit: And Other Museum Poems*. Illus. by R. W. Alley. S & S, 2002.
Lithgow, John. *Micawber*. Illus. by C. F. Payne. S & S, 2002. (Includes CD)

Standard Six: Making connections between the visual arts and other disciplines.

See also Chapter Two: Language Arts Standard Two (Classic Poems)

Standard Six: Collections of Art and Poetry

Several types of poetry collections and picture books directly link the visual arts with the language arts. First, there are the poems and collections in which poets respond to works of art through poetry. This poetry captures the subjects, elements, and materials of the artworks as well as the feeling evoked by each. Jan Greenberg introduces readers to a wonderful word for poems that are inspired by art: *ekphrasis*. Some poets respond to photographs as Jane Yolen does in a series of books created with her son, Jason Stemple. In each volume, Yolen invites young poets to write their own poems in response to the photographs. In *Once Upon Ice*, there are several photographs accompanied by more than one poem; Yolen thus models how we can respond to a photograph quite differently at different times. In another type of anthology, selectors have published poems with works of art. A number of these collections feature the art works of particular museum collections or of particular cultures or subjects.

Some poems have become the text for picture books, with illustrators selecting classic poems to respond to through their art. The few artistic responses to modern poems include Nina Payne's *Summertime Waltz* and Jacques Prévert's *How to Paint the Portrait of a Bird*. Ed Young has combined art and poetry, creating a "visual poem" in *Beyond the Great Mountains*.

Students might try responding to works of art with poetry. Before they see what the poets have to say, students could select a picture and write words of response, thinking about the use of color, texture, line, and other elements, and also the feelings that are evoked. After comparing their responses with one another, they could then read the published poet's response. Activities such as this help students to understand that, just as their own responses to poems can be unique, so can their responses to a work of art. Some students might like to create picture-book-length artistic responses to poems as the picture book artists have done.

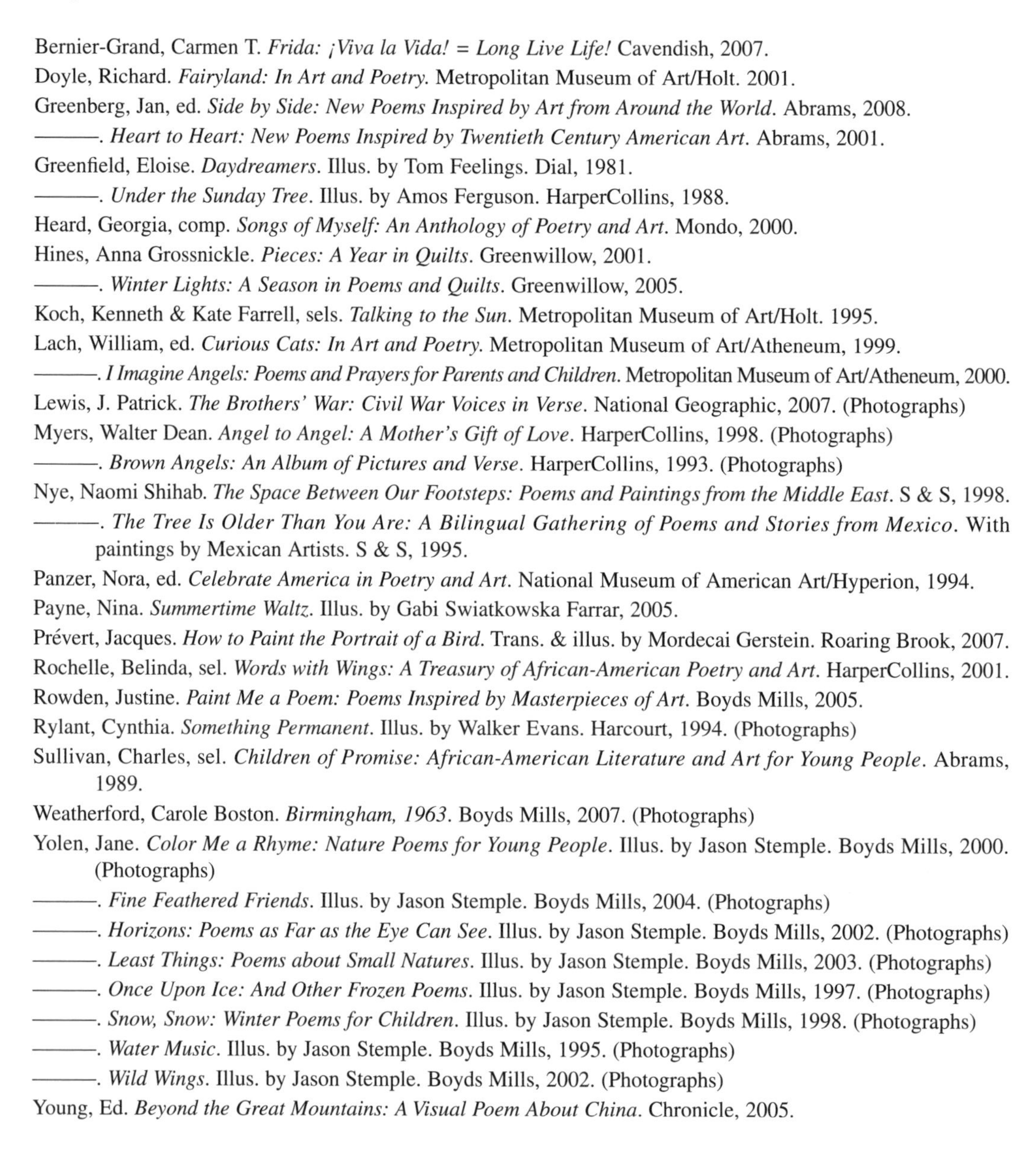

Bernier-Grand, Carmen T. *Frida: ¡Viva la Vida! = Long Live Life!* Cavendish, 2007.
Doyle, Richard. *Fairyland: In Art and Poetry.* Metropolitan Museum of Art/Holt. 2001.
Greenberg, Jan, ed. *Side by Side: New Poems Inspired by Art from Around the World.* Abrams, 2008.
———. *Heart to Heart: New Poems Inspired by Twentieth Century American Art.* Abrams, 2001.
Greenfield, Eloise. *Daydreamers.* Illus. by Tom Feelings. Dial, 1981.
———. *Under the Sunday Tree.* Illus. by Amos Ferguson. HarperCollins, 1988.
Heard, Georgia, comp. *Songs of Myself: An Anthology of Poetry and Art.* Mondo, 2000.
Hines, Anna Grossnickle. *Pieces: A Year in Quilts.* Greenwillow, 2001.
———. *Winter Lights: A Season in Poems and Quilts.* Greenwillow, 2005.
Koch, Kenneth & Kate Farrell, sels. *Talking to the Sun.* Metropolitan Museum of Art/Holt. 1995.
Lach, William, ed. *Curious Cats: In Art and Poetry.* Metropolitan Museum of Art/Atheneum, 1999.
———. *I Imagine Angels: Poems and Prayers for Parents and Children.* Metropolitan Museum of Art/Atheneum, 2000.
Lewis, J. Patrick. *The Brothers' War: Civil War Voices in Verse.* National Geographic, 2007. (Photographs)
Myers, Walter Dean. *Angel to Angel: A Mother's Gift of Love.* HarperCollins, 1998. (Photographs)
———. *Brown Angels: An Album of Pictures and Verse.* HarperCollins, 1993. (Photographs)
Nye, Naomi Shihab. *The Space Between Our Footsteps: Poems and Paintings from the Middle East.* S & S, 1998.
———. *The Tree Is Older Than You Are: A Bilingual Gathering of Poems and Stories from Mexico.* With paintings by Mexican Artists. S & S, 1995.
Panzer, Nora, ed. *Celebrate America in Poetry and Art.* National Museum of American Art/Hyperion, 1994.
Payne, Nina. *Summertime Waltz.* Illus. by Gabi Swiatkowska Farrar, 2005.
Prévert, Jacques. *How to Paint the Portrait of a Bird.* Trans. & illus. by Mordecai Gerstein. Roaring Brook, 2007.
Rochelle, Belinda, sel. *Words with Wings: A Treasury of African-American Poetry and Art.* HarperCollins, 2001.
Rowden, Justine. *Paint Me a Poem: Poems Inspired by Masterpieces of Art.* Boyds Mills, 2005.
Rylant, Cynthia. *Something Permanent.* Illus. by Walker Evans. Harcourt, 1994. (Photographs)
Sullivan, Charles, sel. *Children of Promise: African-American Literature and Art for Young People.* Abrams, 1989.
Weatherford, Carole Boston. *Birmingham, 1963.* Boyds Mills, 2007. (Photographs)
Yolen, Jane. *Color Me a Rhyme: Nature Poems for Young People.* Illus. by Jason Stemple. Boyds Mills, 2000. (Photographs)
———. *Fine Feathered Friends.* Illus. by Jason Stemple. Boyds Mills, 2004. (Photographs)
———. *Horizons: Poems as Far as the Eye Can See.* Illus. by Jason Stemple. Boyds Mills, 2002. (Photographs)
———. *Least Things: Poems about Small Natures.* Illus. by Jason Stemple. Boyds Mills, 2003. (Photographs)
———. *Once Upon Ice: And Other Frozen Poems.* Illus. by Jason Stemple. Boyds Mills, 1997. (Photographs)
———. *Snow, Snow: Winter Poems for Children.* Illus. by Jason Stemple. Boyds Mills, 1998. (Photographs)
———. *Water Music.* Illus. by Jason Stemple. Boyds Mills, 1995. (Photographs)
———. *Wild Wings.* Illus. by Jason Stemple. Boyds Mills, 2002. (Photographs)
Young, Ed. *Beyond the Great Mountains: A Visual Poem About China.* Chronicle, 2005.

MUSIC STANDARDS

Standard One: Singing, alone and with others, a varied repertoire of music.

See also Chapter Two: Language Arts Standard Five (Ballads)

Standard One: Song

Music and poetry are linked through song. We speak of birdsong or cricket song in the animal kingdom. Ballads are songs-stories that may or may not be accompanied by music. Students may recognize the *Song of Solomon* from the Bible, Longfellow's *Song of Hiawatha*, or Walt Whitman's "Song of Myself." "Sing a Song of Sixpence" is a well-known English-language nursery rhyme. This "singing" quality is what poets call lyric poetry. Margaret Wise Brown ends her collection *Nibble Nibble* with "Cadence," a poem about how words themselves have music, and includes a number of songs of nature in her collection.

Brown, Margaret Wise. "Song of the Bugs," "Fish Song," "Song of the Silver Fish," "The Secret Song," "Song of the Bunnies," "Song of Summer," and "Cadence." *Nibble, Nibble.* Illus. by Leonard Weisgard. HarperCollins, 2007.

Bryan, Ashley. "Song" & "Village Voices." *Sing to the Sun.* HarperCollins, 1992. (M)

Fleischman, Paul. "Cicadas." *Joyful Noise.* Illus. by Eric Beddows. HarperCollins, 1988.

Giovanni, Nikki. *The Genie in the Jar.* Illus. by Chris Raschka. Holt, 1996.

Goble, Paul. *Song of Creation.* Eerdmans, 2004.

Hughes, Langston. "April Rain Song," "Song," "Song for a Banjo Dance," & "Sun Song." *The Dream Keeper.* Illus. by Brian Pinkney. Knopf, 1993.

Joyce, James. "Strings in the Earth and Air." In Krull, Kathleen. *A Pot O' Gold.* Illus. by David McPhail. Hyperion, 2004.

Kennedy, X. J. & Dorothy M. Kennedy. sels. Section: "Songs." *Knock at a Star.* Illus. by Karen Lee Baker. Little, 1999.

Kenward, Jean. "Lark." In Nicholls, Judith. *The Sun in Me.* Illus. by Beth Krommes. Barefoot, 2003.

Kirk, Daniel. "Symphony." *Cat Power!* Hyperion, 2007. (Includes CD)

Longfellow, Henry Wadsworth. *Hiawatha.* Illus. by Keith Moseley. Putnam, 1988.

———. *Hiawatha's Childhood.* Illus. by Errol Le Cain. Farrar, 1984.

"My Song: A Toltec Poem from Ancient Mexico" and "A Song of Greatness: A Chippewa Indian Song." In Hoberman, Mary Ann. *My Song Is Beautiful.* Little, 1994.

Tynan, Katherine. "The Wind That Shakes the Barley." In Krull, Kathleen. *A Pot O' Gold.* Illus. by David McPhail. Hyperion, 2004.

Whitman, Walt. "From 'Song of the Open Road' "& "From 'Song of the Answerer.' " In Hopkins, Lee Bennett. *Voyages.* Illus. by Charles Mikolaycak. Harcourt, 1988.

Song Picture Books

In song picture books the lyrics for a song are used as the poetic text and the written music is included in the back. Some books now include CD versions of the song. Song picture books include a variety of types of music. Sometimes a poet will add verses to a traditional song, as Mary Ann Hoberman has done in her songbooks. Joanne Ryder has created all new verses and kept the traditional chorus of the song "Buffalo Gals" in her *Dance by the Light of the Moon.* Children have long created parodies of classic songs. These often violent versions in which schools are burned down and rules are broken are a part of the folk traditions of childhood, passed from one group of children to another orally over time.

Song picture books are valuable in primary classrooms because song rhymes and rhythms make for predictable reading experiences for beginning readers. They can be used in other content areas for any age when they give insight into a time period, a cultural activity, or an aspect of nature. When a song picture book connects with an area of the curriculum it is included the appropriate standards area.

Sometimes, illustrators have interpreted a song in different ways. Three illustrated versions of *Over the River and Through the Wood* and four versions of America *the Beautiful* provide differing artistic responses to these songs. Tomie De Paola's illustrations for *Mary Had a Little Lamb* are true to the time period in which it was written, while Bruce McMillan's bright contemporary photographs give his version a very different feel. Allowing students to look through both of these versions can lead to discussions about how artists respond to the music they hear and about how the meaning of songs might change over time.

Adams, Pam. *This Old Man*. Child's Play, 2000.
Allen, Thomas S. *The Erie Canal*. Illus. by Peter Spier. Doubleday, 2001.
Arnold, Tedd. *Catalina Magdalena Hoopensteiner Wallendiner Hogan Bogan Was Her Name*. Scholastic, 2004.
Bangs, Edward. *Yankee Doodle*. Illus. by Steven Kellogg. S & S, 1976.
Barnwell, Ysaye M. *We Are One*. Illus. by Brian Pinkney. Harcourt, 2008. (Includes CD)
Bates, Katherine Lee. *America the Beautiful*. Illus. by Neil Waldman. Diane, 2004.
———. *America the Beautiful*. Illus. by Chris Gall. Little, 2004.
———. *America the Beautiful*. Illus. by Wendell Minor. Putnam, 2003.
———. *America the Beautiful: A Pop-Up Book*. Illus. by Robert Sabuda. S & S, 2004.
Berlin, Irving. *God Bless America*. Illus. by Lynn Munsinger. Diane, 2006.
Bucchino, John. *Grateful: A Song of Giving Thanks*. Illus. by Anna-Liisa Hakkarainen. New York: HarperCollins, 2003. (Includes CD)
Child, Lydia Maria. *Over the River and Through the Wood*. Illus. by Brinton Turkle. Putnam, 1975.
———. *Over the River and Through the Wood*. Illus. by Christopher Manson, Night Sky, 2008.
———. *Over the River and Through the Wood*. Illus. by David Catrow. Holt, 1996.
Cohan, George M. *You're a Grand Old Flag*. Illus. by Norman Rockwell. S & S, 2008.
Collins, Judy. *My Father*. Illus. by Jane Dyer. Little, 1989.
Cumbayah. Illus. by Floyd Cooper. Morrow, 1998
De Colores = Bright with Colors. Illus. by David Diaz. Marshall Cavendish, 2008.
Fox Went Out on a Chilly Night: An Old Song. Illus. by Peter Spier. Doubleday, 1961.
Frog Went A-Courting. Illus. by John Langstaff. Harcourt, 1955.
Gág, Wanda. *The ABC Bunny*. Putnam, 1978.
Gershwin, George. *Summertime: From Porgy and Bess*. Illus. by Mike Wimmer. S & S, 1999.
Go Tell Aunt Rhody. Illus. by Robert Quackenbush. HarperCollins, 1973.
Goober Peas. The Wright Group, n.d. (Includes CD)
Goodman, Steve. *The Train They Call the City of New Orleans*. Illus. by Michael McCurdy. Putnam, 2003.
Guthrie, Woody. *This Land Is Your Land*. Illus. by Kathy Jakobsen. Little, 1998.
Hale, Sarah Josepha. *Mary Had a Little Lamb*. Illus. by Tomie De Paola. Holiday, 1984.
———. *Mary Had a Little Lamb*. Illus. by Bruce McMillan. Scholastic, 1990.
Hammerstein, Oscar. *My Favorite Things*. Illus. by Renée Graef. HarperCollins, 2001.
He's Got the Whole World in His Hands. Illus. by Kadir Nelson. Dial, 2005.
Hoberman, Mary Ann, adapt. *Bill Grogan's Goat*. Illus. by Nadine Bernard Westcott. Little, 2002.
———, adapt. *The Eensy-Weensy Spider*. Illus. by Nadine Bernard Westcott. Little, 2000.
———. adapt. *Mary Had a Little Lamb*. Illus. by Nadine Bernard Westcott. Little, 2009.
———, adapt. *Mrs. O'Leary's Cow*. Illus. by Jenny Mattheson. Little, 2007.
———, adapt. *Skip to My Lou*. Illus. by Nadine Bernard Westcott. Little, 2000.
Holiday, Billie & Arthur Hertzog Jr. *God Bless the Child*. Illus. by Jerry Pinkney. HarperCollins, 2004.
Hush Little Baby. Illus. by Marla Frazee. Harcourt, 1999.
Hush Little Baby. Illus. by Brian Pinkney. Greenwillow, 2006.
I've Been Working on the Railroad: An American Classic. Illus. by Nadine Bernard Westcott. Hyperion, 1996.
Kennedy, Jimmy. *The Teddy Bears' Picnic*. Illus. by Michael Hague. Holt, 1992.
Key, Francis Scott. *The Star Spangled Banner*. Illus. by Peter Spier. Random, 1992.

———. *The Teddy Bears' Picnic*. Illus. by Alexandra Day. Green Tiger, 1989.
Kovalski, Maryann. *The Wheels on the Bus*. Kids Can, 1987.
Langstaff, John, ret. *Frog Went A-Courtin'*. Illus. by Feodor Rojankovsky. Harcourt, 1955.
———, ret. *Oh, A-Hunting We Will Go*. Illus. by Nancy Winslow Parker. Macmillan, 1983.
LaPrise, Larry, et al. *Hokey Pokey*. Illus. by Sheila Hamanaka. S & S, 1997.
Mallett, David. *Inch by Inch: The Garden Song*. Illus. by Ora Eitan. HarperCollins, 1975.
Norworth, Jack. *Take Me Out to the Ballgame*. Illus. by Alec Gillman. S & S, 1993.
Old MacDonald Had a Farm. Illus. by Jane Cabrera. Holiday, 2008.
Orozco, José-Luis. *Rin, Rin, Rin = Do, Re, Mi*. Orchard, 2005.
Peek, Merle. *Mary Wore Her Red Dress and Henry Wore His Green Sneakers*. Clarion, 1985.
Roll Over! A Counting Song. Illus. by Merle Peek. Houghton, 1981.
Ryder, Joanne. *Dance by the Light of the Moon*. Illus. by Guy Francis. Hyperion, 2007.
She'll Be Comin' Round the Mountain. Illus. by Tom Birdseye. Holiday, 1994.
Simple Gifts: A Shaker Hymn. Illus. by Chris Raschka. Holt, 1998.
Simple Gifts: The Shaker Song. Illus. by Solomon Skolnick. Hyperion, 1992.
Staines, Bill. *All God's Critters*. Illus. by Kadir Nelson. S & S, 2009.
Ten In the Bed. Illus. by Jane Cabrera. Holiday, 2006.
There's a Hole in the Bucket. Illus. by Nadine Bernard Westcott. Harper, 1990.
There Was an Old Lady Who Swallowed a Fly. Illus. by Simms Taback. Viking, 1997.
Weiss, George David & Bob Thiele. *What a Wonderful World*. Illus. by Ashley Bryan. Atheneum, 1995.

Song Adaptations and Parodies

See also Chapter Two: Language Arts Standard Two (Retellings)

Aylesworth, Jim, adapt. *Our Abe Lincoln: An Old Tune with New Lyrics*. Illus. by Barbara McClintock. Scholastic, 2009.
Beaumont, Karen. *I Ain't Gonna Paint No More!* Illus. by David Catrow. Harcourt, 2005.
Canzoneri, David & Bill Martin Jr. "Let There Be Pizza on Earth." In Martin, Bill, Jr. & Michael Sampson. *The Bill Martin Jr. Big Book of Poetry*. S & S, 2008.
Downing, Johnette, adapt. *My Aunt Came Back from Louisiane*. Pelican, 2008.
Ehrhardt, Karen. *This Jazz Man*. Illus. by R. G. Roth. Harcourt, 2006. ("This Old Man")
Grandits, John. "The H-U-P Song." *Blue Lipstick*. Clarion, 2006. ("The Alphabet Song")
Hort, Lenny. *The Seals on the Bus*. Illus. by G. Brian Karas. Holt, 2000.
Jackson, Alison. *The Ballad of Valentine*. Illus. by Tricia Tusa. Dutton, 2002. ("Clementine")
Manning, Maurie. *The Aunts Go Marching*. Boyds Mills, 2003.
"On Top of Spaghetti." In Hopkins, Lee Bennett. *Climb into My Lap*. Illus. by Kathryn Brown. S & S, 1998.
Raffi, adapt. *If You're Happy and You Know It*. Illus. by Cyd Moore. Knopf, 2001.
Salas, Laura. *Move It! Work It! A Song About Simple Machines*. Illus. by Viviana Garófoli. Picture Window, 2009.
Sturges, Philemon. *She'll Be Comin' 'Round the Mountain*. Illus. by Ashley Wolff. Little, 2004.
Tobin, Jim. *Sue McDonald Had a Book*. Illus. by Dave Coverly. Holt, 2009.

Standard One: Singing Performances

Singing together can be a joyous experience. Many of us have fond memories of singing while we played, singing while we are on the school bus, caroling, or singing with choirs. The focus on these occasions is on enjoying the words and sounds, on being loud and enthusiastic, and on being part of a group. Quentin Blake's *All Join In* invites this joyous participation and encourages children to create sound effects for other favorite songs. Sometimes, however, a singer is not very good, as in Sara Holbrook's "I Have to Stand by Susan Todd?" and Jack Prelutsky's "My Sister's Taking Lessons" and "Euphonica Jarre." To appreciate Prelutsky's puns on Euphonica's names, students may want to look for them in the dictionary. Sometimes, the singer is just loud, as in Marchette Chute's couplet, "School Concert." In "Music Lesson," Nikki Grimes describes the embarrassment of hearing one's mother singing off-key in the church choir.

Agard, John. "The Older the Violin, the Sweeter the Tune." In Yolen, Jane & Andrew F. Peters. *Here's a Little Poem*. Candlewick, 2007.

Alarcón, Francisco X. "My Grandma's Songs." In Micklos, John, Jr. *Grandparent Poems*. Illus. by Layne Johnson. Boyds Mills, 2004.

Blake, Quentin. *All Join In*. Little, 1991.

Brooks, Geraldine. "Gertrude." *Bronzeville Boys and Girls*. Illus. by Faith Ringgold. HarperCollins, 2007.

Carlson, Lori Marie. "Grandpa Singing." *Sol A Sol: Bilingual Poems*. Holt, 1998.

Chute, Marchette. "School Concert." In Kennedy, Dorothy M. *I Thought I'd Take My Rat to School*. Illus. by Abby Carter. Little, 1993.

Greenfield, Eloise. "Flowers." *In the Land of Words*. Illus. by Jan Spivey Gilchrist. Harper, 2004.

———. "In the Church." *Night on Neighborhood Street*. Illus. by Jan Spivey Gilchrist. Dial, 1991.

Grimes, Nikki. "Climb Ev'ry Mountain." *Danitra Brown, Class Clown*. Illus. by E. B. Lewis, HarperCollins, 2005.

———. "Music Lesson." *A Dime a Dozen*. Illus, by Angelo, Dial, 1998.

Holbrook, Sara. "I Have to Stand by Susan Todd?" *Nothing's the End of the World*. Illus. by J. J. Smith-Moore. Boyds Mills, 1995.

Johnson, Georgia Douglas. "I've Learned to Sing." In Muse, Daphne. *The Entrance Place of Wonders*. Illus. by Charlotte Riley-Webb. Abrams, 2005.

Johnson, James Weldon. "The Gift to Sing." In Muse, Daphne. *The Entrance Place of Wonders*. Illus. by Charlotte Riley-Webb. Abrams, 2005.

Mandlsohn, Sol. "Basso Profundo." In Booth, David. *'Til All the Stars Have Fallen*. Illus. by Kady MacDonald Denton. Viking, 1989.

Mugo, Micere Githae. "Daughter of My People, Sing!" In Hollyer, Belinda. *She's All That!* Illus. by Susan Hellard. Kingfisher, 2006.

Prelutsky, Jack. "The Dragons Are Singing Tonight." *The Dragons Are Singing Tonight*. Illus. by Peter Sis. Greenwillow, 1993.

———. "Euphonica Jarre." In Janeczko, Paul B. *Seeing the Blue Between*. Candlewick, 2002.

———. "My Sister's Taking Lessons." *My Dog May Be a Genius*. Illus. by James Stevenson. HarperCollins, 2008.

Schotter, Roni. *Doo-Wop Pop*. Illus. by Bryan Collier. HarperCollins, 2008.

Smith, Charles R. *Perfect Harmony: A Musical Journey With the Boys Choir of Harlem*. Hyperion, 2002.

Smith, Hope Anita. "Audition." In Giovanni, Nikki. *Hip Hop Speaks to Children*. Sourcebooks, 2008. (With CD)

Thomas, Joyce Carol. *Shouting!* Illus. by Annie Lee. Disney, 2007. (Gospel)

Turner, Nancy Bird. "From . . . A Popcorn Song." In De Regniers, Beatrice Schenk. *Sing a Song of Popcorn*. Scholastic, 1988.

Singing the Blues

The blues are a notable American form of music that comes out of African American traditions. The blues appear in a number of poems for young people. Paul Janeczko includes Bobbi Katz's "Back-to

School Blues" under "Blues Poem," a form of poetry he describes as "a blues song without music" in *A Kick in the Head: An Everyday Guide to Poetic Forms*.

Appelt, Kathi. "Air Guitar Blues" & "Lost in the Blues." *Poems from Homeroom*. Holt, 2002.

Bryan, Ashley. "Good Flower Blues." *Sing to the Sun*. HarperCollins, 1992.

Greenfield, Eloise. "Little Boy Blues." *Night on Neighborhood Street*. Illus. by Jan Spivey Gilchrist. Dial, 1991.

Hughes, Langston. "Bound No'th Blues," "The Weary Blues," "Po' Boy Blues," "Wide River," "Homesick Blues," & "Night and Morn." *The Dream Keeper*. Illus. by Brian Pinkney. Knopf, 1993.

———. "Hey! Hey! Hey!" "Homesick Blues," and "Weary Blues." In Roessel, David & Arnold Rampersad. *Langston Hughes*. Illus. by Benny Andrews. Sterling, 2006.

Katz, Bobbi. "Back-to-School Blues." In Janeczko, Paul. *A Kick in the Head: An Everyday Guide to Poetic Forms*. Illus. by Chris Raschka. Candlewick, 2005.

Knight, Etheridge. "A Poem for Myself (Or Blues for a Mississippi Black Boy.)" In Panzer, Nora. *Celebrate America*. National Museum of American Art/Hyperion, 1994.

Lewis, J. Patrick. "The Bluesman's Lament" & "Movin' Out, Movin' On Blues." *Black Cat Bone*. Illus. by Gary Kelley. Creative Eds. 2006.

Medina, Tony. "Jazz Makes Me Sing" & "Little Boy Blues." *Love to Langston*. Illus. by R. Gregory Christie. Lee & Low, 2002.

Myers, Walter Dean. *Blues Journey*. Illus. by Christopher Myers. Holiday, 2003.

———. "Tom F." & "Willie S." *Here in Harlem*.Holiday, 2004.

Pinkney, Andrea Davis. *Boycott Blues: How Rosa Parks Inspired a Nation*. Illus. by Brian Pinkney. Greenwillow, 2008.

Weatherford, Carole Boston. "Brand-New Roller Skate Blues (For Bessie Smith)." *Remember the Bridge*. Philomel, 2002.

Rap and Hip Hop

See also Theatre Standards (Performance)

Rap and Hip-Hop are poetic forms that have their roots in traditional African American chants. Nikki Giovanni makes the musical roots of these forms of poetry clear in *Hip Hop Speaks to Children*. This book and its accompanying CD help students to see how much these forms have in common with much older poetic traditions. Middle school students might like to try creating rap songs. Helping young poets to shape their words to give them power in the way of older street performers is important. Poetry slams have also popularized this kind of poetic presentation in clubs and coffee houses.

Fletcher, Ralph. "Venus Flytrap Rap." *A Writing Kind of Day*. Illus. by April Ward. Boyds Mills, 2005.

Giovanni, Nikki, ed. *Hip Hop Speaks to Children: A Celebration of Poetry with a Beat*. Sourcebooks, 2008. (With CD)

Greenfield, Eloise. "Nathaniel's Rap" and "Nathaniel's Rap (Reprise)." *Nathaniel Talking*. Illus. by Jan Spivey Gilchrist. Writers and Readers, 1988.

Katz, Bobbi. "The President's Rap, Part I: Political Pulse, Rap Artist" & "The Presidents' Rap, Part II: Political Pulse, Rap Artist." *We the People*. Illus. by Nina Crews. Greenwillow, 2000.

Myers, Walter Dean. *Amiri and Odette: A Love Story*. Scholastic, 2009. (Hip-Hop)

Nikola-Lisa, W. *Shake Dem Halloween Bones*. Illus. by Mike Reed. Houghton, 1997. (Hip-Hop)

Toure, Askia M. "Rhythms, Harmonies, Ancestors (A Spirit Rap)." In Feelings, Tom. *Soul Looks Back in Wonder*. Dial, 1993.

Standard Two: Performing, alone and with others, a varied repertoire of music.

Standard Two: Musical Performances

The poems included here reflect both the positive and the less positive aspects of playing musical instruments. Jeanne Steig evokes my own experience of piano lessons when I was growing up in "A Pianist Plummets," in which a mother reminds her daughter that playing dead and falling off the piano bench only postpones her practicing of scales. The first group of poems is about practicing or playing a musical instrument. It is followed by a section of poems about playing with a group. David Harrison's *Connecting Dots: Poems of My Journey* includes a plot thread that moves from one of these areas to the next. Poems describing his efforts to play the trombone range from his feeble beginnings ("No Way But Up") to some success playing with the band. Kristine O'Connell George includes a thread of band poems from the point of view of a new flautist (Including "Flute Practice," "More Flute Practice," and "Much More Flute Practice") in *Swimming Upstream: Middle School Poems.*

Sometimes poets compare musical performances or playing an instrument to something else. Eve Merriam's "Rainbow Writing," for example, compares musical instruments to nature. In "Starry Night I" she describes night as an orchestra, as well as alluding to Van Gogh's painting.

Playing Musical Instruments

Bryan, Ashley. "My Dad." *Sing to the Sun.* HarperCollins, 1992. (Saxophone)

Daniels, Shirley. "Drums of My Father." In Booth, David. *'Til All the Stars Have Fallen.* Illus. by Kady MacDonald Denton. Viking, 1989.

George, Kristine O'Connell. "Music Class." *The Great Frog Race.* Illus. by Kate Kiesler. Clarion, 1997. (Also in *The 20th-Century Children's Poetry Treasury*) (Percussion)

———. "Gretchen's Parakeet." In Kiesler, Kate. *Wings on the Wind.* Clarion, 2002. (Flute)

———. *Swimming Upstream: Middle School Poems.* Illus. by Debbie Tilley. Clarion, 2002. (Flute)

Giovanni, Nikki. "The Drum." *Spin a Soft Black Song.* Illus. by George Martins. Hill, 1985. (Also in *My Song Is Beautiful*)

Greenfield, Eloise. "Night on Neighborhood Street" & "When Tanya's Friends Come to Spend the Night." *Night on Neighborhood Street.* Illus. by Jan Spivey Gilchrist. Dial, 1991. (Horn)

Grimes, Nikki. "Handel." *A Dime a Dozen.* Illus. by Angelo. Dial, 1998. (Violin)

Harley, Avis. "Come, Drum." *Fly With Poetry.* Boyds Mills, 2000.

Harrison, David L. "From the Back Row," "The Lesson," "No Way But Up," & "When Words Fail." *Connecting Dots.* Illus. by Kelley Cunningham Cousineau. Boyds Mills, 2004. (Trombone/Oboe)

Hijuelos, Oscar. "Nothing but Drums." In Carlson, Lori M. *Cool Salsa.* Holt, 1994.

Johnson, Angela. "Piano Lesson." *The Other Side.* Orchard, 1998.

Johnston, Tony. "Once an Aztec Had a Flute." *The Ancestors Are Singing.* Illus. by Karen Barbour. Farrar, 2003.

Katz, Susan. "Master Drum." *A Revolutionary Field Trip.* Illus. by R. W. Alley. S & S, 2004.

Kennedy, X. J. "The Girl Who Makes the Symbols Bang." In Hollyer, Belinda. *She's All That.* Illus. by Susan Hellard. Kingfisher, 2006. (Also in *The 20th-Century Children's Poetry Treasury*)

Kuskin, Karla. "Lewis Has a Trumpet." *Dogs and Dragons, Trees and Dreams.* HarperCollins, 1980 (Also in *A Jar of Tiny Stars*)

Lansky, Bruce. "My Violin." In Prelutsky, Jack. *The 20th-Century Children's Poetry Treasury.* Illus. by Meilo So. Knopf, 1999. (Percussion)

Lester, Richard. "My Cello Big and Fat." In Moss, Elaine. *From Morn to Midnight.* Illus. by Satomi Ichikawa. HarperCollins, 1977.

Lesynski, Loris. "Anything's a Drum." *Zigzag.* Annick, 2004.

Lewis, J. Patrick. "Music Lessons at the Hamilton Armories."*Black Cat Bone*. Illus. by Gary Kelley. Creative, 2006. (Bagpipes)

Mora, Pat. "Castanet Clicks." *Confetti*. Illus. by Enrique Sanchez. Lee & Low, 1996.

Olaleye, Isaac. "The Distant Talking Drum." *The Distant Talking Drum: Poems from Nigeria*. Illus. by Frané Lessac. Boyds Mills, 1995.

Prelutsky, Jack. "The Trumpetoos and Tubaboons." *Behold the Bold Umbrellaphant*. Illus. by Carin Berger. HarperCollins, 2006. (Invented instruments)

Roe, Margie McCreless. "The Bagpiper In the Park." In Nye, Naomi Shihab. *Is This Forever or What?* HarperCollins, 2004.

Schertle, Alice. "Ukelele." *Keepers*. Illus. by Ted Rand. Lothrop, 1996.

Sklansky, Amy E. *The Duck Who Played Kazoo*. Illus. by Tiphanie Beeke. Clarion, 2008.

Soto, Gary. "Ode to El Guitarron." *Neighborhood Odes*. Illus. by David Diaz. Harcourt, 1992. (Guitar)

Steig, Jean. "Coaxing Carrotina" & "A Pianist Plummets." *Alpha Beta Chowder*. Illus. by William Steig. HarperCollins, 1992. (Concertina/Piano)

Worth, Valerie. "Bell." *All the Small Poems and Fourteen More*. Illus. by Natalie Babbitt. Farrar, 1987.

Group Performances

Anderson, Peggy Perry. *Chuck's Band*. Houghton, 2008. (Farmyard Band)

Appelt, Kathi. "Elegies for Those We Lost Too Soon." *Poems from Homeroom*. Holt, 2002. (Rock Bands)

Baer, Gene. *Thump, Thump, Rat-a-Tat-Tat*. Illus. by Lois Ehlert. HarperCollins, 1989. (Marching Band)

Bodecker, N. M. "One Year." In Kennedy, X. J. and Dorothy M. Kennedy. *Talking Like the Rain*. Illus. by Jane Dyer. Little, 1992. (Each month described as an instrument)

Grandits, John. "Silver Spandex" & "The Name Your Rock Band Chart." *Blue Lipstick*. Clarion, 2006. (Rock Bands)

Harrison, David L. "A Musical Family." *Connecting Dots*. Illus. by Kelley Cunningham Cousineau. Boyds Mills, 2004.

Hoberman, Mary Ann. *And to Think That We Thought That We'd Never Be Friends*. Illus. by Kevin Hawkes. Crown, 1999. ((Marching Band)

Holman, Felice. "Tuning Up." In Prelutsky, Jack. *The 20th-Century Children's Poetry Treasury*. Illus. by Meilo So. Knopf, 1999. (Orchestra)

Hurd, Thatcher. *Mama Don't Allow*. HarperCollins, 1984. (Jug Band)

Lewis, J. Patrick. "First King of Rock 'n' Roll." *A Burst of Firsts*. Illus. by Brian Ajhar. Dial, 2001. (Elvis Presley)

Lithgow, John. *The Remarkable Farkle McBride*. Illus. by C. F. Payne. S & S, 2000. (Orchestra/Conductor)

Maddox, Marjorie. "A Band of Coyotes." *A Crossing of Zebras*. Illus. by Philip Huber. Boyds Mills, 2008. (Rock Band)

Martin, Bill, Jr. *The Maestro Plays*. Illus. by Vladimir Radunsky. Harcourt, 1996.

Merriam, Eve. "Rainbow Writing" &"Starry Night I." *The Singing Green*. Illus. by Kathleen Collins Howell. Morrow, 1992.

Mole, John. "A Musical Family." In Yolen, Jane & Andrew F. Peters. *Here's a Little Poem*. Candlewick, 2007. (Family band)

Mora, Pat. "Mexican Musicians = Los Musicos Mexicanos. In Greenberg, Jan. *Side by Side*. Abrams, 2008.

Prelutsky, Jack. "Johnny Squeezed a Concertina . . . " *Beneath a Blue Umbrella*. Illus. by Garth Williams. Greenwillow, 1987. (Small Marching Band)

———. "The Underwater Marching Band." *My Dog May Be a Genius*. Illus. by James Stevenson. Greenwillow, 2008.

Stevenson, Robert Louis. "Marching Song." *A Child's Garden of Verses*. Illus. by Diane Goode. Morrow, 1998. (Small Marching Band)

Standard Three: Improvising melodies, variations, and accompaniments.

Standard Four: Composing and arranging music within specified guidelines.

See also Music Standard One (Blues and Rap and Hip Hop)

See also Music Standard Nine (Jazz)

See also Language Arts Standard Five (Forms of Poetry)

Standard Four: Composition

At times, poetry is improvisational. At other times, it has forms and structures that parallel musical arrangements. Poetry is about composing and arranging words on a page. Occasionally poems mention composition. Langston Hughes writes about how a sunrise can stir one to want to compose music in his "Daybreak in Alabama." On a less happy note, Walter Dean Myers writes of "Charles B." whose wish to be a composer was thwarted when he was young.

Hughes, Langston. "Daybreak in Alabama." *The Dream Keeper.* Illus. by Brian Pinkney. Knopf, 1993.
Myers, Walter Dean. "Charles B." *Here in Harlem.* Holiday, 2004.

Standard Five: Reading and notating music

Standard Five: Musical Terminology

Students can learn some of the terminology of music as they read poetry. Lloyd Moss' rhymed picture book, *Zin! Zin! Zin! A Violin* introduces a variety of instruments, and as each is added, the name of the group size is mentioned from "duet" through "chamber group" to a full orchestra. The dancing text and onomatopoeic descriptions make this simple picture book useful for all ages. Melvin B. Tolson's history of African Americans is arranged as the parts of a symphony in "Dark Symphony." The elements of the symphony build to a "Tempo de Marcia," with its transcendent sense of hope.

Sometimes a poem uses musical imagery to describe something else. Jane Yolen, for example, uses the image of birds sitting on a wire as musical notes on a staff in "Song/Birds" and "Nine Swallows: A Haiku." Sometimes, poets use the vocabulary of music in their poetry. Eve Merriam includes "agitato" and "sotto voce" in "Quaking Aspen" to describe the movement of the wind through the trees. The puns on musical terminology in Brian Cleary's *Rhyme and Punishment: Adventures in Wordplay* provide a sillier access point.

Cleary, Brian P. Section: "Music: Going for Baroque." *Rhyme and Punishment: Adventures in Wordplay.* Illus. by J. P. Sandy. Millbrook, 2006.
Harley, Avis. "A Note to the Monarchs." *The Monarch's Progress.* Boyds Mills, 2008.
Merriam, Eve. "Quaking Aspen." *Fresh Paint.* Illus. by David Frampton. Macmillan, 1986.
Moss, Lloyd. *Zin! Zin! Zin! A Violin.* Illus. by Marjorie Priceman. S&S, 1995.
Tolson, Melvin B. "Dark Symphony." In Giovanni, Nikki. *Shimmy Shimmy Shimmy Like My Sister Kate.* Holt, 1995.
Yolen, Jane. "Nine Swallows: A Haiku." *Count Me a Rhyme.* Illus. by Jason Stemple. Boyds Mills, 2006.
———. "Song/Birds." *Bird Watch.* Illus. by Ted Lewin. Putnam, 1990

Standard Six: Listening to, analyzing, and describing music.

Standard Seven: Evaluating music and music performances.

Standards Six and Seven: Appreciating Music

Along with singing and playing music, students should have opportunities to listen to a variety of music. The standards for music don't mention the emotional responses that human beings have to music. They say nothing about being moved to laughter or tears, to want to dance or clap or physically respond in some way to the music that we hear. It is these qualities of appreciation that lead to poetry in response to music. Sometimes poets borrow the rhythms, sounds, and forms of music and capture them in poetry. Sometimes poets use music as a metaphor as Audrey Baird does in "Matinee Storm Concert By the Midsummer Philharmonic." A few poems help the listener to understand the feelings of particular pieces of classical music. Biographical works can allow students to understand the roots of the music they hear. Music can be an important accompaniment to poetry at any time. Students can look for pieces of music that provide the right "atmosphere" in which to read a poem. Some poems respond to a particular piece of music, which can be played as they are read.

Anderson, M. T. *Strange Mr. Satie*. Illus. by Petra Mathers. Viking, 2003.

Baird, Audrey. "Matinee Storm Concert By the Midsummer Philharmonic." *Storm Coming!* Illus. by Patrick O'Brien. Boyds Mills, 2003.

Braithwaite, William Stanley. "Rhapsody." In Rochelle, Belinda. *Words with Wings*. HarperCollins, 2001.

Brooks, Gwendolyn. "Gertrude." *Bronzeville Boys and Girls*. Illus. by Faith Ringgold. HarperCollins, 2007. (Listening to Marion Anderson)

Chernaik, Judith, ed. *Carnival of the Animals: Poems Inspired by Saint Saens' Music*. Illus. by Satoshi Kitamura. Candlewick, 2006. (With CD)

Cole, William. "Here Comes the Band." In De Regniers, Beatrice Schenk. *Sing a Song of Popcorn*. Scholastic, 1988.

Davila, Vianna Risa. "How I Learned to Love Music." In Nye, Naomi Shihab. *Is This Forever Or What?* HarperCollins, 2004.

Fleischman, Paul. *Rondo in C*. Illus. by Janet Wentworth. HarperCollins, 1988.

Greenfield, Eloise. "Grandma's Bones," "My Daddy," & "Who the Best." *Nathaniel Talking*. Illus. by Jan Spivey Gilchrist. Writers and Readers, 1988.

———. "Way Down in the Music." *In the Land of Words*. Illus. by Jan Spivey Gilchrist. HarperCollins, 2004. (Also in *Honey, I Love*.)

Gunning, Monica. "My First Symphony Concert." *America, My New Home*. Boyds Mills, 2004.

Hru, Dakari Kamau. "John Coltrane Ditty." In Slier, Deborah. *Make a Joyful Sound*. Illus. by Cornelius Van Wright & Ying-Hwa Hu. Checkerboard, 1991.

Komaiko, Leah. *I Like the Music*. HarperCollins, 1989.

Lewis, J. Patrick. "Baby Contralto: Marion Anderson." *Freedom Like Sunlight: Praisesongs for Black Americans*. Illus. by John Thompson. Creative Ed. 2000.

Lithgow, John. *Carnival of the Animals*. Illus. by Boris Kulikov. S & S, 2004. (With CD).

Moss, Lloyd. *Music Is*. Illus. by Phillipe Petit-Roulet. Putnam, 2003.

Prelutsky, Jack. "Awful Ogre's Music. "*Awful Ogre's Awful Day*. Illus. by Paul O. Zelinsky. HarperCollins, 2001.

———. "I Love When Someone Whistles." *My Dog May Be a Genius*. Illus. by James Stevenson. Greenwillow, 2008.

Rowden, Justine. "Ziggidy Zaggedy." *Paint Me a Poem*. Boyds Mills, 2005.

Soto, Gary. "Music for Fun and Profit." *Canto Familiar*. Illus. by Annika Nelson. Harcourt, 1995.

Thomas, Joyce Carol. "Remembering Marion Anderson." In Hopkins, Lee Bennett. *Days to Celebrate*. Illus. by Stephen Alcorn. Greenwillow, 2005.

Standard Eight: Understanding relationships between music, the other arts, and disciplines outside the arts.

Standard Nine: Understanding music in relation to history and culture.

Standard Nine Unit: Jazz

Links with Social Studies Theme One (Culture)

Links with Social Studies Theme Two (History and Biography)

Links with Language Arts Standard Six (Conventions of Poetry)

Links with Dance, and Visual Arts

See also Social Studies Theme Three (Harlem)

Units that link music with other subject areas add great depth to any area of the curriculum. A number of the song picture books and the works about pieces of music add richness to studies of the history of time periods or to studies of cultures. Any form of music from any period can be the beginning of such studies. Jazz is used here as an example of these possibilities.

Jazz is a uniquely American form of music, a blending of the rhythms and pentatonic scale of African music brought to this country by slaves and European musical traditions that were added to the mix. Jazz has come into its own in literature for young people in the last few years, appearing as the focus of picture books, novels, biographies, and nonfiction. Most of these works use poetic language, echoing the rhythms, sounds, and feelings of jazz. It is difficult to write about jazz without using its rhythms and sounds, which makes it a valuable unit for poetry study that crosses into several other disciplines.

Walter Dean Myers' *Jazz* provides a good introduction for the unit, with a brief history of jazz and fifteen poems about the range of jazz including bebop, jazz sessions, poems about the musical instruments used to play jazz, and two poems that represent the music of a New Orleans-style jazz funeral. Wynton Marsalis' *Jazz A B Z* complements the Myers text, with a collection of poems in different forms that echo the music of 26 well-known jazz musicians. For younger students *The Jazzy Alphabet* uses alliteration and onomatopoeic words to catch the rhythms of jazz. Muriel Weinstein's *When Louis Armstrong Taught Me Scat* and Lisa Wheeler's *Jazz Baby* are almost entirely made up of onomatopoetic sounds, and would be good performance pieces.

Rachel Isadora's *Bring on that Beat* and Chris Raschka's *Mysterious Thelonius* match colors and shapes to the rhythms of jazz. Students might create their own artistic responses to jazz. Pete Seeger and Paul Dubois Jacobs make rhythm and sound in a different way in *The Deaf Musicians*. When a jazz pianist loses his hearing, he finds other musicians in the same situation in his sign language class. Together with a sign language interpreter who becomes their singer, they create jazz on the subways using the rhythms of their hands and bodies.

Chris Raschka 's *Charlie Parker Played Be Bop* combines the rhythms and onomatopoetic sounds of this form of jazz with striking visuals. Robert Burleigh's *Lookin' for Bird in the Big City* follows teenaged trumpeter Miles Davis on a trip to New York City to find Charlie Parker (Known as "Bird"). The prose text also has the staccato rhythms and onomatopoetic sounds of Bebop. Read these with H. L. Panahi's *Bebop Express*, which takes a train ride to all of the major U.S. cities where jazz is being played. The rhymed, rhythmic text, filled with sound effects, sings out to be read aloud.

Chris Raschka's illustration of John Coltrane's *Giant Steps* visualizes one of Coltrane's compositions. Carole Boston Weatherford's *Before John Was a Jazz Giant: A Song of John Coltrane* uses the title as a litany to tell of how Coltrane heard music in the everyday sounds around him when he was a child. Coltrane's music can be played as these two books are shared.

Carole Boston Weatherford has created *Becoming Billie Holiday*, a full-length biography in verse. This biography can be paired with the wordless picture book, *God Bless the Child*, which includes a CD of Holiday singing her classic swing tune with roots in spirituals. These biographies can be read along with histories of the 1920s and 1930s in the United States and combined with some of the works on Harlem included in the social studies chapter.

Jazz Poetry

Calmenson, Stephanie. *Jazzmatazz!* Illus. by Bruce Degen. HarperCollins, 2008.

Carter, Don. *Heaven's All-Star Jazz Band.* Knopf, 2002.

Clewell, David. "Man Ray Stares into the Future of Jazz: 1919." In Greenberg, Jan. *Heart to Heart: New Poems Inspired by Twentieth Century American Art.* Abrams, 2001.

Dillon, Leo and Diane Dillon. *Jazz on a Saturday Night.* Scholastic, 2007.

Ehrhardt, Karen. *This Jazz Man.* Illus. by R. G. Roth. Orlando: Harcourt, 2006.

Hanson, Warren. *Bugtown Boogie.* Illus. by Steve Johnson & Lou Fancher. HarperCollins, 2008.

Hines, Carl Wendell, Jr. "From 'Two Jazz Poems.'" In Dunning, Steven, et al. *Reflections on a Gift of Watermelon Pickle.* HarperCollins, 1967.

Holiday, Billie & Arthur Herzog Jr. *God Bless the Child.* Illustrated by Jerry Pinkney. HarperCollins, 2004.

Hru, Dakari Kamau. "John Coltrane Ditty." In Slier, Deborah. *Make a Joyful Sound.* Illus. by Cornelius Van Wright and Ying-Hwa Hu. Checkerboard, 1991.

Hughes, Langston. "Dream Boogie" and "Dream Boogie Variation." In Giovanni, Nikki. *Shimmy Shimmy Shimmy Like My Sister Kate.*Holt, 1995.

Isadora, Rachel. *Bring on That Beat.* Putnam, 2002.

Lewis, J. Patrick. "Ella Fitzgerald." *Vherses.* Illus. by Mark Summers. Creative Ed. 2005.

———. "Nickel-A-Bucket Tune: Louis Armstrong" & "Lady Day." *Freedom Like Sunlight.* Illus. by John Thompson. Creative Eds. 2000.

London, Jonathan. *Who Bop?* Illus. by Henry Cole. HarperCollins, 2000.

Marsalis, Wynton. *Jazz A B Z.* Illus. by Paul Rogers. Candlewick, 2005.

Medina, Tony. "Jazz Makes Me Sing." *Love to Langston.* Illus. by R. Gregory Christie. Lee and Low, 2002.

Myers, Walter Dean. *Jazz.* Illus. by Christopher Myers. Holiday, 2006.

———. "Willie Arnold, 30: Alto Sax Player." *Here in Harlem.* Holiday, 2004.

Panahi, H. L. *Bebop Express.* Illus. by Steve Johnson & Lou Fancher. HarperCollins, 2005.

Raschka, Chris. *Charlie Parker Played Be Bop.* Orchard, 1992.

———. *John Coltrane's Giant Steps.* Atheneum, 2002.

———. *Mysterious Thelonius.* Orchard, 1997.

Sandburg, Carl. "From Jazz Fantasia." In Niven, Penelope. *Carl Sandburg: Adventures of a Poet.* Illus. by Marc Nadel. Harcourt, 2003.

Shahan, Sherry. *The Jazzy Alphabet.* Illus. by Mary Thelen. Philomel, 2002.

Weatherford, Carole Boston. *Becoming Billie Holiday.* Illus. by Floyd Cooper. Boyds Mills, 2008.

———. *Before John Was a Jazz Giant: A Song of John Coltrane.* Illus. by Sean Qualls. Holt, 2008.

———. *Jazz Baby.* Illus. by Laura Freeman. Lee & Low, 2002.

———. "Jazz Roots." *Remember the Bridge.* Philomel, 2002.

———. *The Sound That Jazz Makes.* Illus. by Eric Velasquez. Walker, 2000.

Weinstein, Muriel. Harris. *When Louis Armstrong Taught Me Scat.* Illus. by R. Gregory Christy. Chronicle, 2008.

Wheeler, Lisa. *Jazz Baby.* Illus. by R. Gregory Christie. Orlando: Harcourt, 2007.

Prose Works on Jazz

Burleigh, Robert. *Lookin' for Bird in the Big City.* Illus. by Marek Los. Harcourt, 2001.

Collier, James Lincoln. *Jazz: An American Saga.* Holt, 1997.

Curtis, Christopher Paul. *Bud, Not Buddy.* Delacorte, 1999. (Novel)

Daly, Niki. *Ruby Sings the Blues.* Bloomsbury, 2005.

Gourse, Leslie. *Sophisticated Ladies: The Great Women of Jazz.* Illus. by Martin French. Dutton, 2007.

High, Linda Oatman. *Cool Bopper's Choppers.* Illus. by John O'Brien. Boyds Mills, 2007.

Hurwitz, Andy Blackman. *Ella Elephant Scats Like That.* Illus. by Andrew Cunningham. Price, Stern, Sloan, 2007.

———. *Miles the Crocodile Plays the Colors of Jazz.* Illus. by Andrew Cunningham. Price, Stern, Sloan, 2007.

Igus, Toyomi. *I See the Rhythm.* Illus. by Michele Wood. Children's, 1998.

Kimmel, Eric A. *A Horn for Louis.* Illus. by James Bernardin. Random, 2005.

Miller, William. *Rent Party Jazz.* Illus. by Charlotte Riley-Webb. Lee & Low, 2001.

Myers, Walter Dean. *Jazz.* Live Oak, 2007. (With CD)

Parker, Robert Andrew. *Piano Starts Here: The Young Art Tatum.* Random, 2008.

Pinkney, Andrea Davis. *Duke Ellington: The Piano Prince and His Orchestra.* Illus. by J. Brian Pinkney. Hyperion, 1998.

———. *Ella Fitzgerald: The Tale of a Vocal Virtuosa.* Illus, by J. Brian Pinkney. Hyperion, 2002.

Seeger, Pete and Paul Dubois Jacobs. *The Deaf Musicians.* Illus. by R. Gregory Christie. Putnam, 2002.

Selfridge, John W. *John Coltrane: A Sound Supreme.* Watts, 1999.

Stone, Tanya Lee. *Ella Fitzgerald.* Viking, 2008.

Townley, Roderick. *Sky: A Novel in Three Sets and an Encore.* S & S, 2004.

Volponi, Paul. *Hurricane Song: A Novel of New Orleans.* Viking, 2008.

Weinstein, Muriel Harris. *When Louis Armstrong Taught Me Scat.* Illus. by F. Gregory Christie. Chronicle, 2008.

Winter, Jonah. *Dizzy.* Illus. by Sean Qualls. Scholastic, 2007.

———. *Once Upon a Time in Chicago: The Story of Benny Goodman.* Illus. by Jeanette Winter. Hyperion, 2000.

REFERENCES

Bauer, C. F. *The Poetry Break: An Annotated Anthology with Ideas for Introducing Children to Poetry.* H. W. Wilson, 1995.

Eisner, E. "Ten Lessons the Arts Teach." The Arts and the Creation of Mind." Yale University Press, 2002: 70–92.

Holbrook, S. & M. Salinger. *Outspoken! How to Improve Writing and Speaking Skills through Poetry Performance.* Heinemann, 2006.

Martin, Bill, Jr. & Michael Sampson. *The Bill Martin Jr. Big Book of Poetry.* S & S, 2008.

National Standards for Arts Education: http://www.menc.org/resources/view/national-standards-for-arts-education.

O'Conner, J. S. *Wordplaygrounds: Reading, Writing, and Performing Poetry in the English Classroom.* National Council of Teachers of English, 2004.

Roser, N., S. Keehn, & M. Martinez. (2008). "Read for You, Audio Review: Poetry Aloud!" *Journal of Children's Literature* 34 (Spring): 65–69.

Terry, A. *Children's Poetry Preferences: A National Survey of Upper Elementary Grades.* National Council of Teachers of English, 1964.

Vardell, S. *Poetry Aloud Here! Sharing Poetry with Children in the Library.* American Library Association, 2006.

http://www.poetryoutloud.org (National Endowment for the Arts, the Poetry Foundation, and state arts agencies).

CHAPTER 7

Poetry and the Standards for Physical Education; Poetry and the Health Education Standards

PHYSICAL EDUCATION

Standard One: Student demonstrates competency in motor skills and movement patterns needed to perform a variety of physical activities.

Standard Two: Student demonstrates understanding of movement concepts, principles, strategies, and tactics as they apply to the learning and performance of physical activities.

Standards One and Two: Sports

Opportunities to participate in formal and informal sporting activities help students to develop physical strength and skills, to understand the importance of practice, and to learn about rules. One has only to look at John Grandits' concrete poems of various sports to see how much movement and activity take place as one plays. Both boys and girls enjoy poetry about sports, especially if they have enjoyed (or suffered) the feelings expressed in the poems included here.

Baseball and basketball are popular subjects of poetry, featured not only in individual poems, but in entire subject collections. Baseball has been treated as a metaphor for American ideals because it combines teamwork with individual accomplishment. Poems about the history of baseball reveal much about American history. In Walter Dean Myers' poem "John Reese, 70" reflects on baseball from the Negro Leagues through integration of teams. Kam Mak uses baseball as a metaphor for his young narrator's acceptance into his new community.

Poems about basketball feature action and graceful movements, and highlight some of the game's well-known players. Basketball poems feature both boy and girl players. *Swish!* by Bill Martin Jr. and Michael Sampson and *Hoop Queens* by Charles R. Smith Jr. are about girls' basketball teams. Although widely played, football and soccer do not appear as frequently in poetry. Some sports don't appear at all. Students might want to write a poem about their own favorite sport after reading some of these poems.

One of the important lessons students gain from sports is that it takes practice to be a good player. Moving into the rhythms of a sport is the same as moving into the rhythms of mathematics or reading. Some of these poems are about young people who only dream of being great; others are about those who work at being great; still others are about those who have a bad day. Students who are active in sports will enjoy collections and poems about them, as they compare their experiences with those the poets capture.

Ferris, Helen, ed. Section: "It's Fun to Play." *Favorite Poems Old and New.* Illus. by Leonard Weisgard. Random, 1957, 2009.

Ghigna, Charles. *A Fury of Motion.* Boyds Mills, 2003.

Hopkins, Lee Bennett, sel. *Sports! Sports! Sports!* Illus. by Brian Floca. HarperCollins, 1999.

Lewis, J. Patrick. *A Burst of Firsts: Doers, Shakers, and Record Breakers.* Illus. by Brian Ajhar. Dial, 2001. (Many sports figures)

Morrison, Lillian. *Way to Go! Sports Poems.* Illus. by Susan Spellman. Boyds Mills, 2001.

———, sel. *Sprints and Distances: Sports in Poetry and Poetry in Sport.* HarperCollins, 1990.

Prelutsky, Jack. *Good Sports.* Illus. by Chris Raschka. Knopf, 2007.

Rex, Michael. *Dunk Skunk.* Putnam, 2005.

Baseball

Adoff, Arnold. *Outside, Inside Poems.* Illus. by John Steptoe. Harcourt, 1981.

Adoff, Jaime. "Whack." *Small Fry.* Illus. by Mike Reed. Dutton, 2008.

Elya, Susan Middleton. *Eight Animals Play Ball.* Illus. by Lee Chapman. Putnam, 2003.

Fehler, Gene. *Change-Up: Baseball Poems.* Illus. by Donald Wu. Clarion, 2009.

Florian, Douglas. "Fly Ball." *Summersaults.* HarperCollins, 2002.

———. "Last Licks" & "Off Season." *Autumnblings.* HarperCollins, 2003.

———. "Spring Training" & "Play Ball." *Handsprings.* HarperCollins, 2006.

Francis, Robert. "The Base Stealer." In Dunning, Stephen, et al. *Reflections on a Gift of Watermelon Pickle.* HarperCollins, 1967.

Grandits, John. "Robert's Four at-Bats." *Technically, It's Not My Fault.* Clarion, 2004.

Graves, Donald. "First Baseball Glove." *Baseball, Snakes, and Summer Squash.* Boyds Mills, 1996. (Also in *Daddy Poems*)

Grimes, Nikki. "Play Ball & "Baseball Surprise." *Oh, Brother!* Illus. by Mike Benny. HarperCollins, 2008.

Hulme, Joy N. "Play Ball." In Hopkins, Lee Bennett. *Oh, No! Where Are My Pants?* Illus. by Wolf Erlbruch. HarperCollins, 2005.

Kunitz, Stanley. "The Testing Tree-Part One." In Paschen, Elise. *Poetry Speaks to Children.* Sourcebooks, 2005. (With CD)

Lewis, J. Patrick. "Father Time Is Coming." *Freedom Like Sunlight.* Illus. by John Thompson. Creative, 2000. (LeRoy "Satchel" Paige)

Mak, Kam. "The Baseball." *My Chinatown.* HarperCollins, 2002.

Merriam, Eve. "Associations." *The Singing Green.* Illus. by Kathleen Collins Howell. Morrow, 1992.

Morrison, Lillian, sel. *At the Crack of the Bat: Baseball Poems.* Illus. by Steve Cieslawski. Hyperion, 1992.

Myers, Walter Dean. "John Reese, 70." *Here in Harlem.* Holiday, 2004.

Nevius, Carol. *Baseball Hour.* Illus. by Bill Thompson. Cavendish, 2008.

Norworth, Jack. *Take Me Out to the Ballgame.* Illus. by Alec Gillman. S & S, 1993.

Shields, Carol Diggory. "Baseball." *American History, Fresh Squeezed!* Illus. by Richard Thompson. Handprint, 2002.

Smith, Charles R. *Diamond Life: Baseball Sights, Sounds, and Swings.* Orchard, 2004.

Soto, Gary. "Black Hair." *A Fire in My Hands*. Harcourt, 2006.

Swenson, Mae. "Analysis of Baseball." *The Complete Poems to Solve*. Illus. by Christy Hale. Macmillan, 1993. (Also in *Knock at a Star, Celebrate America*)

Testa, Maria. *Becoming Joe DiMaggio*. Candlewick, 2005. (Novel in Verse)

Thayer, Ernest Lawrence. *Casey at the Bat*. Illus. by Joe Morse. Kids Can, 2006.

———. *Casey at the Bat: A Ballad of the Republic Sung in the Year 1888*. Illus. by Patricia Polacco. Putnam, 1988.

Basketball

Burgess, Michael. "Lightning Jumpshot." In *In Daddy's Arms I Am Tall*. Illus. by Javaka Steptoe. Lee & Low, 1997.

Butcher, Grace. "Basketball." In Hollyer, Belinda. *She's All That!* Illus. by Susan Hellard. Kingfisher, 2006.

Carroll, Lewis. *Jabberwocky*. Retold & illus. by Christopher Myers. Hyperion, 2007.

Dakos, Kalli. "Five Seconds Left in the Game." *Mrs. Cole on an Onion Roll*. Illus. by JoAnn Adinolfi. S & S, 1995.

Giovanni, Nikki. "Basketball." *Spin a Soft Black Song*. Illus. by George Martins. Farrar, 1987.

Glenn, Mel. *Jump Ball: A Basketball Season in Poems*. Dutton, 1997. (Novel in Verse)

Grandits, John. "The Lay-Up." *Technically, It's Not My Fault*. Clarion, 2004.

Greenfield, Eloise. *For the Love of the Game: Michael Jordan and Me*. Illus. by Jan Spivey Gilchrist. Harper Collins, 1997.

Grimes, Nikki. "Shoe Surprise." *Thanks a Million*. Illus. by Cozbi A. Cabrera. HarperCollins, 2006.

Hoey, Edwin A. "Foul Shot." In Dunning, Stephen, et al. *Reflections on a Gift of Watermelon Pickle*. Harper Collins, 1967.

Martin, Bill, Jr. & Michael Sampson. *Swish!* Illus. by Michael Chesworth. Holt, 1997.

Morrison, Lillian, comp. *Slam Dunk: Basketball Poems*. Illus. by Bill James. Hyperion, 1995.

Myers, Walter Dean. "Lawrence H." *Here in Harlem*. Holiday, 2004.

Prelutsky, Jack. "Stringbean Small." *The New Kid on the Block*. Illus. by James Stevenson. Greenwillow, 1984.

Smith, Charles R. *Hoop Queens*. Candlewick, 2003.

———. *Rimshots: Basketball Pix, Rolls, and Rhythms*. Dutton, 1999.

Sullivan, John. "Basketball Seasons." In Hopkins, Lee Bennett. *Incredible Inventions*. Illus. by Julia Sarcone-Roach. HarperCollins, 2009.

Troupe, Quincy. "A Poem for Magic." In Slier, Deborah. *Make a Joyful Sound*. Illus. by Cornelius Van Wright & Ying-Hwa Hu. Checkerboard, 1991.

Soccer

Ahlberg, Allan. "The Betsy Street Booters." In Hollyer, Belinda. *She's All That!* Illus. by Susan Hellard. Kingfisher, 2006.

Brug, Sandra Gilbert. "Soccer Feet." In Hopkins, Lee Bennett. *Sports! Sports! Sports!* Illus. by Brian Floca. HarperCollins, 1999

Greenfield, Eloise. "Zigzag." *Brothers and Sisters*. Illus. by Jan Spivey Gilchrist. HarperCollins, 2009.

Holbrook, Sara. "The Greatest Fun." *Which Way to the Dragon!* Boyds Mills, 1996.

Hopkins, Lee Bennett. "Soccer." *Days to Celebrate*. Illus. by Stephen Alcorn. HarperCollins, 2005.

Shapiro, Karen Jo. "Soccer Land." *I Must Go Down to the Beach Again*. Illus. by Judy Love. Charlesbridge, 2007.

Strickland, Michael R. "Guess What!" In Hopkins, Lee Bennett. *Sports! Sports! Sports!* Illus. by Brian Floca. HarperCollins, 1999.

On Wheels

Anderson, Peggy Perry. *Joe on the Go*. Houghton, 2007.

Carlson, Lori Marie. "I Like to Ride My Bike." *Sol a Sol*. Illus. by Emily Lisker. Holt, 1998.

Grandits, John. "Skateboard." *Technically, It's Not My Fault*. Clarion, 2004.

Lewis, J. Patrick. "The Highest Air on a Skateboard." *The World's Greatest*. Illus. by Keith Graves. Chronicle, 2008.

Livingston, Myra Cohn. "74th Street." In Hollyer, Belinda. *She's All That!* Illus. by Susan Hellard. Kingfisher, 2006. (Roller Skating)

McGinley, Phyllis. "We're Racing, Racing down the Walk." In DePaola, Tomie. *Tomie DePaola's Rhyme Time*. Grosset, 1988. (Roller Skating)

Morrison, Lillian. "The Sidewalk Racer." In Hollyer, Belinda. *She's All That!* Illus. by Susan Hellard. Kingfisher, 2006. (Skateboard)

Track and Running

Butcher, Grace. "Track." In Hollyer, Belinda. *She's All That!* Illus. by Susan Hellard. Kingfisher, 2006. (Running)

Creech, Sharon. *Heartbeat*. HarperCollins, 2004. (Novel in Verse) (Running)

Dakos, Kalli. "I'm Going to Die." *If You're Not Here, Please Raise Your Hand*. Illus. by G. Brian Karas. MacMillan, 1990. (Running)

George, Kristine O'Connell. "Long Jump." *Swimming Upstream*. Illus. by Debbie Tilley. Clarion, 2002.

Grimes, Nikki. "Running." *It's Raining Laughter*. Illus. by Myles C. Pinkney. Boyds Mills, 1997.

Haraway, Fran. "In New Running Shoes." In Hopkins, Lee Bennett. *Incredible Inventions*. Illus. by Julia Sarcone-Roach. HarperCollins, 2009.

Lewis, J. Patrick. "First Lady of Twentieth Century Sports." *A Burst of Firsts*. Illus. by Brian Ajhar. Dial, 2001. (Mildred "Babe" Didrikson Zaharias; also golf)

———. "I Decided . . . to Stay Up in the Air Forever" & "The Black Gazelle." *Freedom Like Sunlight*. Illus. by John Thompson. Creative, 2000. (Jesse Owens & Wilma Rudolph)

Paul, Ann Whitford. "Wilma Rudolph." *All by Herself*. Illus. by Michael Steirnagle. Harcourt, 1999.

Ridlon, Marci. "Running Song." In Prelutsky, Jack. *The 20th Century Children's Poetry Treasury*. Illus. by Meilo So. Knopf, 1999.

Weatherford, Carole Boston. *Jesse Owens: Fastest Man Alive*. Illus. by Eric Velasquez. Walker, 2007.

Whitman, Walt. "The Runner." In Kennedy, X. J. & Dorothy M. Kennedy. *Knock at a Star*. Illus. by Karen Lee Baker. Little, 1999.

Water Sports

Harley, Avis. "First Jump." *Fly with Poetry*. Boyds Mills, 2000.

Hillyer, Robert. "Lullaby." In Pearson, Susan. *The Drowsy Hours*. Illus. by Peter Malone. HarperCollins, 2002. (Canoeing) (Also in *Reflections on a Gift of Watermelon Pickle*)

Lewis, J. Patrick. "Swim, Girl, Swim." *Vherses*. Illus. by Mark Summers. Creative, 2005. (Gertrude Ederle)

Prelutsky, Jack. "Awful Ogre Swims." *Awful Ogre Running Wild*. Illus. by Paul O. Zelinsky. HarperCollins, 2008.

———. "I'm Chasing After Porpoises" & "Though I Like to Swim." *Good Sports*. Illus. by Chris Raschka. Knopf, 2007.

Smith, William Jay. "The Outrigger Canoe." *Here Is My Heart*. Illus. by Jane Dyer. Little, 1999.

Snow and Ice Sports

Florian, Douglas. "Sled," "Winter Blades" & "Figure 8." *Winter Eyes*. Greenwillow, 1999.

George, Kristine O'Connell. "Skating in the Wind." In Paschen, Elise. *Poetry Speaks to Children*. Sourcebooks, 2005. (Includes CD)

Hovey, Kate. "Patch Lesson." In Hopkins, Lee Bennett. *Sports! Sports! Sports!* Illus. by Brian Floca. Harper Collins, 1999. (Ice Skating)

Prelutsky, Jack. "My Mother Took Me Skating." *It's Snowing! It's Snowing!* Illus. by Yossi Abolafia. Harper Collins, 2006.

Schimel, Lawrence. "Ice Hockey." In Hopkins, Lee Bennett. *Sports! Sports! Sports!* Illus. by Brian Floca. HarperCollins, 1999.

Yolen, Jane. "Skier." *Snow, Snow*. Illus. by Jason Stemple. Boyds Mills, 1998.

Tennis

Kulling, Monica. "Tennis, Anyone?" In Janeczko, Paul B. *A Poke in the I*. Illus. by Chris Raschka. Candlewick, 2001.

Lewis, J. Patrick. "Double Doubles (A Verse Served up by Two Booming Voices)." *Vherses*. Illus. by Mark Summers. Creative, 2005. (Williams Sisters/Tennis)

———. "The Man Who Became a Word." *Freedom Like Sunlight*. Illus. by John Thompson. Creative, 2000. (Arthur Ashe)

Boxing

Grimes, Nikki. "Training Season." *My Man Blue*. Illus. by Jerome Lagarrigue. Dial, 1999.

Smith, Charles R., Jr. *Twelve Rounds to Glory: The Story of Muhammad Ali*. Illus. by Brian Collier. Candlewick, 2007.

Spires, Elizabeth. "Jack Johnson." *I Heard God Talking to Me*. Farrar, 2009.

Weatherford, Carole Boston. "The Brown Bomber." *Remember the Bridge*. Philomel, 2002. (Joe Louis)

Football

Adoff, Jaime. "Recess." *Small Fry*. Illus. by Mike Reed. Dutton, 2008.

Arnold, Tedd. *Hooray for Fly Guy!* Scholastic, 2008.

Dakos, Kalli. "David Grabs Me." *The Bug in Teacher's Coffee*. Illus. by Mike Reed. HarperCollins, 1999.

Florian, Douglas. "The Winter Field." *Winter Eyes*. Greenwillow, 1999.

Morrison, Lillian. "In the Beginning Was the Field." In Panzer, Nora. *Celebrate America*. Smithsonian/Hyperion, 1994.

Soto, Gary. "Manuel and the Football Scrubs." *A Fire in My Hands*. Harcourt, 2006

Other Sports and Physical Activities

Adoff, Jaime. "Air Shortness." *Small Fry*. Illus. by Mike Reed. Dutton, 2008. (Dodgeball)

Cheng, Andrea. "Tai Chi." *Shanghai Messenger*. Illus. by Ed Young. Lee & Low, 2005.

Grandits, John. "Volleyball Practice" & "The Bowling Party." *Blue Lipstick*. Clarion, 2007.

Grimes, Nikki. "Zuri at Bat." *Danitra Brown Leaves Town*. Illus. by Floyd Cooper. HarperCollins, 2002. (Softball)

Little, Jean. "Cartwheels." *Hey World, Here I Am!* Illus. by Sue Truesdell. HarperCollins, 1989.
Shaw, Nancy. *Sheep Take a Hike*. Houghton, 1994.
Sidman, Joyce. "I Got Carried Away," "Dodge Ball Crazy," & "Dodge Ball Kings." *This Is Just to Say*. Illus. by Pamela Zagarenski. Houghton, 2007.
Soto, Gary. "Ode to Weight Lifting." *Neighborhood Odes*. Illus. by David Diaz. Harcourt, 1992.
Wong, Janet. *Twist: Yoga Poems*. Illus. by Julie Paschkis. McElderry, 2007.

Standard Three: Student participates regularly in physical activity.

Standard Four: Student achieves and maintains a health-enhancing level of physical fitness.

Standard Five: Student exhibits responsible personal and social behavior that respects self and others in physical activity settings.

Standard Six: Student values physical activity for health, enjoyment, challenge, self-expression and social interaction.

Standard Six: Free Play

Children's free play at recess, in parks and playgrounds without the restrictions of adult coaching and supervision is important not only to physical health but to mental and social health as well. One modern pressure on students is long periods of rote instruction to prepare for tests; in some schools this has led to the cancellation of recess in order to provide content instruction in other areas. Long sedentary periods are very difficult for children both physically and mentally. Students do not develop the social and imaginative skills that come from free play. Participation in both formal and informal physical activities on a regular basis is necessary for students' self-expression and social interaction.

Many playground games belong to folk traditions. Game rules and techniques, and the folk rhymes and chants that accompany movements, are part of the oral culture of childhood passed down from child to child, often with small differences depending upon who taught the rules. Students argue and negotiate these rules as they play. Ayana Lowe has collected some of these folk rhymes from around the world in *Come and Play: Children of Our World Having Fun*. The accompanying photographs show that children don't need a lot of equipment to have a good time in their play.

Students may have opportunities for both free and organized play in Gym classes. Sometimes, the focus of physical education seems to be on obeying the rules, rather than the rule negotiation that comes during free play. Like many of us, poets have less-than-fond memories of their gym classes.

Lowe, Ayana, ed. *Come and Play: Children of Our World Having Fun*. Bloomsbury, 2008.

Recess and Gym

Dakos, Kalli. "Gym," "Monkey Bars," & "Slide." *The Bug in Teacher's Coffee*. Illus. by Mike Reed. Harper Collins, 1999.
———. "I Live for Gym." *Don't Read This Book, Whatever You Do!* Illus. by G. Brian Karas. S & S, 1993
———. "Muddy Recess." *Mrs. Cole on an Onion Roll*. Illus. by JoAnn Adinolfi. S & S, 1999.
George, Kristine O'Connell. "Dressing for P. E." *Swimming Upstream*. Illus. by Debbie Tilley. Clarion, 2002.
Holbrook, Sara. "Gym." *The Dog Ate My Homework*. Boyds Mills, 1996.
Salas, Laura Purdie. "King of the Jungle (Gym)" & "Playground Sparrows." *Stampede!* Illus. by Steven Salerno. Clarion, 2009.

Jump Rope Rhymes

Children use poetry regularly on the playground in the songs and chants that accompany jump rope, hand clapping, ball bouncing and other games. When students look at print versions of traditional rhymes they may discover that their versions of these rhymes differ from those of others. Sometimes it is just a difference in a word or two, sometimes there are more verses, and sometimes the same rhythmic beat is used but with entirely different words. Students might collect versions of jump rope rhymes that their parents and teachers remember and compare them with their own.

Several jump rope rhymes have been illustrated in picture book form including *A My Name Is Alice* and *The Lady with the Alligator Purse*. Students might want to add verses to these rhymes or make their own illustrated book featuring a favorite jump rope rhyme. Poets like the rhythms of jump rope rhymes and have created their own jump rope poems. These poems are fun to perform because of their beat, and students could jump role as they perform them. Students might also want to try writing their own rhymes.

Agard, John. "Skipping Rope Spell." In Janeczko, Paul B. *A Poke in the I*. Illus. by Chris Raschka. Candlewick, 2001.

Bayer, Jane A. *A My Name Is Alice*. Illus. by Stephen Kellogg. Dial, 1984.

Brand, Dionne. "Skipping Rope Song." *Earth Magic*. Illus. by Eugenie Fernanades. Kids Can, 2006.

Chambers, Veronica. *Double Dutch: A Celebration of Jump Rope, Rhyme, and Sisterhood*. Hyperion, 2002.

Cole, Joanna, sel. *Anna Banana: 101 Jump-Rope Rhymes*. Illus. by Alan Tiegreen. Morrow, 1989.

Dotlich, Rebecca Kai. "Double Dutch Song," "Jump Rope Rhyme," & "Jump Rope Talk." *Lemonade Sun*. Illus. by Jan Spivey Gilchrist. Boyds Mills, 1998.

———. "Jump Rope." *In the Spin of Things*. Illus. by Karen Dugan. Boyds Mills, 2003.

———. *Over in the Pink House: New Jump Rope Rhymes*. Illus. by Melanie Hall. Boyds Mills, 2004.

Fisher, Aileen. "Jump Rope Jingle." *Sing of the Earth and Sky*. Illus. by Karmen Thompson. Boyds Mills, 2001.

Florian, Douglas. "Double Dutch Girls." *Summersaults*. HarperCollins, 2002.

Franco, Betsy. "Jump Role Jingle." *Messing Around on the Monkey Bars*. Illus. by Jessie Hartland. Candlewick, 2009.

Grimes, Nikki. "Jump Rope Rhyme." *Meet Danitra Brown*. Illus. by Floyd Cooper. Lothrop, 1994.

"José Canseco (Jump Rope Rhyme)." In Morrison, Lillian. *At the Crack of the Bat*. Illus. by Steve Cieslawski. Hyperion, 1992.

Merriam, Eve. "A Rhyme Is a Jump Rope" & "Supermarket, Supermarket (A Jump Rope Rhyme)." *The Singing Green*. Illus. by Kathleen Collins Howell. Crowell, 1992.

———. "Skip Rope Rhyme for Our Time." In Cullinan, Bernice E. *A Jar of Tiny Stars*. Illus. by Andi MacLeod. NCTE/Boyds Mills, 1996.

Rice, John. "Skipping Rhyme." In Foster, John. *A Very First Poetry Book*. Oxford, 1980.

Turner, Ann. "Red-Dress Girl." *Street Talk*. Houghton, 1986.

Watson, Clyde. "Uptown, Downtown." *Father Fox's Pennyrhymes*. Illus. by Wendy Watson. HarperCollins, 1971.

Westcott, Nadine Bernard. *The Lady with the Alligator Purse*. Little, 1988.

Other Traditional Playground Games

See also Chapter Six: Dance Standard One (Rhythmic Poetry)

See also Chapter Six: Music Standard One (Song Picture Books)

Playground chants accompany various types of games or are performed as sassy verbal play. *Miss Mary Mack: And Other Children's Street Rhymes* collected by Joanna Cole and Stephanie Calmenson and *Street Rhymes around the World* collected by Jane Yolen are good resources for these rhymes. Children may learn these traditional chants at camp or at other organized group activities. Swinging, hopscotch, and ball bouncing are all inherently rhythmic activities. When combined with action rhymes they help students with motor skills, coordination, and balance.

Ada, Alma Flor & F. Isabel Campoy. *Mamá Goose: A Latino Nursery Treasury.* Illus. by Maribel Suárez. Hyperion, 2004.

Cole, Joanna & Stephanie Calmenson. *Miss Mary Mack: And Other Children's Street Rhymes.* Illus. by Alan Tiegreen. Morrow, 1990.

Hastings, Scott E. *Miss Mary Mack All Dressed in Black.* August, 1990.

Hoberman, Mary Ann, adap. *The Eensy-Weensy Spider.* Illus. by Nadine Bernard Westcott. Little, 2000.

———. *Miss Mary Mack: A Hand-Clapping Rhyme.* Illus. by Nadine Bernard Westcott. Little, 1998.

Opie, Iona & Peter Opie, sels. *I Saw Esau: The Schoolchild's Pocket Book.* Illus. by Maurice Sendak. Candlewick, 1992.

Schwartz, Alvin, sel. Section: "Fun & Games." *And the Green Grass Grew All Around.* Illus. by Sue Truesdell. HarperCollins, 1992.

Sierra, Judy, sel. *Schoolyard Rhymes: Kids Own Rhymes for Rope Skipping, Hand Clapping, Ball Bouncing, and Just Plain Fun.* Illus. by Melissa Sweet. Knopf, 2005.

Yolen, Jane. *Street Rhymes around the World.* Illus. by Jeanette Winter, et al. Boyds Mills, 1992.

Swinging

Allingham, William. "A Swing Song." In Kennedy, X. J. & Dorothy M. Kennedy. *Talking Like the Rain.* Illus. by Jane Dyer. Little, 1992.

Berry, James. "Swinging." *A Nest Full of Stars.* Illus. by Ashley Bryan. Greenwillow, 2004.

Dotlich, Rebecca Kai. "Summer Swinging." *Lemonade Sun.* Illus. by Jan Spivey Gilchrist. Boyds Mills, 1998.

Frost, Robert. *Birches.* Illus. by Ed Young. Holt, 1988. (On trees)

George, Kristine O'Connell. "Ghost Children" & "Winter Swing." *The Great Frog Race.* Illus. by Kate Kiesler. Clarion, 1997.

Hoberman, Mary Ann. "Hello and Good-by." *The Llama Who Had No Pajama.* Illus. by Betty Fraser. Harcourt, 1998.

Mordhorst, Heidi. "Singing the Swing." *Squeeze.* Illus. by Jesse Torrey. Boyds Mills, 2005.

Stevenson, Robert Louis. "The Swing." *A Child's Garden of Verses.* Illus. by Diane Goode. Morrow, 1998.

Hopscotch and Ball Bouncing

Cole, Joanna & Stephanie Calmenson. Section: "Ball Bouncing Rhymes." *Miss Mary Mack: And Other Children's Street Rhymes.* Illus. by Alan Tiegreen. Morrow, 1990.

Grimes, Nikki. "Hopscotch Love." *Hopscotch Love.* Illus. by Melodye Benson Rosales. Lothrop, 1999.

———. "Time to Play." In Hudson, Wade. *Pass It On.* Illus. by Floyd Cooper. Scholastic, 1993.

Kulling, Monica. "Hop to It." In Katz, Bobbi. *Pocket Poems.* Illus. by Marylin Hafner. Dutton, 2004.

HEALTH STANDARDS

Health Standard One: Students will comprehend concepts related to health promotion and disease prevention to enhance health.

Standard One: Getting Sick

Colds, the flu, various childhood diseases and accidents occur in every school and classroom. While the Health Standards are intended to encourage healthy behaviors, students still manage to get sick. Poets write about illnesses, rather than staying healthy, but these poems can accompany health lessons.

Colds and Sneezing

In spite of what we try to do to prevent communicable diseases, the common cold visits every classroom on a regular basis. The poems included here can be shared along with lessons about covering your mouth when you sneeze, keeping your hands clean, and other preventative measures. Poets like to play with the way we sound when we have a cold, as Jack Prelutsky does in "Sprig Id Here" and Carol Diggory Shields does in "Code." Ogden Nash's classic poem "The Sniffle" misspells "cheerful" so it rhymes with "sniffle," to create the same effect.

Fitch, Sheree. "The Sneeze." In Booth, David. *'Til All the Stars Have Fallen.* Illus. by Kady McDonald Denton. Viking, 1989.

Kumin, Maxine. "Sneeze." In Prelutsky, Jack. *The 20th Century Children's Poetry Treasury.* Illus. by Meilo So. Knopf, 1999. (Also in *Read-Aloud Rhymes for the Very Young*; *Poetry Speaks to Children*)

Milne, A. A. "Sneezles." *Now We Are Six.* Illus. by Ernest H. Shepard. Dutton, 1988.

Nash, Ogden. "The Sniffle." In Prelutsky, Jack. *The 20th Century Children's Poetry Treasury.* Illus. by Meilo So. Knopf, 1999.

Prelutsky, Jack. "Sprig Id Here." *My Dog May Be a Genius.* Illus. by James Stevenson. HarperCollins, 2008.

———. "Awful Ogre Causes a Commotion." *Awful Ogre Running Wild.* Illus. by Paul O. Zelinsky. Harper Collins, 2008. (Giant Sneeze)

———. "I Am Freezing." *It's Raining Pigs and Noodles.* Illus. by James Stevenson. Greenwillow, 2000.

Ridlon, Marci. "Sick." In Prelutsky, Jack. *The 20th Century Children's Poetry Treasury.* Illus. by Meilo So. Knopf, 1999.

Shields, Carol Diggory. "Code." *Lunch Money.* Illus. by Paul Meisel. Dutton, 1995.

Silverstein, Shel. "Bad Cold." *Falling Up.* HarperCollins, 1996.

Soto, Gary. "Winter Cold." *Canto Familiar.* Illus. by Annicka Nelson. Harcourt, 1995.

Spinelli, Eileen. "Granddad Has a Cold." *In Our Backyard Garden.* Illus. by Marcy Ramsey. S & S,, 2004.

Weeks, Sarah. *Baa-Choo!* Illus. by Jane Manning. HarperCollins, 2004.

Winters, Kay. "Runny Nose." *Did You See What I Saw?* Illus. by Martha Weston. Viking, 1996.

Wong, Janet S. "The Best Dreams." *Night Garden.* Illus. by Julie Paschkis. McElderry, 2000.

Illnesses and Accidents

Poets have written on a variety of illnesses, in both serious and lighthearted ways When illnesses are serious, some poets choose to use the format of the novel in verse. Sometimes, the young person must miss something that is important to him as in Ron Koertge's novel in verse, *Shakespeare Bats Cleanup.* The book consists of the poems a young boy with mononucleosis writes when he has to miss baseball season. Sometimes the illness of the parent or sibling affects every aspect of the young person's life, as in Ann Turner's novel in verse, *Hard Hit* and Sonya Sones' *Stop Pretending: What Happened When My Big Sister Went Crazy.* The length of the novel in verse allows the author to explore the subject with more depth.

In a few poems, the young person deals with a chronic illness, as in Emily Hearn's "Courage," about a child with allergies who must turn an invitation to spend the night with a friend with new kittens. Sometimes children who are sick can take advantage of this time-out from busy lives. Judith Viorst's "Oh, Wow! Book" suggests that sometimes when you are sick a good book is the best medicine.

Sometimes, children must stay home to take care of others in their families, as "Jim" does in Geraldine Brooks' poem. Sometimes it is a friend, as in Nikki Grimes' "A Friend in Need," It is surprising how few poets have written about the accidents and broken limbs which seem a part of student life. "The Cast" by John Grandits is one of the few. Students might want to write poems about their own experiences with wearing casts and healing bones.

There are also poems about times, as in Shel Silverstein's "Sick," when children feign illness to avoid school. Silverstein's narrator realizes it's Saturday; the young narrator of Shirley Neitzel's *I'm Not Feeling Well Today* discovers it's a snow day and school has been cancelled. Bruce Lansky's narrator is hoping to avoid a test by painting himself with "measles." Jack Prelutsky's narrator in "I'm Off to the Infirmary" has not done his homework.

Brooks, Gwendolyn. "Charles" & "Jim." *Bronzeville Boys and Girls*. Illus. by Faith Ringgold. HarperCollins, 2007.

Cheng, Andrea. "Sick." *Shanghai Messenger.* Lee & Low, 2005. (Novel in Verse)

Collis, John. "Job Satisfaction." In Janeczko, Paul B. *Dirty Laundry Pile*. Illus. by Melissa Sweet. HarperCollins, 2001. (Food poisoning)

Dakos, Kalli. "The Bugs Are Out." *Don't Read This Book, Whatever You Do!* Illus. by G. Brian Karas. S & S, 1993.

———. "Happy Hiccup to You" & "Don't You Remember How Sick You Are?" *If You're Not Here, Please Raise Your Hand*. Illus. by G. Brian Karas. S & S, 1990.

Fletcher, Ralph. "Broken Ice," "The Story," & "King for a Day." *Relatively Speaking*. Illus. by Walter Lyon Krudop. Orchard, 1999. (Accident)

Grandits, John. "The Cast" & "Sick Day." *Technically, It's Not My Fault*. Clarion, 2004.

Graves, Donald. "Chicken Pox." *Baseball, Snakes, and Summer Squash*. Boyds Mills, 1996.

Grimes, Nikki. "A Friend in Need." *Danitra Brown, Class Clown*. Illus. by E. B. Lewis. HarperCollins, 2005.

Hoban, Russell. "Sick in Winter." *Egg Thoughts*. Illus. by Lillian Hoban. HarperCollins, 1972.

Hearn, Emily. "Courage." In Booth, David. *'Til All the Stars Have Fallen*. Illus. by Kady MacDonald Denton. Viking, 1990

Hoberman, Mary Ann. "Sick Days." *Fathers, Mothers, Sisters, Brothers*. Illus. by Marylin Hafner. Little, 1991.

Holbrook, Sara. "Earache." *Which Way to the Dragon!* Boyds Mills, 1996.

Koertge, Ron. *Shakespeare Bats Cleanup*. Candlewick, 2003. (Novel in Verse)

Lansky, Bruce. "Measles." In Hopkins, Lee Bennett. *Hamsters, Shells, and Spelling Bees*. Illus. by Sachiko Yoshikawa. HarperCollins, 2008.

McCord, David. "The Doctor." *One at a Time*. Illus. by Henry B. Kane. Little, 1986.

Merriam, Eve. "Bella Had a New Umbrella." *Blackberry Ink*. Illus. by Hans Wilhelm. Morrow, 1985.

Mordhorst. Heidi. "The Skin Giver: For Satchel." *Squeeze*. Illus. by Jesse Torrey. Boyds Mills, 2005. (Scraped Knee)

Nash, Ogden. "The Germ." In Rogasky, Barbara, *Winter Poems*. Illus. by Trina Schart Hyman. Scholastic, 1994.

Neitzel, Shirley. *I'm Not Feeling Well Today*. Illus. by Nancy Winslow Parker. Greenwillow, 2001.

Prelutsky, Jack. "I'm Off to the Infirmary." *What a Day It Was at School!* Illus. by Doug Cushman. Harper Collins, 2006.

———. "I've Got an Incredible Headache" & "I've Got an Itch." *The New Kid on the Block*. Illus. by James Stevenson. Greenwillow, 1984.

Reader, Willie. "When Paul Bunyan Was Ill." In Kennedy, X. J. & Dorothy M. Kennedy. *Knock at a Star*. Illus. by Karen Lee Baker. Little, 1985.

Shapiro, Karen Jo. "A Red, Red Nose." *Because I Could Not Stop My Bike*. Illus. by Matt Faulkner. Charlesbridge, 2003. (Sunburn)

———. "This Rotten Lousy Flu." *I Must Go Down to the Beach Again*. Illus. by Judy Love. Charlesbridge, 2007.

Silverstein, Shel. "Sick." *Where the Sidewalk Ends*. HarperCollins, 1974.

Sones, Sonya. *Stop Pretending: What Happened When My Big Sister Went Crazy* HarperCollins, 1999. (Novel in Verse)

Starbird, Kaye. "Measles." In Prelutsky, Jack. *The Random House Book of Poetry for Children*. Illus. by Arnold Lobel. Random, 1983.

Stevenson, Robert Louis. "The Land of Counterpane." *A Child's Garden of Verses*. Illus. by Diane Goode. Morrow, 1998.

Turner, Ann. *Hard Hit*. Scholastic, 2006. (Novel in Verse)

Viorst, Judith. "My Oh-Wow! Book." *If I Were In Charge of the World*. Illus. by Lynne Cherry. Atheneum, 1981.

Westcott, Nadine Bernard. *The Lady with the Alligator Purse*. Little, 1988.

Whitehead, Jenny. "Mom, I'm Coughing" & "First Aid." *Lunch Box Mail*. Holt, 2001.

Winters, Kay. "Lots of Spots." *Did You See What I Saw?* Illus. by Martha Weston. Viking, 1996. (Chicken Pox)

Wong, Janet S. "Grandmother's Cure." *Good Luck Gold*. McElderry, 1994. (Chicken Pox)

Health Standard Two: Students will analyze the influence of family, peers, culture, media, technology, and other factors on health behaviors.

Standard Two: Students with Disabilities

In spite of legislation and much education, people can be very hard on those who have disabilities. There is not a great deal of poetry about this subject, but the few poems we have often try to get to the feelings and abilities of children who may look or act different from their peers. Being overweight is another social issue that is getting a lot of attention. Children who are overweight are often teased or bullied by their peers. Judith Viorst's "See the Jolly Fat Boy" gets at the feelings of someone who struggles with weight. Kalli Dakos' poem is a poignant conversation between an overweight child and a teacher.

Anderson, Peggy Perry. *Joe on the Go*. Houghton, 2007. (Grandmother Uses a Wheelchair)

Creech, Sharon. *Hate That Cat*. HarperCollins, 2008. (Novel in Verse) (Mother is Deaf)

Dakos, Kalli. "Four Eyes." *Don't Read This Book Whatever You Do!* Illus. G. Brian Karas. S & S, 1993. (Eyesight)

———. "Were You Ever Fat Like Me?" *If You're Not Here, Please Raise Your Hand*. Illus. by G. Brian Karas. S & S, 1990.

George, Kristine O'Connell. "Margo," "Award Assembly," & "Worth Hearing." *Swimming Upstream*. Illus. by Debbie Tilley. Clarion, 2002. (Mental Disability & Stutter)

Grimes, Nikki. "Dyslexia." *Bronx Masquerade*. Dial, 2002.

———. "Four Eyes." *It's Raining Laughter*. Illus. by Miles C. Pinkney. Boyds Mills, 1997.

LeZotte, Ann Clare. *T4: A Novel in Verse*. Houghton, 2008. (Deafness)

Seeger, Pete & Paul Dubois Jacobs. *The Deaf Musicians*. Illus. by R. Gregory Christie. Putnam, 2002.

Sones, Sonya. *Stop Pretending: What Happened When My Big Sister Went Crazy*. HarperCollins, 1999. (Novel in Verse) (Mental Illness)

Soto, Gary. "Eyeglasses." *Canto Familiar*. Illus. by Annika Nelson. Harcourt, 1995.

Viorst, Judith. "See the Jolly Fat Boy." *Sad Underwear*. Illus. by Richard Hull. Atheneum, 1995.

Zimmer, Tracie Vaughan. *Reaching for the Sun.* Bloomsbury, 2007. (Novel in Verse) (Cerebral Palsy)

Health Standard Three: Students will demonstrate the ability to access valid information and products and services to enhance health.

Health Standard Four: Students will demonstrate the ability to use interpersonal communication skills to enhance health and avoid or reduce health risks.

See also Health Standard Two

See also Chapter Five: Social Studies Theme Four (Individual Development and Identity)

Standard Four: Bullying

Interpersonal communication skills are necessary for those who are bullied and those who support them. Learning how to confront and defuse bullies is a valuable skill throughout one's life, as bullying does not stop as we grow up. Poets describe the fear bullying induces or use humor to deal with that fear as Jack Prelutsky does in "The New Kid on the Block." Victims of bullies will get a bit of satisfaction from J. Patrick Lewis's epitaph for a bully who has died.

Girls are just as likely to bully as boys. The sense of power one can feel over another is an all too human if not very likeable trait. Peer pressure and admiration for students in in-groups causes people to do things they later regret. Gary Soto's poem "Cruel Boys" talks about wanting to be one of those tough kids, but not quite managing it. Intolerance of differences, whether of ability, appearance, gender, religion, or of ethncity, is at the root of much destructive bullying. Poems about name-calling and intolerance are also included here.

Adoff, Jaime. "Very Big Mark." *Small Fry.* Illus. by Mike Reed. Dutton, 2008.
Graves, Donald. "The Bully" & "Muscles." *Baseball, Snakes, and Summer Squash.* Boyds Mills, 1996.
Grimes, Nikki. "Class Bully." *My Man Blue.* Illus. by Jerome Lagarrigue. Dial, 1999.
Lewis, J. Patrick. "Bully." *Once Upon a Tomb.* Illus. by Simon Bartram. Candlewick, 2006.
Prelutsky, Jack. "The New Kid on the Block." *The New Kid on the Block.* Illus. by James Stevenson. Greenwillow, 1984.
Sidman, Joyce. "To Maria: Not Really, by Bobby." *This Is Just to Say.* Illus. by Pamela Zagarenski. Houghton, 2007.
Soto, Gary. "Cruel Boys." In Kennedy, Dorothy M. *I Thought I'd Take My Rat to School.* Illus. by Abby Carter. Little, 1993.
Swados, Elizabeth. "Tough Kids." *Hey You! C'Mere: A Poetry Slam.* Illus. by Joe Cepeta. Scholastic, 2002.
Viorst, Judith. "Stanley the Fierce." *If I Were in Charge of the World.* Illus. by Lynne Cherry. Atheneum, 1981.
Walker, Alice. "Primer." In Clinton, Catherine. *I, Too, Sing America.* Illus. by Stephen Alcorn. Houghton, 1998.

Intolerance

Castillo, Ana. "We Would Like You to Know." In Carlson, Lori M. *Cool Salsa.* Holt, 1994.
Cullen, Countee. "Incident." In Rochelle, Belinda. *Words With Wings.* HarperCollins, 2001. (Also in *Shimmy Shimmy Shimmy Like My Sister Kate*)
Hopkins, Lee Bennett. "Clutching." *Been to Yesterdays.* Boyds Mills, 1995.
Saroyan, Gladys Alam. "From . . . Unveiled." In Nye, Naomi Shihab. *The Space Between Our Footsteps.* S & S, 1998. (Also in *The Flag of Childhood*)
Steig, Jeanne. "Intolerance." *Alpha Beta Chowder.* Illus. by William Steig. HarperCollins, 1992.
Wong, Janet S. "Speak Up," "Waiting at the Railroad Café, " & "Noise." *Good Luck Gold.* McElderry, 1994.

Health Standard Five: Students will demonstrate the ability to use decision-making skills to enhance health.

See Chapter Four: Math Standard One (Shopping)

See Chapter Three: Science Standard Four (Gardening)

Health Standard Six: Students will demonstrate the ability to use goal-setting skills to enhance health.

Health Standard Seven: Students will demonstrate the ability to practice health-enhancing behaviors and avoid or reduce health risks.

Standard Seven: Teeth

Of all of the health-enhancing behaviors that children might learn, the poets seem to prefer taking care of your teeth. Poems about teeth range from losing baby teeth and the subsequent visit from the tooth fairy to braces and dental visits. Just as poets play with the sounds of stuffed up noses when children have colds, they also play with how children sound with loose or missing teeth. Few people know the important contribution George Washington made to dental health. As Deborah Chandra and Madeleine Comora point out in their amusing and informative book, *George Washington's Teeth*, Washington struggled with tooth pain and lost teeth all of his life. His search for a comfortable set of false teeth contributed to the rise of modern dentistry. Some poetic portraits of dentists are not positive, but they can be the basis for discussions about why we needn't fear a trip to the dentist.

Alarcón, Francisco X. "Magica Dental = Tooth Magic." *Angels Ride Bikes = Los Ángeles Andan en Bicicleta*. Illus. by Maya Christina Gonzalez. Children's, 1999.

Chandra, Deborah & Madeleine Comora. *George Washington's Teeth*. Illus. by Brock Cole. Farrar, 2003.

Dakos, Kalli. "I Lost My Tooth in a Doughnut" & "Dear Tooth Fairy." *Mrs. Cole on an Onion Roll*. Illus. by JoAnn Adinolfi. S & S, 1995.

Dotlich, Rebecca Kai. "Steel Strong and Silver Bright . . . " *When Riddles Come Rumbling*. Boyds Mills, 2001. (Braces)

Elya, Susan Middleton. *Tooth on the Loose*. Illus. by Jenny Mattheson. Putnam. 2008.

Florian, Douglas. "If I Eat More Candy." *Bing Bang Boing*. Harcourt, 1994.

Holbroook, Sara. "The Tooth Comes Out." *Which Way to the Dragon!* Boyds Mills, 1996.

Hopkins, Lee Bennett. "This Tooth." *Good Rhymes, Good Times*. Illus. by Frané Lessac. HarperCollins, 1995. (Also in *The Bill Martin Jr. Big Book of Poetry* & *Talking to the Sun*)

McCord, David. "Tooth Trouble." *One at a Time*. Little, 1986.

McGinley, Phyllis. "Reflections Dental." In Dunning, Stephen, et al. *Reflections on a Gift of Watermelon Pickle*. HarperCollins, 1967.

Perry, Andrea. "Tooth Fairy Forklift." *Here's What You Do When You Can't Find Your Shoe (Ingenious Inventions for Pesky Problems)*. Illus. by Alan Snow. Atheneum, 2003.

Prelutsky, Jack. "I Went Hungry on Thanksgiving." *It's Thanksgiving!* Illus. by Marylin Hafner. HarperCollins, 2007. (Braces)

———. "I Ate a Tooth This Morning." *It's Raining Pigs and Noodles*. Illus. by James Stevenson. Greenwillow, 2000.

———. "I Have Got a Steamship Anchor." *Monday's Troll*. Illus. by Peter Sis. Greenwillow, 1996. (A Giant's good dentist)

Rex, Adam. "The Dentist." *Frankenstein Makes a Sandwich*. Harcourt, 2006.

Silverstein, Shel. "The Crocodile's Toothache." *Where the Sidewalk Ends*. HarperCollins, 1974.

———. "Dentist Dan." *Falling Up*. HarperCollins, 1996.

Ulrich, George. "My Tooth Ith Loothe." In Prelutsky, Jack, sel. *The 20th Century Children's Poetry Treasury*. Illus. by Meila So. Knopf, 1999.

Viorst, Judith. "Well, Shut My Mouth." *Sad Underwear*. Illus. by Richard Hull. Atheneum, 1995.

West, Colin. *The King's Toothache*. Illus. by Anne Dalton. HarperCollins, 1988.

Whitehead, Jenny. "I Loth My Tooth." *Lunch Box Mail*. Holt, 2001.

Willard, Nancy. "Magic Story for Falling Asleep." In Hopkins, Lee Bennett. *Climb Into My Lap*. Illus. by Kathryn Brown. S & S, 1998.

Wolf, Alan. "One Tooth, Two Tooth, White Tooth, Looth Tooth." In Janeczko, Paul B. *A Foot in the Mouth*. Illus. by Chris Raschka. Candlewick, 2009.

Health Standard Eight: Students will demonstrate the ability to advocate for personal, family and community health.

Links with Chapter Three: Science Standard Seven (Science in Personal and Social Perspectives)

Links with Chapter Five: Social Studies Theme Four (Individual Development and Identity)

Links with Chapter Five: Social Studies Theme Ten (War and Peace)

Standard Eight Unit: Talking About Race

Scientists have long known that race is a social and cultural construction, and that human beings are more alike than different. In spite of this, too often people use race as a way of dividing us. In his "I Have a Dream "speech in 1963 Martin Luther King spoke of a time when his own children would " . . . not be judged by the color of their skin but by the content of their character." We judge people by the color of their skin, the look of their hair, the ways they speak, their religion, their national origins, and their gender. In her poem, "Labels" Sara Holbrook writes that looking at someone and labeling them doesn't mean you know them, " . . . you have to take a taste." That taste means getting to know and understand both similarities and differences on a deeper level. A unit that combines biology, human anatomy, community health, and social studies gives students a chance to explore differences and similarities in the human race. Arnold Adoff says it quite succinctly in *All the Colors of the Race*: "Stop Looking, Start Loving."

Julius Lester's matter-of-fact and humorous prose picture book *Let's Talk About Race* is a good way to begin. In clear language Lester makes the case for our commonalities and the beauty of differences, and this book can be shared with all ages. Older students can watch the PBS series *Race: The Power of an Illusion*, which sets out the scientific and cultural issues surrounding race. For younger students Jamie Lee Curtis' *Is There Really A Human Race?* works well. This book plays on the word "race" as a contest, suggesting that in the end no one wins if we don't get along. Maya Angelou's poem "Human Family" provides both a beginning and an ending point for a unit. The poem ends with a repeated stanza: "We are more alike, my friends, than we are unalike. We are more alike, my friends, than we are unalike."

Adoff, Arnold. *All the Colors of the Race*. Illus. by John Steptoe. Morrow, 1982.

Angelou, Maya. "Human Family." In Rochelle, Belinda. *Words with Wings*. HarperCollins, 2001.

Curtis, Jamie Lee. *Is There Really a Human Race?* Illus. by Laura Cornell. HarperCollins, 2006.

King, Martin Luther, Jr. *I Have a Dream*. Scholastic, 1997.

Lester, Julius. *Let's Talk About Race*. HarperCollins, 2005. (prose)

The Color of Our Skin

It is useful to begin a discussion of skin with a poem that makes the point that we all have it such as Debra Chandra's "Tent." Science reveals the reasons that skin colors differentiated because of geography and exposure to sunlight. Poets more often focus on the way we label skin colors. As "black and white." In *Black Is Brown Is Tan*, Arnold Adoff says that in his family the skin colors are more brown and pink than black and white. Black skin comes in many shades, and poets find the beauty in all of them. Langston Hughes compares the color of his skin to the pale cool of the evening in "Dream Variation." Both Nikki Grimes and Joyce Carol Thomas have used the saying "The blacker the berry, the sweeter the juice" as a way to help children fend off the taunts of others about the color of their skin. Asian Americans, American Indians, Latinos, and African Americans have felt judged by the "color of their skin." Some have conveyed these feelings in their poems.

Adoff, Arnold. "All the Colors of the Race" & "I Think the Real Color Is Behind the Color." *All the Colors of the Race*. Illus. by John Steptoe. Morrow, 1982.

———. *Black Is Brown Is Tan*. Illus. by Emily Arnold McCully. HarperCollins, 2002.

———. "Flavors." In Cullinan, Bernice E. *A Jar of Tiny Stars*. Illus. by Andi MacLeod. NCTE/Boyds Mills, 1996.

Allison, Madeline G. "Children of the Sun." In Muse, Daphne. *The Entrance Place of Wonders*. Illus. by Charlotte Riley-Webb. Abrams, 2005.

Bennett, Gwendolyn B. "To a Dark Girl." In Clinton, Catherine. *I, Too, Sing America*. Illus. by Stephen Alcorn. Houghton, 1998.

Berry, James. "Okay, Brown Girl, Okay." In Paschen, Elise. *Poetry Speaks to Children*. Sourcebooks, 2005. (With CD)

Chandra, Deborah. "Tent." In Hopkins, Lee Bennett. *Climb into My Lap*. Illus. by Kathryn Brown. S & S, 1998. (Also in *The 20th Century Children's Poetry Treasury*)

Cuney, William Waring. "No Images." In Giovanni, Nikki. *Hip Hop Speaks to Children*. Sourcebooks, 2008. (With CD)

Grimes, Nikki. "Sweet Blackberry." *Meet Danitra Brown*. Illus. by Floyd Cooper. Lothrop, 1994.

hooks, bell. *Skin Again*. Illus. by Chris Raschka. Hyperion, 2004.

Hughes, Langston. "Dream Variation," "The Negro," "My People," & "Color." *The Dream Keeper*. Illus. by Brian Pinkney. Knopf, 1994.

Hughes, Langston. *My People*. Illus. by Charles R. Smith Jr. S & S, 2009.

Mahone, Barbara. "What Color Is Black?" In Slier, Deborah. *Make a Joyful Sound*. Illus. by Cornelius Van Wright & Ying-Hwa Hu. Checkerboard, 1991.

Nelson, Gordon. "Science." In Slier, Deborah. *Make a Joyful Sound*. Illus. by Cornelius Van Wright & Ying-Hwa Hu. Checkerboard, 1991.

Perkins, Useni Eugene. "Black Is Beautiful." In Slier, Deborah. *Make a Joyful Sound*. Illus. by Cornelius Van Wright & Ying-Hwa Hu. Checkerboard, 1991.

Pinkney, Sandra L. *Shades of Black: A Celebration of Our Children*. Illus. by Myles C. Pinkney. Scholastic, 2000.

Redhouse, Mary. "Red Girls." In Ochoa, Annette Piña, et al. *Night Is Gone, Day Is Still Coming*. Candlewick, 2003.

Sanchez, Trinidad, Jr. "Why Am I So Brown?" In Carlson, Lori M. *Cool Salsa*. Holt, 1994.

Thomas, Joyce Carol. *The Blacker the Berry*. Illus. by Floyd Cooper. HarperCollins, 2008.

Walker, Margaret. "Mother of Brown-ness." In Feelings, Tom. *Soul Looks Back in Wonder*. Dial, 1993.

Wong, Janet S. "All Mixed Up." *Good Luck Gold*. McElderry, 1994.

Wright, Richard. "Laughing Boy." In Rogasky, Barbara. *Winter Poems*. Illus. by Trina Schart Hyman. Scholastic, 1994.

Our Hair

In a society with set notions of what is beautiful, we tend to judge others by the texture, look and feel of their hair. A preschool teacher heard children taunting a child with wildly curly dark hair and decided to address the subject. She set up a hair salon as a center in the corner of her classroom, with a large mirror and many types of brushes, picks, and combs. She gently talked with the children about how different in color and texture and curl each child's hair was, and let them tell stories about hair in their families. She shared Sandra Cisneros' *Hairs = Pelitos* in which the members of a family have many types of hair. As children played in the hair salon corner, she gradually began to see them lovingly touching one another's hair, gently brushing and combing it and talking about its beauty. These children had begun to understand Arnold Adoff's "Stop Looking, Start Loving."

Adoff, Arnold. "I Can Do My Hair." *All the Colors of the Race*. Illus. by John Steptoe. Morrow, 1982.

Cisneros, Sandra. *Hairs = Pelitos*. Illus. by Terry Ybañez. Knopf, 1994.

Fatchen, Max. "Hair." In Rosen, Michael. *Poems for the Very Young*. Illus. by Bob Graham. Houghton, 1993.

Hru, Dakari Kamau. "Crown." In Slier, Deborah. *Make a Joyful Sound*. Illus. by Cornelius Van Wright & Ying-Hwa Hu. Checkerboard, 1991.

Johnson, Dinah. *Hair Dance!* Illus. by Kelly Johnson. Holt, 2007.

Medina, Jane. "Braids = Trenzas." *The Dream on Blanca's Wall = El Sueño en la Pared de Blanca*. Illus. by Robert Casilla. Boyds Mills, 2004.

Mellage, Nanette. "Willimae's Cornrows." In Slier, Deborah. *Make a Joyful Sound*. Illus. by Cornelius Van Wright & Ying-Hwa Hu. Checkerboard, 1991.

Miller, Kate. "My Mother's Hair." *Poems in Black and White*. Boyds Mills, 2007.

Nichols, Grace. "Granny Granny Please Comb My Hair." In Micklos, John, Jr. *Grandparent Poems*. Illus. by Layne Johnson. Boyds Mills, 2004. (Also in *The Fish Is Me*)

Nye, Naomi Shihab. "Hairdo." *A Maze Me*. HarperCollins, 2005.

Thomas, Joyce Carol. *Crowning Glory*. Illus. by Brenda Joysmith. HarperCollins, 2002.

Weatherford, Carole Boston. "Bea the Beautician" & "Lou's Barbershop." *Sidewalk Chalk*. Illus. by Dimitrea Tokunbo. Boyds Mills, 2006.

Wong, Janet S. "Hair." *Knock on Wood: Poems About Superstitions*. Illus. by Julie Paschkis. McElderry, 2003.

———. "Joyce's Beauty Salon." *A Suitcase of Seaweed*. Booksurge, 2008.

Our Hands

See also Chapter Two: Language Arts Standard Six (Figurative Language)

We use our hands for so many purposes that our language is filled with "handy" expressions. Shari Griffin's fourth and fifth graders brainstormed a list that included: "Keep your hands off!" "Lend a hand." "Put your hands together for . . ." "Helping hands," "Many hands make light work," "Need a hand?" and "Holding hands." One student altered a cliché to come up with "Two hands are better than one." Students might want to look in books of idioms for more expressions about hands and parts of the hand. Being "all thumbs" and "putting your finger" on the problem are just the beginning of lists of these phrases. These expressions exist in our language because our hands are useful and distinctive. In "Love Poem for My People" Pedro Pietri writes, "if you want to feel very rich look at your hands." It's useful to take a close look at our hands.

Cheryl Willis Hudson's *Hands Can* gives a brief rhymed introduction to some of the things hands can do, from their use to feel texture, to the language of hands, to how we use them to create, caress, and keep time. Hope Lynne Price also uses rhyme to list the uses of hands. Amanda Hahn's *I Call My Hand Gentle* uses a repeated phrase, "It can . . . " to list some of these activities, but to also make the point that what she doesn't want her hand to do is to hit or to hurt.

Some poems books help students understand how we may differ by skin color, age, or ability, but our hands are more alike than different. Several poets have written about gloves, and the ways that these can take on the shape of the owner's hands over time. Our hands may look like those of a parent or other relative, with the same long fingers or double-jointed thumb. Students may notice other qualities of hands around them. Some people are missing a finger; others cannot use their hands, and have found other ways to touch, hold, and caress. Some hands are smooth and others are rough from hard work. Some people wear distinctive rings or decorative designs on their hands. Some students might try art activities that celebrate what their hands reveal about them. Sometimes, our hands are used to reach out and connect with others. Pat Mora's *Join Hands! The Ways to Celebrate Life* is an exuberant wish for this. Art activities in which hands are linked in some way or recreating the circles Mora describes can add to the feelings of this poem.

Alarcón, Francisco X. "My Mother's Hands = Las Manos de Mi Madre." *Angels Ride Bikes = Los Ángeles Andan en Bicicleta*. Illus. by Maya Christina Gonzales. Children's, 1999.

Brown, Calef. "Bear Paws." *Soup for Breakfast*. Houghton, 2008.

Cedering, Siv. "The Red Gloves." In Janeczko, Paul. *Dirty Laundry Pile*. Illus. by Melissa Sweet. HarperCollins, 2001. (Also in *Here Is My Heart*)

Cole, Joanna and Stephanie Calmenson. "Hand-clapping Rhymes." *Miss Mary Mack and Other Children's Street Rhymes*. Illus. by Alan Tiegreen. Morrow, 1990.

Dakos, Kalli. "The Hand Collection," "A Gift for Ms. Roys," and "Fingernails on a Stick." *Put Your Eyes up Here*. Illus. by G. Brian Karas. S & S, 2003.

Dotlich, Rebecca Kai. "A Father's Hands." In Hopkins, Lee Bennett, *Days to Celebrate*. Illus. by Stephen Alcorn. HarperCollins, 2005.

Dove, Rita. "Fifth Grade Autobiography." In Rochelle, Belinda. *Words with Wings*.HarperCollins, 2001.

Florian, Douglas. "Hand To Hand." *Laugh-eteria*. Harcourt, 1999.

George, Kristine O'Connell. *One Mitten*. Illus. by Maggie Smith. Clarion, 2004.

Grimes, Nikki. "Brown Hands, by Lupe Algarin." *Bronx Masquerade*. Dial, 2002.

———. "Grandma's Gloves" and "Radio City." *Stepping Out with Grandma Mac*. Illus. by Angelo. Scholastic, 2001.

———. "His Hands." *My Man Blue*. Illus. by Jerome Lagarrigue. Dial, 1999.

Haan, Amanda. *I Call My Hand Gentle*. Illus. by Marina Sagona. Viking, 2003.

Hoberman, Mary Ann. "Magic Hands." *The Llama Who Had No Pajama*. Illus. by Betty Fraser. Harcourt, 1998.

Hubbell, Patricia. "Starfish." *Earthmates*. Illus. by Jean Cassels. Cavendish, 2000.

Hudson, Cheryl Willis. *Hands Can*. Illus. by John-Francis Bourke. Candlewick, 2003.

Hughes, Langston. "Daybreak In Alabama" and "As I Grew Older." *The Dream Keeper*. Illus. by Brian Pinkney. Knopf, 1993.

Johnson, Angela. "Her Daddy's Hands." In *In Daddy's Arms I Am Tall*. Illus. by Javaka Steptoe. Lee & Low, 1997.

Majaj, Lisa Suhair. "I Remember My Father's Hands." In Nye, Naomi Shihab. *The Space Between Our Footsteps*. S & S, 1998. (Also in *The Flag of Childhood*)

Merriam, Eve. "Secret Hand." *The Singing Green*. Illus. by Kathleen Collins Howell. Morrow, 1992.

Micklos, John, Jr. "Grandpa's Hands." *Grandparent Poems*. Illus. by Layne Johnson. Boyd's Mills, 2004.

Mora, Pat. *Join Hands! The Ways We Celebrate Life*. Illus. by George Ancona. Charlesbridge, 2008.

Nelson, Kadir. *He's Got the Whole World In His Hands*. Dial, 2005.

Nye, Naomi Shihab. "Yellow Glove." In Janeczko, Paul B. *Poetry from A to Z*. Illus. by Cathy Bobak. S & S, 1994.

Pietri, Pedro. "Love Poem For My People." In Giovanni, Nikki. *Hip Hop Speaks To Children*. Sourcebooks, 2008. (With CD)

"A Pretty Little Hand." In Delacre, Lulu. *Arroz con Leche: Popular Songs and Rhymes From Latin America.* Scholastic, 1989.

Prelutsky, Jack. "The Truth Is." *It's Snowing! It's Snowing!* Illus. by Yossi Abolafia. HarperCollins, 2006.

Price, Hope Lynne. *These Hands.* Illus. by Bryan Collier. Hyperion, 1999.

Silverstein, Shel. "Hand Holding." *Falling Up.* HarperCollins, 1996.

Spires, Elizabeth. "Hands." *I Heard God Talking to Me.* Farrar, 2009.

Swenson, May. "An Extremity." *The Complete Poems To Solve.* Illus. by Christy Hale. Macmillan, 1993.

Thurston, Harry. "Fingerprint." In Booth, David. *'Til All the Stars Have Fallen.* Illus. by Kady MacDonald Denton. Viking, 1989.

"Up To the Ceiling." In Hopkins, Lee Bennett. *Climb Into My Lap.* Illus. by Kathryn Bown. Simon &Schuster, 1998.

Valdes, Gina. "The Hands." In Carlson, Lori Marie. *Red Hot Salsa.* Holt, 2005.

Viorst, Judith. "Mending." *If I Were in Charge of the World.* Illus. by Lynne Cherry Atheneum, 1981.

Weisburd, Stefi. "Mehndi Party." *Barefoot.* Illus. by Lori McElrath-Eslick. Boyds Mills, 2008.

Worth, Valerie. "Seashell." *All the Small Poems and Fourteen More.* Illus. by Natalie Babbitt. Farrar, 1994.

Prose Works About Hands

Aliki. *My Hands.* Crowell, 1990.

Barasch, Lynne. *Hiromi's Hands.* Lee & Low, 2007.

Crandell, Rachel. *Hands of the Maya: Villagers at Work and Play.* Holt, 2002.

Ehlert, Lois. *Hands: Growing Up to Be an Artist.* Harcourt, 2004.

English, Karen. *Nadia's Hands.* Illus. by Jonathan Weiner. Boyds Mills, 1999.

Lorbiecki, Marybeth. *Sister Anne's Hands.* Illus. by Wendy Popp. Dial, 1998.

Rankin, Laura. *The Handmade Alphabet.* Dial, 1991.

Ryder, Joanne. *My Father's Hands.* Illus. by Mark Graham. Morrow, 1994.

Coming Together

Teachers and librarians can address our differences and similarities through science, social studies, or community health units or weave them together. Depending upon the events in classrooms and school, the unit might focus on skin color, on hair, or on the hands. The end result of any of these studies should lead students to understand Maya Angelou's being "more alike, my friends, than we are unalike." We need to honor our unique selves and our cultural differences, but we also need to come together to celebrate them with one another. The poems listed here are celebrations of community, in classrooms, neighborhoods, the country, and around the world.

Adoff, Arnold. *All the Colors of the Race.* Illus. by John Steptoe. Morrow, 1982.

Angelou, Maya. "Human Family." In Rochelle, Belinda. *Words with Wings.* HarperCollins, 2001.

Berry, James. "People Equal." In Giovanni, Nikki. *Hip Hop Speaks to Children.* Sourcebooks, 2008. (With CD)

Clifton, Lucille. "Listen Children." In Rochelle, Belinda. *Words with Wings.* HarperCollins, 2001.

Cullen, Countee. "Tableau." In Muse, Daphne. *The Entrance Place of Wonders.* Illus. by Charlotte Riley-Webb. Abrams, 2005.

Dillon, Leo & Diane Dillon. *To Every Thing There Is a Season.* Scholastic, 1998.

Dotlich, Rebecca Kai. "Kaleidoscope." *When Riddles Come Rumbling.* Boyds Mills, 2001.

Edelman, Marion Wright. *I Can Make a Difference.* Illus. by Barry Moser. HarperCollins, 2005.

Fox, Mem. *Whoever You Are.* Illus. by Leslie Staub. Harcourt, 1997.

Gilchrist, Jan Spivey. *My America.* Illus. by Ashley Bryan & Jan Spivey Gilchrist. HarperCollins, 2007.

Hamanaka, Sheila. *All the Colors of the Earth.* Morrow, 1994.

Hoberman, Mary Ann, sel. *My Song Is Beautiful*. Little, 1994.
Hughes, Langston. "Little Song." In Kennedy, X. J. & Dorothy M. Kennedy. *Talking Like the Rain*. Illus. by Jane Dyer. Little, 1992.
King, Martin Luther, Jr. *I Have a Dream*. Scholastic, 1997.
Kuskin, Karla. *I Am Me*. Illus. by Dyanna Wolcott. S & S, 2000.
Mora, Pat. *Join Hands! The Ways We Celebrate Life*. Illus. by George Ancona. Charlesbridge, 2008.

REFERENCES

National Health Education Standards. American Alliance for Health, Physical Education, Recreation, and Dance. 2007. http://www.aahperd.org/aahe/pdf_files/standards.pdf
National Standards for Physical Education. American Alliance for Health, Physical Education, Recreation, and Dance. 1995. http://www.aahperd.org/naspe/publications-nationalstandards.html
Race: The Power of an Illusion. http://www.pbs.org/race

APPENDIX

Directory of Publisher Addresses

Addresses listed here are current as of the time of publication. Web addresses are included here as they will most directly lead readers to changes in the status or addresses of the publishers.

Abrams, 100 Fifth Ave. New York, NY 1001 (www.abramsbooks.com)
Albert Whitman, 6340 Oakton St. Morton Grove, IL 60053 (www.awhitmanco.com)
Annick Press, 15 Patricia Ave. Toronto M2M 1H9, Ontario, Canada (www.annickpress.com)
Arté Público, 4800 Calhoun Rd. Houston, TX 77004 (www.arte.uh.edu)
Atheneum, see Simon and Schuster August House, P.O. Box 3233, Little Rock, AR 72203 (www.augusthouse.com)
Barefoot Books, 2067 Massachusetts Ave. 5th Floor, Cambridge, MA (www.barefoot-books.com)
Black Butterfly, see Writers and Readers
Bloomsbury, 175 Fifth Ave. Suite 300, New York, NY 10010 (www.bloomsburyusa.com)
BookSurge (Self-publishing) (www.BookSurge.com)
Boyds Mills Press, 815 Church Street, Honesdale, PA 18431 (www.boydsmillspress.com)
Bradbury Press, see Simon and Schuster
Candlewick Press, 2067 Massachusetts Ave. Cambridge, MA 02140 (www.candlewick.com)
Capstone Publications, 151 Good Counsel Dr. P.O. Box 669, Mankato, MN 56002 (www .capstonepress.com)
Carolrhoda Books, see Lerner Publications
Cavendish, see Marshall Cavendish
Charlesbridge Publishing, 85 Main St. Watertown, MA 02472 (www.charlesbridge.com)
Children's Book Press, 246 First St. Suite 101, San Francisco, CA 94105 (www.childrensbookpress .org)
Child's Play, USA, 250 Minot Ave. Auburn, ME 14210 ('www.childs-play.com)
Chronicle Books, 85 Second St. 6th Floor, San Francisco, CA 94105 (www.chroniclekids.com)
Cinco Puntos Press, 701 Texas Ave. El Paso, TX 79901 (www.cincopuntos.com)
Clarion Books, see Houghton Mifflin
Creative Education, 123 S. Broad St. Mankato, MN 56001 (www.thecreativecompany.us)
Crowell (Thomas Y. Crowell), see HarperCollins

Crown, see Random House
Dawn Publications, 12402 Bitney Springs Rd. Nevada City, CA 95959 (www.dawnpub.com)
Delacorte, see Random House
Dial, see Penguin Putnam
Diane Publishing, P.O. Box 617, Darby, PA 19023 (www.dianepublishing.net) (Out of Print and Hard to Find Books)
Disney Press, 114 Fifth Ave. 12th Floor, New York, NY 10011 (www.disneybooks.com)
Dover Publications, 180 Varick St. New York, NY 10014 (www.doverpublications.com)
Dutton, see Penguin Putnam
Farrar, Straus & Giroux, 19 Union Square West, New York, NY 10003 (http://us.macmillan.com/fsg.aspx)
Feiwel and Friends, see Macmillan
Front Street, see Boyds Mills
Gareth Stevens, PO Box 360140, Strongsville, OH 44136 (www.garethstevens.com)
Godine (David R. Godine), 9 Hamilton Place, Boston, MA 02108 (www.godine.com)
Green Tiger, see Simon and Schuster
Greenwillow, see HarperCollins
Grosset (Grosset & Dunlap), see Penguin Putnam
Groundwood Books, 720 Bathurst St. Toronto M5S 2R4, Ontario, Canada (www.groundwoodbooks.com)
Handprint Books, 413 Sixth Ave. Brooklyn, NY 11215 (www.handprintbooks.com)
Harcourt, see Houghton Mifflin Harcourt
HarperCollins Children's Books, 1350 Ave. of the Americas, New York, NY 10019 (www.harperchildrens.com)
Heyday Books, Box 9145, Berkeley, CA 94709 (www.heydaybooks.com)
Holiday House, 425 Madison Ave. New York, NY 10017 (www.holidayhouse.com)
Holt (Henry Holt), see Macmillan
Houghton Mifflin Harcourt, 222 Berkley St. Boston, MA 02116 (www.houghtonmifflinbooks.com)
Hyperion, see Disney
Kane/Miller Book Pubs. P.O. box 8515, La Jolla, CA 92038 (www.kanemiller.com)
Kids Can Press, 2250 Military Road, Tonawanda, NY 14150 (www.kidscanpress.com)
Kingfisher, see Simon and Schuster
Knopf, see Random House
Lee & Low Books, 95 Madison Ave. New York, NY 10016 (www.leeandlow.com)
Lerner Publications, 241 1st Ave North, Minneapolis, MN 55401 (www.lernerbooks.com)
Little, Brown & Co. 3 Center Plaza, Boston, MA 02108 (http://www.hachettebookgroup.com/publishing_little-brown-and-company.aspx)
Lothrop, Lee & Shepard, see HarperCollins
Macmillan, see Simon & Schuster
Maple Tree, see Publishers Group West
Marshall Cavendish, 99 White Plains Rd. B 2001, Tarrytown, NY 10591 (www.marshallcavendish.com)
McElderry (Margaret McElderry), see Simon and Schuster
Milkweed, Open Book Building, Suite 300, 1011 Washington Ave South, Minneapolis, MN 55415 (www.milkweed.org)
Millbrook Press, see Lerner
Mondo Publications, 980 Ave. of the Americas, New York, NY 10018 (www.mondopub.com)
Morrow, see HarperCollins

National Geographic Press, 1147 17th St. NW, Washington, DC 20036 (www.nationalgeographic.com)
Northland Books (Out of business, but stock is still available)
North-South Books, 1123 Broadway, Suite 1016, New York, NY 10010 (www.northsouth.com)
Northwords, see T & N Children's Publishing
Orchard, see Scholastic
Oxford University Press, 198 Madison Ave. New York, NY 10016 (www.oup-usa.com)
Peachtree Publishers, 1700 Chattahoochee Ave. Atlanta, GA 30318 (www.peachtree-online.com)
Pelican Publishing, 1000 Burmaster St. Gretna, LA 70053 (www.pelicanpub.com)
Penguin Putnam, 375 Hudson St. New York, NY 10014 (www.penguinputnam.com/readers)
Philomel, see Penguin Putnam
Picture Window Books, see Capstone
Publishers Group West, 1700 Fourth Street, Berkeley, CA 94710 (www.pgw.com)
Putnam, see Penguin Putnam
Random House, 1540 Broadway, New York, NY 10036 (www.randomhouse.com)
Roaring Brook see Holt
S & S, see Simon and Schuster
Scholastic, 555 Broadway, New York, NY 10012 (www.scholastic.com)
Schwartz & Wade, see Random House
Scribners (Charles Scribners), see Simon and Schuster
Sierra Club Books for Children, 100 Bush St. San Francisco, CA 94104 (www.sierraclub.org/books)
Simon and Schuster, 1230 Avenue of the Americas, New York, NY 10020 (www.simonsayskids.com)
Sourcebooks, P.O. Box 4410 Naperville, IL 60567 (www.sourcebooks.com)
Star Bright Books, The Star Building, 42-46 28th St. Suite 2B, Long Island City, NY 11101 (www.starbrightbooks.com)
Sterling, 819 Fulton Ave. Falls Church, VA 22046 (www.sterlingpublishing.com)
T & N Children's Publishing, 8500 Normandale Lake Blvd. Minneapolis, MN 55437 Ticknor and Fields, see Houghton Mifflin Harcourt
Tricycle/Ten Speed Press, P.O. Box 7123, Berkeley, CA 94707 (www.tenspeedpress.com)
Tundra Books, 481 University Ave. # 802, Toronto M5G 2E9, Ontario Canada
Viking, see Penguin Putnam
Villard Books, see Random House
Walker, see Macmillan
Weston Woods, see Scholastic
Whitecap Books, 351 Lynn Ave. North Vancouver V7J 2C4, British Columbia, Canada (www.whitecap.ca)
Whitman, see Albert Whitman
Wordsong, see Boyds Mills
Writers and Readers, 625 Broadway, New York, NY 10012

Index

ABOUT THE AUTHOR

BARBARA CHATTON, Ph.D. is a professor at the University of Wyoming in Laramie. She wrote *Blurring the Edges: Integrated Curriculum Through Writing and Children's Literature* with N. Lynne Decker Collins, and has most recently published articles in *Book Links*, *The Journal of Children's Literature*, *The Dragon Lode*, and *Language Arts*.

Dr. Chatton received the Ellbogen Award for Excellence in Teaching from the University of Wyoming in 1990 and the College of Education Faculty Award for Outstanding Teaching in 1996. In 2002, she was the first College of Education faculty member to present the University of Wyoming Presidential Lecture.